W9-BJK-913

# Thumbing a Ride

LINDA MAHOOD

# Thumbing a Ride

## Hitchhikers, Hostels, and Counterculture in Canada

UBCPress · Vancouver · Toronto

© UBC Press 2018

All rights reserved. No part of this publication may be reproduced, stored in a retrieval system, or transmitted, in any form or by any means, without prior written permission of the publisher, or, in Canada, in the case of photocopying or other reprographic copying, a licence from Access Copyright, www.accesscopyright.ca.

27 26 25 24 23 22 21 20 19 18    5 4 3 2 1

Printed in Canada on FSC-certified ancient-forest-free paper (100% post-consumer recycled) that is processed chlorine- and acid-free.

---

**Library and Archives Canada Cataloguing in Publication**

Mahood, Linda, 1960-, author
Thumbing a ride : hitchhikers, hostels, and counterculture in Canada / Linda Mahood.

Includes bibliographical references and index.
Issued in print and electronic formats.
ISBN 978-0-7748-3733-0 (hardcover). – ISBN 978-0-7748-3734-7 (pbk.). – ISBN 978-0-7748-3735-4 (PDF). – ISBN 978-0-7748-3736-1 (EPUB). – ISBN 978-0-7748-3737-8 (Kindle)

1. Counterculture – Canada – History – 20th century. 2. Hitchhiking – Canada – History – 20th century. 3. Hippies – Canada – History – 20th century. 4. Youth hostels – Canada – History – 20th century. I. Title.

HM647.M346 2018            306'.1            C2018-900992-6
                                                                C2018-900993-4

---

Canadä

UBC Press gratefully acknowledges the financial support for our publishing program of the Government of Canada (through the Canada Book Fund), the Canada Council for the Arts, and the British Columbia Arts Council.

This book has been published with the help of a grant from the Canadian Federation for the Humanities and Social Sciences, through the Awards to Scholarly Publications Program, using funds provided by the Social Sciences and Humanities Research Council of Canada.

A reasonable attempt has been made to secure permission to reproduce all material used. If there are errors or omissions they are wholly unintentional and the publisher would be grateful to learn of them.

Printed and bound in Canada by Friesens
Set in Goudy Sans and Minion by Artegraphica Design Co. Ltd.
Copy editor: Robert Lewis
Proofreader: Helen Godolphin
Indexer: Cheryl Lemmens
Cover designer: Jessica Sullivan

Cover images: *front,* Rita Daly *(left)* and Barb Sneyd hitchhiking outside Moose Jaw, Saskatchewan, 1972 | photo by Patricia Daly, courtesy of Rita Daly; back, Kelly Ziolkoski waiting for a ride in 1976 | photo courtesy of Kelly Ziolkoski

UBC Press
The University of British Columbia
2029 West Mall, Vancouver, BC V6T 1Z2
www.ubcpress.ca

*To my son, Jack Satzewich*

*We had longer ways to go. But no matter, the road is life.*
— Jack Kerouac

## Urban Legend: The Disappearing Hitchhiker
*Told by Tanys Howell, 16, Toronto, 1973*

Well this happened to one of my girlfriend's best friends and her father. They were driving along a country road on their way home from the cottage when they saw a young girl hitchhiking. They stopped and picked her up and she got in the back seat. She told the girl and her father that she just lived in the house about five miles up the road. She didn't say anything after that but just turned to watch out the window. When the father saw the house, he drove up to it and turned around to tell the girl they had arrived – but she wasn't there! Both he and his daughter were really mystified and decided to knock on the door and tell the people what had happened. They told them that they had once had a daughter who answered the description of the girl they supposedly had picked up, but she had disappeared some years ago and had last been seen hitchhiking on this very road. Today would have been her birthday.

*– Quoted in Edith Fowke,* Folklore
of Canada *(1976), 265*

# Contents

List of Illustrations / ix

Acknowledgments / xi

1   Get Your Motor Running: Risk, Ritual, and Rite of
    Passage Travel / 3

2   Thumb Wars: Adventure Hitchhiking / 25

3   Rucksack Revolution: Quest in the Age of Aquarius / 63

4   Cool Aid: The Transient Youth Movement / 101

5   Crash Pads: Blue-Jean Bureaucrats versus the Canadian
    Youth Hostels Association / 135

6   Head Out on the Highway: Stories from the Trans-Canada
    Highway / 173

7   Car Sick: Hitchhiking Dos and Don'ts / 205

    Conclusion: The Vanishing Hitchhiker Eulogy / 239

    Notes / 249

    Index / 317

# Illustrations

3 / Hitching in Saskatoon

25 / Hitchhiking back to Edmonton after climbing to Morro Peak, 1961

38 / Early youth hostel in the foothills of the Canadian Rockies, Priddis, Alberta, 1940

41 / Valeen Pon travels the hitch and hostel way, circa 1953

43 / "Having a Cup of Coffee before Leaving," Bragg Creek hostel, August 22, 1959

44 / "'L.A.' Was the Cry of Two Hiking Vancouver Girls," circa 1924

63 / Hitchhikers from Toronto and British Columbia taking a break near Winnipeg, 1970

69 / A few of the 55,000 attendees leaving the Strawberry Fields Rock Festival, Bowmanville, Ontario, 1970

87 / "After you're through with the Army of Transient Youth ...," cartoon, 1970

101 / The Battle of Jericho, October 15, 1970

120 / People forced out of the Jericho hostel before the statement to the press from the Vancouver Liberation Front, October 1970

124 / The Battle of Jericho, October 15, 1970

128 / The Battle of Jericho, October 15, 1970

135 / Elk Island hostel spring work party, 1974

139 / Alberta Youth Hostels Association Klondike Days parade float, Edmonton

143 / Prime Minister Pierre Elliott Trudeau's memorandum to the Canadian Youth Hostels Association

152 / "... no ... this is my house ...," cartoon, 1971

164 / Youth hostel birthday party, Jasper hostel, 1975

173 / Toronto-bound hitchhikers from California, April 27, 1972

179 / Paul Orlowski hitchhiking from British Columbia to Toronto for a Crosby, Stills, Nash & Young concert, 1974

180 / Mealtime at the Winnipeg youth hostel with L. Alfred Dubree and Sandi Ogden of Hamilton, 1972

183 / Bed and board, Winnipeg youth hostel, January 1, 1970

184 / Men's section of Winnipeg youth hostel, July 19, 1974

197 / Kel Ziolkoski in the Fraser Valley on a hitchhiking trip from Saskatoon to Vancouver, 1976

205 / "One of 42 billboard crews across Canada pastes a sign seeking 14-year-old Ingrid Bauer ...," August 6, 1972

211 / Female hitchhikers with dog, July 21, 1971

217 / Facts on venereal disease, *On the Road: A Guide for Youth Travelling Canada,* 1972

217 / Travel advice for youth, *On the Road: A Guide for Youth Travelling Canada,* 1972

225 / Carole Lebrec and Monique Fouquet of Quebec City hitchhiking on Highway 401, August 1, 1970

# Acknowledgments

I left my home in Saskatoon in 1978, when I was seventeen, to join a new federal youth program called Katimavik. My plan was to travel and volunteer with other young Canadians in different provinces. I quickly learned that Katimavik had three rules: no sex, no drugs, and no hitchhiking. In November we stayed at the youth hostel in Baie-Saint-Paul, Quebec. My diary entry says, "I broke the hitchhiking rule today ... After work we hitchhiked to St. Irene. On the way home, we stopped at the top of the hill and philosophized for a while." Next I wrote, "Fate is what happens when your past catches up with your future!" This unique project would not exist in its present form without the help of many special baby boomers: Katimavikers Branca Verde and Alan Dickson; my delightful travelling companions and confederates Shawn Koeckeritz, Duff Sigurdsen, Arleen Rainbow May, and Kim Hunter; Douglas Williams, who sent me his book *Promised Lands* (2012); Robert Miller, who dug out his copy of *On the Road: A Guide for Youth Travelling Canada* (1972); and former blue-jean bureaucrats and long-haired civil servants Cam Mackie, Brian Gilhuly, Teddy Mahood, Byron Rogers, and Patrick Esmonde-White, who generously granted me interviews, the latter two also providing me with copies of private papers. Additional thanks to Renee and Sandra Bohun, Kel Ziolkoski, Ken Zakreski, Paul Orlowski, and Rita Daly for permission to use photographs. Finally, deep gratitude to the army of hitchhikers, regretfully too numerous to name, who shared their good and bad road stories with me. Yes, indeed, it was a "different time!"

This research was generously supported by the Social Sciences and Humanities Research Council of Canada's grants program and Aid to Scholarly Publications Program and by the College of Arts, University of Guelph. Archivists and librarians of the following collections must also be mentioned: Vancouver City Archives, Glenbow Museum Archives, Saskatoon Public Library, University of Manitoba Archives, Archives of Ontario at York University, Thunder Bay City Archives, London Public Library, and McGill University Archives. Many associates, colleagues, and students have helped me in different ways. My thanks to Professors Vic Satzewich, Kevin James, David Murray, Catherine Carstairs, and Andrew Bailey, as well as to my University of Guelph "Summer Work-in-Progress" colleagues, especially Alan Gordon and Mathew Hayday, for their patience with my persistent questions. It was a privilege to work with my talented research assistants and proofreaders, who provided the perspective of travelling youth today, Brad Larkin, Alicja Grzadkowska, Emily Martin, Sarah Mortimer, and Jack Satzewich. The staff at UBC Press is wonderful to work with. Darcy Cullen steered the manuscript through the review process, Nadine Pedersen provided essential editorial coordination, Ann Macklem guided it through production, and copy editor Robert Lewis was very patient and helped me to make it readable. Material in this book appears in abridged forms in "Thumb Wars: Hitchhiking, Canadian Youth Rituals and Risk in the Twentieth Century," *Journal of Social History* 49, 3 (2016): 647–70, and in "Hitchin' a Ride in the 1970s: Canadian Youth Culture and the Romance with Mobility," *Histoire sociale/Social History* 47, 93 (2014): 205–27. Every attempt has been made to contact other copyright holders, and I apologize if copyrighted material has been used inadvertently. No doubt, mistakes due to deteriorating documents and misjudgments have crept in. I hope that they are few, and I take full responsibility for them. Finally, thanks go to Coach Miguel Vadillo and all the EMBRACE, L.O.S.T., and Marlin swimmers who have kept me afloat. Thank you Vic, Lucy, Jack, and Alysha for past, present, and future journeys.

# Thumbing a Ride

Youth culture is an essay in ... the mini-politics of rebellion against obscure social forces. During a brief period, youth step outside the stark reality of industrial society to explore a symbolic identity, to celebrate being young, optimistic and joyous – a moment all too brief in personal biography.

– *Mike Brake,* Comparative Youth Culture *(1985)*

When you give a lift to a ragged boy he is, perhaps, a potential Prime Minister, an unlikely Trudeau in blue jeans, in hope or in despair.

– *"The Young in Summer,"* Winnipeg Free Press *(1971)*

# 1
# Get Your Motor Running
## Risk, Ritual, and Rite of Passage Travel

Hitching in Saskatoon, n.d.
*Local History Archive, CFQC qc42091, Saskatoon Public Library*

**In July 1970** a young man named Gary Barclay sent a protest letter to the Vancouver weekly the *Georgia Straight*. Under the headline "Hitch Bitch," Barclay listed the negative consequences of the mayor of Vancouver's efforts to prohibit hitchhiking in the city and other parts of British Columbia. Barclay called Mayor Tom Campbell's hitchhiking ban "fascistic" because it would harm the environment, the young, the poor, and the students, "who must travel to and from school."[1] A month later, a young man in Faro, Northwest Territories, wrote directly to the mayor. Rik Morgan drew a peace sign on a piece of paper and wrote, "Dear Mayor Campbell ... several of my friends told me that for some 'moralistic reason' you were going to clamp down on hitchhikers?" Morgan was also offended because the mayor called people with long hair "undesirables." He said, "I am, as you would say, a hippie, but I work and I support myself as all my long haired friends do."[2] For young people in the late 1960s and the 1970s, the struggle over the right to hitchhike epitomized more than just a struggle for access to a cheap means of transportation.

To open the mayor's "mind" to "different perspectives," Morgan enclosed a cartoon by Dave Berg from *Mad* magazine with his letter. The first frame of the cartoon showed a scruffy hitchhiker in blue jeans, headband, and sandals. In the second frame, a middle-aged motorist in a suit and tie pulls over to give the hippie a lift. He shouts, "Hop in!" and the bearded young man cheerfully replies, "Thanks," as he scrambles in beside the driver. In the remaining frames, as the car accelerates, the camaraderie between the men vanishes. The anxious motorist thinks, "What am I doing, giving a lift to this perfect stranger? After all, I'm a father and a husband! I've got responsibilities! He could be a dope fiend! He could hold me up, or bash me over the head, or ..." The nervous hitchhiker is also thinking, "What am I doing asking for a lift from a perfect stranger?! After all, I've got my whole life ahead of me. He could be some kind of a nut, or pervert! He could have a knife, or ..."[3] Berg's references to dope fiends, nuts, and perverts illustrate the contested meaning associated with hitchhiking and the underlying risks, tension, and fear it produced on both sides of the so-called generation gap.

Teenagers of the baby boom era were not the first generation to hitchhike. In *The Hitchhiker's Field Manual* (1973), Paul DiMaggio says the first "automobile begat the ride-beggar, who begat the hitchhiker, who discovered that thumbing down rides" was quicker and safer than hopping freight trains.[4] "Hitchhike," originally "hitch-hike," is an American term that appeared in the 1920s and is believed to have evolved from older terms like "ride beggar" and "hobo-hike."[5] There were approximately 1 million automobiles in Canada in the 1920s. Automobile ownership doubled between 1945 and 1962 and had doubled again by 1964. Half of householders owned a car in 1953, and by 1960 two-thirds had a motor vehicle.[6] The more cars on the road, the more likely a thumb-traveller was to get a lift. The most avid hitchhikers prior to the Second World War were girls and boys looking for rides to the beach or the ball diamond or simply seeking the novel experience of riding in a car.[7] College students thumbed to campus, and universities had hitchhiking clubs and contests. During the Depression, entire families were on the road thumbing toward greener pastures.[8] Wartime servicemen and women hitchhiked to military bases and munitions factories. After the Second World War, the Trans-Canada Highway neared completion. The beatnik subculture and folk music scene constructed hitchhiking as an activity for "hip youth," and the rituals of hobo "thumb-travel" were embraced by young adults wishing to reject consumerism and materialism. This generation linked hitchhiking to membership in the "radical youth scene."[9] In 1970 Barclay and Morgan were correct that due to the so-called hippie sensibilities of free love and anti-establishment nomadism, mayors, town councillors, community groups, and motorists called for a nationwide clampdown on hitchhiking. The hitchhikers fought back. They equated hitchhiking with liberty and freedom. For them, the hitchhiking ban was an undemocratic attempt to "deny the people freedom to help one another."[10]

This book examines youth mobility, risk taking, and the rite of passage of travel in Canada. Popular wisdom regarded the desire to travel as a normal part of adolescence, so picking up a young hitchhiker was perceived as an act of paternalism, an investment in the next generation, or in the case of female hitchhikers, chivalry. The focus of this research is how "hitchin' a ride" and youth hostelling during liminal moments in early adulthood came together in the 1970s when the so-called "transient youth movement" was formed in response to the intervention of social workers and government programs.[11] Archival research and oral history narratives with baby boom youth not only highlight the pleasures and dangers of alternative travel but can also be read as key biographical moments when understandings of landscapes, national identity, and citizenship in Canada were formed.

### Wanderlust: Wandering Theory and the History of Adolescence

The wandering child has a unique place in the settler history of Canada. The equation of travel with colonial discovery, adventure narratives, and greater global awareness has long been associated with youth and nation building. The Dominion of Canada, as historians Neil Sutherland and Susan Houston point out, is a nation built by tens of thousands of travelling apprentices, abandoned orphans, juvenile migrants, and refugees for whom the transition to adulthood is marked by saying goodbye to hearth and home, both psychologically and geographically, in order to seek their fortune, immigrate to a new country, marry, wander with a youth club or alone, or run away.[12]

Historical forms of youth travel include numerous class-based coming of age rituals. In the eighteenth century, affluent families believed that educational travel provided their children with important cultural capital. Wealthy parents sent their children on "self-improving" tours to study high culture and architecture in European cities. The Grand Tour was an elite rite of passage that marked entry into the ruling class.[13] Descending the social ladder, craft guilds, teachers, and professional fraternities sent students and apprentices off travelling in search of scholarship or training.[14] Working-class boys and girls travelled from town to town in order to attend hiring fairs and look for seasonal work in factories and agriculture. A "readiness to tramp" was taken as a sign of a young person's "readiness to work."[15] Along the way, they developed their own traditions and rituals, learned about life, and mastered the skills needed for their trades.

In the late 1890s, a unique recreational travel game called "tramping" was developed by the children of the new industrial bourgeoisie. Well-to-do youth did not copy the highbrow Grand Tour. Instead, they copied the migrant labour traditions of apprentices, hoe-boys, and fruit tramps, which were dwindling due to railway construction and urbanization. For affluent Victorians and Edwardians, it was fun to rove the countryside masquerading as tinkers, vagabonds, and hobos. "Tramp Trips" and games enabled them to play with contemporary codes of social distance, experience the daily lives of working people, and explore landscapes in ways that were off limits to members of the better-off classes to which they belonged.[16]

Around the turn of the century, politically conscious students, feminists, socialists, and artists took the cross-class masquerade from the countryside to the city. Young suffragists, journalists, and social workers went "slumming" in urban spaces dressed as tramps.[17] Well into the twentieth century, slumming provided an educational, temporary release from stifling social class, gender, and family expectations while preparing future pillars of society for careers in social service and politics. Dressing below their social class enabled them to sleep in cheap lodging houses and to receive the handouts that were normally reserved for the poor. English essayist George Orwell described the experience of living in cheap lodging houses disguised as a tramp in *Down and Out in Paris and London* (1933) and *The Road to Wigan Pier* (1937). In the latter, he wrote, "I was very happy. Here I was, among 'the lowest of the low,' at the bedrock of the Western world! ... Down there in the squalid and, as a matter of fact, horribly boring sub-world of the tramp I had a feeling of release, of adventure."[18] In *The Autobiography of a "Newspaper Girl"* (1902), American journalist Elizabeth Banks told of disguising herself as a flower girl, crossing sweeper, laundress, dressmaker's apprentice, strawberry picker, and servant to live and work among the poor, for whom she discovered deep empathy. She wrote,

> I could even feel myself growing, growing in grace, growing in charity, putting aside such narrow creeds and prejudices as had been a part of my up-bringing ... Life! Life! Seething life was all about me. The life of a great city, its riches, its poverty, its sin, its virtue, its sorrows, its joyousness – there it was, and I was in it.[19]

As Ellen Ross notes, charitable work by genteel ladies in London slums took them into places "exotic and unknown enough to the reading public before 1918 to enable these women to be thought of as real 'travelers' ... Their close contact with 'the natives' ... solidified this image."[20]

Despite the occupational and educational value of travel, youth mobility patterns have long been a concern of civil society. In the eighteenth century, young aristocrats misbehaved on their European tours, which caused their parents and tutors to order them to return home. Middle-class parents worried that their daughters' attraction to cross-class "slumming" encounters could ruin their chances for marriage.[21] The British colonies were dumping grounds for the "inconvenient children" of libertines and paupers who posed "social problems" for the church and state. On long voyages aboard dirty, overcrowded ships and in urban settlements, itinerant and abandoned boys and girls banded together and clashed with the authorities over appropriate moral codes and public decorum. Child savers lamented the loose morality of roving seasonal agriculture gangs, especially the sexual behaviour of working-class girls.[22] Under the authority of the Indian Act, Aboriginal children were confined to Indian residential schools, and the mobility of young adults was restricted by the pass system.[23] Missionaries, Indian Agents, parents, and police feared that an "addiction to travel" could cause juvenile delinquency.[24]

In the early twentieth century, youth mobility became the focus of new research in the psychology of adolescence. In 1904 American psychologist G. Stanley Hall wrote his authoritative two-volume text *Adolescence: Its Psychology and Its Relation to Physiology, Anthropology, Sociology, Sex, Crime, Religion, and Education.* Hall said that adolescence was a biologically driven "stage of life" when all young people went through some degree of emotional and behavioural upheaval, called "storm and stress," before establishing a more stable equilibrium in adulthood. Between the ages of fifteen and twenty-four, adolescents experienced an array of restless impulses characterized by "ennui, malaria, space-hunger, horror of familiar environments and habitual duties, and spring fever."[25] Behavioural disruptions included the need for constant excitement and the desire to test one's self in risky, sensation-seeking situations and in conquests that challenged intellectual and physical strength. Hall's scientific grounding of the "instability" of this vulnerable age group dovetailed nicely with early-twentieth-century social reformers' protective measures to replace youth labour with a longer time in school and more leisure time supervised and structured by adults.[26]

G. Stanley Hall's theory of adolescent restlessness and sensation seeking influenced other experts. In the 1920s German psychologist Eduard Spranger called "wanderlust" the internal restlessness that manifested itself in young adults' desire to get away from home and family and be on their own. In the teen years, boys and girls consciously began to seek out role models and peer-based activities related to a striving for emancipation.[27] The creation of the "modern or psychological" adolescent is part of what French philosopher Michel Foucault calls the nineteenth-century regulation, disciplining, and policing of individual bodies, or "biopower."[28] Biopower enabled experts to discover, categorize, and observe groups of people, including children and teenagers. Through the "discoverable adolescent," cultural theorist Hans Arthur Skott-Myhre says, "modern youth work was born."[29] Today, popular attitudes, professional counsellors, and various social policy initiatives still regard adolescence as a "traumatic" time of storm and stress. Neuroscientists believe that the "unstable" adolescent brain is incapable of assessing risk and danger or making sound moral judgments. In effect, the "teen brain" is more likely than ever to make teenagers a risk to themselves and others.[30]

In the second quarter of the twentieth century, theories of wanderlust were associated with teaching children and young adults impulse control, rational decision making, and ways to guard their personal safety. In the 1930s child psychologist John B. Watson traced juvenile delinquency back to the parental mishandling of early childhood fears. He believed that children had very few natural fears and that delinquent youth had therefore learned to use aggression and bullying to conceal their terror. Watson told parents not to frighten children with stories of "the old bogyman" but rather to encourage them to face psychological and physical challenges with bravery, rationality, caution, and confidence.[31] Neither Hall nor Watson called fearfulness a feminine characteristic, and popular fiction for Edwardian girls showed them hiking, cycling, swimming, and playing team sports. Brave girls did not run away screaming at the sight of spiders and snakes. Instead, "modern girls," like "new women," demonstrated habits of self-discipline, emotional control, a business-like respect for order, and bravery.[32]

Well into the twentieth century, wanderlust was a recurring theme in child psychology. Wanderlust was assumed to be a natural expression of romantic individualism, bravery, confidence, and the collective, youthful gang instinct.[33] Psychoanalyst Erik Erikson associated teenagers' wanderlust, restlessness, and risk taking with identity exploration and lifestyle experimentation, which included the formation of cliques and gangs where collective behaviour, values, and ideals could be expressed.[34] Youth workers and guidance counsellors urged parents to become involved in the day-to-day management of childhood environments and to pay close attention to the emotional development of older children, especially middle-class children. Adults sought to channel the traditions of youth mobility for their own purposes and to harness the supposed "gang" instinct of teenagers through games that tested moral and physical strength, fraternity, and natural leadership.[35] In the 1950s and 1960s the parents of baby boomers who followed the "child-centred" advice of Dr. Benjamin Spock freed their kids from the premature pressure of adulthood by treating youthful impulses as healthy, innocent, and pure.[36] This focus resulted in the expansion of sports activities, recreation clubs, the Boy Scouts, the Girl Guides, the YMCA and YWCA, and Junior Red Cross Lifesaving programs. Participation in communal and individual outdoor activities and recreational programs became shared experiences for thousands of Canadian youngsters and "important contributors to the evolution of a nation-wide youth culture."[37]

### Wandering Youth: Automobility and Rites of Passage

Throughout western Europe and North America, G. Stanley Hall's "stage of life" theory was complicated by the commercialization of youth recreation and leisure activities. For this reason, sociologist Stanley Cohen says that the youth of a generation are rarely remembered in terms of a particular chronological period but rather for their unique "fads, fashions, crazes, styles or – in a less ephemeral way – a certain spirit or *kulturgeist*."[38] The commercialization of youth subcultures involved the "innovative marrying of high culture and folk culture," which occurred organically and spread by word of mouth, music, dancing, film, intellectual discussion, and domestic and international travel.[39] Each generation embraces social change by adjusting to technology and consumerism in order to create a unique style of life. In the 1920s, dance halls, cinemas, sports, and automobiles excited the generation that came of age in the aftermath of the First World War.[40] For anyone who could afford one, the automobile was equated with luxury, status, freedom, and the good life.[41] Following the Depression era's road-building relief programs and the Second World War, the federal government passed the Trans-Canada Highway Act (1949), which provided joint funding to build roads that would unite the nation.[42] Numerous postwar youth subcultures equated status with consumerism, and youth were preoccupied with clothes, hair, music, the cars they drove, and what "constitutes being 'cool.'"[43] In the final quarter of the twentieth century, new roads were incorporated into rite of passage rituals that opened new avenues for teenagers to explore automobility and travel.

Historian Tamara Myers notes that baby boom children came of age just in time to "collide" with automobility.[44] Metaphors of automobility reflect sociologist Mimi Sheller's observation that people make powerful "emotional investments" in cars that exceed any rational economic calculation of ownership. One does not have to own a vehicle to experience the pleasure it provides. Teenage passengers and drivers absorb a tremendous emotional, affective, and libidinal energy from "dwelling" in cars, which are key status markers that advertise individual and collective mobility potential through what Sheller calls "automotive emotions."[45] Beat generation novelist Jack Kerouac's *On the Road* (1957) employed "the metaphor of motoring" to explore youth alienation from society.[46]

Youth subcultures may be distinguished by their various elements of style, dress, demeanour, and argot, as well as by the modes of automobility they use or lust over.[47] These could be Vespas, Volkswagen Microbuses, Jeeps, Chevy vans, or hot-wired cars. For youth, old jalopies, choppers, pickup trucks, and even skateboards become extensions of the ego formation of the apprentice traveller and shape the forms of automobile-related rituals and coming of age. In the case of hitchhiking, the rite of passage began by slinging on a backpack and thumbing down the road in search of a good ride.

Traditionally, the youth subcultures that became social problems were the ones that appeared to be hedonistic, irresponsible, and threatening to collectively shared social values.[48] In the age of automobility,

North American youth incorporated increasingly efficient and affordable automobiles into their mobility rituals.[49] Unlike the worst years of
the Great Depression when unemployed youngsters took to the open
road in search of work, in the late 1960s when thousands of self-styled
"freaks" were spotted hitchhiking and sleeping in parks and ditches
along the Trans-Canada Highway, motorists from the Atlantic to the
Pacific complained because they could not see "any difference between
the long-haired lazy and rebellious bums who live off welfare," young
people looking for jobs, and student travellers out enjoying themselves.[50]
Moreover, due to the values of rock lyrics, which seemed to denounce
"the Establishment" and to promote drug use and sexual freedom, it
was hard for many older Canadians to understand where fashion trends
stopped and true rebellion began.[51] It is not known how many youth
took to the roads. In 1971, under the headline "Canada's Great Trek," the
*Vancouver Province* proclaimed, "Hitchhiking has become a national
phenomenon."[52] The public spectacle of youth hitchhiking and complaints about moral indecency in the youth hostels – which were under
the auspices of the Secretary of State via the National Hostel Task Force,
founded in 1970, Transient Youth Services, and Opportunities for Youth
from 1971 to 1977 – resulted in surveillance, resistance, violence, and
finally the multigenerational collaboration of travellers and locals in cities
and towns all over Canada.[53]

In this research, youth mobility and alternative travel are conceptualized as a rite of passage that sometimes occurred in retreat or isolation
from the community but inevitably marked the transition to adulthood.
Travellers develop what tourism scholars, led by John Urry, call the "tourist gaze,"[54] which from an anthropological perspective is a new way of
sightseeing. Jane Desmond says the tourist gaze is "always performed in
contradistinction to everyday looking."[55] The romantic form of the gaze
emphasizes solitude, privacy, and a personal semi-spiritual relationship.
The other type of tourist gaze is the "collective" gaze, which necessitates
the presence of large numbers of other people and takes on a feeling
of "carnival." It is "the place to be" – in other words, what the young in
the 1960s called making the scene.[56] Both gazes emphasize the visual and
bodily nature of the tourist performance.[57] In his work on youth travel,
cultural anthropologist Victor Turner and others use "liminality" and

"communitas" as analytical concepts that make up rite of passage travel. Liminality begins when the ritualist decides to separate from home and community, and it lasts until one's reaggregation into society.[58] According to the rite of passage heuristic, a ritualist's wanderlust or escape is driven by the desire for authentic, spontaneous, and communal experiences beyond the tourist bubble, which creates a collective "drifter culture," or in counterculture jargon, a "trip."[59] The "anti-structural" state of being "betwixt and between" consecutive stages in a social milieu is called "communitas" (togetherness); it is where honesty, sensuality, openness, and lack of pretensions are sought and valued. In communitas, co-ritualists join together and undergo deep personal experiences and seek out and share family-like feelings of solidarity with peers.[60] At any point in a journey or quest, betwixt-and-betweeners are vulnerable to long-term negative consequences of risk taking. However, when a journey is successful, rite of passage travellers return home having discovered the secrets and traditions of the culture.[61] Both physically and metaphorically, then, coming of age travel is the time when the young citizen apprentice embarks on a quest and undergoes a series of tests prior to rejoining society as a responsible adult. The completion of the journey is tantamount to the completion of the self.[62]

The profound psychological impact of rite of passage travel for young people is well documented in literature, poetry, and folklore, but the historical origins of how backpacking, hitching, hostelling, and trekking off the beaten track came to be regarded as cultural capital for citizenship in the late twentieth century are largely unknown. As we shall see, adventure, quest, and risk are inherent parts of every journey. In this book, risk is conceptualized in four ways. First, risk is a very real part of good and bad holiday travel, as commercial package tours, insurance waivers, accidents, illness, and crime rates indicate. Second, facing the dangers of the unknown enables travellers to construct new self-identities, heroic personas, and exciting autobiographical travel narratives.[63] Third, historically, unwanted tourism poses risks to travellers, especially to those whose quests take them beyond the beaten track. Darya Maoz's anthropological study of Israeli backpackers in India shows that in the eyes of locals, backpackers have embodied "the most negative characteristics of Western culture."[64] Locals create boundaries between the community and unwanted guests through surveillance, veiled resistance, and open aggression; this negatively affects how guests treat hosts and increases risk for everyone.[65] Finally, adults' perceptions of youth mobility and risk-taking behaviour have been a barometer of emergent social ills. The interplay of the social structure with real and imagined youth behaviour tells us more than one story about the adult construction of normal and abnormal risk taking and communicates broader cultural imperatives for society to protect, monitor, and sustain youth.[66] This research examines coming of age in the twentieth century, the "transient youth problem," state and civil society intervention in youth culture, and the surveillance of youth mobility. It scrutinizes adult-led judgments, authority, and control respecting what constituted acceptable and unacceptable risk exposure largely for girls and boys of the late baby boom who were in transition to adulthood.[67]

### (Auto)Biography Methodology: Oral History and Road Stories

The social and historical construction of childhood and youth should not, as historian Cynthia Comacchio says, divert us from remembering that growing up is a deeply personal experience that we all share.[68] The catalyst for this book comes from my students' astonishment when I told them I had hitchhiked with my friends in the late 1970s and early 1980s. My hitchhiking days ended over thirty years ago, and I fully appreciate why getting into cars with strangers is risky – but at the time, hitchhiking was a mode of ride sharing that made sense to Canadians of all ages, and it received a great deal of attention in the press, which indicates acute public interest in both good and bad road stories.[69] This book uses hundreds of articles from Canadian newspapers and magazines published between 1924 and the late 1980s. Newspapers and magazines provide a valuable encapsulation of attitudes and sentiments about hitchhiking and serve as living catalysts, influencing future attitudes. Although it may not be the best source of unbiased fact, the popular press provides us with "ephemeral feelings" that capture the mood of the moment.[70]

Another insightful printed source of information about hitchhiking was written by hitchhikers and published by the newswire service Canadian University Press. Founded in 1938, Canadian University Press distributed the stories written by its student journalists to local campus newspapers. Due to the ample room for "free expression" that university administrators gave student journalists in the 1960s, James Pitsula says the scanning of articles and editorials enables historians to "re-enter their world and get a feeling for the emotional penumbra" of life on university campuses.[71] For the past seventy-five years, the campus press has been an agent for social change. Charles Levi argues that there is no "controversial cultural subject that has not been written about in a student newspaper."[72] Campus administrators, municipal leaders, and the Royal Canadian Mounted Police monitored student papers for information about campus events, student opinions, and the names of political activists.[73] Contemporary hitchhikers also published advice manuals and guidebooks.[74] These sources are the textual medium that comes closest to diaries and conversations.

In addition to contemporary written accounts, the hitchhiker's perspective is rounded out by open-ended interviews and email correspondence with thirty-six women and forty-two men born roughly between 1946 and 1965. To enlist the assistance of hitchhikers of the baby boom generation, I created a snowball sample of interviewees. I used Google to locate former youth hostel and Transient Youth Services staff members who were quoted in contemporary newspaper reportage. Following public talks and press interviews that I gave on the topic, many hitchhikers contacted me to offer their travel stories from the 1960s and 1970s. In the interviews, I asked hitchhikers to recall where they went and with whom, what they packed and ate, and where they slept, as well as to describe good and bad encounters with motorists and in youth hostels and the circumstances surrounding their decision to leave home to travel. The lift-givers provide us with the motorist's side of the story, which is inferred from oral history, mainstream and university newspaper accounts, and government and police reports.

When I began my interviews, I had no idea what I was going to hear. Some road stories, like the one about the hitchhiker who waited so long for a ride in Wawa, Ontario, that he married a local waitress, are told so often that they have acquired the status of urban legends. Other stories were shared for the first time. There were a lot of gasps, laughter, knowing silences, and in a few cases, tears. Recorded interviews were conducted over the telephone, via Skype, or face-to-face in Nova Scotia, Quebec,

Ontario, Manitoba, Saskatchewan, and British Columbia. Former hitch-hikers usually met me for coffee. Special thanks to Branca Verde for organizing a brown bag lunch and to Kim Hunter and Arleen Rainbow May for hosting a potluck to swap hitchhiker stories. In compliance with the protocols of the Social Sciences and Humanities Research Council of Canada and the wishes of interviewees who requested anonymity, I have not used names or other identifying information, unless otherwise indicated.

Shortly after I began the archival research, I came across a series of social work reports about hitchhiking by the Canadian Welfare Council. They reminded me of Stanley Cohen's warning in 1985 that scholars should "imagine" a time when "a complete cultural dummy – the Martian anthropologist" – found social work reports, client directories, and field studies written in the 1970s. How would they interpret the new "social action" experiments developed by the baby boom generation? How would they explain the "anti-social-worker"? How would they understand community care models and networks of paraprofessionals, semi-professionals, students, and volunteers in state-funded drop-in centres and hostels?[75] I became this Martian when I read the CWC's reports and others by middle-class professionals and senior bureaucrats who used words like "groovy," "far out," and "hassle-free" to describe federal government programs for youth. On the face of it, in 1969 the Department of Health and Welfare gave the council a grant to investigate why an excessive number of youth were hitchhiking on the roads and highways in the summers of 1967 and 1968. The first report, called *Transient Youth: Report of an Inquiry in the Summer of 1969* (1970), is 142 pages. It includes three appendices with graphs, tables, and question-naires, a twelve-page scholarly bibliography, and submissions by over 250 academic experts, governmental and nongovernmental agencies for youth social services, urban-planning councils, city hospitals, church groups, local charities, and graduate students. A few months later, the council changed its name to the Canadian Council on Social Development, and three supplementary reports appeared: *More about Transient Youth* (1970), *Transient Youth, 70–71* (1970), and *Youth '71* (1972).[76] In the summer of 1970, the Liberal government funded an "emergency" youth hostel program to help youth on the road. The following year, Opportunities for

Youth and Transient Youth Services took over the youth hostels. Some background on these programs appears in a publication by the Secretary of State titled *It's Your Turn* (1971). The Department of Health and Welfare also published a road safety guide titled *On the Road: A Guide for Youth Travelling Canada* (1972).[77] The federal youth hostel program ran until 1976 when the Independent Hostel Association and the Canadian Youth Hostels Association merged to form the Canadian Hostel Association, founded in 1977.

Additional information on youth travel was found in the archives of the Canadian Youth Hostels Association for 1933 to 1995 at the Glenbow Museum in Calgary. In addition, well-thumbed files titled "hippies," "youth hostels," or "transient and alienated youth" containing surveys and reports by local officials and volunteer agencies are kept in public libraries and municipal archives in Montreal, Toronto, Winnipeg, Thunder Bay, Windsor, London, Saskatoon, Calgary, Victoria, and Vancouver, as well as in the Ontario Provincial Police Archive at the Archives of Ontario. In the summer of 1970, Patrick Esmonde-White was the National Hostel Task Force's advisory coordinator. He gave me permission to take notes from copies in his possession of RCMP intelligence and operations files, which describe the youth hostel riots in Vancouver in 1970.[78] Byron Rogers, former program researcher for Transient Youth Services in 1971, gave me permission to transcribe unpublished hostelling and kiosk reports and notes from meetings in his possession. Interviews with Cam Mackie, formerly of Opportunities for Youth, and with Ken Rubin, an interviewer for the Canadian Welfare Council's initial report, *Transient Youth*, as well as Cool Aid volunteer and Jericho Beach hostel staffer Teddy Mahood's vivid description of the standoff there on October 15, 1970, have all greatly enhanced this project.

Hitchhiking stories are special types of autobiography that use methodology from oral history.[79] The challenge of oral history travel narratives is how to interpret the way people re-create tales over time. In this study, interviewees in the role of the teller-as-responsible-adult were asked to reflect upon their self-imposed rite of passage and the reactions of significant others to their adolescent risk taking. Like letters and diaries, autobiographical stories capture the interplay between the teller's adolescent "self" and the "other," including family, friends, and community, and what it felt like to be a young student or worker in Canada in the latter half of the twentieth century. To convey the full public reaction to the transient youth phenomenon, I compare interviewees' travel accounts with the official version of events that appeared in media coverage, in the reports of social welfare and voluntary youth agencies, and in government and police records. No doubt, in the construction of a generation's coming of age story, some details about "back in the day" when "everyone was hitchhiking" have been romanticized, manipulated, exaggerated, or omitted.[80]

### Roadside Rituals: What Is Hitchhiking?

Folklorists and anthropologists regard hitchhiking as a begging ritual that is visual rather than secret like a prayer or a wish. Lift giving is a benevolent gesture that rests on the understanding that the motorist's only responsibility is to provide a lift, not other forms of charity such as a hot meal, money, liquor, or a bed for the night. Hitchhikers, in turn, assume that motorists are acting the part of the Good Samaritan and that they expect nothing in return except good conversation and the pleasure of having done a good deed.[81] By the 1930s provincial traffic laws regulated nonmotorists and motorists and reduced the status of the pedestrian because riding in an automobile was regarded as a more esteemed mode of transportation than walking, cycling, or buying a ticket on public transit. People with access to cars were attributed greater prestige vis-à-vis pedestrians; therefore, automobile historian Stephen Davis says, automobility should not be confused with freedom for everyone.[82] Conversely, privately owned automobiles drive on public roads provided for them by taxpayers, who regard public roads as communal property and have a vested interest in what happens on them. Showing charity, kindness, compassion, or at the very least tolerance toward wayfaring strangers, like the thirsty beggar or road-weary vagabond, has long been considered a golden rule in Judeo-Christian ethics and liberal-democratic society. Indeed, in Western culture, the hitchhiker's "thumbs up" gesture has long been interpreted as a positive sign meaning "good."[83] It grants permission to go ahead and seals a bargain. Conversely, as suggested by the popular mid-1970s bumper sticker "Gas, Grass or Ass – Nobody Rides for Free," any act of charity can be read as an unequal power relationship between haves and have-nots. Graeme Chesters and David Smith point out that given that civil society depends upon charity, trust, diversity, and tolerance, we have much to learn from the intimacy and risk taking that hitchhiking implies.[84]

For alternative and noncommercial travellers, destinations and sightseeing are less important than "the performance of the journey."[85] In his work on mobility and microadventures, Michael O'Regan regards hitchhiking as a performance through which one makes provocative statements and acquires status.[86] Backpackers and hitchhikers regard themselves as special types of travellers who participate in a sublifestyle rather than profit-making tourism. Hitchhiking is an alternative mode of mobility that grants travellers cultural and social capital in the form of credible narrative capital, which actually serves as an admittance rite to a mobility subculture, thereby giving them a valid claim to a new collective self-identity and a chance to show off their "fictive selves."[87] Traditionally, heroic travel stories are built on quest, risk, and agency.[88] They are reproduced in travel literature, poems, and epics and are vital to the genre's survival. They contain easily identifiable tropes such as the "brave intrepid explorer," the "daring deed," the "lone individual against nature," and the "savage 'Other.'"[89] In 1970 Chandra Mukerji interviewed male hitchhikers in the southern United States. She said that their stories lay somewhere between "road reality," a "fish-story," and "scary bullshit," noting that the pleasure of telling and listening to a road story was just as important as the content of the story itself. More recently, in *Mobility without Mayhem*, Jeremy Packer has argued that hitchhikers swap stories to establish their credibility among other travellers and to produce an alternate identity by situating their experience within a "truly hip or beat" social structure.[90]

Hitchhiking is a gendered and sexualized performance. Each hitchhiker rides on the contradiction between the freedom of the road and the confinement of a car, specifically a stranger's car. Tourism anthropologist Chaim Noy's study of Israeli men's narratives of their backpacking trips shows how men subvert dominant and hegemonic masculine gender expectations when they are on the road.[91] The male domination of automobiles and public spaces reflects the cultural assumption that women have a different relationship to cars and roads than men do.[92] Ethnographic observations of solo women backpackers indicate that women's risk-taking achievements do not have the same "meaning to them" as male travellers' experiences do. Gender and sexuality are negotiated on the road. In her work on solo women travellers, Torun Elsrud discovered that some women choose to "keep quiet about their actions after home-coming."[93] Twenty-first-century hitchhiker Vanessa Veselka says it was difficult for motorists and onlookers to imagine a rewarding future for a woman on the road. In her experience, women and girls pay a higher "social cost" for hitchhiking than men do. She argues that "a man with a quest ... makes the choice at every stage about whether to endure the consequences or turn back," whereas female hitchhikers are "fetishized" by the onlooker. "The onlooker can choose to save her, choose to watch, or choose to ignore her as her fate plays out."[94] The sexual politics of hitchhiking mean that thumb-travellers encounter unequal power relations, conflicting gazes and stereotypes, physical obstacles, and danger.

The intersection of history and biography is an important variable in research on childhood, youth, and gender because it opens up a line of inquiry that enables us to see the choices of girls and boys in the past and present.[95] The main focus of this book is the period now called the "long sixties (1965–1974)."[96] The concept of "the 'sixties' as an *idea*" is said to reveal the ethos of the postwar era, whereas the long sixties "implies that a period contains a unity of experience defined by events, values, and political and social hierarchies."[97] Cultural historians, such as Thomas Hine and other scholars believe that with the end of the innocence and idealism of the 1960s counterculture came the "decline" of the "teenager" as the icon of the twentieth century.[98] In Canada contemporaneous youth services experts, urban planners, and academic scholarship state that, as an "idealistic cult," the original youth subculture identified as the "hippie movement" had in fact come and gone by 1966.[99] In *Canada's 1960s*, Bryan Palmer argues that as the first wave of baby boomers aged, they lost the radical exuberance they had felt.[100] Stuart Henderson challenges the "days of hope/days of rage" narrative. His work reveals that there were still teenagers and twentysomethings in Yorkville coffeehouses and clubs who were defying the status quo, getting busted with drugs, and "playing at free love" in the 1970s and beyond.[101]

So who were the youth that made up what a 1970 *Globe and Mail* article called the "summer army of hitchhikers" who marched "across this land"?[102] Drawing on older and newer scholarship, my emphasis on the long sixties allows for a sharper historical analysis of age cohorts by permitting the introduction of a new historical actor on the youth scene, variously called the late boomer, final-waver, and trailing-edger.[103] Demographers William Strauss and Neil Howe argue that children born between 1954 and 1965 came of age amid "a lost civility" surrounded by "a gray generational drizzle of sex, drugs, unemployment."[104] In the 1970s challenges to patriarchy and the nuclear family by feminism, the sexual revolution, an increasingly vocal gay rights movement, the decline of trade unions, the reduced security of white-collar jobs, immigration, economic turmoil, and the sociological discovery of child abuse and domestic violence all challenged the cultural hegemony of white men and their sons. In Canada the period of childhood innocence was extended to the age of eighteen and in some cases to twenty-five.[105] Today, youth rebellion, resistance, and agency are well documented in academic studies of juvenile delinquency, yet we know very little about risk-taking subcultures, lifestyle mobility, and how girls and boys from diverse walks of life negotiate cooperative relationships with adults and peers to create new forms of community and ways of living.

### *Outline: On the Road*
Historians barely mention the rise or fall of hitchhiking, so we do not know how Canadians responded in the 1920s to hitchhiking flapper girls, Depression-era "kids," or soldiers and bomb girls, for whom "flipping the duke" to "land a hop" was "Thumb Fun!"[106] The focus of Chapter 2 is the opposing perceptions of adventure hitchhiking in the first half of the twentieth century. In tandem with adventurous road stories by polite, rucksack-wearing youngsters and members of the YMCA and YWCA, Young Communist League, Canadian Youth Hostels Association, and Canadian Youth Congress, a counternarrative appeared in popular culture and crime reports in the 1940s and 1950s. Hollywood depictions of roadside maniacs, femme fatales, and teenage gangs transformed hitchhiking from an embodiment of trust and sharing into a risky, nerve-racking,

and dangerous activity. Chapter 3 examines why the baby boom generation ignored the risks, as well as discussing parents' fear that if a child dropped out of school or left work to drift around, it was a sign of their failure to raise a child who was a productive citizen. In the late 1960s and the 1970s, ride-thumbing adventure trips appealed to teenagers, workers, students, and Aboriginal youth during liminal moments in early adulthood, when hitchhiking was equated with the search for meaningful spiritual, political, and anti-materialist encounters.

Chapters 4 and 5 switch the focus from inside the hitchhiking subculture to the development of youth policy. Hitchhikers were a relatively unfamiliar sight on the roads in the 1950s, so when the numbers shot up to the thousands in the late 1960s, town councillors, the police, and members of Parliament were deluged with complaints. Following the publication of *Transient Youth: Report of an Inquiry in the Summer of 1969* (1970),[107] the Canadian Welfare Council hosted a three-day National Youth Consultation in Sainte-Adèle, Quebec, in May 1970, which led to the formation of the National Hostel Task Force, and the Secretary of State announced that it would provide free temporary hostels for summer travellers. The responses of host communities to unwelcome travellers ranged from cooperation and veiled surveillance to violence against hostellers. In Vancouver the tensions that erupted in the "Battle of Jericho" on October 15, 1970, illustrate how youth mobility and travel became a pressing social problem that turned young travellers into transients.

Any history of youth culture must confront youth crime and conflict, but it is also important to examine cooperation among rival youth subcultures and conformity with adult-run agencies. In the wake of 1967's Summer of Love, headlines in Canadian newspapers switched from the scourge of juvenile delinquency to bands of wandering bearded boys and lank-haired girls who talked about peace and love. The tide also turned in professional social work when a new generation of "blue-jean bureaucrats" entered the system. Although youth wanderlust and mobility continued to be contested, some cities developed innovative community youth-hostelling and drop-in programs. Chapter 5 examines the years of conflict and rivalry between the Canadian Youth Hostels Association's European-style hostels and the new "hassle-free" independent hostels run by the Secretary of State until 1976 when the two merged to form the Canadian Hostel Association, founded in 1977.

Chapter 6 moves back inside the transient youth subculture to see what hitchhikers' time on the road, codes of ethics, and survival strategies meant to them. Late-twentieth-century thumb-travellers passed time on the road telling stories about their adventures, the longest wait, the nastiest meal, the biggest bugs, the dirtiest youth hostel, wild rides, dark and scary nights, and heroic feats and rescues. Contemporary writing and "road talk" reveal the survival strategies and ethical codes that enabled many young travellers to feel "untouchable" in the communitas stage of the rite of passage, when co-ritualists become outsiders, explorers, lovers, and wanderers. Risk-taking and pleasure-seeking, riders and drivers met each other across the dashboard of every type of automobile, where harsh words, cruel weather, and tough surroundings were among the challenges of life on the road.

Chapter 7 shows that the publication of gender-biased sociological research and police reports, criminal judicial rulings, and cases of missing teenagers raised uncomfortable questions about adolescent risk taking, hitchhiking safety, and the nature of sexual violence against youth in everyday life. The truth of the hitchhiking ritual is that one never knew the true identity of the hitcher or the true motives of the motorist. There was nothing about the late boomers' hitchhiking that should have threatened social order more than the conduct of any other generation, yet civil society's anxiety about freaks, dropouts, and youth unrest cast a dark shadow over youth mobility, especially for girls.

In the book's Conclusion, I discuss how Canada's last hitchhiking "craze" ended in the late 1970s due to pressure on the police and municipalities to pass bylaws banning hitchhiking. Pro- and anti-hitchhiking information about safety and "dos and don'ts" reignited the old debate about youth mobility traditions in Canadian society.

### Life's Long Detour

We roast the kids for doing it,
But it can't be denied.
Most of us often wish we had
The nerve to "thumb" a ride.

*— Anonymous poem (1927)*

### Motorist Mistakes Bear for Hitchhiker

On a foggy night around Wiarton, Mr. E. Skene
stopped to pick up what he thought was a hitchhiker, only to be frightened when a large brown
bear reared on its hind legs and "landed a hay-
maker on the car." Mr. Skene drove on alone,
leaving the bear swinging wild punches in the air.

*— Globe and Mail (1948)*

# 2
# Thumb Wars
## Adventure Hitchhiking

Hitchhiking back to Edmonton after
climbing to Morro Peak, 1961.
*Scrapbook 1959–1966, North West Region, Edmonton, M7832, file 290,*
*Canadian Youth Hostels Association, Glenbow Museum Archives, Calgary*

**One afternoon in** March 1937, three students from Welland High School realized they were going to be in trouble for playing hooky, so they sold their bicycles and set off to hitchhike from southern Ontario to Florida. William Mudle, Jack Smith, and Jack Noxel thumbed to Buffalo, New York, without raising any questions. At the Peace Bridge, a transport driver promised to give them a lift to Toledo if they helped him unload his truck before dark. It was hard work and the exhausted boys got a hotel room for the night. Unfortunately, they overslept and the trucker left them behind. Later in the day, a state trooper spotted the boys thumbing along on the interstate near Erie, Pennsylvania. He guessed that they were the three missing teenagers mentioned in a police dispatch, so he drove them back to the Canadian border at Niagara Falls, where their parents were anxiously waiting. A few weeks later, an account of their misadventure appeared as a human-interest story in the *Globe and Mail*.[1]

Children learned to hitchhike by imitating their older siblings and friends. The ride-thumbing ritual was not regarded as a serious social problem, so a neighbour or passing stranger with a car might offer a lift to a girl or boy hitching to a swimming hole, ball diamond, or school and be perceived as a Good Samaritan.[2] Helping out a youngster was regarded as a valuable opportunity for a car owner to participate in the civic education and moral development of a youngster.[3] The idea that someone might violate the moral boundaries of the ride-sharing ritual was remote enough in 1932 that the children's columnist for the *Toronto Globe* said that hitchhiking was an excellent opportunity for children to show their good manners when people showed them "small and large courtesies."[4] In the Welland case, there was no indication that Mudle, Smith, and Noxel's truancy was linked to prior crimes or misdemeanours, so no appearance in the juvenile court was ordered.[5] Newspaper readers likely regarded the Welland hitchhiking story as an amusing tale about a trucker who taught three boys a valuable lesson. In all likelihood, their families eventually chuckled about it, and the boys never ditched school again.

Childrearing experts regarded "wanderlust" and "sowing wild oats" as normal stages in adolescent development, so for most of the century hitchhiking was perceived as a rite of passage that enabled boys and girls growing up in wartime and the Great Depression to visit locations and see sights far beyond the financial means of most families. Hitchhiking also enabled Canadian youngsters to participate in leisure activities and to join clubs as diverse as the YMCA and YWCA, Young Communist League, Canadian Youth Hostels Association, and Canadian Youth Congress. However, in tandem with the adventurous road stories of polite, well-adjusted, rucksack-wearing youngsters, a counternarrative appeared in the press and popular culture that challenged the assumption that a hitchhiking adventure during moments of youthful liminality created social cohesion between classes, genders, and generations. The focus of this chapter is the diverging perceptions of adventure hitchhiking in the first half of the twentieth century. By the 1950s police reports and true crime fiction had dramatized the violence perpetrated upon innocent motorists by hitchhiking ex-cons, femme fatales, and teenage gang members, so suspicion of strangers deterred motorists from offering rides to thumb-travellers. Hitchhiking was transformed from the embodiment of trust and sharing into a risky, nerve-racking, dangerous activity.

### *"Canada's New Main Street": Road Travel and Youth Tourism*

Hitchhiking in Canada emerged in tandem with the popularity of automobiles and road construction. There were approximately 1 million automobiles in Canada in the 1920s. That equals one car for every 9.9 people. During the Depression and war years, austerity reduced this ratio to one car for every 10.4 people. The number of automobiles increased again after 1945 when prosperity returned and people bought new cars. The registration of motor vehicles doubled between 1945 and 1954 and had doubled yet again by 1964. Half of householders owned a car in 1953; by 1960 two-thirds had a motor vehicle.[6]

These new cars required roads to drive on. In Canada road and rail transportation were regulated under the auspices of the federal and provincial governments. Initially, many Canadians had mixed feelings about federal-provincial road construction schemes due to the crushing burden they placed on taxpayers. Nevertheless, between 1930 and 1938 the Government of Canada was committed to spending on roads, and during the Depression thousands of men on unemployment relief were put to work under provincial and federal schemes that committed $19 million to the construction of highways.[7] The selling point for these roads was that they would boost tourism and, for the first time, permit

Canadians to drive from one part of Canada to the other without "traveling south of the border."[8]

Following the Second World War, the provincial road network continued to expand.[9] In 1949 the federal government passed the Trans-Canada Highway Act, which provided joint funding to build the country's initial "first-class, hard-surface road" linking each province across the "shortest practical east-west route."[10] In 1952, to facilitate travel in Ontario between Hamilton Harbour and the Welland Canal, the Queen Elizabeth Way, which had been unpaved until after the war, was improved, and new high-level bridges were added in 1958 and 1963. The Ontario government also began an ambitious highway project with the creation of the 400-series highways. On the other side of the country, the events of war also invigorated highway construction. In 1941, after the bombing of Pearl Harbor, British Columbia built a northern highway through the province to improve national defence. From 1937 to 1949, $4.5 million were spent on the construction of mining roads for extraction and transportation of natural resources in remote locations.[11] After decades of planning, the official grand opening of the Trans-Canada Highway took place in 1962.

The federal government hoped that new high-quality highways would eventually be paid for by selling Canada as a tourist destination to Americans and by convincing Canadians to holiday at home. In 1932 the mandate of the newly founded Canadian Government Travel Bureau was to make Canada a "tourist nation."[12] Everything from the position of the Trans-Canada Highway to the location of new national parks and campgrounds, airports, and resort sites fell within the bureau's purview. Between 1937 and 1949 the federal government allocated $5 million to boost the tourist industry through tourist-related highways. To further encourage American tourism, access routes from the United States and the roads to national parks were upgraded.[13] Generations of Canadians were eager to explore their new highways, and hitchhiking adventure trips quickly became a cheap travel game for teenagers and young adults. In 1953 the National Film Board of Canada dubbed the envisaged Trans-Canada Highway "Canada's New Main Street."[14] As early as 1935, the *Toronto Globe* reported that one could not go very far without seeing "scores of people standing by the roadside vigorously waving their thumbs in an attempt to secure lifts for short or long distances."[15]

## The Car: Teenagers and Automobile Rituals

The age of automobility arrived in the 1930s when motor vehicles were transformed from a means of basic transportation for the farming and labouring classes into a lifestyle necessity.[16] Technological advances in the late 1920s in the automobile industry and mass-market advertising discovered the buying power of the Canadian family. Automobiles were no longer a "rich man's toy."[17] In the 1930s "automobiles ranked third – behind food, clothing, and shoes – as a percentage of every dollar Canadians spent on consumer goods."[18] Advertisers targeted every member of the family, including the future drivers. A Chevrolet advertisement said that the members of a family without a car were like "prisoners on a limited range – like hobbled horses on a pasture."[19] Automobile industrialist Henry Ford advertised directly to children. One advertisement said, "The Ford car is the friend of childhood ... the modern Magic Carpet that will transport them ... from the baking asphalt."[20]

The first "modern teenagers" appeared in the 1920s, and they grew up under the spell of automobility. Economic prosperity meant that people from a wider range of social classes were able to keep their children in school longer and that middle-class girls enjoyed far more unchaperoned leisure time activities than their mothers had. Technology, mass marketing, and spare time allowed for a common teenage consumer culture to develop. After the First World War, girls and boys embraced lifestyles based on freedom and new social codes that ritualized events such as high school proms, dance styles, unique fashions, music, slang, and automobiles.[21] It was not necessary to own a car in order to appreciate the pleasure it might bring.[22] Youngsters sat for hours watching mechanics straighten tires and repair engines in old and new automobiles. Numerous automobility coming of age rituals included getting a driver's licence, driving cars for pleasure rather than employment, cruising, drive-in movies, drive-thru restaurants, drunk driving, drag racing, dating and courtship, playing pranks on other drivers, and just simply hitting the road.[23] Teenagers rode on rumble seats and truck beds, in backseats, or nestled romantically alongside a newly licensed driver. When the economic crisis in the 1930s greatly reduced the use of personal automobiles, youngsters became avid hitchhikers to save money, have fun, and escape the troubles of everyday life.[24] Any of these activities instantly shifted a teenager's status from immobile to mobile. Ford was correct. The automobile was a "Magic Carpet" waiting to transport young Canadians anywhere they wished "to play."[25]

### Thumb Fun: "Wild Boys of the Road"

Lara Campbell's oral history narratives from the 1930s "reveal the creative ways in which children and youth found opportunities for pleasure and enjoyment in the midst of deprivation."[26] Like the "gentleman-adventurers" of old and like fictional heroes such as Mark Twain's Huckleberry Finn and Herman Melville's Ishmael, "purposeful hitchhikers [had] discovery, exploration and self-education in mind."[27] The potentialities of a hitchhiking adventure were described in 1928 by twenty-two-year-old P.E. Stollery, who listed his occupation as "hitch-hiker." Edinburgh's *The Scotsman* newspaper caught up with the Ontario man after he had travelled two-thirds of the way around the world. Stollery began his world tour chopping wood in Ontario. He hitched to Vancouver. Then, with the help of carts and motorcars while living on bread and sleeping in sand trenches, he journeyed through California, Mexico, and Florida. Along the way, he found work as a doctor's assistant, a ranch cowboy, a tomato picker, and a postcard seller. He sailed to England, cycled to France and Spain, resumed thumbing, and bought a ticket on a steamer bound for Egypt. Stollery disembarked and "hiked" the Pyramids, later visiting Palestine, India, and Australia.[28]

Over the next two decades, hitchhiking caught on as a "novel holiday habit" for lower-middle-class and working-class youth in Europe and North America. The "three E's of hitchhiking" were to economize, escape, and experience.[29] In 1938 the *New York Times* sent reporter H.L. Verry to England to investigate the new fad. He discovered the hitching custom was "spreading across England like a harmless summer rash." In nearly every youth hostel, he met hitchhikers, predominantly "clerks and typists" and "Colonials" of "both sexes" from the Dominions. Typically, they were well-spoken, well-educated, and industrious men and women on tramping holidays. British motorists were "good-humored" and obligingly offered rides, making "hitchhiking as easy as falling off a log."[30] Travellers slept rough or joined the International Youth Hostel Federation, founded in 1932, so that they could stay in private youth hostels as stopping-places.[31]

Verry noted that thumb-travellers "delight in the sense of adventure born of hazarding their destination upon what rides come their way."[32]

During the darkest days of the Depression, when 100,000 Canadians lived hand to mouth, many people applauded anyone who could beat big businesses and bankers by getting something for free. Newspapers published many upbeat hitchhiking stories that emphasized the speed, distance, pleasure, and freedom that the new motor vehicle technology afforded. The *Toronto Globe* provided readers with ample details about the time taken by thumb-travellers to go great distances and about the cost involved. In 1934 two nineteen-year-old boys from Edmonton thumbed 3,700 kilometres to meet Prime Minister R.B. Bennett at the Chicago World's Fair. The headlining entertainment at the fair included cha-cha girls, an automated life-size dinosaur exhibit, a 191-metre Sky-ride, a "Midget City" with "sixty Lilliputians," and Chrysler Motors' latest "dream car," which went 80 kilometres per hour. On a scroll, the young men collected the signatures of the mayors of every city and town they passed through and showed it to Prime Minister Bennett, who gave them his "blessing" and his signature.[33] In 1937 two seventeen-year-old boys, Stanley Levine and Charles Dangelmajer, hitchhiked a total of a hundred rides from Niagara Falls to Vancouver in twenty-two days. Their longest lift was 1,247 kilometres between Lexington, Nebraska, and Salt Lake City, Utah. Their final destination was Charles's grandmother's house in Victoria, British Columbia, with a side trip to visit an uncle on Salt Spring Island. The boys planned to work their way home along the southern route through San Francisco and Denver.[34] A "knight of the road" from Saskatchewan hitchhiked through Europe, Algeria, and Japan. He told a gripping story about the time the French Foreign Legion recruiters lured him into the backroom of a saloon. He made a "wild dash" and "leapt out the window."[35]

People seemed the most impressed by stories of thrift. Hitchhiking enabled John Nalon of Gananoque, Ontario, to travel 64,374 kilometres through various parts of the world without paying "one cent for transportation." He worked on tramp steamers and hitchhiked on motorcars, trucks, and trains through half a dozen countries until he caught malaria in Africa.[36] In 1936 the Reverend Sylvester Toll gave his sons, Ellsworth and LeRoy, permission to take a year away from their studies at the

University of Toronto in order to hitchhike around the world. They hitch-hiked in France, Germany, Belgium, Italy, Palestine, and India. They ran out of money in China and sailed back to Canada on a freighter bound for Vancouver. By the time they got back to Toronto, they had travelled 61,155 kilometres across twenty-seven countries and had spent a mere $75.[37] The Depression era affected everyone who lived through it. The dearth of job opportunities and decent wages was especially hard on men in their twenties, and according to Heidi MacDonald, their transition to adulthood was blocked by unemployment, underemployment, and little chance for advancement. Such "liminality made people vulnerable."[38] For young men who were betwixt-and-betweeners, hitchhiking enabled them to travel as far as possible for very little money while exercising masculine independence and testing their capacity and mettle during economic and individual liminality.[39]

*Wandering Daughters on the Road*

Women and girls were also "avid hitchhikers."[40] Early-twentieth-century social workers observed that young women possessed the same sprit of "wanderlust" and the "irresistible yearning to see the world" that their brothers did.[41] The automobile industry recognized this yearning, too. Manufacturers assured women that cars were a safe way to escape and discover "new and untried places."[42] A 1915 Model T advertisement prom-ised "Freedom for the Woman Who Owns a Ford."[43] Canadian women were interested in hearing the tales of women who made "adventurous" hitchhiking trips. For instance, in 1930 the Women's Immigration Soci-ety invited Miss Lillian Schoedler to Toronto in order to give a lecture about her three-year hitchhiking trip across French Indochina, Malaya, Sumatra, and the interior of Persia. The forty-year-old businesswoman had been "vagabonding" since 1922. Her talk concluded, "to the intense interest of the audience," with a demonstration of the use of the chador, the "all-enveloping garment of the Mohammadian woman."[44]

   Like other rites of passage, hitchhiking is a gendered performance. The newspaper editors realized this and sent curious reporters to inter-view and photograph women thumb-travellers. In 1924 the *Vancouver Sun* covered the story of two women in their early twenties who hitchhiked from Vancouver to Los Angeles. Bella Rigby and Rheta Watson said that with $30 in their pockets, it took six and a half days, 1,520,000 steps, and twenty-four lifts to get to Los Angeles and only three and a half days and twenty-three lifts to get home. Rigby and Watson hitched rides in coupes, sedans, and a truck loaded with sawdust. The "hog fuel" blew into their eyes and made it impossible to read signposts. Early in the trip, they "solemnly declared" that they hated rumble seats. On the road through prohibition-era Washington and Oregon, they got rides with a bootlegger who drilled them on Vancouver's liquor laws, from Mr. Henry "Human Fly" Roland, who was on his way to scale the seven-storey Eugene Hotel blindfolded, and from a Spanish psychologist, who told them that he "believed in murder, thieving – in fact, everything – except lying," which he said was an "unpardonable sin." This caused the women to worry that "fate" had "matched them with a lunatic." Using lunchtime as the excuse to "get out," they left him at a filling station. Later, they thumbed a lift from state trooper Charles Reardon, who advised them to carry a revolver while hitchhiking. Editorializing about the "glorious trip!" the journalist encouraged *Vancouver Sun* readers to consider taking such a journey.[45]

Coming of age was also a time of liminality for young women. The adventures and uncertainty of life on the road enabled them to postpone taking on traditional feminine roles and duties. In 1930 Katharine Trevelyan's decision to leave Oxford University and thumb lifts across Canada was driven by her struggle against societal expectations. She said, "I failed four times in a Latin Examination at Oxford. The hour for taking it the fifth time was approaching, and I was ... cramming ... Suddenly ... I thought: I am a fool to waste my time and money on what I cannot do ... I will take a change of clothes, my tent and will cross Canada."[46] Katharine was the twenty-two-year-old daughter of Sir Charles Philips Trevelyan, minister of education in Great Britain's Liberal government. Inspired by stories about her famous aunt, archaeologist and political spy Gertrude Bell, Trevelyan put her rucksack on her back and spent three months hitchhiking from Quebec to British Columbia. She occasionally made use of influential "letters of introduction" that her grandfather Hugh Bell insisted she carry and stayed in private homes, but most of the time she hitchhiked, camped, and lodged at the YWCA.[47] When there was no one interesting to talk to at the YWCA, she called it the "Old Women's Christian Association." The high points of her trip were traversing the Rocky Mountains, attending the Calgary Stampede, and climbing Mount Edith Cavell.[48]

Women who were less well-to-do also embarked on hitchhiking adventures for self-discovery and personal growth.[49] In 1939 Nora Harris hitchhiked from Victoria to Halifax because she thought it would be "educational to travel." Her father wanted her to cycle, but the twenty-three-year-old insisted on hitching, sleeping outdoors, and cooking her meals over a fire. The most challenging leg of her journey was between Ontario and Quebec. Due to the absence of a passable road around the north shore of Lake Superior, Harris was stranded for a week in Fort William before a grain-boat captain took her through the Great Lakes to Port Colborne. From there, she walked over 645 kilometres to Montreal. Harris made the long trip alone because she wanted the freedom to move when and where she wished. "I am a timid person," she confessed, "and thought it would help me to get over my self-consciousness."[50]

Not only was coming of age in Canada stalled by the Depression, but the transition to adulthood was also disrupted by the Second World War both for youths who went off to fight and for those who remained at home. During the war, the labour of thousands of teenage girls kept the war industries operating. Joyce Hill and Margaret Smith built Avro Lancaster Mk X bombers in an ammunitions factory in Malton, Ontario. In 1945, when the restriction on wartime travel to the United States was lifted, the twenty year olds decided to hitchhike across the continent before starting university. The girls slept in a haystack in Michigan, saw a rodeo, visited Glacier National Park, helped with "Victory over Japan Day" celebrations in Seattle, took a ferry from Victoria to Vancouver, hitchhiked to Banff, Calgary, Regina, and Winnipeg, continued down to Chicago, and finished at the border in Windsor.[51] They learned that the art of "the first-class hitch-hiker" required charming motorists with enlivened conversation and sociability.[52] Smith wrote her mother, "Everybody we've met has been so kind and courteous that we are simply amazed ... We haven't walked 2 miles in the 2,000 we have travelled so far ... This transcontinental hitchhike is the big adventure of our lives."[53]

Canadian country girls may not have known much about the elite tradition whereby well-to-do girls travelled to Europe to finish their education, but it probably dawned on them that presenting their travel plans as educational would be a good way to get their parents' permission. On the evening of the class of 1949's graduation dance at the Macdonald Institute, two home economics students caught the train from Guelph to Banff in order to start their "college-girl waitress" jobs. Nineteen-year-old Helen "Lenny" Burton and Jacqueline "Johnny" Cochrane fell in love with the Canadian West and hitchhiked to Jasper and Vancouver, as well as into the Okanagan Valley to work the apple harvest. Over the Christmas holiday, they realized that the "travel bug" had not left them. They began 1950 working as waitresses at a ski resort in the Laurentian Mountains. By spring they had enough money for two one-way passages to England.[54]

Cochrane and Burton wanted to prove that two girls willing to work their way across Europe could have a pretty good time and see a lot of a country. They toured museums and galleries, they saw architecture, ballet, the *Merchant of Venice,* and *South Pacific* in London, and they followed the funeral procession of King Gustav in Stockholm. On the road, they ate cold pork and beans scooped out of a ragged-edged tin on the blade of a hunting knife. In Norway they slept in a bomb shelter, in Cornwall they slept on rocks, and in France they slept on the banks of the Loire, their clothes soaked by the rising tide and "crawling with live slugs." In Calais they slept in a graveyard, and in Scandinavia they slept in a Salvation Army church, where they woke the next morning to "the congregation filing in." Once, they bedded down in Rotterdam's largest park and woke surrounded by ducks, a crowd of staring people, and a burly policeman "indignantly kicking our bottoms." Their journey ended on Bastille Day in Paris, where the "broke" travellers were invited to join a group of students and "danced and feasted and drank champagne 'til dawn."[55]

### Swinging the Duke: Youth Clubs and Contests

In the 1930s thumb-travel represented more than the quest for adventure. Thrifty young people attracted to various transnational youth clubs also adopted the drifter's mode of travel. Similar to other youth culture rituals that involved a shared taste in music, dancing, hairstyles, and fashion, hitchhiking aided in social bonding. A willingness to hitchhike enabled youth to participate in many popular "character-forming agencies," such as the YMCA and YWCA, Young Communist League, Canadian Youth Hostels Association, and Canadian Youth Congress, which was formed in 1936 in response to the Depression.[56] At its peak, the Canadian Youth Congress represented the interests of almost 400,000 young people, including students, veterans, workers, and members of the YMCA, YWCA, church groups, and the youth wings of the Conservative, Liberal, Co-operative Commonwealth Federation, and Communist Parties. In 1939 many of the five hundred delegates hitchhiked to the annual meeting of the Canadian Youth Congress in Winnipeg. The *Globe and Mail* explained that the object of the meeting was to "foster a spirit of national unity among people that make up Canada's population."[57] It said, "From every corner of Canada youth were coming together, stirred by the ideal of a united country ... knit through common interest." Lloyd Birmingham, secretary of the Christian Student Association at the University of New Brunswick, was so passionate about the meeting that he hitchhiked for two and a half days to get there.[58]

Hitchhiking was a popular mode of travel for young political activists and protesters. In the 1930s Ben Swankey joined the Young Communist League of Northern Alberta. He used his time alone with the motorists who picked him up to talk about the merits of socialism but admitted that drivers were usually more impressed by his hitchhiking than by the "Red Bogey."[59] Hitchhiking was also a mode of travel used by young members of the Co-operative Commonwealth Federation. In 1938 Emerson Parks thumbed over 4,025 kilometres in eight days to attend its conference in Edmonton.[60] In 1948 the discussion items at its national convention were chartered banks and approval of a socialist blueprint for Canada. David Lewis, the party's national secretary, emphasized the "grass-roots character" of the convention, and the *Globe and Mail* said that "a lack of train fare" would not stop "young CCFers from travelling" because they would "hitchhike as they have in the past."[61] Hitchhiking created instant publicity for student protesters. In 1939 four University of Western Ontario students thumbed their way from London to Toronto carrying "a stack of papers which bore 20,482 names." The petition asked the government of Premier Mitchell Hepburn to reconsider the $25,000 cut to university grants.[62]

None of this is to suggest that hitchhiking was not perceived as subversive. Judith Adler notes that "freedom of movement" has never attained "the status of a universal human right."[63] The authorities have always strictly controlled the travel traditions of the poor. The treatment of unemployed youth and strikers revealed the fear of mobility and the unsettling encounters it could bring.[64] Hitchhiking, like riding the rails, could be regarded as a stigmatized mode of travel used by the aimless destitute and the troublesome tramps who lived hand to mouth. The Depression escalated the rise of the labour movement, so picking up a hitchhiker could be a gesture of solidarity with an unemployed worker on his way to a protest march, whereas not picking someone up might be due to fear that the young trekker in a sooty coat and cap was a Communist.[65]

In the 1930s hitchhiking created an underground railway for labour organizers and striking workers during the Regina Riot and On-to-Ottawa Trek. In 1932 the federal government tried to force single men on government relief to live in relief camps, but some preferred the freedom of travelling to the constant discipline of the camps.[66] Jobless men and boys gathered in their own makeshift camps; before long, many main railway divisions had "hobo jungles," which former residents describe as "boot camps and intellectual storm centres for a generation of the unemployed and labour radicals." Edmund Francis lived in a relief camp in 1935. He observed that young men like him were "truly a lost league of youth – rotting away for want of being offered an outlet for our energies. Something to do and something for that doing."[67]

In the spring of 1935, internees at a government unemployment-relief camp, most of them in their early twenties, angry and eager for adventure, went on strike for decent wages. After two months of inaction, protesters decided to take the train to Ottawa and present their grievance directly to Prime Minister Bennett.[68] The trek to Ottawa entered Saskatchewan on June 12. The plan was to meet up with thousands of their Manitoban brethren who were congregating in Winnipeg. To stop them, the Tory government gave the Royal Canadian Mounted Police orders to stop them from getting on Canadian National Railway trains in Regina, and the protest bogged down. On June 28, to "dodge" the RCMP, some trekkers escaped from Regina on freight trains bound for Winnipeg, and others dotted provincial highways hitchhiking west. The whole time, the police pulled workers off the freight trains and announced that any transport truckers caught picking up hitchhiking strikers would be prosecuted. The trucks would be sealed and the strikers arrested.[69] On July 1 a rally turned into one of the most violent riots of the decade when the RCMP and Regina police tried to disperse the crowd. Trekkers threw rocks and bricks, and the police fired bullets. Two people were killed, and 130 rioters were arrested.[70]

### Hitch and Hike: The Canadian Youth Hostels Association

In Europe and North America, many youth clubs, with mottos such as "Be Prepared" and their ethic of the "good deed," reflected the idea that "wanderlust" was a creative energy that could be channelled individually and collectively in positive directions that would serve the nation.[71] In Germany hiking clubs like the Wandervogel (literally "wandering bird"), whose shelters were called "nests," placed extensive emphasis on outdoor rambling and camping trips to forests and lakes, as well as on educational excursions to castles and churches in order to enjoy national history,

Early youth hostel in the foothills of the Canadian Rockies, Priddis, Alberta, with the Canadian Youth Hostels Association's "Magic Triangle" logo beside the door, 1940.
*NA 2468-6, Canadian Youth Hostels Association, Glenbow Museum Archives, Calgary*

heritage, and comradeship.[72] The YMCA, YWCA, Boy Scouts, and Girl Guides shared a similar creed. Adult-supervised leisure activities and forms of outdoor education like tramping and camping in one's *vaterland* (fatherland) were exhilarating ways to liberate youth from the social and physical oppression of modern city life.[73]

The German youth-hostelling movement became popular in Europe in the early twentieth century. It is said that during the First World War, a young German schoolteacher named Richard Schirrmann spent Christmas Eve of 1914 in the trenches of the Western Front. When the German and French soldiers came out of their dugouts to fraternize and sing together, Schirrmann was so profoundly affected by the camaraderie that in his mind grew the idea of an international network of youth hostels where the travelling young people of all nations, classes, and regions could meet and make friends.[74] In reality, Schirrmann had already established eighty-three youth hostels in the Rhineland before the war. There were 1,200 hostels in Germany by 1921 and 2,100 in 1931.[75] It is, therefore, not without irony that the hostel movement spread throughout Germany when Adolf Hitler created a well-funded network of youth hostels along the Rhine for Nazi youth. The International Youth Hostel Federation was formed in the 1930s. Under the leadership of Jack Catchpool in the postwar reconstruction period, hostellers became "youthful ambassadors" promoting international cooperation and bonds of friendship, and hostels were "the nursery for our democracy."[76]

Good citizenship and sharing fellowship in natural spaces were also appealing to Canadian youth. In 1933 two Calgary schoolteachers, sisters Mary and Catherine Barclay, founded the first branch of the Canadian Youth Hostels Association (CYHA).[77] The sisters regretted that so many teenagers were wasting money on picture shows and on jukeboxes and jive dancing. Anti-modernist philosophy alleged that society had spawned a mass culture that bought and "consumed" excessive amounts of ready-made pleasures "catering only to baser instincts, serving at once to titillate and stupefy."[78] The Barclays believed that youth hostelling united the "best elements" of body, mind, and a "wholesome spirit" and that it led to the "revival of the pioneer spirit." Catherine said, "The open and silent spaces of this vast land ... give moments of deep inspiration to the youth of Canada."[79]

Regional branches of the CYHA worked tirelessly to educate the public about the educational value of the "European-style" youth hostel movement, but it was slow to catch on in Canada due to the distance between suitable settings, the weather, the cost of memberships, and parental disapproval. In 1939 the CYHA executive invited Harriet Mitchell of the National Council of Women and the director of education at the Montreal Mental Hygiene Institute to explain the merits of hostelling to anxious parents. Mitchell addressed mothers, specifically those whom child psychologist John B. Watson called "emotional over-protective mothers."[80] Mitchell's children were CYHA members, and she playfully mocked mothers who worried that a fifteen-year-old son might not be strong enough to carry a packsack or able to do his own cooking or who fretted over a daughter who had never "washed out a thing in her life." Mitchell admitted that hostelling "almost inevitably involves some degree of risk ... but the benefits are immeasurable."[81] She was adamant that if a child was not afraid to try a new experience, parents must not generate anxiety by harping on the dangers of a strange situation. In 1939 the president of the University of Toronto, H.J. Cody, shared his vision of youth hostelling in the Canadian Youth Hostels Association's first annual *Handbook:* "It is better to build bridges of international understanding than to dig ditches of separation and hatred ... Our young people can gain the thrill of adventure, the enrichment of wider experience, the physical and mental discipline which will make for good citizenship."[82]

In the 1940s and 1950s, youth hostellers' stories revealed the pleasure of experiential education through the hitch and hike traditions of hostelling.[83] In 1954 the Alberta branch of the CYHA invited Lydia Paush, Diane Marchment, and Imogene Walker to describe the "thrills of [their] hitch-hike across Europe." The three College of Education co-eds at the University of Alberta strapped knapsacks onto their backs and stayed in hostels in Germany, Denmark, Holland, England, and Scotland. They saw St. Peter's Basilica, the Sistine Chapel, and a production of Richard Wagner's opera *Tristan und Isolde,* and they enjoyed fireworks and street dancing in Paris on Bastille Day.[84] At the CYHA information booth in Edmonton, backpacker Shirley Herdman said, "Hitchhiking is not frowned upon." Over 50 percent of hostellers hitchhiked. She advised

## Hitchhike Across Europe Adventure For Miss Pon

Edmonton still is a wonderful place to live according to petite Valeen Pon, 10137 97 st., who returned to the city from Europe shortly before Christmas.

During the past week Miss Pon has been busy re-acquainting herself with home and the many changes that have taken place in the past three years while she has been abroad. In recent months she has visited the celebrated capitals all over Europe.

The story of Valeen's adventures and achievements in Europe and England began about three years ago in Edmonton.

A graduate from the University of Washington in journalism, the ambitious young student decided she would like to travel and study in England.

Of course there was the matter of money, but that failed to daunt Valeen's spirit and she set to work saving and cutting

**MISS VALEEN PON**

was welcomed by Miss Georgi Christopoulu, president of the Greek Federation of University Women and a friend she had met in London, Mrs. Elli Papazachariou, a prominent woman lawyer, who last year represented the Women's Bar Association of Greece at the International Congress of Lawyers held in Istanbul.

Valeen Pon travels the hitch and hostel way, circa 1953.
*Scrapbook 1953–1956, North West Region, Edmonton, M7832, file 289,*
*Canadian Youth Hostels Association, Glenbow Museum Archives, Calgary*

western Canadians to "learn about the different customs as one can easily be embarrassed in breaking a rule."[85] In 1953 arts students Georgia Papas and Loraine Irving hitchhiked the whole length of Europe, with the exception of Greece, where there were very few cars on the road. They told fellow backpackers that $10 would last a long time and that American Express traveller's cheques were "better known than Canadian cheques."[86]

Valeen Pon was another hitch-hostel adventurer of the early 1950s. Valeen, whose Chinese name was Mei Ti Pon, and two girlfriends were unprepared to settle down after graduation in 1948, so they saved money for three years to travel to Europe. Pon worked at the welfare department in Edmonton and at her parents' restaurant, Lingnan Chop Suey. In Europe she discovered that the "only way" college and university students could ever hope to see Europe was by hitchhiking and hostelling. Pon traded her suitcase for a knapsack and joined in. Soon, she was living on $1 a day. By travelling the "youth hostel way," Pon said, "now I can define the various schools of art, literature, music and architecture."[87]

*Gospel of the Toothbrush: Drifter's Demeanour "Dos and Don'ts"*
The road from elite Grand Tours of Europe to thumbing across Canada during the Depression was a rocky one. For many, adventure hitchhiking was a serious vocation that must be understood within the context of the 1930s and the Second World War, as well as through the lens of class, gender, and generational liminality. Canada was a young nation that prided itself on being a land of opportunity, where the social class barriers of the old country no longer hindered social advancement.[88] Canadian-ization was associated with a willingness to embrace hard work, soap and water, purity and salvation – in other words, respectability.[89] Social purity campaigns maintained clear distinctions between rough and respectable members of the working class.[90] The belief that if people worked hard they would be successful was shared by Canada's wandering youth, who hoped that somewhere in the future the experience of travel could be an educational or economic asset.[91]

In the process of writing a hitchhiking story, journalists created an idealized image of young hitchhikers that set them apart from hobos and tramps, who were driven to thumb and bum due to dire economic cir-cumstances. Class-based social status was in flux, and foreign travel was a way to acquire social capital. By hitchhiking at home and abroad, working odd jobs, and sleeping rough, young Canadians were able to take self-directed tours of prestigious museums, cathedrals, ancient ruins, and romantic geographical sites, explore exotic destinations and monu-ments, and have direct encounters with art and culture at a time when such travel was well beyond a family's means. Typically, adventuring hitchhikers were the offspring of clergymen, immigrants, farmers, and labourers who shared economic hardships in their families before and during their travels. Youth on the road were well-spoken, industrious Jacks- and Janes-of-all-trades as well as students.[92] Socialist hitchhiker Ken Woodsworth said that the youth of his generation were "quite con-ventional in their dress and social behaviour."[93] In 1942 Ontario Veterin-ary College student Lloyd Mitton hitchhiked home on weekends to work on his family's farm. To attract motorists' attention and engage sympathy, he always wore his college jacket. During the lift, he let the driver know that he was working his way through college making 20 cents per hour at the Veterinary Barns.[94] After the war, future film director Norman

"Having a Cup of Coffee before Leaving,"
Bragg Creek hostel, August 22, 1959.
*Scrapbook 1959–1966, North West Region, Edmonton, M7832, file 290,*
*Canadian Youth Hostels Association, Glenbow Museum Archives, Calgary*

Jewison of Montreal hitchhiked around the southern United States still wearing his uniform.[95] To observers, hitchhikers' dress and demeanour indicated that they shared the dominant culture's belief in the value of cleanliness, respectable dress, and deportment; and unlike middle-class Victorian youth who wore vagabond disguises on "slumming" and "tramping" trips, Canadians dressed up when they went out on the road. Hitchhiker Samuel Zeidman said that the only possessions the thumb-traveller "really needs is a razor and tooth brush."[96]

In the period before 1960, the stereotype of the "college student" was still positive, and people enjoyed hearing about students' antics. When the Toll brothers returned from Europe, they discovered that they could make money selling tickets to people who wanted to see their "unusual" travelogue, called "Hitchhiking 'Round the World." The reviewer of the Kingsville Community Hall performance said there were "peals of laughter and applause" as "hundreds of the most beautiful colour pictures were

## L. A.' Was the Cry of Two Hiking Vancouver Girls

"We made our exit from Seattle, seated in the midst of a truckload of sawdust."

"'L.A.' Was the Cry of Two Hiking
Vancouver Girls," *Vancouver Sun,* circa 1924.
*In the scrapbook of Henrietta Lethbridge Watson Nickel,
courtesy of Renee and Sandra Bohun*

thrown on the screen." The audience's favourite photographs were taken at night inside an Egyptian pyramid: "[The] boys slept in an empty coffin in the big pyramid in Egypt, and the flashlight picture of Ellsworth as he rose out of the coffin was weird enough to catch the fancy of the entire audience."[97]

Journalists who wrote women's hitchhiking stories also went to great lengths to emphasize their respectability. Unlike the spoiled debutante hitchhiker in film director Frank Capra's *It Happened One Night* (1934), who raised her skirt with her right hand to show a tempting bit of leg and thigh in order to catch a lift, female adventure hitchhikers did not regard hitchhiking as an erotic performance. In the 1920s, newspaper representations of women replaced the dreary middle-aged "new woman" with a controversial girlish style embodied by "the flapper." As the name implied, this style was focused on the spatial freedoms of youth.[98] In 1924 the *Vancouver Sun* published a collage of cartoons and photographs of California-bound Bella Rigby and Rheta Watson. The careful artwork showed two smiling twenty year olds, with haircuts in the fashion of aviation pioneer Amelia Earhart, sitting in the back of a hay truck. To onlookers, they were the epitome of what gender historian Jane Nicholas calls "a quintessential Modern Girl: cool by disposition, somewhat masculine in appearance, athletic, and mobile."[99] Unlike the spinsters and bluestockings before the war, the bobbed-haired girl was regarded by the public at large as likely to be more interested in fun and shopping than politics or women's rights.

Watson liked the *Vancouver Sun* cartoon enough to paste it into her scrapbook for safe keeping. Katharine Trevelyan was unimpressed with the article that the *Toronto Star* printed about her in 1930, which described her as a "Shy Miss" with

a Will of her own – Camping Out ... like a shy English deer ... She is no flapper. Get that idea at the very start. She is sturdy Nordic, robust and strong, almost six feet tall, but thoroughly good-looking and feminine. She has the stature of an army officer, and wears a military raincoat and no hat. Her golden bobbed hair blows free in the wind. Her frail skin is bronzed, but with the pink cheeks of England.[100]

This description infuriated Trevelyan. She retorted, "It indicates what I did *not* say, what I do *not* look like, and what I am *not* going to do."[101] If being a flapper meant being independent and taking control of one's life, Trevelyan was certainly a flapper. She wrote, "I am a fool to let people try to make me into a fashionable lady. I am a fool to go to dances when I hate them. The time has come when I will stop trying to be someone I am not."[102]

In the 1950s the Canadian press continued to focus on what women hitchhikers wore. In 1954 the *Edmonton Journal* said that Lydia Paush, Diane Marchment, and Imogene Walker wore "grey pleated skirts, T-shirts and dark blazers."[103] Backpacker Shirley Herdman advised Canadian girls not to wear "slacks or blue jeans" in Europe because they "were not popular."[104] Valeen Pon wore a black skirt and black twin-sweater set and added coloured scarves for "variety." She said, "All my friends knew when I was really dressed up [because] I would wear a strand of pearls and earrings."[105] A photograph in *Maclean's* magazine shows Helen "Lenny" Burton and Jacqueline "Johnny" Cochrane with tidy haircuts, identical Royal Navy horn-toggle duffle coats from a military surplus store, two "stout army rucksacks," and good-quality leather footwear. Burton had on penny loafers, and Cochrane wore saddle shoes. Their 10-kilogram rucksacks contained sleeping bags, cooking utensils, and a few threadbare jerseys, washcloths, and one tube of lipstick to share. After wearing tattered jeans for a month, the women felt the contradiction when they got jobs at the London bureau of the *Reader's Digest* and "found it strange and unnatural to be 'ladies' again in skirts and blouses and pearl necklaces."[106]

Feminist geographers stress that for any generation, a woman's freedom to venture to untried places has depended upon where she was going and why.[107] When travel was an extension of a traditional feminine role, whether a woman was rich or poor, there were many cultural moments when her presence on the road promoted sociological, psychological, and gender cohesion. During the toughest years of the 1930s, there was strong social approval of "trios and pairs" of "job-seeking" women and girls, whom the *Globe and Mail* reported were often seen "trekking along near Norfolk County looking for work in the tobacco fields." In August 1938 eight women from the Cooper family, including an eight-month-old baby girl, posed for the newspaper's photographer. They had hitchhiked more than 320 kilometres to work in the tobacco fields. The sixteen-year-old "girl-wife," Joyce, said "it was awfully cold some nights."[108] Emily Post admired the way reputable women shared in the war effort by working in ammunition industries during the Second World War, prompting her to write to the US Office of War Information in order to give her nod to hitchhiking for "defense debutantes," provided they followed her list of "dos and don'ts" and thumbed to their factory jobs in a "patriotic" manner. Post instructed factory girls to "remember that the rides are not social gatherings and conversation is not necessary." She told them to wear defence identification tags in order to indicate "why she needs a lift ... If they must talk, girls should stick to impersonal subjects [like weather and scenery]. Talking about their personal concerns to or before strangers would be in very bad taste! Talking about their jobs might give out dangerous information."[109]

In a study of Canadian teenagers, Mary Louise Adams notes that in the reconstruction period following the Second World War, many adults saw "teens as symbols of the modern age." The peacetime image of confident young women like Joyce Hill and Margaret Smith was the assurance that the devastation of war had not produced another lost generation."[110] In a somewhat tarnished Grand Tour fashion, the *Newmarket Era and Express* dubbed Hill and Smith Canada's 1945 "hitchhiking ambassadors."[111] In 1951 Jacqueline "Johnny" Cochrane celebrated her twenty-first birthday in Paris. She said that it was "the most exciting coming-of-age party any girl ever had."[112] As we have seen, the Canadian Youth Hostels Association encouraged female members to finish their education with hitching and hostelling tours of Europe. The *Edmonton Journal* called Valeen Pon a "brilliant scholar." The paper printed her graduation photograph and said that "the small Chinese girl" counted many prominent members of the International Federation of University Women and the Greek Women's Bar Association among the friends she had stayed with along the way.[113] The media travel narratives represented girl hitchhikers as educated, career-minded, and forward-looking women participating in educational travel. They were not tramps, objects of pity, shunned, helpless, or in trouble.[114] They had their parents' consent, they knew that they would be missed, and they kept in touch with family and friends by letters, postcards, and telegrams.

### Road Rage: "Thumbs Down on Hitchhikers!"

On a summer afternoon in 1935, Frank Fitzgerald and William Hill went on a sightseeing tour from Toronto to Goderich. A Huron County farmer spotted them hitchhiking "from town to town" and wrote a letter to the *Toronto Globe* complaining that too many "tourists are hitchhiking for the fun" and for the handouts "they get out of it."[115] Given Canada's seemingly positive response to thumb-travel, it is instructive to note that many provinces restricted where it could be done. In Ontario hitchhiking was a violation of the Highway Traffic Act (1934). The Ontario Provincial Police could charge hitchhikers with "soliciting a ride from any motor vehicle on the travelled portion of the public highway." Fines ranged from $5 to $25, and repeat offenders could be incarcerated.[116] Furthermore, vagrancy was an offence under the Criminal Code of Canada. A penniless traveller was a vagrant in the eyes of the law and a "depraved savage" in the eyes of many generations of working people who disliked the tramping lifestyle and the "get something for nothing" attitude.[117] In the 1930s "tourists" like Fitzgerald and Hill flouted local customs, broke the law, and set a bad example for local youth. When the young men stopped at the Goderich Police Station to ask for a meal, Chief Postlethwaite told them that "they would be welcome" at the dinner table of a nearby farmhouse, provided they spent a few hours in "the hayfield." Failing that, he gave them "half an hour to get out of town," or else he would put them in jail.[118] The focus of this section is the inherent ambiguity of the hitchhiking ritual. Some Canadians regarded hitchhikers as abusers of local charity and hospitality on the path toward delinquency.[119]

In the early twentieth century, there were people who did not like that motor tourism was becoming a popular new leisure activity. Prior to the First World War, road construction was a touchy subject in many regions of the country. In 1910 an angry farmer told an Ontario legislative committee that motorists were "scoundrels" who "should be shot."[120] Automobiles were banned in Prince Edward Island until 1913, when the newly elected provincial legislature permitted motor vehicles on public roads only on Mondays, Wednesdays, and Thursdays. Western prairie farmers had been the principal impetus behind the "highway movement" because they sought a farm-to-market connection and relief from rural isolation, but they were reluctant to pay taxes in order to build roads that did not facilitate their needs.[121] Farmers regarded "motor touring" as a destructive urban phenomenon; tensions arose when hordes of city cars invaded the countryside. Noisy cars and reckless drivers frightened horses, and macadamized roads disintegrated rapidly under the impact of their whirling wheels, which turned stones or gravel into dust. Infuriated farmers complained when the dust descended on their fields and ruined crops. Some farmers retaliated against urban road hogs by sabotaging their travel. They buried planks with spikes, scattered tacks, and strung wires across roadways, and they charged tolls and extortionate prices for gasoline and towing.[122]

*Something for Nothing: "Give Us a Ride, Piker"*

The attraction of free automobile travel was a temptation to all but the most morally disciplined young person. American psychologist G. Stanley Hall observed that when wanderlust appeared in teenagers, their world suddenly felt "dull by want, and perhaps even nauseating because of familiarity." He argued that in a well-adjusted child, "wanderlust" could be the "elementary expression of the romantic interest in life," yet he noted that wanderlust was also the root of both adolescent vulnerability and the restless and rebellious impulses in "young hobos."[123] Child psychologist Cyril Burt's studies of boy criminals affirmed that running away led to "far more desperate misdemeanours."[124] In the 1920s Robert E. Park's sociological studies of adult tramps' childhood and adolescence indicated that "the hobo, who begins his career" by breaking the physical and emotional ties that bind well-adjusted people to their families, friends, and the community, will eventually break all other associations. Accordingly, the hobo was not just a "homeless man, he was a man without a cause and without a country."[125]

After the 1929 stock market crash, there were over 1 million Canadian families on relief and 300,000 unemployed youth. Cynthia Comacchio emphasizes that the "economic deprivation did bear down especially hard on the young," stating that the "unreliable statistics" of the period indicate an unemployment rate of more than 50 percent for youth aged fourteen to twenty-five, higher than that of any other age group.[126] Social workers dealt with case files of teenagers who had been pushed from home due to family discord or had left altruistically to reduce burdens of poverty. They feared that on the road these impressionable youngsters would be exposed to low company, gangsters, and hoodlumism.[127] In 1934 a young American sociologist, Thomas Minehan, disguised himself in tattered clothes and hopped freight trains across the Midwestern United States. The result was a study called *Boy and Girl Tramps of America,* which surveyed five hundred homeless and wandering boys and girls. Minehan showed that the youngsters torn from home due to the Depression had less education than average and had never enjoyed "the normal pleasures and contacts of childhood and youth" or participated in Boy Scouts, Girl Guides, or community activities such as baseball, basketball, or dramatics.

Equally disturbing was Minehan's observation that wandering without direction was contagious among youth. No sooner had it arisen in one part of the country than it spread, causing a "mob psychology" and a "mass movement" in the nation's boys and girls.[128]

In Ontario an officer of the Dominion-Provincial Youth Training Programme told guests at a Lions Club luncheon in 1939 that the boys and girls he picked up on the road between Fort William and Cornwall had informed him that "they had to sleep in surroundings that would rouse protests from the Humane Society if somebody's dog was substituted."[129] He repeated Minehan's concern that the hordes of boys and girls who spent years on the road would have great difficulty reintegrating into society when prosperity returned to the country.[130] This being the case, the staff of the Dominion-Provincial Youth Training Programme recommended early intervention whenever possible. Wandering boys should receive industrial training, and girls on the road should be found places in domestic service, where they would be under the supervision of respectable people.[131]

Wanderlust was not solely an affliction of the rough and impulsive social classes. Unlike traditional forms of juvenile delinquency, such as theft, precocious sexuality, and gang membership, which were supposedly rooted in the homes of the poor and immigrant families, hitchhiking was singled out by social workers, teachers, and the police as a universally bad habit that also fostered laziness, poor manners, and a "get something for nothing" attitude in middle-class children.[132] In the 1920s the negligent child-rearing customs of affluent "uplifters" were said to be producing a generation of "well-nourished" looking, albeit annoying, "boy ride-beggars."[133] A YMCA spokesman urged well-meaning motorists to let touring pedestrians "keep walking" and told parents to "advise" their children not to hitchhike. He cautioned that "the small boy is the most persistent solicitor of free motor rides,"[134] adding that "even going only a few blocks to school, he often prefers to stand in the road waiting for a ride rather than walk the short distance."[135]

Working people sent letters to newspapers complaining about all ranks of hitchhikers, including school pupils who stuck their heads into automobiles, demanded lifts, and then muttered insults like "piker" (cheapskate) when motorists turned them away.[136] In 1935 a driver described for the *Toronto Globe* the all too frequent occurrence of a "smartly dressed young lad" poking "his impudent head" inside a car and yelling, "Give us a ride." An article entitled "Injury Peril Grows with Hitch-Hiking among Students" quoted a member of the Toronto School Board:

> Some of these young fellows get as much pocket money in a week as poor children get in a year, yet they disdain streetcars. Not good enough for the likes of them, I guess. They settle back in somebody else's car with a lordly air, and think they are pretty smart ... When I went to school I walked three miles through the snow and rain ... Now these young gaffers get pretty impertinent if some hardworking citizen doesn't give them a lift for ten blocks.[137]

After a motorist picked up five boys who put their feet on his car seats, rifled through his belongings, and stole his driver's permit, which later turned up in a garbage bin, he said, "This, you see, is why one more driver gives no more rides."[138] For Torontonians, the sight of lazy pupils and schoolgirls hitchhiking home dismayed their teachers. The Toronto School Board tried to stop the "heart-breaking spectacle." Police officers made fools of themselves when they "lectured and warned" the youngsters, who only pretended to be "crestfallen and apologetic." The junior culprits knew hitchhiking was a violation of the Highway Traffic Act, but they doubted the police would arrest them or take them to the juvenile court, as some American states were doing. The next day, police officers spotted the same children out on the road hitchhiking.[139]

### Hitchhikers in Khaki: "The Nation's Shame"

Much of the anti-hitchhiking sentiment was ignored until the Depression era when child psychologists became concerned about the impact of economic disruption on family life.[140] The lack of employment opportunities for teenagers was the topic of articles in *Maclean's*, *Saturday Night*, and *Chatelaine*. Social workers asserted that unemployed fathers' "shame" upset the status of men in the home and impacted the development of boys' masculine traits. The Depression appeared to be crushing young men, who became disillusioned, emasculated, indolent, and stuck in "the liminal phase between youth and adulthood," ultimately regressing from men back into boys again.[141]

One youth organization that took a proactive stance against the slack behaviour of boys was the Boy Scouts.[142] The mandate of the scouting organization was to produce the "'right kind of boy' citizen" through character training and "manly self-reliance."[143] Scoutmasters were uneasy about their members hitchhiking. In 1932 the Executive Board of the Canadian General Council of the Boy Scouts Association decided that the popular hitchhiking habit was "a complete negative to the spirit of Scouting and should be forbidden."[144] Nonetheless, like other boys, Scouts were enthusiastic hitchhikers and ignored the rule. On Victoria Day in 1933, an "innocent hike became a hitchhike" that resulted in a countywide search for four "inconsiderate" Toronto Scouts whose parents had to fetch them home from North Bay. The Executive Board responded to this misadventure by reasserting an anti-hitchhiking stance. Scoutmasters appealed to motorists to stop offering lifts to Scouts because it "tempted" them to "cheat on their 14-mile hiking badges."[145] Scouts should not be classified with "other thumbers" even when they were caught behaving "unscoutly." In the 1930s the Boy Scouts of Canada created new mottos: "Real Scouts don't hitchhike!" and "Scouts hike, they don't hitchhike!" The Boy Scouts of Canada regarded hitchhiking as "a disease" to be "stamped out."[146]

When Canada entered the Second World War in 1939, the average age of the Canadian Armed Forces volunteers was 19.5 years. Overnight, teenagers were expected to become soldiers.[147] In every province, teenagers like Ed Cyples and his friends "thought it would be nice to get in the forces." "Fresh out of high school," sixteen-year old Cyples left home and hitchhiked hundreds of kilometres to enlist in the Highland Light Infantry in London, Ontario.[148] Around the time that thousands of young men like Cyples put on military uniforms, youth gangs from Montreal to Prince George, British Columbia, appeared wearing a counteruniform called the zoot suit, which consisted of an Edwardian-style jacket, wing-tipped shoes, and a wide-brim fedora. For some people, boys' zoot suit costumes were an affront to wartime austerity, patriotism, and sacrifice. In the 1940s and 1950s flashy clothes were regarded as dangerous to social

order and were linked to juvenile delinquency.[149] Tailors were investi-
gated for violations of fabric rationing, and high school principals for-
bade boys to wear pleated trousers to school.[150] Anti-zoot campaigns
illustrated just how angrily adults reacted when youth violated normative
dress codes.[151]

In 1939 the public's anxiety about boy hitchhikers expanded from Boy
Scouts to the Canadian military as "hitchhikers in khaki" became a familiar and controversial sight.[152] Military historians Geoffrey Hayes and
Kirk Goodlet suggest that by the Second World War an altered patriotic
ethos had replaced the Great War's heroic "discourses of sacrifice."[153] In
the 1940s new recruits were familiar with the conduct expected of the
ideal soldier, but new institutions, economic uncertainties, commercial
technologies, and a "live for today" mentality influenced the type of
soldiers and officers that Canadian youth wanted to be.[154] Consequently,
the early years of the war saw mounting alarm over moral laxity and poor
social decorum in the military, which was piqued by displays of rudeness,
beverage room intoxication, and brawls and street fighting that affronted
hegemonic ideas about manliness and patriotism.[155]

Many First World War veterans and civilian onlookers continued to
picture the military through a lens coloured by romantic paternalism.[156]
For them, the soiled image of the drifter did not transfer well to the
discipline expected of a soldier in uniform. In the early stages of the war,
the army did not issue any general orders against hitchhiking and the
Ministry of Defence did not develop an extensive ride-sharing program
with civilians like the British government did.[157] Soldiers were not permitted to keep private vehicles on military bases; therefore, a debate
quickly arose in the press after enlisted men were seen hitchhiking back
and forth to military camps. Letters to the *Globe and Mail* put hitchhiking at the centre of public anxiety about lax military discipline. One
writer said that soldiers "thumbing" along the highway were a "distressing
sight to behold." Another said that it was "belittling to the dignity of
uniformed men." Another called it "behaviour unfitting" for the "King's
Army." It was against the law in Ontario and, therefore, "degrading to the
soldier" and "the nation's shame." There was some consensus that hitchhiking made the Canadian military look like a "bad organization and
insufficient in regard to the morale and the reputation of the army."[158]

Enlisted men and women were still "wild boys [and girls] of the road."[159] The pleasure and freedom of hitchhiking outweighed both the risk of violating the hitching ban and the precious time and money that would be wasted on bus or train tickets.[160] During their long furlough, Captain Marie Spearman and Private Barbara Dennison of the Canadian Women's Army Corps hitchhiked over 4,800 kilometres to California. They said, "We got a flip all the way from Detroit to San Francisco." The trip was "interesting and exciting," and they wired home that they were "having a wonderful time."[161] The suggestion that one must not hitch-hike because it made the "King's Army" look bad caused a soldier to sourly remark, "There will always be an England ... but to heck with the soldiers."[162]

In wartime or peacetime, one of the dominant ambiguities of the hitchhiking experience was that the true identity of a hitchhiker could never be known. The clauses of Ontario's Highway Traffic Act that pro-hibited soliciting rides were in place to protect "kind-hearted car drivers" from feeling guilty for passing by stranded pedestrians. In 1942 a soldier from the Peterborough training centre was given six months in jail for beating up the motorist who had picked him up while hitchhiking.[163] That spring, a Montreal motorist drove two hitchhikers "clad in khaki trousers and blue work shirts" to the Canadian border. Later, it was discovered that the men were really "fugitive Nazis" who had "hitchhiked away" from Bowmanville's prisoner of war camp.[164]

## The Vanishing Hitchhiker: Unadjusted Girls

Folklorists of the early twentieth century observed that hitchhiking could flourish only in a culture that saw "nothing strange in the use of auto-mobiles over long distances ... nothing exotic in the casual intimacy between complete strangers which hitchhiking implies, and no breach of etiquette" in making a roadside "pickup."[165] Feminist geographers challenge this notion, arguing that spaces are gendered and that histor-ically women who took to the open road were "deemed to be erratic misfits."[166] The gendered ambiguity of hitchhiking reveals the cultural assumption that women have a different relation to cars and the road than men have. Mimi Sheller and John Urry suggest that the male dom-ination of public space appears in the practice of "kerbcrawling" by men in motorcars. For women, the road is a stage where their hitchhiking bodies perform for the "prevalent male gaze."[167] Whereas social workers had always maintained that when girls went "astray" they headed straight for the streets, mid-twentieth-century tracts on social problems said that if wanderlust was not monitored, it could lead both boys and girls toward juvenile delinquency.

Female hitchhikers were aware that fellow travellers regarded them as "intruders."[168] In folklore and Western travel narratives, Vanessa Veselka writes, "a man with a quest, internal or external, makes the choice at every stage about whether to endure the consequences or turn back, and that choice is imbued with heroism." In contrast, there was a "prohibition against quests for women" because girls on the road worried people.[169] In the twentieth century, cars enhanced the mobility of the daughters of immigrants and suburban middle-class girls, whose parents sometimes brought them to court to curtail their "hitchhiking escapes to nearby towns" and joyriding with boys.[170] These defiant rule breakers became the subjects of detailed case studies by social workers concerned that bad things happened to girls who defied patriarchal expectations, left home, and stayed out late. Neither motorists nor male hitchhikers considered it in bad taste to "defame the general character" of girls on the road.[171] Female students were not permitted to join the Hitchhiking Club at Berkeley College.[172] In the 1920s Vancouver hitchhikers Bella Rigby and Rheta Watson noticed that whenever married couples passed them, the wives forced a "look of disdain."[173] In 1938 social workers in Ontario compiled psychometric descriptions of the "mental state" of teenage girls "bitten by the wanderlust bug." A total of 76 girls under sixteen and 152 girls over sixteen ran away from home. Their psychological profiles revealed that they had left home because they were unhappy there, were following a boyfriend, wanted to join the circus, or had dreams of stardom in New York and Hollywood. From these facts, the social workers concluded, "It is generally agreed that home conditions – the economic status of the family, restrictions of freedom and other factors – are not the cause of most cases of 'itchy feet.' The irresistible yearning to see the world, if only a small portion, in a few days is the answer to most instances of wanderlust."[174] As mentioned, during the Second World War, Emily Post reminded hitchhiking factory girls that car "rides are not social gatherings."[175] As we have seen, in the 1950s, women thumb-travellers tried to mitigate the risk to their character through what Torun Elsrud calls "identity reading" – in their case, by adopting the easily recognized appearance of a "lady-like" sportswoman and dressing up when hitchhiking.[176]

None of this is to say that rebellious, rude, inconsiderate, and angry young women did not exist.[177] In the summer of 1951, twenty-year-old Everett Amaral encountered some of them when he picked up three teenage girls hitchhiking. The *Globe and Mail* reported that the "handsome, curly-haired" Everett was terrified by three girls with a long-bladed knife who sexually assaulted him. One hitcher had red hair, and another was a brunette; they "were pretty." Everett told the police that "the short dumpy one" forced him to have sexual intercourse. "Knife girl held the weapon almost at my face and the third girl drove the car to a lonely road," he said. Afterward, the hitchhikers forced him to drive to a drugstore to buy a bottle of peroxide because "they'd decided to become blondes." The police charged the "amorous trio" with lewd behaviour and disorderly conduct.[178]

Girls paid a high social cost for hitchhiking. In the cultural imagination, patriarchy values women as agents of social preservation rather than social change; it is their job to wait patiently at home while men quest, pilgrimage, and adventure. The low social and gender status of female vagrants is revealed by the harsh way that unmarried, unemployed, and homeless women were treated in the Criminal Code of Canada in 1892. The Criminal Code equated homelessness and unemployment with prostitution; therefore, a police officer could arrest any woman for vagrancy whom he suspected to be a streetwalker if she was unable to give a "good account of herself."[179] Joan Sangster notes that in the early decades of the twentieth century, very few girls and women had accurate sexual knowledge, that they frequently had only their sexuality with which to barter for food, lodging, and transportation, and that their transgressions were seen as less reversible than those of boys.[180] The best solution the police had was to apprehend hitchhiking girls and get them off the road, rescued, and resettled as soon as possible. In New York, state troopers offered them coffee and sandwiches and sent them to church-run Homes for Wayward and Fallen Girls, to Girls' Service Club Homes, and to the Florence Crittenton Home.[181] In Canada fifteen-year-old Mary Walsh hitchhiked more than 24,100 kilometres from Toronto to Wadena, Saskatchewan, before turning herself over to the police after a driver put her out in the middle of nowhere. The police questioned the driver and sent Mary to the Manitoba Home for Girls to await her appearance in juvenile court for running away.[182] Two sisters from Hamilton were picked up hitchhiking to Toronto. They sat huddled together in the prisoner's box, refusing to go home. The court social worker took them to the Catholic Welfare Home.[183] These residential facilities stigmatized the girls and punished them, although they had not committed any crimes.

### "Don't Pick Up Trouble:" The Vanishing Hitchhiker and the Criminal Law

Alongside adventurous road stories by well-adjusted rucksack-wearing youngsters, a counternarrative appeared in the press and popular culture that transformed hitchhiking from the embodiment of trust and sharing into a risky, nerve-racking, and dangerous activity. In the 1940s and 1950s, popular culture, crime reports, and official narratives put a spotlight on scary road stories, which altered the hitchhiking ritual drastically.

In the 1920s typical hitchhikers were middle-class youth who hitched because they were wealthy enough to afford the leisure time and sufficiently carefree to heed their yearning for adventure; however, in the 1930s and 1940s a "grim earnestness replaced the insouciance of earlier years."[184] In the United States, state legislatures and automobile insurance companies took a proactive stance against hitchhiking. Various states passed traffic laws with clauses that made it an offence "for anyone to ask for a ride or offer a ride on the open highway."[185] The tightest restrictions were in the southern states and the Los Angeles area, where virtually all trucks carried the sign "Sorry, No Riders." Anti-hitchhiking laws were regarded as a weak deterrent because the number of state troopers was too low for their adequate enforcement.[186] Anti-hitchhiking rhetoric was made flesh in the 1950s by the director of the Federal Bureau of Investigation, J. Edgar Hoover, who feared a spreading Communist menace. In 1957 Hoover warned motorists against picking up hitchhikers. FBI posters said, "Don't Pick Up Trouble!" Hoover added, "The beckoning thumb of the hitchhiker can be a lure to disaster in disguise."[187]

The most effective anti-hitchhiking campaigns were played out in the national press, which reported the details of American hitchhiker crimes as constant reminders to Canadians of the risks of picking up strangers. For instance, the Canadian press joined American papers in reporting the details of the 1943 execution by electric chair of William Haggard, found guilty of murdering two thirteen-year-old caddies whom he had picked up hitchhiking home from a golf course. Haggard, who had shot each boy in the head, "stuck his tongue out at the jury" when the guilty verdict was announced.[188] In 1950 the trustworthy *Reader's Digest* published a lengthy article called "Thumbs Down on Hitchhikers! Too Many Rob and Kill," in which Don Wharton summarized the gruesome details of twenty years of hitchhiking-related crimes, murders, rapes, and accidents.[189] And in 1951 the *Globe and Mail* described a blood-spattered, bullet-ridden car found in Oklahoma; the "ignition keys still hung from the dashboard." The bodies of the driver, his wife, and their three small children were missing and police suspected that the family had been murdered by a hitchhiker.[190] Canada had its own tales of thumb-travel gone wrong due to car accidents, highway injuries, and police interventions. In 1938 a Saskatchewan farmer was shot in the back by a young, transient hitchhiker he had befriended.[191] In 1944 Ernest Teale murdered Alexander Vansickle, a sixty-five-year-old Melfort farmer, who had picked up Teale when the "fair-faced youth" was hitchhiking in the district.[192] In 1963, in Lillooet, British Columbia, a rancher found the hacked-up remains of a young Quebec hitchhiker, Henri Meriguet, in a ravine by the old Cariboo Cattle Trail. The Royal Canadian Mounted Police were confounded because parts of his body were found in three sacks, one containing the torso, one the arms, and one the upper parts of the legs; missing were the head and the lower parts of the legs.[193]

The press reported the details of numerous hitchhiking-related accidents. A twenty-five-year-old Ontario man broke his neck when he fell off the back of a lumber truck in Vancouver while hitchhiking. A fifteen-year-old girl was killed when the freight truck that picked her up plunged more than 20 metres down a rocky cliff on the Fraser Canyon Highway. In 1937 a Saskatchewan hitchhiker said that very reckless drivers and "hop heads that were weaving all over the roads" had picked him up.

"You were taking your life in your hands" when you "stepped into some cars."[194] Motorists were annoyed too. In 1943 a motorist said, "I have been imposed on by professional road lice, liquor addicts, charmers who bring their boyfriends out of hiding when the car pulls up, hard luck guys who break my heart before I have travelled 10 miles ... I have been thumbed, shouted at, insulted, and often crowded into the oncoming traffic."[195]

By the 1950s everyday Canadians feared that they no longer knew their neighbours, which gave rise to a sense of insecurity that could quickly be mobilized against strangers. In addition to highway legislation, the passing in 1948 of Canada's new legislation on "the criminal sexual psychopath" contributed to public anxiety about dangerous strangers.[196] In the 1950s Lunacy Acts of the Victorian era were repealed. The new trend in psychiatry was to release people with mental illnesses from hospitals and return them to their communities, where they depended on drugs to control their behaviour. Criminologist Andrew Scull argues that "decarceration" increased the visibility of psychiatric patients in the community. Included among the conspicuous strangers who occasioned increased anxiety and distrust were hitchhikers.[197] In Canada the Cold War era marked the beginning of the "child molester scare." Parents urged children to report sightings of strange men in cars.[198]

At the same time that social workers' theories of juvenile delinquency linked hitchhiking to the nerve-racking behaviour of girls, the predatory femme fatale hitchhiker became a stock character of Hollywood movies, true crime novellas, and television shows. The hitchhiker in film director Edgar Ulmer's *Detour* (1945) was a venomous femme fatale who, we are told, "looked like she'd just been thrown off the crummiest freight train in the world."[199] In 1955 viewers of the popular television series *Dragnet* watched an episode where a female hitchhiker beat and robbed male motorists.[200] Thumbsploitation movies for the teen market, with names like *The Violent Years* (1956) and *The Night Holds Terror* (1955), dramatized the violence perpetrated upon innocent motorists by teenage girls and youth gangs. These stereotypes, fiction or fact, fuelled public fear and fantasies about strangers on the road. Henceforth, occasions for roadside chivalry collapsed when gentleman motorists discovered that the "pretty travellers" were only pretending to be farmers' daughters; their boyfriends were hiding in the bushes ready to beat and rob them.[201]

As the decades passed, good ride stories about well-adjusted boys and girls were overshadowed by stories about the survivors of hitchhikers' assaults and the "folly of motorists picking up hitchhikers."[202] In 1964 the *Stouffville Tribune* called picking up hitchhikers "bad business." The *Newmarket Era and Express* reported that out of every "100 hitchhikers that pass through a small town, it was found that 84 had criminal records and twelve others were either juvenile runaways or absent-without-leave servicemen. Only four out of 100 were without police records."[203] The *Era and Express* also wrote,

> Some people believe they can pick out a respectable hitchhiker. However, too often they guess wrong. Some provinces prohibit hitchhiking but the law is not rigidly enforced. Despite all warnings, motorists continue to invite strangers into their cars ... Some drivers seem to feel guilty when they turn down an upturned thumb on the road. Don't. You wouldn't open your home to them, why admit one to your car?[204]

The subsequent decline in hitchhiking was explained by the improvement of the economy and the "democratization of car ownership," which meant that more people, especially men, without ownership and access to cars were marginalized and stigmatized.[205]

### Conclusion: "No Riders"

In the first half of the twentieth century, adventurous young women and men thumbing for cars, trains, and even horses became common figures of the North American roadscape. Their stories caught the imagination of everyday Canadians who respected the educational value of travel as a means of entry to "the school of the world."[206] Hitchhikers also became fictional characters in magazine stories, movies, and other forms of popular culture. The most famous literary example comes from John Steinbeck's *The Grapes of Wrath* (1939), which begins with Tom Joad hitchhiking home after being released from prison. A trucker points to a sign on his windshield that says, "No Riders." Tom replies, "Sure – I seen it. But sometimes a guy'll be a good guy even if some rich bastard makes him carry a sticker."[207] Tom got a lift.

Steinbeck put hitchhiking at the centre of solidarity among working people; almost fifteen years later, the title character of director Ida Lupino's film *The Hitch-Hiker* (1953) was shown as a murderer who would "stop at nothing." But *The Hitch-Hiker* was based on a crime spree in 1951 that began with the killing of a family of five in Oklahoma, as referred to earlier.[208] Such real-life crime stories, and the urban legend of the vanishing hitchhiker, revealed the dominant truth of hitchhiking: one never knew the true identity of people they met on the road. In tandem with adventurous road stories, then, a counternarrative appeared in the press and popular culture challenging the assumption that a hitchhiking adventure created social cohesion between classes, genders, and generations.[209] Following the Second World War, hitchhikers became statistically and by definition deviant, morally suspect, disreputable, abnormal, and dangerous. Ironically, despite the creation of laws in Prince Edward Island, Nova Scotia, New Brunswick, Quebec, Ontario, and British Columbia that prohibited soliciting car rides on "the roadway," Canadian highways were again "swarming with hitchhikers" in the late 1960s when the children born after the war came of age.[210] It was still a risky thing to play the part of a Good Samaritan, but people from all walks of life appreciated a lift from time to time.

The Buddha left home as a young man, leaving behind family and wealth, in search of knowledge ... One day during his wanderings he encountered an aged man, a sick man, and a corpse. From these encounters he realized that suffering was an inescapable part of life, whereupon he determined to forsake wealth and power in the quest for truth – in the quest for answering the question why life exists in the first place.

– *Marcel Danesi*, Geeks, Goths, and Gangstas *(2010)*

"Sal, we gotta go and never stop going till we get there."
"Where we going, man?"
"I don't know, but we gotta go."

– *Jack Kerouac*, On the Road *(1957)*

# 3
# Rucksack Revolution
## Quest in the Age of Aquarius

Hitchhikers from Toronto and British
Columbia taking a break near Winnipeg, September 18, 1970.
*Photographer unknown, Winnipeg Tribune Fonds, PC 18/3518/18–2747–006,*
*University of Manitoba Archives and Special Collections*

**In 1966 a** twelve-year-old girl met some "hippie people" in Ontario who were hitchhiking through Peterborough on the way to Vancouver. She fell in love with the way they were dressed. She went home and "furiously" started drawing pictures of teenage travellers "with backpacks ... and bellbottoms, sandals, long hair and beards, and guitars and stuff ... Each one was different." She plastered the walls of her bedroom with her art because it looked "so cool." When her mother asked her what she was doing, she replied, "These are all the people I'm going to meet when I go to Vancouver."[1] Between 1961 and 1971 the population in Canada aged fifteen to twenty-four increased by 53 percent.[2] The adult world watched them come of age and struggle to run as much of their own lives as they could by "doing their own thing," even when it meant being called dropouts, hippies, radicals, and troublemakers.[3]

Cold War childhood socialization was shaped by the numerous challenges of modernity. Understanding this generation's behaviour requires exploring the interactions between the subjective world of youth subculture and the dynamics of the larger social structure in the postwar period. This chapter examines why ride-thumbing adventure trips were appealing to teenagers, students, workers, and Aboriginal youth at liminal moments in early adulthood, when hitchhiking was equated with freedom and meaningful spiritual, political, and anti-materialist encounters. The news that a youngster was planning to hit the road sometimes met with parental approval, but the drifter identity was often disapproved of due to parents' fear that if their child left home to drift around, it was a sign of their failure to raise a child who was a productive citizen. In the 1960s and early 1970s, young people adopted drifter, wanderer, and transient identities by consulting peer networks, hitchhiker guidebooks, and university newspapers for advice. By resisting hegemonic class and gender expectations, they put a new twist on the rituals associated with traditional Canadian tourism. Their oral history stories highlight biographical moments when understandings of Canadian landscapes and citizenship were formed.

### *"Something to Sing About": Intersections and Automobility Rituals*
Canada's birthrate was among the highest in the industrial world in the period after the Second World War.[4] Like generations before them, school

children were taught stories, poems, and songs that ignored Aboriginal peoples and praised the bravery of European explorers, pioneers, and national heroes who made their fortunes through risk, adventure, and travel. In the mid-1960s preparations began for the country's hundredth anniversary celebrations, which included the new Maple Leaf flag and a Centennial train that chugged across the country like "a history book on rails."[5] The assumption that children should be proud ambassadors in their "home and native land" was embodied in the national anthem. "O Canada" (1906) was sung at public gatherings, sports events, and symphony concerts, whereas "God Save the Queen," "if played at all, [was] rendered at the end." National pride was also embodied in Bobby Gimby's bilingual Expo 67 theme song, "Ca-na-da" (1967),[6] and in Oscar Brand's spirited phrase "this land of ours" in the song "Something to Sing About" (1963). All over the country, children sang, "I have walked on the strand of the Grand Banks of Newfoundland / Lazed on the ridge of the Miramichi ... From the Vancouver Island to the Alberta Highland / 'Cross the Prairies, the lakes to Ontario's towers / From the sound of Mount Royal's chimes, out to the Maritimes / Something to sing about, this land of ours." Cold War schoolbooks, patriotic songs, and picture atlases undoubtedly sparked the wanderlust and imagination of many young people whose heroes broke ties with family and friends to seek their fortunes and move onward and upward.[7]

Tarah Brookfield argues that the ethos of prosperity inherent in pediatrician Benjamin Spock's childrearing theories, which replaced child psychologist John B. Watson's behaviourism, must have sounded like "the voice of God" to baby boom parents.[8] Spock gave parents permission to forget about the Depression and advised them not to frighten their children unnecessarily with stories of battlefield atrocities or the grim facts of nuclear war. Hardworking Canadians wanted children to have stability, prosperity, and choices that had been unknown to many families in the 1930s and 1940s. In 1967 the *Toronto Daily Star* announced that Canadians were on a "spending spree." The cash registers throughout the country rang up $22 billion in retail sales and $4 billion in construction and redevelopment. In 1966 trends in car sales indicated that the three-car family would soon be the norm and that $900 million was spent on trips outside Canada that year, an increase of 13 percent over

1965.[9] Economists announced that the middle class was "no longer in the traditional middle, but upwardly mobile." Social workers fretted that the gap "between the have somes, which used to be the middle-class objective, and the have nothings" was widening, but their concerns were drowned out by "the din of earthmoving equipment and speeches at the opening of yet another Centennial museum, library, park, or planetarium."[10] By the time of the grand opening of the 7,821-kilometre Trans-Canada Highway in 1962, those youth who had arrived with the wave of Spock babies born in 1948 were in high school. The nation expected them to be confident and proud of their citizenship in the "fashionable young country."[11]

Doug Owram asserts that most boomer babies were driven home from hospital maternity wards in the family car. They were the first generation for whom "automania" was "unexceptional."[12] To persuade upwardly mobile families to focus their leisure time on consumerism, advertisers put the automobile at the centre of modern life. The "family car" should be used to explore, buy services, and consume modern lifestyle conveniences, such as a drive-in meal at an A&W. Children wanted Matchbox cars, Dinky Toys, and a pink convertible for Barbie. The new middle-class holiday craze was a major cross-provincial summer vacation in a camper van or motor home, beginning with a road trip to see Expo 67 pavilions in Montreal.

As they grew up, hitchhiking offered young people the same excitement and immediate way to participate in multiple forms of youth culture that it had offered their parents and grandparents. Like the youth of earlier generations, they ignored adults' warnings not to stand out in busy traffic or take rides from strangers. There were very few school buses for high school students. A Windsor girl said, "There would be fifty kids hitchhiking in waves at one point in the intersection from four o'clock on."[13] In Prince Edward Island, "normally girls would hitch in pairs ... For guys, it didn't really matter."[14] Young people hitchhiked in the autumn and winter when their bikes and motorcycles weren't any good.

Richard Ivan Jobs notes that modern society offered very "few rites to mark major life changes."[15] Hitchhiking embodied the spirit of wanderlust and facilitated puberty rituals, courtship, and a chance to acquire artefacts and experiences in order to enhance one's subcultural capital. Three Ottawa Valley boys once hitchhiked 56 kilometres "just to get a *Playboy* magazine."[16] A teenager from rural British Columbia hitchhiked to Surrey every Saturday to buy the latest 45-rpm records. He said, "It was easy ... The drivers would say, 'I'll give you a ride if you put out your cigarette.'"[17] In 1963 fourteen-year-old "aspiring" poet Rod Willmot heard "that some of Canada's most important poets were in Montreal." On the day that Robert F. Kennedy was shot, Willmot left his home in Ajax, Ontario. He said, "I secretly hitchhiked to Belleville to see a girl I'd met ... I packed a haversack with my binder of poems, and nothing else I recall, and hit the road."[18] Hitching also advanced social capital. On Friday nights, in the mid-1970s, west-side girls in Saskatoon dressed in bomber jackets and Frye boots hitchhiked up and down Broadway Avenue and 8th Street. "It was a great way to meet kids from other schools."[19]

Independent youth travel was not confined to short hitchhiking trips. The travel rituals of baby boomers had historic roots in the self-improving Grand Tours, the self-education "finishing" traditions of elite girls, working-class journeyman's apprentices, and migrant and seasonal labourers. The tramping and slumming traditions of Edwardian middle-class youth required minimizing personal possessions, toting a rucksack, playing a cross-class masquerade, and sleeping rough in cheap lodgings and locations normally off limits to elite members of society.[20] In the late 1960s sociologists said that millions of youth were hitchhiking their way through major centres like London, Amsterdam, and Copenhagen. They called them "drifters" and "wanderers." Initially, the majority were western European and North American middle-class youth, but by the early 1970s an increasing number of working-class youth and young women had joined the subculture because they also wanted to travel "outside the tourism bubble" and live as simply as possible. Erik Cohen wrote,

The drifter is a genuine modern phenomenon. He is often a child of affluence, who reacts against it. He is young, often a student or a graduate who has not yet started to work. He prolongs his moratorium by moving around the world in search of new experiences, radically different from those he has been accustomed to in his sheltered middle-class existence. After he has savoured these experiences for a time, he usually settles down to an ordinary middle-class career.

Cohen observed that by 1973 the frontiers of the "nomads from afflu-ence" had expanded to the Middle East, Asia, Africa, Australia, and North America.[21] In 1976 sociologist Jay Vogt said that "wanderers" appeared to be driven by "the quest for personal growth, autonomy in decision-making, learning through exposure and detachment, and transient yet intense interpersonal relationships." The travel style was a product of and reaction to affluent society:

> By merging with the culture the wanderer can know it without de-stroying it. He travels in ecological harmony with the land and people. With few needs, he makes few demands on the culture. He values cultural areas in their native state, not those transformed by the tourist industry ... Rather than accept familiarity, convenience, and guidance, the wanderer embraces novelty, necessity, and independence.[22]

With hindsight, and in view of the turbulent events of the years be-tween 1965 and 1975, it is easy for scholars of the 1960s to understand why baby boom children, notably those from middle-class families, had different ideas than their parents had about what it meant to be productive citizens.

Schoolroom curriculum influenced by the Cold War instructed pu-pils to be cooperative, responsible, and globally aware.[23] As they came of age, many baby boomers turned away from their parents' materialist values, which equated conformity and consumption with moral character, to seek out "authentic" experiences beyond the "cookie cutter post-war suburbs."[24] Cyril Levitt says that many in his generation were frustrated by the "cautious superficial conformity" of postwar Canadian social life, especially values that equated a person's self-respect with a willingness to live by established social norms.[25] In 1975 Kenneth Westhues said that the result was the formation of a left-wing student movement and a countercultural youth movement that articulated the generational idea that youth should, as Brookfield says, "do something ... to help children in need, to stop war, end poverty, or for world peace."[26] One value that baby boomers did not reject was automobility. Soon thousands of Canadian youth were on the road. In 1970 a student at Simon Fraser University announced that the "hitchhiking era" had begun.[27]

*Setting the Mood of the Hitchhiking Era*
Youth subcultures are often deliberate solutions to issues that develop when adolescents "experience gaps between what is happening and what they have been led to believe should happen."[28] In popular culture of the 1960s and 1970s, car travel was predominantly associated with various coming of age rituals, the freedom of movement and the anticipation of new adventures.[29] This vision of automobility was reflected in the new forms of music that replaced the high-energy rock and roll songs that

A few of the 55,000 attendees leaving the
Strawberry Fields Rock Festival in Bowmanville, Ontario,
August 10, 1970. The police were happy the entire group did
not head out at the same time, clogging the roads.
*Photo by Frank Lennon via Getty Images/* Toronto Star

1950s teenagers would bop, swing, and twist to.[30] By the mid-1960s young adults were producing their own writing, art, music, and activities that denounced "apathy, warmongering, racism, gender inequality, stereo-typing, and other social ills," while encouraging young people to explore new ways of living.[31] On Canadian university campuses, newspapers shifted their focus from stories about football games and sock hops to coverage of the movements that "were reshaping society and culture." James Pitsula says student journalists with the University of Regina's *Carillon* wrote about civil rights, women's liberation, Aboriginal rights, and the peace movement.[32] In campus newspapers readers found stories about musicians like Bob Dylan, Janis Joplin, Joan Baez, Neil Young, Gordon Lightfoot, and Joni Mitchell who sang about the freedom of life on the road unencumbered by domestic responsibilities and material possessions.

All over Canada, students and workers were getting ideas about travel from the songs they were listening to on AM radio stations. The University of Lethbridge's newspaper, *The Meliorist*, published an inter-view with folk singer Ian Tyson – one of the icons of the duo Ian & Sylvia. Tyson was "a fine arts student" who quit art college in Vancouver to hitchhike around North America. While thumbing in the southern United States, he learned the Kentucky mountain music that inspired the folk songs that would launch his career in Yorkville coffeehouses and at the Newport Folk Festival in 1965.[33] In his dorm room on Burnaby Mountain at Simon Fraser University, student Ron Verzuh made a list of hit songs about hitting the road for his "Trip Tips" column in the campus newspaper, *The Peak*. It included "Hitchin' a Ride" (1969) by Vanity Fare, "The Long and Winding Road" (1970) by the Beatles, and "Ride Captain Ride" (1970) by Blues Image. Verzuh said that the songs set the "mood ... They tell you to move, to go to another place."[34] Undeniably, music influ-enced listeners. In Quebec two sisters quit their factory jobs in Montreal to hitchhike the California coastline. Danielle Laurence said that they got the idea for their destination from the song "California Dreamin'" (1965) by the Mamas & the Papas, which had been playing on Quebec radio stations. She explained, "We spoke zero English" and did not know "much about the world at that time ... but we knew the song about

California dreams." They set out to see if you could "dream a lot in that place."[35] After watching Michael Wadleigh's documentary *Woodstock* (1970) "about a dozen times," an eighteen-year-old Ontario hitchhiker and her best friend hitchhiked to Banff for the summers of 1971 and 1972, having lied to their parents about taking the train. They tormented each other by singing Simon & Garfunkel's "Homeward Bound" (1966) every morning on the road back to Ontario.[36]

Women folk singers also wrote and performed songs about hitchhikers and nomadic lifestyles. In 1971 Janis Joplin "immortalized the practice" of hitchhiking with her rendition of "Me and Bobby McGee" (1969).[37] In "Carey" (1971), Joni Mitchell sang, "My fingernails are filthy / I've got beach tar on my feet ... Maybe I'll go to Amsterdam / Or maybe I'll go to Rome." In "The Hitchhikers' Song" (1971) Joan Baez sang,

> *When the mist rolls in on Highway One*
> *like a curtain to the day*
> *A thousand silhouettes hold out their thumbs*
> *and I see them and I say*
> *You are my children*
> *My sweet children*
> *I am your poet*
>
> *So walk to the edges of a dying kingdom*
> *There's one more summer just around the bend*
> *The amber in your smile is brave and winsome*
> *For though your highway has no end, it never ends*
> *There is still the sky*
> *The windy cliff*
> *And the sea below it*

The impact of music and lyrics on the "mood of youth" was commented upon in the publication *It's Your Turn* (1971) by the Secretary of State's Committee on Youth. The authors of the report told parents that songs like Joni Mitchell's "Woodstock" (1970), which communicated resistance to entrapment, environmental poisons, and calculated killing in the world, played to "a far different audience" than the one described by sociological analysts of teenagers in the 1950s.[38] Sophisticated singer-songwriters criticized mainstream values and incorporated anti-establishment and anti-materialist themes into songs that shifted imagery from the confinement of the car to the freedom of "tripping" down the highway.[39] The Committee on Youth observed that pop music had a greater effect on virtually all youngsters than most adults realized. Teenagers' language had become filled with figures of speech and slang drawn from popular music that encouraged "the casual adventurousness of the flower children."[40] In Quebec the proliferation of folk music, art, and the vibrant coffeehouse scene gave "French youth a sense of community spirit and an interest in politics" that differentiated them from preceding generations.[41] Most worrisome were the multiday rock festivals where communal values generated by participants led peer groups to regard these festivals as "liberating and ecstatic" collective experiences.[42] Aggressive merchandizing, weekend-long rock concerts, and psychedelic headshops inspired by the ones in San Francisco became major tourist attractions for youth seeking freedom and fun around the country.[43]

For Canadian youth, the urgency of "making the scene" meant joining others on the road. It was unclear to adults where rock and roll lyrics stopped and true rebellion began. In the spring of 1971, the Prince Edward Island legislature hastily passed anti-rock-festival Bill 55, the "Act to Provide for the Prohibition of Certain Public Gatherings," in order to stop plans for Junction '71, a two-day rock concert in a Charlottetown suburb. The entertainment lineup for Junction '71 included the Toronto gospel pop band Ocean, which had the hit "Put Your Hand in the Hand," and singer-songwriter Bruce Cockburn, who had just performed on the soundtrack of film director Donald Shebib's *Goin' Down the Road* (1970).[44] The concert promoters promised to donate 50 percent of the proceeds to the Easter Seal Campaign, but anti-rock-festival taxpayers and protesters thought that the risks outweighed the benefits. They said that the community would never permit drug dealers to get away with the "exploitation of children" or allow the hippie lifestyle to ruin local tourism.[45] Young people viewed the active discouragement of rock concerts by politicians and the police as an "instance of anti-youth discrimination."[46] Music and travel bound youth together by promising shared empathy, emotional intimacy, and communal experiences.

*"Tripping" Out: Transition through Travel*
There was more to hitchhiking than something to sing about. In the late 1960s a number of global, social, and economic factors put youth in the mood to travel. For teenagers, workers on holiday, and students without summer jobs, a cross-country hitchhike during moments of liminality seemed appealing for a variety of reasons. It was a way to celebrate a personal or cultural milestone, such as a sixteenth birthday, completing high school, or the end of a semester of college. Interviewees recalled that "lots of kids left for cross-country trips the morning following graduation."[47]

Young people across the political and ideological spectrums considered a journey with a "bulging knapsack" to be a more educational and satisfying experience than living at home, looking for work, or staying in school.[48] In 1964 British traveller Katharine Whitehorn said, "Ever since the Twelfth Century students have been poor, adventurous and on the move ... Begging lifts nowadays is what walking the roads once was; and anyone who brakes reluctantly to admit the hairy knees and bulging knapsack of a hitchhiker can reflect that even now there is a certain amount of hallelujah about being a bum."[49] What was new in the era after the Second World War was that the demand for a well-educated and highly trained workforce increased. Subsidized tuition, low-interest student loans, and the promise of high-paying jobs in business and industry upon graduation made it possible for young people from diverse backgrounds to try college or university after high school. Between 1964 and 1965 the number of full-time university students in Canada was 178,000. Between 1961 and 1968 nearly 20 percent of those aged eighteen to twenty-one were in university, which was the highest concentration that the university system had ever seen. Unfortunately, in 1969 an economic recession pushed the overall youth unemployment rate from 4.7 percent in 1969 to 6.3 percent in 1972. The unemployment rate for young men was 11.6 percent, which was more than twice what it had been in 1967.[50]

The result was the rise of the student movement, tensions on university campuses, and the belief among the left wing and counterculturalists that students could be a force to reshape society. The federal voting age was twenty-one, and many young adults felt like "another persecuted minority group" locked out of the decision making that governed their lives. The assistant director of the Company of Young Canadians, Stewart Gooding, criticized the subservient status of youth in society. He said, "whether you are a slum-dweller, an Indian, a university student, or a 4-H club-member, you have a right to be a part of decision-making." For him, "student power" meant a "full-scale attack" on the "theory of apprenticeship," which propounded that young people needed to be protected and therefore must endure "a long period of play-acting at citizenship."[51] As for students involved in left-wing politics, Levitt says they regarded "the school as prison," and American essayist Jerry Farber's 1967 phrase "Students as Niggers" embodied their critique of capitalist values and of the mass regimentation and depersonalization of academic life.[52] In 1970 the leader of the Canadian Union of Students, Jim Harding, disparaged university education as an illustration of the "false consciousness that governs most people's lives."[53] He dubbed hitchhiking the mode of transportation of "the new transient class" and challenged students to "unlearn."[54] There was nothing new in this view of youth transience, as the On-to-Ottawa Trek of 1935 had shown Depression-era adults the collective power of restless youth; youth mobility frightened people. In Vancouver the *Georgia Straight* called the mayor's proposed hitchhiking ban "oppressive," "fascistic," and "a step away from democracy."[55] Whitehorn said restrictions on movement were among "the first actions of tyranny." It was "no wonder Hitler rounded up the gypsies."[56]

Disappointing experiences in high school and university inspired would-be travellers to seek more authentic experiences on the road. A University of Waterloo student was fed up with learning about life in Canada from *Maclean's* magazine and textbooks. In a letter to the university's newspaper, *The Chevron,* he said that *Maclean's* was "too hung up on Pierre Trudeau, Anne Murray, or Bobby Orr." He wrote, "You don't really get to know anyone or any place from a book or magazine. There is only one way to do that – by talking to people first and/or travelling down the road away from your hometown ... You are bound to meet other Canadians ... some doing the same thing you're doing – namely tripping."[57] Young women also wanted to run their own lives without schedules and obligations.[58] An eighteen year old in Guelph turned down her university admission in order to hitchhike to Victoria. She "didn't want to go to university and get a job and get married and be miserable like everybody else."[59] Susan Rome quit college because she thought hitchhiking from Colorado to Santa Fe would be "a real adventure" and a well-deserved "break" before finishing her degree.[60] In the winter of 1971, the newswire service Canadian University Press distributed a story about the previous summer that said there had been "more hitchhikers on the roads than there were cars."[61]

Youth mobility was not confined to middle-class students, although campuses were the most visible strongholds of unrest and media publicity. Hitchhiking in the 1930s had been an important mode of travel for workers in the Young Communist League, Canadian Youth Congress, and Co-operative Commonwealth Federation. Ian Milligan points out that 87 percent of the baby boom generation entered the workforce for wage labour after leaving school.[62] For them, unemployment was more than a "sore point." Workplace-bound youth wanted fairer labour laws, minimum wage legislation, greater labour force mobility, and jobs that were "relevant to the satisfaction of human needs in a community context."[63] The material realities they faced produced a different class consciousness from that of university students but the same frustration with the conservatism of older workers and age discrimination within trade unions.[64]

For young workers, alternative travel was also an expression of anti-authoritarian values and a symptom of global social and political forces. In 1964 a high school teacher quit her job to hitchhike around Europe. She said that her parents were devastated because "they spent all that money to send me to university, and here I was going off."[65] In his memoir *Promised Lands* (2012), Douglas Williams describes leaving Kingsville, Ontario, in 1966 for Greece, Istanbul, and other points to the east. He was twenty years old. Inspired by Allen Ginsberg's beatnik poem *Howl* (1955), he wrote, "I saw the best minds of my generation go off to university in the mid-Sixties. Some of the rest of us – wanderers, riffraff, bohemians, freaks, wayfarers, beatniks, hippies, and the broken hearted, we who had decided to sidestep participation in becoming the most educated generation in history – saved up U[S]$167.00 and flew Icelandic Airways to Luxembourg."[66] In 1967 a twenty-one-year-old from BC was "making good money" at a tire plant in Vancouver, but "the factory was really disappointing." He did not want to become like the "middle-aged" men who were "getting divorced." He recalled that the "hippie thing was starting, and there was a lot of questioning going on." His friend "started going off hitchhiking." After one trip, he "came back and shared his experience. I said, 'You know I would like to do that ...' My friend was talking about his really great life ... One day I decided – that's it. I quit!"[67] From his point of view, hitchhiking to the Maritimes would be a new form of self-discipline.

The same year, a waiter at a Brother John's restaurant asked for a day off, but his boss would not give it to him, so he called in sick "and was immediately fired." He was delighted. He was twenty-one, with "new friends from California and time on my hands. For the first time in my life, I was homeless and on the road."[68] In 1971 two sixteen year olds from North Bay were working at a car wash in west Toronto. They were horsing around throwing wet sponges when the boss pulled up, and they "got fired on the spot."[69] They decided then and there to hitchhike to Vancouver.

Travelling young people did not see their behaviour in negative terms like "dropping out" but were opting for self-education by exploring the world.[70] Williams's "knapsack was loaded with books that I knew would be read by the kind of person I wanted to be." They included Jack Kerouac's semi-autobiographical novel *Desolation Angels* (1965), Eric Josephson and Mary Josephson's edited anthology *Man Alone: Alienation in Modern Society* (1971), which he describes as a collection of "really depressing essays about alienation, mental illness and existentialism," William H. Whyte's *The Organization Man* (1956) – "*being one* was about as un-cool as you could get" – and Paul Goodman's *Growing Up Absurd* (1960) because "being absurd" was what the twenty year old wanted to be "before becoming part of the army of pipsqueaks that makes up the face of modern man – Organization Men."[71] An anonymous letter to the editor of the University of Lethbridge's *The Meliorist* in 1968 dreamingly described the opportunities that travel offered this generation:

> To find what this short period of being on earth is all about (if it is indeed possible to find this out) a person must get away from all he has already lived with, he must travel, he must meet, he must give, he must take, he must love, he must hate, he must run, he must crawl, he must fly, he must swim, and he must be reborn and die several times in one lifetime. Many people are afraid to throw away the security they have been raised with; challenge the standards on which they have been brought up ... The risk to their security would be too great. Life without insecurity must be sheer Hell.[72]

Hitchhiking travel was a form of self-education that required the same commitment and discipline as studying or paid work. A young woman from a small town on Vancouver Island recalled that in 1972 everyone "I wanted to be like was hitchhiking."[73]

*Native Youth: "On the Pow Wow Trail"*
Beyond class and gender, youth culture needs to be understood as having important racial cleavages.[74] Young hitchhikers of Aboriginal heritage were also on the road. Hitchhiking had always been a practical way to get on and off reserves and away from northern towns with underserviced bus routes. First Nations youth came from cultural and demographic situations that were very different from those of middle-class youth of European heritage. Material wealth was unevenly distributed in postwar Canada but for none more so than for First Nations people, who did not gain full citizenship until 1960. The Secretary of State's publication *It's Your Turn* (1971) made no mention of the residential school system but admitted, "In the present system, the Indian student's cultural background is denigrated." According to this report, Aboriginal youth faced "special challenges" because they identified only "slightly" with the values taught by the white education system.[75] A former student of the Kamloops Indian Residential School recalled the "three things" he remembered most from

his years at school: "hunger; speaking English; and being called a heathen because of my grandfather."[76]

In the 1960s the global civil rights movement influenced Aboriginal youth who were fully aware that education and job training were essential to their future roles in society. Prior to the appearance of the federal government's White Paper on Indian policy (1969) and the National Indian Brotherhood's policy statement *Indian Control of Indian Education* (1972), young people expressed their powerlessness to shape the oppressive colonial system of education "by dropping out" of school. Ninety-four percent did not graduate from high school.[77] Dene Nation leader and Assembly of First Nations chief Georges Erasmus was a volunteer with the Company of Young Canadians in 1967. He recalled that in the late 1960s "things started to change" for his generation.[78] Like Erasmus, youth leaders came forward and allied themselves with the Red Power movement in the United States, which saw the complex position of Native people in the context of colonization and saw the struggle for self-determination as "part of a Fourth World of anti-colonial resistance."[79]

In her semi-autobiographical novel *Slash*, Jeannette Armstrong shows how her generation felt torn between the desire to succeed and the fear that if they stayed in school or left home, they ran the risk of alienation from their Indian culture.[80] Those leaving residential and provincial schools experienced complex cultural clashes with their families, friends, and communities. The Department of Indian Affairs refused to build seemingly simple facilities like sport and recreation centres on reserves, so there was little for young men and women to do there. Youth in Uranium City, Saskatchewan, said that the only recreation in town was "billiards and drinking."[81] After arriving in the cities, Aboriginal youth were exasperated by the continuous assault on the Indigenous way of life. They moved from "the bush to the metropolis" only to discover that they lacked education and job skills and faced discrimination from the "dominant white culture." Many quickly fell prey to unemployment, substance abuse, homelessness, criminalization, and recidivism.[82] In its study of travelling youth and youth at risk, the Canadian Welfare Council noted that social workers encountered "victims of racial prejudice" with "Indian backgrounds" who were runaways from Children's Aid Society foster homes and other institutions.[83]

In 1974 CBC Radio announced, "This summer, like a lot of other summers, young people and Native people particularly are travelling across the country ... And many of us see them."[84] Whether angry, militant, confused, or out enjoying freedom, they were motivated to "see the world as it really is."[85] Cree activist and journalist Bernelda Wheeler's program, "On the Pow Wow Trail," featured conversations with hitchhikers of Aboriginal heritage who were "on the road" hoping to form cross-border links with youth and elders in the Red Power movement. Hitchhiking adventures resembled traditional rites of passage that had been outlawed in the 1940s and 1950s. Individually and collectively, they were seeking travel experiences that would enhance their own ideas about colonization. One traveller told Wheeler that her generation wanted to find "something of a spiritual nature ... that doesn't have a price tag attached to it."[86] Another said she needed to get "away from the plastic cities ... I can't hack the cities ... I like to leave ... It's the moving feeling. It is the natural trait in me. I have to move to learn."[87]

Bryan Palmer argues that one distinction between youthful Native militants and New Left militants was Indigenous young people's appreciation of elders and their desire to "seek sustenance" through developing a connection with them. They situated "their challenges to the colonizing white state within a return to traditional customs" and "Indigenous spirituality."[88] First Nations hitchhikers sought spiritual knowledge from medicine men to learn things "about our connection with Mother Earth." Wheeler spoke with a young man who said that he liked to hitchhike across the US border to Canada so that he could get "in tune" with a culture he felt he had lost. He said, "I like to travel to learn more about the different people across Canada, other than Indian people. I just want to get to know them and find out about their religion ... Is it similar to ours?"[89] His destinations were pow wows, sun dances, Hopi snake dances, and the early Indian Ecumenical Conference in Morley, Alberta, which attracted over ten thousand people from the "North America Island" in 1973.[90] A young traveller said,

> I've got a job just for travelling expenses. I came up here ... to see lots of places I've heard of ... You can't just find answers from people in the city ... and you can't find an answer from people just in the country ...

I want to know more about these pow wows and these Indian traditions ... I am going to go by a lot of other people's ideas ... That will broaden my knowledge about traditional ways of life and the culture itself.[91]

For some travellers, learning included helping their own people to learn how to live "the Indian way." Julie and her boyfriend found jobs with the Department of Health and Welfare working with "our own people."[92] Julie met two little boys caught in what we now call the Sixties Scoop. Due to the federal welfare agency's practice of removing Aboriginal children from their families, Native children were almost eight times more likely than non-Aboriginal infants and adolescents to be placed in childcare programs by various government social services.[93] Julie told Wheeler that the boys had been in fourteen different foster homes. Before she "moved on," she tried to teach them "to respect themselves as Indian people." She said, "I travel across the land and find other Native people. I never feel separate from people in British Columbia or Nova Scotia." Her boyfriend agreed: "Unity and togetherness ... If it's done together, that's right on!"[94]

*Thumb Power: Anti-Car Hitchhikers*
Hitchhiking was not only central to low-budget, freewheeling lifestyles that linked voluntary simplicity with freedom but also central to environmentalism. Public debates about the environment and natural resources were focused on the energy crisis and access to wild, unspoiled parks and wetlands. Canadians, especially children, were told not to litter and to preserve wild habitats and endangered species. Environmentalism entered popular culture in the 1970s in songs like Joni Mitchell's "Big Yellow Taxi" (1970) and Marvin Gaye's "Mercy Mercy Me (The Ecology)" (1971).[95] By the mid-1970s understanding of ecological issues broadened to include nuclear energy, food additives, and pharmaceuticals. Sharon Weaver's study of the back-to-the-lander movement says counterculturalists focused on finding new ways of living but also protested pollution and challenged the scientific evaluation of the impact of chemical reactions on the environment and on the body.[96] Environmentalists' discussions about how pollution and roads were destroying landscapes and wildlife were part of what Mimi Sheller calls the "emotional geographies of power and inequality."[97]

Environmentalists argued that what you drove was as important as where you drove it to. They disparaged automobile "consumerism" by boycotting the automobile industry, especially Detroit automakers, which changed models and designs so that consumers were pressured to buy new cars every year. The "tail fin" was the target of "special scorn" due to its opulence and wastefulness. Hippies who could afford them bought Volkswagen Beetles and Microbuses to show their rejection of mass society.[98] For many, hitchhiking was both an anti-materialistic performance and a political platform for anti-car environmentalism. Thumb-travellers' city and country hitchhiking trips were personal protests against society's emotional investment in, and dependence upon, automobiles. An article in *The Martlet* at the University of Victoria stated, "If you have to be somewhere fast, ride a bike, [and] if you have to go too far to walk or ride, use public transport, hitchhike. If you positively have to drive, pick up people hitchhiking."[99]

The new ethic of anti-automobility involved discussions about pollution, the energy crisis, and ways to "save the planet." Students cited information from the World Health Organization that said automobiles emitted carbon monoxide, oxidants, nitrogen oxide, and lead into the air. At the University of Victoria, a group called Environmental Action administered a transportation survey to students in 1970 and discovered that 70 percent of the student population drove a car to campus. Drawing on early Black Panther Party leader Eldridge Cleaver's famous remark that "if you are not part of the solution, you are part of the problem," ecologically minded students demanded "parks over parking lots" for the city of Victoria and hitchhiking posts, especially after the 1973 "energy crisis."[100] A letter from Lorna Rasmussen to the editor of the University of Lethbridge's *The Meliorist* praised the hitchhiking posts at Simon Fraser University and the University of British Columbia. Rasmussen wrote, "Our affluent society has deemed the car a necessity for all, but such an attitude will inevitably add to the destruction of our society as we misuse our environment. I urge more people to walk and hitchhike, and for those who choose to drive, to pick these people up."[101] Environmentalists challenged the assumption that "it is within the rights of the individual to drive a machine that harms others by polluting the air they breathe."[102] The thumb-power counternarrative privileged the moral character of hitchhikers over selfish motorists in private vehicles. The irony, of course, is that thumb-travellers had little difficulty accepting rides in such environmentally harmful machines.

### Flower Power: Embodiment and Subculture

Historically, all youth subcultures, whether punk, preppy, or hippie, use fashion and bodily performance to advertise a uniquely constructed class and gender identity that conveys a subliminal intellectual and emotional message about one's personality, values, and lifestyle.[103] Academic studies of the composition of youth subculture indicate that, like music, fashion is a way that youth distinguish themselves from each other and the "parent culture." Thus youth fashion is a "text which can be read at a level beyond the verbal."[104] Interviewees recalled that to become hitchhikers, they watched other teenagers, copied posture, emotional expression, and slang, and voiced similar likes, dislikes, and opinions. Some adopted the artistic style of the bohemians, the illegal drug use of the delinquents, the "cool" demeanour of beatniks and 1960s mods, and automobility – albeit alternative mobility.[105]

The beatniks and hippies did not descend directly from the late-Victorian era's well-to-do youth who went on tramping trips dressed as tinkers and rovers. As we have seen, Depression-era and wartime hitch-hikers had firsthand experience of material hardships, and when they hitchhiked, they dressed up, not down. In doing so, hitchhikers in the 1930s communicated their social distance from the down-and-outs who depended upon soup kitchens and government relief. In contrast, it dawned on the Spock babies that the best way to disarm "the establish-ment" was to make their clothing into "untrustworthy indicators of caste and caliber."[106] For counterculturalists, the scene is a performance. The hippie script reflected an old, romantic, bohemian idea of "breaking puritan shackles" and exploring "the wisdom and teaching of old cul-tures, wildness and primitive places."[107] The complexities of cross-class dressing have been examined by Angela Carter, who writes, "Clothes are so many things at once. Our social shells, the system of signals with which we broadcast our intentions, are often the projections of our fantasy selves ... Clothes are our weapons, our challenges, our visible insults."[108] For example, long hair, a marijuana-leaf appliqué on a T-shirt, and love beads transformed suburban teenyboppers, workers, and "non-political, non-activist students" into foot soldiers in the generational struggle against adult authority.[109]

It worked; the sight of the unisex styles of shabby clothing annoyed the older generation, especially older conservative adults. In 1967 hippie-hating sociologist Bennett Berger scorned the "flowers, ice cream, kites, beads, bells, bubbles and feathers, and sitting on the ground, like Indians, or legs outstretched in front of one, like Charlie Brown and his friends." He said that beneath the "symbolic" childhood innocence was hostility, such as when antiwar protesters taunted "a policeman by insistently offering him flowers."[110]

The high visibility of hitchhikers on the roads in the summers of 1968 and 1969 was the catalyst for the Canadian Welfare Council's inquiry on transient youth. The social workers who wrote first and second volumes of the report noted that Canadians put "a tremendously high value on personal appearance and especially on clothes."[111] It was customary to appraise the calibre of a person on "the basis of externals, such as modes of dress." Therefore, the preference of "the stereotyped transient" youth for faded blue jeans, T-shirts, unkempt hair, and bulky haversacks, "all coated with dust from the Trans-Canada Highway," infuriated adults, who associated their appearance with "laziness, rebellion against authority, shiftlessness, and promiscuity."[112] For non-Aboriginal boys and girls whose youth included playing "Indian" games at Boy Scouts and Girl Guides, time around campfires, and canoeing at summer camp, the choice of attire, headbands, beads, feathers, long hair, and natural fibres was tied to an imagined aesthetic of freedom "dominated by symbols of Native American identity."[113] "Playing at Indian-ness" enabled Euro-Canadian youth to "transcend and distance themselves from their own colonial Euro-Canadian heritage and privileged status."[114]

Tourism scholars call "travelscapes" the foundations, spaces, and opportunities of "imagined communities." These "scapes" are the building blocks that lead backpackers toward new "imagined worlds."[115] Special gear and clothing afforded entry into one's desired alternative social arena. Interviewees admitted that they self-consciously enhanced their subcultural capital by copying their role models to create a unique persona. The idea was that to be a true wanderer, one had to become "spontaneous and fun."[116] Carefree dress and demeanour made an impression on other hitchhikers and distinguished insiders from pretenders. Travellers recalled wearing their hair in braids and beads and adorning themselves with amulets and crosses. When a thirteen-year-old hitchhiker got to Greenwich Village, he bought a purple leather vest and John Lennon sunglasses to wear with a belt he made from beer-can tabs. He was delighted when word got around his school that he had bought these items when he hitchhiked to New York.[117] In the summer of 1968, a young man in Wawa, Ontario, bought a raincoat like poet and singer-songwriter Leonard Cohen's and walked along the main street carrying a flower "just for something to do."[118] Some hitchhikers prepared their bodies for natural experiences by shunning commercial soaps, shampoos, and deodorants. One traveller commented on the natural bodies of the back-to-the-landers: "It was just the way they felt they could be ... Once we picked up a guy who stunk so bad ... we asked the driver to let him out."[119] Douglas Williams says that despite all the emphasis on individuality, all the young men on his flight to Europe looked like him, "deep in the hippie-larval stage of development: longish-hair, thin beards and moustaches, rumpled jeans."[120]

Gender in Canada was equated with a work ethic. Mike Brake argues that "work and commitment to work separate one from the idle and unsuccessful members of the working class, or from the ungrateful immigrant."[121] Young men without jobs knew they were transgressing the Protestant work ethic's mainstream codes of successful masculinity, material acquisitions, and employment status, so many hitchhikers tried spiffing themselves up as their predecessors in the 1930s and 1940s had done.[122] By adopting a respectable bodily demeanour, they hoped to overcome the "deficit of a beard and a ponytail."[123] One Edmonton hitchhiker said, "Don't wear a hat ... Don't stand with your hands in your pockets. Always use the thumb ... All these trivial things might make the difference ... when people are driving along and they think, 'Should I pick him up or not?'"[124] The son of a college vice-principal carried a hammock so he could claim to be camping and "wouldn't get picked up as a vagrant."[125]

To counter the dirty-hippie stereotype, a Montreal teenager carried a sign that said, "I Just Took a Bath."[126]

Newspaper stories about young women backpackers in the 1940s and 1950s emphasized that they were respectable, college-educated girls and members in good standing of highly regarded youth organizations. These details set them apart from the erratic misfits described in police reports, who left home in such a hurry "that they took no more than a set of curlers and a can of hair spray."[127] Interviews with middle-aged women who travelled in their twenties show how clearly they remember the clothes they brought on holidays. Jennie Small's research shows that decades after a holiday women travellers recalled which outfits were physically uncomfortable and inappropriate for the strange situations they found themselves in.[128] My interviews with female hitchhikers indicate that they also remembered the contents of their backpacks and the central role of their clothing, hairstyles, and jewellery in drawing attention to their new identities. For her first trip out West, a Guelph teenager with granny glasses said, "I only packed my hippie clothes ... I was ready to fit in with the hippies, as soon as I found them."[129]

A teenager in Toronto discovered that the hippies' androgynous clothing style enabled her to explore her new queer identity. She said, "I wanted to *be* John Lennon."

> I was born in 1953 ... I was the first hippie in my district. Nobody was wearing the type of clothes I wore ... I trotted around Lawrence Park, which was the posh district for the upper-middle-class kids in Toronto, with my bare feet and ratty jeans and jacket from the Army Surplus store ... I embroidered appliqués of big felt flowers all over everything and wandered around in my hair band ... hitchhiked around Toronto and up to Ottawa and around. I was not running away. I was going somewhere.[130]

Androgynous backpacks and symbolic resistance to sexist mobility stereotypes like Barbie, with her pink plastic luggage, did not change negative stereotypes about why women travelled. In Simon Fraser

University's *The Peak*, student-traveller Ron Verzuh advised young women to pack a "skirt or even a wash and wear wig. It's up to you, but it is a good idea to keep the weight of the backpack to about 10 or 15 pounds."[131] In 1972 *Globe and Mail* book reviewer Marilyn Dawson mocked the advice to women backpackers provided by travel guide publisher Fodor's because it was out of step with the idea that women could be on the road. Fodor's advised girls to pack "a nylon slip, a half slip, 3 pairs of bras, a garter belt and 5 pairs of stockings." Dawson pointed out that women had not worn that "paraphernalia" for at least a decade.[132] As we shall see in Chapter 7, women and girls in the 1970s faced new cultural stereotypes about the alleged loose sexual morality of lank-haired hippie girls.

### *"My Parents Had a Fit!" Intergenerational Conflict or Value Stretch*

Behind every sociological and historical study of childhood and youth, we find the influence of the family. Would-be thumb-travellers' announcement of an approaching hitchhiking trip often meant a tough negotiation with disapproving and disappointed parents who were confused because their growing children wanted to criticize their lifestyle values and the happiness that consumerism promised. In many Canadian homes in the 1950s and 1960s, the values of church and conformity were reinforced by strong traditions based on ideas of maternal and paternal authority mediated by class, ethnic background, and the economic and emotional insecurities of the Depression and the Second World War.[133] Hard work and thrift were values that parents hoped to pass on to their children. The children of immigrants, especially girls, had a harder time convincing their parents to grant them freedom and unsupervised leisure time.[134]

Parents' fear that their child's desire for freedom and independence meant that they had failed to bring them up right was also compounded by the contradiction of childrearing under capitalism. Meg Luxton's interviews with working-class mothers in Flin Flon, Manitoba, revealed the tension between the futures mothers wanted for their children and the situation that their kids were encountering in the early 1970s. Women said they did not want to seem "old-fashioned," but neither did they want their children to face the insecurity inherent in wage labour, so they

"After you're through with the Army of Transient Youth,
don't forget Super Batboy's on at 5, supper's at 6, the low tonight is 40
and it's dark by 7," *Vancouver Sun*, October 3, 1970.
*Cartoon by Leonard Matheson Norris, courtesy of the Leonard Matheson Norris estate*

scrimped, saved, and nagged about homework so that their children could
go to university. A woman born in 1937 said "we lived really frugally" and
she told the children "to work hard," go to university, and "get good jobs,"
but in the 1970s graduates with bachelor's degrees discovered that a degree
did not guarantee a good job. After college, her son was in the factory
with his dad, and her daughter was working in a bank. She added, "Well,
if I'd known that would happen, I wouldn't have scrimped so hard."[135]
Parents experience their child's adolescence as an emotional time,
especially if it involves the child's participation in a youth subculture
that seems to disrespect and disregard their family's values. Twentieth-
century childrearing experts like G. Stanley Hall and Freudian-infused

pop psychology told parents to anticipate that adolescence would be a time of storm and stress, so impulsiveness, wanderlust, and grumpiness were normal. Erik Erikson assured parents that adolescent risk taking correlated with "negative identity" and "self-destruction" only in extreme cases.[136] Benjamin Spock said that children were more likely to rebel if their democratic rights were suppressed in the home. His Cold War endorsement of a permissive parenting style was based on his belief that democracy was fragile and could be easily lost, as the example of Weimar Germany appeared to show.[137] By the late 1960s critics of permissive parenting said that parents had "unwittingly" instilled in their children "a tendency to be critical but not constructive."[138] In response to youth hitchhiking on the Trans-Canada Highway, disapproving adults blamed Spock's childrearing theories for causing youth unrest. Spock's detractors did not see "any difference between the long-haired lazy and rebellious bums who live off welfare and the sincere travelling students intent upon seeing Canada."[139]

To discover what was behind the hitchhiking craze, in 1969 the Canadian Welfare Council asked travellers in youth hostels and drop-in centres about their relationship with their parents. Travellers talked openly about fights with their parents over hair, clothes, lifestyles, and values. "Very anti-hippie" parents called their children lazy, ungrateful, selfish, too advanced, stupid, and degenerate.[140] A boy said, "They think I'm nuts." A girl explained that "her parents are always putting down hippies and she feels that they hate her." Another said, "We have no communication. I don't know what they think and they don't know how I feel. They don't know who I am, so whatever they think is irrelevant." Fathers fared worse than mothers due to their greater use of corporal punishment. Children said their fathers could be harsh, brutal, narrow-minded, unpredictable, and moody. One hitchhiker pitied his parents because they were unable to give him the "love and understanding he sought from them."[141]

Whether or not travellers' perceptions of their parents' feelings were accurate, parental reaction to the announcement of a hitchhiking trip ranged from worry and disappointment to anger, either resulting in a tough negotiation or causing a child to decamp and run away. In 1969 a fifteen-year-old boy was disappointed when his parents refused to let him hitchhike from Banff to Vancouver. He complained, "My parents had a fit. They wouldn't even let me go on the train."[142] Susan Rome said, "You'd have thought somebody died. In my Jewish family, quitting school was a big deal."[143] Many hitchhikers did not tell their parents the truth about their transportation plans. A Toronto teenager and his sixteen-year-old girlfriend decided to hitchhike out West for the summer after his graduation. He said, "We lied through our teeth ... We said we're taking the bus and ... I had relatives to stay with."[144] In 1977 a Saskatoon teenager got his mother's permission to go to Victoria after Grade 11 by promising to register with local branches of the Royal Canadian Mounted Police along the way, but "of course we didn't."[145] In 1977 two women from northern British Columbia decided to thumb to Quebec because India "was too expensive." One said, "I didn't tell my mother ... It was just our generation ... You kept your mouth shut."[146] In Winnipeg two boys and two girls aged sixteen decided to hitchhike to Vancouver together. One of the girls said that she was tired of being controlled by her strict Catholic family. As she explained, they did not get very far:

> We bolted ... I can't remember whose idea it was ... We were safe in the sense that we had the boys with us ... We snuck out early. I lived in a very creaky house. I went down the stairs really slowly. It did not take them long to realize that we were together. They called the police. In fact, we were in Saskatchewan, and the police stopped the car because the person was driving too fast. He looked in the car and saw these young people and started getting suspicious and got us out of the car.[147]

Many would-be hitchhikers admitted that they had a hard time hurting their parents' feelings. Various psychological defence mechanisms enabled them to feel less guilty. A seventeen year old said that his hitchhiking trip was his only option in the summer of 1972: "I was doing poorly at school from having too much fun ... I was also having difficulties with my parents and a girlfriend. I knew I was going to have to repeat Grade 13 anyhow." He decided to do his family a favour and hitchhike to Florida and "just hang out for a while."[148] A young woman on Vancouver Island "just announced" that she was hitchhiking to the Maritimes. She suspected her parents "were just so glad I was leaving." She added, "I was so obnoxious ... They thought, 'At least she'll smarten up' ... They were at their wits' end."[149]

Values stretch in many directions. Stuart Henderson reminds us that a "hippie never can exist wholly outside his or her cultural context."[150] Like the child's role, that of the adult is a negotiated one. In their roles as parents, these adults got caught in the same social movements that teenagers did, and the family norms of the middle class were changing. In liberal-democratic society, "doing your own thing" was not very different from broader entrepreneurialism, individualism, and the value of self-growth.[151] Many adults were questioning the prescribed sex and gender roles. In 1963 liberal feminist Betty Friedan described how medicine, social science, and media created the "vision of the happy modern housewife" and then mocked homemakers for feeling unfulfilled.[152] In popular culture, family-centred values were the butt of numerous working-class and middle-class situation comedies on television. Naomi Wolf argues that by the 1970s parenting had become devalued. The message to men was "that a family man" tied down with a mortgage, a wife, and kids was a "square." Wolf's own parents were doing "their own thing." Her father grew a beard, and her mother quit setting her hair and returned to graduate school. "Up and down the block, the roar of social upheaval grew louder and closer. One by one, the families began to come apart," with numerous classmates' parents getting divorced.[153] The Canadian Welfare Council commented that in English Canada parents referred to their children by the "deprecating" term "kids."[154]

Parenting advice columns indicate that anxious adults were unsure how much freedom to give their teenagers. In 1971 a mother asked the *Globe and Mail*'s advice columnist, Elizabeth Thompson, whether she should allow sixteen-year-old Marvin to hitchhike to Vancouver. Marvin's father wanted him to go, but she was afraid that "Marvin was not mature enough to handle himself if he got into trouble or a fight and there were drugs." She suspected that he was "just the type to fall for the line about how the stuff won't hurt you." Thompson advised her to let Marvin go because some independence would enable him to develop self-esteem and confidence:

Independence and the experience of trying to survive on little money are good for youngsters his age ... Good things happen to a boy's feelings about himself, if he finds he can successfully get himself across the country and back without help from home. But if he runs into serious trouble, you're only as far away from him as the telephone and he can always call collect if he's broke.[155]

Many adults saw the value of encouraging their children to take chances. A cross-country hitchhiking adventure could be good for a teenager. A traveller from a large family remembered his mother driving his older brothers "to the edge of town to hitch a ride to a faraway destination."[156] In 1966 the mother of a seventeen-year-old boy confessed that she was upset when her son went hitchhiking and was robbed, but she decided that "it was a valuable educational experience for him."[157] A Sault Ste. Marie teenager's parents gave him permission to miss a week of school in order to hitchhike to Winnipeg with his best friend. One of his teachers made it clear that no child of his would be allowed to do such a thing.[158] In 1966 Rod Willmot "hitched out West." He was seventeen and said that he left

with my parents' knowledge and $32 in my pocket. My father drove me out to Highway 400 to see me off. Just as I was getting out of the car, a car coming the opposite way went out of control and veered into the median, bouncing the occupants around before rolling to a stop. No one wore seatbelts in those days, so there was a fair amount of blood. My father told my brothers, "Don't say anything about this to your mother!" And off I went.[159]

A Vancouver girl suspected that her "dad wanted to be a hippie, but he was a dentist, so he used to pick up a lot of hippies and squeeze them into our car with the whole family ... Part of him really related to it."[160] Many travellers told the Canadian Welfare Council's researchers that "they loved and were loved by their parents." Put colloquially, their parents were "'OK' (spoken affectionately, not indifferently)." A girl said, "My mother digs a lot of what's happening and my father's tolerant." A

boy said that he "digs his folks and his dad is growing a beard and letting his hair get longer." Another said "his parents think they are part
of today's youth." He liked them in spite of "their attitude of pseudo-
youthfulness and hip." The council's report on transient youth observed
that few travellers cut all family ties. They kept in touch through long-
distance phone calls, letters, and postcards, and they respected their parents for "trying to understand that times were changing."[161]

### Handbooks: "My Knapsack on My Back"

There is no way of knowing how many young people were on the road.
Following Arnold van Gennep, Victor Turner calls the first stage of rite
of passage travel "liminality." It begins when the ritualist decides to separate from home and community and to embark on a quest or journey
of self-discovery.[162] From that moment, the ritualist's "touristic consciousness" is driven by "inner desires" for authentic and spontaneous
experiences.[163] The completion of the journey was associated with the
completion of the self. The traveller returned home with a new adult
status.[164]

The hitchhiker's "career" began with the backpack. The backpack, also
called a rucksack or haversack, was the equipment of respectable, patriotic occupations such as mountaineer, explorer, and soldier. Backpacking
has always been perceived as an alternative to the mainstream's suitcase-
toting tourist. Symbolically, its roots are traceable to earlier modes of
historic Western travel, notably early European exploration and colonial
domination. However, the backpack entered youth culture in the late
1950s with the publication of Jack Kerouac's autobiographical novel *The
Dharma Bums* (1958). Kerouac called for "a rucksack revolution," and his
books became a canon for Western youth culture. The character Japhy
Ryder was a true dharma bum:

> He hasn't got any money: he doesn't need any money, all he needs is
> his rucksack with those little plastic bags of dried food and a good pair
> of shoes and off he goes and enjoys the privileges of a millionaire ...
> [He said,] "All over the West, and the mountains in the East, and the
> desert, I'll tramp with a rucksack and make it the pure way."[165]

Self-discovery through rite of passage travel existed long before folk singers and beatniks. For generations of Canadian children, powerful and pervasive pioneer stories, summer camp games, and youth clubs revisited tropes of exploration and colonialism. Popular childhood tropes praised adventurers whose "natural" and "traditional" survival skills enabled them to live on very little. Like the "mundane technology" of the hiking boot, the backpack enabled trekkers to magically display their true selves.[166] A prairie girl said, "Give any '60s kid a backpack, and we'll march around singing, 'Val-deri, val-dera, my knapsack on my back'" and other verses from Friedrich-Wilhelm Möller's "The Happy Wanderer," composed after the Second World War, which a German children's choir sang on the radio in the mid-1950s and on *The Ed Sullivan Show* in 1964 and again in 1966.[167] In 1968 an Ontario teenager filled his backpack with "a sleeping bag, WWII poncho (that was like a one-man tent in rain events), a couple of canned goods from my mom's pantry, a can of tobacco, rolling papers, and two bucks in cash."[168] A Montreal girl always carried a "bag of weed" in her pack "to share with the drivers."[169] It was hoped that the backpack would magically enable its wearers to traverse environments and live out their anti-materialist critique of corporate capitalism beyond the tourist bubble; however, motorists and the residents of the towns that backpackers passed through did not always share this illusion.

Travelling is a learned activity with culturally constituted sets of behaviours that ensure boundaries between locals and travellers as well as safety. First-time would-be travellers were nervous, and with no previous experience, they did not know where to begin. Guidebooks and travel manuals indicate that hitchhiking and youth hostelling had become part of an international youth mobility phenomenon throughout the Americas and Europe. Canadian travellers going to Europe used an old budget travel book from 1957 by Arthur Frommer called *Europe on Five Dollars a Day,* but by the 1960s it was out of touch with the contemporary youth scene. A female hitchhiker in 1963 said that five dollars was "a huge budget; it included your food and everything."[170] In 1966, when Douglas Williams and his friend Paul Keele "embarked on a poor man's tour of the world," Frommer's book was "discarded as 'frat-boy bullshit.'"[171] Publishers of international travel books discovered the baby boom market. In 1973 the student travel guide *Let's Go: Europe* adopted a hitchhiker thumb logo, and Fodor's tried to reach out to affluent travellers by throwing in "young-ish phrases" like "crash pad."[172]

For most of the twentieth century, the police in Canada took a laissez-faire approach to hitchhiking. In the late 1960s they were not "officially" concerned with what thousands of "footloose" and "fashionably penni-less" transients were doing on the Queen's highways, so the numbers of hitchhikers grew. To improve safety and prevent traffic accidents, the Ontario Provincial Police printed 200,000 brochures in 1971 that ex-plained where hitchhiking was permitted in Ontario.[173] The editors at the *Globe and Mail* were alerted to the transient youth phenomenon, and twenty-one-year-old Martin Dorrell was sent out to report on the "thousands of young Canadians short on funds and long on dreams."[174] He wrote eight articles in 1971 documenting his Trans-Canada Highway hitchhiking trip. That same summer, twenty-one-year-old freelancer Duncan McMonagle sent the *Winnipeg Free Press* accounts of his trip across the Prairies to the West Coast. He was pleased that the "conserv-ative" newspaper published every word he sent to the editor.[175] In 1972 the Department of Health and Welfare published 600,000 copies of a booklet called *On the Road: A Guide for Youth Travelling Canada.* The message written under the photo of a boy and a girl on the first page said, "School's out for most, young people are beginning their trek across Canada."[176] The thirty-one-page booklet contained a map of the Trans-Canada Highway, first aid information, and the addresses of youth hostels.

Numerous hitchhikers mocked these government and commercial initiatives to regulate behaviour and control destinations. They wrote their own traveller's guides and sent advice to university newspapers. In 1972 David Rideout and Ray Amiro self-published *Handbook Canada: A Traveller's Manual,* with tips on what to eat, what to pack, maps, a com-prehensive list of hostels run by the federal government, universities, the Canadian Youth Hostels Association, the YMCA and YWCA, and the Salvation Army, the names of drop-in centres and legal aid organiza-tions, first aid tips, "wilderness out-of-doors stuff," and "happenings across Canada," including where to get an abortion in Montreal. *Handbook Canada* also offered tips on how to handle a drunk driver, get rid of lice, and prevent venereal disease and information on the best way to enter the United States or cross the Atlantic. There was a separate section called "Company," which asked questions about whether hitchhiking with a girl was an "asset or liability?"[177] Rideout and Amiro emphasized that in many places in Canada hitchhiking was against the law:

> Legally "no person shall be on a roadway for the purpose of soliciting a ride from any vehicle." Stand well off the roadway, which is "that portion of the highway or road that is designed, improved or originally used for traffic," but does not include the shoulder ... Toronto is particularly bad, as is Montreal. Often the best bet is to take a bus "out a ways" and then start hitchhiking. The police don't want hitchhikers endangering themselves or others ... This is understandable.[178]

Rideout and Amiro's central message was that hitchhiking was a "Zen Art." The hitchhiker must be "prepared to do more hard work than just stand on the side of the road with your thumb out ... For every hardship there is the reward of a good memory."[179] American postgraduate student and veteran hitchhiker Paul DiMaggio wrote *The Hitchhiker's Field Manual* (1973). He informed American readers that "hitchhiking in Canada is a summer sport and a gas" and that the roads were "unplagued by most of the nemeses of U.S. hitchhikers – nasty cops, unpleasant locals, billboard strewn highways and small towns that load their coffers with the vacation money of students and young people."[180]

By and large, campus newspapers were the best source of what tourism scholars call "metaphorical mobilization of performance"; in other words, students tutored each other in the appropriate protocols of engagement, conventions, pre-understandings, and the rituals of alternative travel.[181] Under the slogan "Hitch-Hikers of the World Unite," Ron Verzuh wrote a column for Simon Fraser University students called "Trip Tips." He invited his comrades to drop by his dorm room at 407 Shell House to talk about hitchhiking. He said hitchhikers should "erase inborn fears and inhibitions that most of us develop about moving to foreign places." A cheap trip to Europe should begin "with a warm up of hitchhiking across Canada." For Verzuh, "It's always refreshing and informative to rap over 'un verre de Chianti ou Beaujolais, n'est-ce pas?'"[182]

Members of the Canadian Youth Hostels Association also had advice for young hitchhikers. Just like their predecessors in the 1930s and 1950s, they used a variety of venues, including campus presses, to promote their style of "European hostelling." One member told readers of *The Martlet* at the University of Victoria, "When you are on the move there is nothing of course as economical as hitchhiking." Travellers going to Europe should find a charter flight, plan to stay between six weeks and three months, and have $1,000 in pocket and a return ticket. Hitchhiking in Europe "was easy going," but "Spanish customs officers carry sub-machine guns ... They do not like people with long hair and packsacks and they do not have a sense of humour."[183]

Cultural and regional differences produced "dos and don'ts" for Canadian travellers, too. A Toronto hitchhiker advised fellow easterners, "Don't go west thinking you're a big shot from Toronto or wherever and you know the answer to everything. It just won't work."[184] A student at Memorial University apologized on behalf of young Newfoundlanders because hitchhiking had been so slow to gain acceptance on the East Coast. He compared hitchhiking on the Rock to catching a fish: "A lot depends on the time of day, the weather, the place, and the temperament of the driver. Some days they won't even bite. But they think you do and that's why they won't pick you up."[185] A cross-Canada hitchhiker used *The Chevron* at the University of Waterloo to warn fellow travellers using the Trans-Canada Highway to "be prepared to be stopped and checked out at least once along the way." Specifically, they should avoid Dryden and Moose Jaw and should "watch yourself going into Calgary." One could expect two-hour hassles by the Royal Canadian Mounted Police and "local fuzz and complete car stripping ... If you dig hair, that gets doubled."[186] Dorrell told *Globe and Mail* readers, "The farther west you hitch in Ontario the more conscious you become of the stares, mostly disapproving old citizens." A hitchhiker from Matane, Quebec, told Dorrell, "There's a lot of grease (freak haters) in Winnipeg" and "lots of people ready to beat you up in Dryden and Kenora."[187]

In 1973 student Myles Stasiuk sent his views on hitchhiking to *The Sheaf* at the University of Saskatchewan: "Transients travel not for the sake of travel alone, but in search of a new life and a new identity."

The "best advice" he had was to be oneself because not only "will you get more out of travel ... you will be more appreciated by fellow travellers."[188] Jack English, a student at the University of Victoria, advised hitchhikers not to get angry or frustrated when motorists passed them by. He compared the hitchhiker's life to the life of Buddhist monks. He described the profound impact hitchhiking had on him:

> I have hitchhiked in many countries ... I have had rides with people whose language I could not speak; had rides with madmen and executives, college-students and professors, men and women, and I think I have learned (in a Whitmanesque sense) a great deal from hitchhiking. It's something I have truly come to love, and hence respect. For me hitchhiking is flowing with the tide of life, it is movement, and the tapping and understanding of that movement (I may sound overly enthused about this, but seemingly "insignificant" actions can and do "mean" a great deal if you've got eyes and ears to sense the meaning).[189]

### Conclusion: "The Happy Wanderer"

One spring afternoon in 1968, suddenly and without warning, the prime minister of Canada, Pierre Elliott Trudeau, arrived at the youth hostel in Jasper National Park. He wanted to do a little trail riding in Tonquin Valley before officiating at the opening of a law convention in Vancouver. The newly elected leader took a few minutes to meet the hostellers and told them how he had hitchhiked around Europe and the Middle East in the late 1940s and stayed in youth hostels in Europe and Quebec. An excited hosteller sent an account of the meeting to the Canadian Youth Hostels Association's monthly publication, *Pathfinder*. Under a photograph of Trudeau talking to "a pretty, blushing" backpacker named Penny Gardner, the association's member wrote,

> Both the PM and Penny, dressed in very "with it" shorts, looked as though they were about to set out on a hike together ... Cameras clicked and the elite of park users wondered what on earth the PM was doing, talking to a bunch of hippies ... A discussion of boots ensued ...

Having inspected our array of packboards, Mr. Trudeau had to leave
us ... The most pleasing thing about the occasion was its complete
informality.[190]

Prime Minister Trudeau followed up his visit with a bilingual letter to
the Canadian Youth Hostels Association urging Canadian youth to follow
his footsteps by hitchhiking, hostelling, seeing the nation, and learning
about the world. Over the next couple of summers, the "transient
youth" scene flourished the way other subcultures do, namely by borrow-
ing values, artefacts, and bricolage from the dominant culture and other
youth subcultures to form a unique constellation of symbolic behaviours
and rituals that attract new recruits.[191] Teenyboppers, young workers,
Aboriginal youth, and students made the connection between a hitchhiking trip and the personal growth and freedom to be found in an
"imagined otherness" where cars provided an escape from the pressures
of restrictive families and community control. Oral history and contemporary newspaper headlines capture the impression that no sooner had
one traveller returned home than the kid next door hit the road. Former
hitchhiker Patrick Esmonde-White recalls, "Forty years ago, Canadians
did not hesitate to stop their car and give a ride to strangers ... It seemed
as if everybody had a friend or family member who had been on the
road, and drivers thought nothing of giving a strange kid a ride."[192]
    From the adult perspective, it was the nonconformity to social class
and gender norms that lay behind "defiant" modes of dressing as much
as it was the rebellious and nonconformist behaviour itself that they
found threatening. The Secretary of State's Committee on Youth tried to
soften the blow of the "generation gap" by advising parents not to attrib-
ute more "revolutionary power" than necessary to "ostentatious dress,
a surreally inarticulate argot, spasmodic forms of dance, casual sex, [and]
aggressive merchandizing of everything under the sun."[193] A university
professor urged parents to try to "respect and admire youth for being
able do what they could not do."[194] The *Winnipeg Free Press* assured parents
that they were not alone, noting that "individual stories" were essentially
the same. "Behind the traveller are strict parents and frustrating school
regulations which made the free wandering life attractive."[195] Some

motorists were delighted that hitchhiking had become a unique manifestation of the Age of Aquarius, and they were quick to give roaming youngsters a lift. However, for many anxious motorists, hitchhikers were the "folk devils" of the Trans-Canada Highway, and they feared that Armageddon lay around the next bend.[196]

The phenomenon of travelling ... is closely tied to the general mobility of the population, the ease of transportation and the increasing volume of motor traffic on the Trans-Canada Highway.

– *Canadian Welfare Council,* Transient Youth: Report of an Inquiry in the Summer of 1969 *(1970)*

They feel that anyone who slings a knapsack over his back during the summer and takes off travelling is nothing more than a Commie Pinko slob. Travel has always played an important part in an individual's education, but not, it seems, in North America where the Puritan ethic receives far more attention than the broadening of one's personal scope.

– Georgia Straight *(1970)*

# 4
# Cool Aid
## The Transient Youth Movement

The Battle of Jericho, October 15, 1970.
Youth staying at the temporary hostel on the Jericho
army base in Vancouver were evicted by police.
*Vancouver Sun Archives, byline PGN, Merlin ID 24003042,
used with permission of Postmedia*

***The "Battle of Jericho"*** lasted almost three hours. It began on the afternoon of October 15, 1970, when 150 members of the Vancouver City Police in full riot gear, flanked by members of the Royal Canadian Mounted Police and the Canadian Armed Forces, advanced upon a group of youth hostellers who had been "occupying" the Jericho Beach youth hostel since October 2. There was no need for the heavy artillery that the police concealed on a nearby side street. The only ammunition the hostellers had was insults and rocks, which they hurled freely at the police officers.[1] Unofficially, the standoff, or rather the sit-in, began weeks earlier when two hundred "transients and hitchhikers" refused to vacate one of the twelve federally funded summer youth hostels set up in armouries by the National Hostel Task Force.[2] In reality, the conflict began months earlier when it became evident to thumb-travellers and folks of all ages in host communities that a few youth hostels across the country would not "keep the kids quiet."[3]

Following the publication of *Transient Youth: Report of an Inquiry in the Summer of 1969* (1970), the Canadian Welfare Council and the Department of Health and Welfare jointly sponsored the three-day National Youth Consultation at the historical Hôtel Le Chantecler, in Sainte-Adèle, Quebec, in May 1970, which led to the formation of the National Hostel Task Force and the announcement that the Secretary of State would provide free "temporary" hostels for summer travellers. Rapidly, the social work construction of the "transient youth movement" became a framework for multigenerational reactions to youth on the road. This chapter focuses on the response of community and youth welfare agencies to youth mobility. Tourism research shows that when faced with unwelcome travellers, locals may either cooperate or erect physical and psychological barriers to preserve local customs, or in extreme cases they may react with violence against unwanted tourists.[4] Opposition and hostility toward federal hostels emerged all over Canada. In Vancouver tensions erupted in the "Battle of Jericho," which illustrates how a travel and tourism problem became a pressing moral and social issue that turned young travellers into transients.

### Thumb Tourism: The "New Style of Vagrancy"

The stereotype of the friendly Canadian suggests that people are warm and welcoming, but in many regions of Canada, people harboured hostility toward strangers in their midst. Summer travellers on provincial roads caused congestion and irritated rural communities. In 1910 a farmer told an Ontario legislative committee, "If any Nabob of Toronto" touring the countryside in his automobile "injured members of my family, or my neighbors, I would, if I could do nothing else to punish him, blow his brains out."[5] Wealthy tourists spent millions in northern Ontario visiting the Dionne Quintuplets, gazing at Niagara Falls, and enjoying the rivers and lakes of the national parks. They also tested the patience of locals who struggled to accommodate diverse tastes and constant demands.[6] Parochial attitudes explain why federal bodies worked so hard to promote guest-host tourist relations.

Between 1930 and the 1950s, the Canadian government's Tourist Board and films produced by the National Film Board of Canada urged Canadians to be hospitable when the annual "friendly invasion" of 6 million tourists arrived by car, train, and boat. A tourism film by the National Film Board called *Welcome, Neighbour* (1949) coaxed Canadians to remember that their most valuable asset was "the warm friendliness of the Canadian people," and the film *Travellers' Cheques* (1952) featured an animated segment with "Mr. Tourist Dollar" walking in and out of shops, restaurants, and the bus station.[7] Chasing tourist dollars was a necessary evil that people in many regions of the country were used to, but in the late 1960s local people were unprepared for the influx of fashionably penniless "young strangers" who hitchhiked through town.[8]

Hitchhikers had not been a familiar sight on the roads in the 1950s, so when the numbers shot up to the thousands, followed by rumours of tens of thousands in 1970, town councillors, the police, and members of Parliament were deluged with complaints about young people begging rides and sleeping in roadside ditches. Adults in postwar Canada were less likely than their grandparents had been to appreciate how youthful wandering might open up avenues to education in the "school of the world."[9] From the perspective of mainstream culture, the values that separated the idle members of the working class from decent people were a good work ethic, cleanliness, and nice manners. Local charities, like the Salvation Army, provided food, shelter, and spiritual comfort to the deserving poor, "indigent transients," and "vagrants," but donors resented "squatters, loiterers [and] freeloaders" who could not pay for the things they enjoyed.[10] In the late 1960s, motorists and townsfolk were puzzled to discover that ride-beggars of the baby boom generation were not thumbing toward greener pastures but were mostly well-spoken, highly educated, middle-class "drop-outs."[11] Anxious taxpayers could not understand educated, middle-class young people who "flaunted idleness" and saw "no reason why they should work," nor did critics see any difference between long-haired hippies, idle students, and "lazy bums who want[ed] to see the country at the taxpayer's expense."[12]

A feature of the small-town lifestyle that everyday Canadians of all ages wished to preserve was the minimal public display of the generational conflict between parents, teenagers, and the police that dominated media descriptions of teen trouble in Europe, the United States, and large metropolitan areas.[13] Conservative-minded teenagers shared their parents' values. A teenager from Elora, Ontario, said, "Drifters are frowned upon everywhere ... Grandparents had not allowed moms and dads to race off to Toronto."[14] The executive officer of the evangelical Christian Action organization spoke for many everyday people when he said that postwar affluence, materialism, liberalism, and wrong-headed parenting were "expelling a social waste product" of "social misfits" whose "new style of vagrancy" was entrenched in a "private world of rootlessness, drink, drugs and madness."[15] It was evident to numerous hitchhikers in many provinces that observing the "the Puritan ethic" was more important than the "broadening of one's personal scope."[16]

### "The Establishment:" Social Workers as Moral Entrepreneurs

In the early twentieth century, the field of child welfare was profoundly shaped by the development of new ideas or "truths" about adolescent behaviour. Due to G. Stanley Hall's articulation of a modern psychology of adolescence, the teenage body and brain became objects of scrutiny, definition, and control, which pushed the upper age of the life stage of youth to twenty-five years.[17] Michel Foucault later referred to this as biopower, which encompasses the global regulation, surveillance, and "disciplining of individual bodies."[18] In Canada child welfare and the family court were under the purview of the federal Juvenile Delinquents Act (1908) and its revision of 1929. Provincial ministries hired social workers and experts in child guidance from the public sector to carry out reforms, to design new programs for family courts, police depart-ments, and health and welfare departments, and to initiate joint projects with children's charities.[19]

Professional social workers saw themselves as ethical policy experts, clinicians, and social technicians who played leading roles in shaping Canadian society. It was their duty to step in when families suffering from cycles of deprivation failed. Franca Iacovetta argues that social workers' understandings of "at-risk" youth were affected not only by the Depres-sion, wartime disruptions in marital and familial arrangements, and the subsequent postwar economic transition but also by the rise of Cold War hysteria, mass migration, and threats posed by the atomic bomb, the Soviet Union, and homosexual spies.[20] The middle-class bias of social work theory and practice inevitably caused caseworkers to use a frame-work of "them" and "us" that saw juvenile delinquency as a by-product of working-class and immigrant family values. The "youth problem" nar-rative was kept alive in the 1960s and 1970s in professional journals, sex education classes, documentaries produced by the National Film Board, newspapers, magazines, and pulp fiction. Countless articles on "family values" reported the cases of boys and girls who defied curfews, drank liquor, vandalized private property, and engaged in promiscuous sex. "Young punks" assaulted police officers, harassed innocent bystanders, and engaged in petty theft. Among rural, urban, and suburban girls, the nonconformist behaviour that landed many of them in court included breaking rules, staying out late with disreputable friends, runaway at-tempts, hitchhiking escapades to meet boys, and joyriding.[21]

An important, early social work lobby group was the Canadian Welfare Council (CWC), founded by Charlotte Whitton in the 1920s. Nancy Christie observes that for decades the CWC was the leading centre in interpreting social statistics and shaping the direction of social policy. Through four name changes – Canadian Council on Child Welfare (1920–29), Canadian Council on Child and Family Welfare (1930–35), Canadian Welfare Council (1935–71), and Canadian Council on Social Development (1971 to present) – the CWC was the "clearing house" for health and welfare policy and program reforms.[22] Due to its propensity for issuing knowledge claims and expertise, Stanley Cohen would have called its members "control professionals."[23] In the 1950s the CWC's most prominent work was on the reform of old-age pensions. In the late 1960s the staff began to hear of complaints from member agencies about the behaviour of young clientele and the difficulty that child welfare agencies were having keeping abreast of changes in youth culture, especially the new phenomenon of young hitchhikers who were sleeping rough in ditches or at rest stations or were turning up at the doors of the Salvation Army begging for handouts. Sensing a gap in youth services, the CWC discovered that very little "firm data" had been compiled on the "young itinerants."[24] In June 1969 the CWC initiated its involvement with the "'youth' welfare scene" by applying for a welfare grant from the Department of Health and Welfare to study a situation that had become "obvious to everyone who travels by car"[25] – the "alarming" sight since 1967 and 1968 of "large numbers of young people travelling the summer road," which occurred alongside "increasing motor traffic on the Trans-Canada Highway."[26]

### The Transient Youth Inquiry

The Canadian Welfare Council employed social workers, not travel agents, so their inquiry was not intended to assess the transportation and accommodation needs of low-budget tourists. In fact, initially, they did not know what to call their research subjects. They tried "drop-outs" and "itinerants" before coining the term "transient youth," which was subsequently adopted by other agencies, Secretary of State departments, the media, and some young travellers. The purpose of the study that would produce the publication *Transient Youth: Report of an Inquiry in the Summer of 1969* (1970) was to discover which youth were hitchhiking, what the experience was like, and what problems they encountered and created. In other words, were they "carefree travellers on the roads," or were they running away from "disturbing personal and family tensions?" If the latter, were their problems exacerbated by life on the road? In short, what steps were being taken to provide community services for the young travellers?[27]

Three senior Canadian Welfare Council researchers, Michael Wheeler, Lillian Thomson, and Cenovia Addy, led the inquiry.[28] The initial plan was to hire university students to infiltrate the transient subculture, but funding delays pushed the project into September, so many travellers had already returned to school and work. Undeterred, the CWC hired post-graduate students Mary Fenyor and Ken Rubin and eight regional inter-viewers "identified with the contemporary youth scene" to interview travellers at drop-in centres and hostels in Vancouver, Winnipeg, Toronto, Ottawa, and Montreal.[29] The researchers interviewed seventy-two men and forty-seven women between the ages of fourteen and twenty-four. The typical interviewee was a seventeen year old who had spent from six months to a year on the road. Over half had travelled only in Canada, with the most frequent route being the Trans-Canada Highway between Vancouver and Montreal. A few had also visited the United States, Mexico, South America, and Europe.[30]

The questionnaire was designed to identify "youth at risk" by eliciting deeply personal feelings about family life, educational goals, drug use, encounters with police, foster care, and psychiatric centres. The results challenged the CWC's preconceived biases about youth because the "typical" transient was not a hoodlum or runaway from a foster home, abusive parents, or the police. Instead, over half of the travellers were from middle- and upper-income families whose fathers were professionals and mothers were predominantly suburban homemakers.[31] The discovery that drifting boys and wandering girls were from materially comfortable homes challenged the North American myth of serene suburban family life and blocked the CWC from attributing youth delinquency to crude eugenic and environmental-deprivation theories.

The inquiry on transient youth also asked questions about travellers' educational achievements and feelings about school. Sixty percent of the travellers under age eighteen had not graduated from high school. Unsurprisingly, their case histories included trouble in school, truancy, expulsions, suspensions, corporal punishment, and arguments with teachers about long hair and smoking. Travellers described school as boring, irrelevant, restrictive, authoritarian, and disrespectful of individ-ual creativity and freedom. Travellers criticized "out of touch" guidance counsellors, irrelevant drug-education films, the power of student councils, and the curriculum. At the same time, they offered thoughtful suggestions on how to improve governance rules, vocational training, dress codes, and the curriculum.[32] None of the interviewees described themselves as "drop-outs." Most planned to return to school, but for the time being, travelling was the educational format that enabled them to "acquir[e] knowledge of life and people at first hand." Apart from a few girls who said that they "wanted to get away from home," the most frequent response to the question "Why are you traveling?" was that the question was "irrelevant."[33]

The purpose of the inquiry was to focus on the unmet needs of travellers and on the needs of agencies affiliated with the CWC. To better contextualize the transient youth phenomenon, the CWC invited submissions from the nationwide network of 250 youth service agencies, government and nongovernment social service departments, urban-planning councils, city hospitals, churches, schools, recreation centres, and law enforcement agencies. Notable among them were the federal Departments of Youth and Education, Parks and Recreation, Health and Welfare, and Labour (then called "Manpower"), the Canadian Mental Health Association, Jewish Child and Family Services, the Travellers' Aid Society, the Canadian Youth Hostels Association, the Children's Aid Society, the Royal Canadian Mounted Police, Catholic Family and Child Services, the University Settlement, the Student Christian Movement, and the YMCA and YWCA. The survey results revealed that sick, broke, and hungry hitchhikers were turning up at the doors of "long-established" shelters looking for handouts and a place to sleep. Many faith-based charities, including the Salvation Army, YMCA, and YWCA, felt overrun and ill-equipped to receive middle-class young people whose needs were at odds with their usual clientele.[34]

The Canadian Welfare Council made two additional unanticipated observations. First, in practice, support payments to children who were "in need," destitute, disadvantaged, or orphaned were paid directly to their appointed caregivers. Recently, child welfare agencies had been pressured to expand services in order to include a new category of juvenile welfare recipient, namely middle-class kids with drug problems. Social workers were admittedly unable to relate to middle-class drug users who contravened "traditional definitions of a possible welfare recipient" because, strangely enough, the new clientele were in effect like "their own children."[35] Second, the CWC discovered that a generational rift had opened between "long-established" social work agencies and new youth-operated agencies formed by recent university graduates and hippie volunteers. These new grassroots groups were poorly funded, informally structured, and highly critical of existing social work methods and of the "impersonal bureaucratic practices" used by the Children's Aid Society and the YMCA because they seemed to perpetuate "the very miseries they sought to palliate by their piece-meal approach to social problems."[36] The CWC faced the grim reality that all over the country its affiliated agencies were being forced to compete with the hippie services that sprang up to "serve the unmet needs" of transients and local youth.[37] The CWC's report of its inquiry on transient youth raised the possibility that "non-authority adult figures" in their "shoddy," financially "unstable" agencies were actually more effective doing outreach work with travelling and local youth than were highly trained social workers in federal agencies.[38]

*Reinventing the Youth Travel Tradition*
Between 1950 and 1960 the first baby boomers came of age, graduated from postsecondary education, and were anxious to make their mark on society. The Canadian Welfare Council was correct that a new breed of social workers had entered the profession. The ideological tensions between old and new social work practices were not imaginary. Stanley Cohen argues that the community care model of the late 1960s was focused on "weakening or bypassing professional power" through "deprofessionalization, demedicalization, delegalization, anti-psychiatry, [and] client self-help."[39] In their inquiry, the CWC encountered new community-controlled programs run by anti-social-workers, paraprofessionals, graduate students, volunteers, former addicts, and ex-cons working in drop-in centres, group homes, and hostels that they had started themselves.[40] The largest "hippie organizations" working with Canadian travellers were the Committee Representing Youth Problems Today (CRYPT), started in Winnipeg, the Greater Vancouver Youth Communications Centre Society, called Cool Aid, and the Inner City Service Project, also in Vancouver. As we shall see below and in chapter 5, the founders were disruptive, defiant, creative, and in a rush to impose their vision of the future on existing social institutions or to sidestep them altogether.[41]

The inquiry on transient youth was correct about another observation. Travellers were indeed complaining that "establishment" agencies were "non-receptive to their needs" and that services were often provided in a "judgemental, prying and withholding" manner. The social workers and nurses could be "moralistic, punitive or condescending."[42] A founder of Cool Aid in Victoria agreed. "Kids will often turn to us for help, just because we ourselves are kids."[43] Cool Aid's nonjudgmental staff included dozens of university, high school, and professional volunteers. The volunteers at CRYPT also discarded Dickensian casework methods. They provided unstructured counselling and ran interference with parents looking for runaways. With very little stable funding from the province or federal bodies, CRYPT and Cool Aid canvassed door-to-door and held rock concerts to raise money in order to rent old buildings that it used as hostels and drop-in centres. Unlike the residences of the Canadian Youth Hostels Association and the YMCA and YWCA, which were subsidized partly or fully by private memberships, CRYPT's and Cool Aid's "crash pads" had very few rules and no annual membership fees. The staff aimed to empower youth to solve their own problems without assistance from the police or the Children's Aid Society. CRYPT coordinator Laurie Rubin said,

> CRYPT has no formal organization. We operate on a consensual basis ... We don't believe in running and telling the police or parents about a problem that a person has, because those people don't always understand. This leaves us open to the charge that we are too permissive but we like to develop each personality at its own speed. The police expect us to cooperate with them but they don't cooperate with us. Actually we are taking a workload off their shoulders when we get kids off the street and get them places to stay.[44]

To claim back some institutional authority over the provision of services to transient youth, Lillian Thomson and her team amassed an arsenal of books and articles by international experts in adolescent psychology. Canadian information was drawn from recent social work dissertations on youth subcultures and the generation gap.[45] Following the eminent sociologist Talcott Parsons's positivist – and chauvinistic – theory of the family, which was undeniably popular in conventional Canadian sociology in the 1950s and 1960s, the CWC revised the age-old narrative about youth wanderlust. Parsons's system theory stated that peer socialization and participation in youth rituals were necessary to integrate each new generation of young people into society.[46] An additional valuable study by social work professor John Byles of the University of Toronto focused on "unreached youth." Byles hypothesized that "youth alienation" increased as distinctions of social class increased, with working-class delinquents becoming further alienated – isolated and stigmatized – as a consequence of their lawbreaking behaviour. In contrast, middle-class youth became deviant as a consequence of their alienation from social institutions, specifically family, church, school, and work. The CWC accepted Byles's conclusion that the "transient youth problem" was simply a manifestation of "alienation," which led teenagers and young adults from good homes to drop out of school or quit work in order to drift around.[47] In functionalist terms, it was expected that a well-functioning, integrated society like Canada should be able to accommodate a certain level of disequilibrium and dysfunction from its younger generation and still achieve long-term social stability.

The inquiry's report identified three groups of travellers among the thousands congregating in countercultural enclaves across the country. All were "vulnerable" to illness, drug arrests, poverty, crime, and "adult hostility" toward "non-conformist young people."[48] The first group, the least troublesome travellers, comprised students and workers on a "carefree holiday" and out to see Canada.[49] They had enough money to buy Canadian Youth Hostels Association membership cards and were unlikely to regard the YMCA as "square." The second group, at the opposite end of the spectrum, comprised "alienated" and "troubled youth," for whom "wandering" was a "self-destructive" means of escape from broken families, mental health problems, and addiction.[50] These travellers included "victims of racial prejudice." They lacked education and job skills and faced discrimination from the "dominant white culture." The majority in this group had lived in Children's Aid Society foster homes or were runaways from other institutions.[51]

The third group, the most interesting to the CWC, comprised middleclass, suburban teenyboppers, weekend hippies, and bored students for whom "travel was a form of rebellion and a passing fad."[52] The CWC had no intention of handing them over to poorly trained hippies who could not protect them from the pressures and dangers of gang violence, drug dealers, vagrancy arrests, and disease.[53] The CWC asked its colleagues to broaden traditional understandings of middle-class family values and gender roles and to develop new "social action methods for engaging modern youth in society."[54] That said, hitchhiking as a rite of passage of the middle class was accepted more easily for boys than for girls. A female social worker told Thomson,

> The problems of girl transients are quite different from the problems of the boys and young men on the road ... Boys, when they wish to do so, can return to a settled and ordinary life but in many cases a girl's whole chance of happiness is destroyed. Typically the transient girl leaves a home where she has known no affection and is in search of a close personal relationship ... [Girls are] travelling with boys of disordered character, sometimes of poor mentality, and sometimes in wretched physical condition.[55]

Gendered theories of juvenile delinquency maintained that girls on the road had transgressed further from respectable gender norms and feminine behaviour. The CWC did not agree with CRYPT's statement that girls involved with drugs and sex did not "really have a problem" or with CRYPT's insistence that it was the "up-tight" social worker who "had the problem."[56] Although only 8 percent of the travellers were from one-parent families, they tended to be girls whose mothers worked outside the home. Evidently, working mothers could not give daughters adequate attention, so the lonely daughters sought attention by wandering. In an interview with the *Ottawa Journal*, Michael Wheeler called the road "dismal" for "pathetic girls" seeking affection from "a home where none existed ... Nomadic girls" took the "greatest risk in every way" since "older young men with convictions for assault and robbery used them as drug carriers." Wheeler added, "Transient youth had their own network. Private crashpads are dangerous for everyone."[57] The CWC's report *Transient Youth* (1970) stated that girls survived on handouts from friends and strangers as well as by panhandling and shoplifting. They carried drugs for longhaired dealers and allowed themselves to be "pick[ed] up" by strangers when cheap sleeping accommodation was scarce.[58] Wheeler and Thomson were optimistic that, with timely intervention, empathetic social workers could bring girls on the road back into the mainstream.

The orchestrators of inequity on transient youth updated the wanderlust narrative inherent in historical coming of age travel rituals and in the "self-improving" Grand Tours of Europe by recommending that services be provided to rescue and resettle young people ready to leave the road.[59] The new "truth" about youth wanderlust was that few transients, including girls, had "abandoned mainstream society" completely. Bored suburban betwixt-and-betweeners were simply imitating "the hippie lifestyle in terms of dress and language."[60] If they were well managed and monitored, roving young Canadians from "every province and economic class" could know a life history that included a Grand Tour of sorts.[61] Thomson said,

> We want youth to know Canada. This means knowing the Trans-Canada Highway and the new Yellowhead Highway and the big cities on them, but it also means the North and Newfoundland and Windsor; it means Eskimo land and an acquaintance with the marvelous seamen in Atlantic waters. It means encounters with the non-materialistic culture of the continent's earliest inhabitants.[62]

## The Birth of the National Hostel Task Force

Stuart Henderson says that in the mid-1960s Canadians saw a "re-evaluation of the very conception of youth." He quotes cultural historian Peter Braunstein's view that "no longer simply an age category, youth became a metaphor, an attitude toward life, a state of mind that even adults could access." Kids saw adults as "corrupt, conformist, racist, sexist, violent, boring, lonely, [and] unhappy."[63] The often-repeated phrase "Don't trust anyone over thirty" shifted the power dynamic to youth. Consequently, Lillian Thomson said that if the CWC was going to compete with "new innovative" hippie organizations, her colleagues would have to "regain lost initiative" and "reassert their influence in the area of unmet youth welfare needs" by getting out from "behind desks" and finding out what was "happening in the streets."[64] At the time, most social workers treated youth at risk only in clinical settings. Dealing with kids on their own turf put social workers in vulnerable positions. Nevertheless, phase two of the inquiry on transient youth involved giving youth the opportunity to speak directly to powerful government representatives. In the spring of 1970, the CWC asked twenty-five social work agencies and ten drop-in centres to designate young people in their communities to attend the three-day National Youth Consultation in Sainte-Adèle, Quebec, jointly sponsored by the Department of Health and Welfare.

The CWC anticipated a great deal of generational hostility from youth delegates as well as from civil servants, so it was with some trepidation that Cenovia Addy, program director for social policy, set about organizing the three-day meeting at Sainte-Adèle. She felt there was "no place at such a gathering for adults who had only hostility and contempt for transient youth" or for "youth who were so disenchanted with the establishment that their only purpose would be to disrupt the meeting."[65] The federal government was represented by sixty-nine civil servants, most of whom were under the age of forty, from the Departments of Justice, Manpower and Immigration, and Health and Welfare, as well as from the Office of the Solicitor General. To ensure that the "voice of youth" was reflected in the discussion and decisions, 34 percent of the youth delegates were under twenty-two years of age.[66]

On March 30, 1970, civil servants, social workers, and youth leaders arrived at the Hôtel Le Chantecler in Sainte-Adèle, north of Montreal. In the second volume of the inquiry report, *More about Transient Youth* (1970), Lillian Thomson described how the delegates arrived dressed in "the so-called hippie style." In the spirit of "flower power," a young man planted himself in the dining room and handed out flowers to guests. Tension between the "hips" and the "straights" was not generational. Delegates across the political spectrum had their own ideas about what was wrong with society. The most extreme demands included nothing short of the "humanization" of the whole system. The items for discussion were youth-friendly reforms in social services and hospitals, the creation of a youth bureau, more drop-in centres, summer volunteering and job-training schemes, lowering the voting age to eighteen, and the legalization of marijuana.[67] In her keynote speech, Thomson masterfully directed attention toward the pressing problem of youth travel:

Youth mobility is beyond a doubt a social phenomenon that sweeps across provincial and regional boundaries ... All evidence indicates that this is not a temporary problem ... Many more youth will take to the road this summer ... A lack of physical accommodation for transient youth ... was a real hassle for at least a third of the boys and 40 percent of girls.[68]

The civil servants present were relieved when the topic of youth travel and federally subsidized youth hostels took over the agenda. For the duration of the weekend, young people stretched out on the floor and got to work planning "a network of hostels."[69] Civil servants and Hôtel Le Chantecler staff turned a blind eye to the delegates when they began "smoking grass" and left the rooms littered with "cans, mugs and plastic cups."[70] The delegates wanted "the establishment" to see summer travel as "education for living in a world of great mobility" and as training "through actual experience for a worldwide society that demands un-shocking encounters with different cultures." Delegates favoured the residential model used by Cool Aid hostels because of its "co-operation" with the community, nonjudgmental staff, and "worthwhile and mean-ingful work."[71] They envisaged "cooperative projects," free schools, and free clinics where youth would have a "controlling voice," not only "cheap hotels."[72]

The final step was to "get the bread" with no "strings [and] no rules" from the government. Addy gave her "personal commitment" to pass along the message that the country would face a "hostel crisis" unless the Secretary of State made money available by May 1, 1970.[73] The consultation ended with the formation of an ad hoc committee called the National Hostel Task Force. The appointees included Andy Cohen and Vince Kelly from the Secretary of State's Committee on Youth, one delegate from each city represented, and three members-at-large from the CWC. The task force's mandate was to lobby for youth hostels and appoint and co-ordinate local staff. The CWC's role was to manage financial matters on behalf of the Secretary of State.[74]

In the spring of 1970, the national media predicted that there would soon be as many as "one million Canadian youth on the road."[75] The

Liberal government was anxious to maintain the appearance of a strong commitment to youth, and hostels were visible, tangible, and good for public relations. Secretary of State Gérard Pelletier committed $200,000 to a "temporary hostel program" that offered free accommodation and modest meals to travelling youth. Approximately forty hostels were opened in St. John's, Charlottetown, Montreal, Hull, Kingston, London, Thunder Bay, Winnipeg, Calgary, Edmonton, Quebec City, Toronto, Victoria, Banff, Revelstoke, and Vancouver, ten of which were at Department of National Defence armouries and military bases. Pelletier wanted to keep the focus off the growing youth unemployment problem, so the budget was moved from the Department of Health and Welfare to the Department of Citizenship, making Canada's approach to the issue of youth travel a "social animation" project. The first person Andy Cohen hired was Patrick Esmonde-White, a twenty-one-year-old, "well-travelled hitchhiker" with a political science degree from Carleton University.[76] His job title was task force advisory coordinator, and he was given a $200,000 budget, an office in the CWC's building, a four-month contract, and permission to hire his roommate. He said, "There was no time for all the planning ... but by having someone like me take on the job, the government and the CWC could both claim an arms-length relationship, so if things got screwed up they could pass the blame."[77] A few month later, the Canadian Welfare Council changed its name to the less welfarist-sounding Canadian Council on Social Development and recommended replacing "counsellor" with "social worker" when working with clients. From then on, transient youth reports were embroidered with countercultural jargon that praised community engagement, rapping, no hassles, and doing your own thing.[78]

### Hostel Gaze in "Mecca": Unwanted Youth Tourism in Vancouver

After the minister of defence was informed that a dozen of his armouries had been commandeered as youth hostels, the Secretary of State sent telegrams to mayors, town councillors, and school boards asking municipal leaders to "cooperate with the scheme."[79] When the press learned of the government-funded youth hostel program, there was a great deal of excitement. On the face of it, the hostels felt like a "godsend" to young travellers faced with the prospect of arriving in strange cities.[80] However, free sleep accommodation did not stop people from complaining when hippies hitchhiked into town. The reaction was "extremely bad" in Charlottetown, Prince Edward Island, when people heard that the distinguished armed forces training base Brighton Compound C was about to become what would be known as the "Far East Hostel." The hostel was still amidst a storm of controversy when it closed in September 1970. The following summer, angry taxpayers "blocked the access to the road by felling trees during the night."[81] The most negative response to federal hostels occurred in Vancouver, the focus of this section, where public reaction ranged from confusion to outrage, sit-ins, and a riot between hostellers and the police.

In the late 1960s Vancouverites were embroiled in a battle with the "beatnik" element in the Kitsilano neighbourhood on the south shore of English Bay. Local teenagers nicknamed West 4th Avenue "Love Street," after a song by the Doors about a hippie street in Los Angeles. The Kitsilano Ratepayers' Association, the Kitsilano Chamber of Commerce, and the Vancouver City Police were determined to prevent Kitsilano from becoming an American-style "Beatnik Village."[82] The Kitsilano Ratepayers' Association became the city's most vocal anti-hippie lobby group. Its members regarded beatniks and diggers, later called hippies, as inferior to respectable people, and they did not want to attract more to the neighbourhood.[83] They said that "suspected" marijuana and LSD traffickers made their living by running dubious "head-shops," like the Psychedelic Shop, which sold "obscene books." It was alleged that the woman who ran a second-hand clothing shop called Rags and Riches was a felon and that the Horizon Book Store had a "crash pad" for youth coming down from drug trips.[84] The association wanted to prosecute hippies for contributing to the delinquency of minors; however, there was little the police could do because many of their activities, although deemed offensive, were not illegal.[85]

When Pelletier announced the "crash" youth hostel program, public reaction ranged from cooperation to overt acts of violence and resistance. Vancouver alderman Art Phillips said that hostels were a better option for travellers than sleeping on the beaches and in parks. The mayor of

Victoria, John Haddock, thought that young people were "going through a phase" and that people should "be tolerant."[86] In contrast, as will be discussed in Chapter 5, many cities declared public relations wars on the National Hostel Task Force's youth hostel program. The mayor of Vancouver, Tom Campbell, was the most vocal.[87] He was outraged by the news that the old drill hall on Beatty Street was to be converted into a 350-bed men's hostel. Young women between the ages of thirteen and twenty-one would continue to stay at the YWCA and Alexandra House.[88] Since his election in 1966, Campbell had become an outspoken enemy of the hippies. He called them a "decaying" and "rotten" part of society. In a 1968 CBC interview, Campbell said,

> This is not a racial group, and this is of their own choice ... to drop out of society, onto society. [They] want to contribute absolutely nothing to the welfare of the community and yet they look to us for all the services. They expect hospital care when they take bad trips. They expect police protection when they get into trouble and yet when the police are around they shout "Fuzz." They expect to use the public library and the parks, yet they don't want to pay taxes ... They want to take every-thing and give nothing. They are parasites on the community.[89]

Campbell was angry because Prime Minister Pierre Elliott Trudeau's clarion cry to young people to "See Canada First" pointed them in the direction of Vancouver, which had replaced Yorkville as the centre of the Canadian counterculture.[90] Campbell called it a "national disgrace" for the army to knowingly house "drifters, bums and freeloaders." He predicted that the hostels would become "a rallying point for radicals and encourage sexual misbehaviour."[91] To worsen matters, appointed to run the Beatty Street youth hostel were three men under surveillance by the Royal Canadian Mounted Police due to their radical political activities. Campbell said that with them in charge there "would be no supervision at all." His first act of resistance was to instruct the city to delay the "sewer hook-up," which it did for so long that the "hostel staff rented port-a-potties."[92]

Campbell's meddling did not prevent the Beatty Street youth hostel from opening, but his prediction that travellers' hostels would psychologically prepare people for trouble was prophetic. Articles in the *Vancouver Sun,* the *Vancouver Province,* and the *Georgia Straight* indicate that the Beatty Street hostel became the lightning rod for right- and left-wing activism. One sector of the community with a professional interest in cooperating with the hostel program was the RCMP, which had a long history of using undercover surveillance to infiltrate radical political organizations. With the development of the counterculture movement, Red Power, student activism, feminism, peace demonstrations, environmental groups, and the lobby to legalize marijuana, the RCMP followed the lead of the US Federal Bureau of Investigation and broadened the scope of what it labelled as "subversive." Under the directorship of John Starnes of the RCMP's Security Services, the youth counterculture was the target of numerous intelligence operations.[93]

A federal youth hostel was the ideal location for the RCMP to set up covert operations. In Vancouver, Cool Aid's youth shelters were already under surveillance for allegedly sending "American draft deserters to terrorist camps" disguised as "hippie communes" in a remote BC mountain valley.[94] Junior officers grew their hair, dressed as hippies, moved into the hostels, and immediately began recording the comings and goings of residents and staff associated with the Youth International Party (Yippies), Students for a Democratic Society, and an "anarchist" youth group out of Simon Fraser University called the Vancouver Liberation Front (VLF).[95] Philosophically linked to the ideas of Youth International Party founders Abbie Hoffman and Jerry Rubin, the VLF refused to tune out. Its members intended to fight the establishment by mobilizing young people to resist mainstream political organizations.[96] The VLF caught the attention of the RCMP after it organized a sit-in at the Hudson's Bay Company store on Granville Street to protest management's refusal to serve hippies at the store's lunch counter.[97]

The CWC and the RCMP were not the only organizations to attempt to benefit from the hostel program. Darya Maoz argues that unwanted tourism creates many entrepreneurial opportunities and both friendly and hostile strategies that ordinary people use to gain power by manipulating travellers; in this way, the tourist gaze is really a "mutual gaze."[98] Transient youth were good for hippie businesses and the clubs on Vancouver's 4th Avenue. A federal youth hostel was an ideal location for

People forced out of the youth hostel before the statement
to the press from the Vancouver Liberation Front, October 1970.
*Vancouver Sun Archives, byline Dan Scott, Merlin ID 240030033,*
*used with permission of Postmedia*

the VLF to continue stirring up "trouble for the establishment" through
ongoing people's education rallies, street theatre, sit-ins, and the group's
Marxist-Leninist *Yellow Journal*.[99] An RCMP intelligence file says that
VLF leaders "disguised as young transients" infiltrated the Beatty Street
youth hostel.[100]

By all accounts, the Beatty Street hostel ran smoothly until September 1970. The record books indicate that 6,280 men aged sixteen to
twenty-nine stayed there. Thirty-nine percent were from English Canada,
30 percent from Quebec, 16 percent from the United States, 8 percent
from Europe, and the rest from British Columbia. Fifty percent said that
they were out "to see the country."[101] Teddy Mahood was a staff member
at the time. He recalled that everything was fine until "we got word from
the Big Enchiladas that the youth hostel was closing in six days."[102]
The residents had begun to regard the youth hostel as home and saw no
reason why it should close. An emergency meeting was announced, and

six hundred hostellers, VLF members, and local supporters voted to stage a nonviolent "sit-in" and to "resist passively" when the police and military arrived to reclaim the building. The hostellers created a list of demands, called "The People's Proposal," and sent it to Pelletier's office. Their demands included permission to allow resident occupants to run the hostel with federal money year-round. They also asked the Secretary of State to find them "meaningful work" so that they might be of service to the community, possibly working with children or the elderly.[103]

On September 8, when the janitors arrived to clean up the hostel, they found the hostellers barricaded inside.[104] The RCMP responded to the occupation by leaking information to the press that agitators had armed themselves "with everything from bazookas to machine guns."[105] However, the only sounds inside the hostel were bongo drums and hoots and hollers. While everyone waited for Pelletier's reply, the hostellers read back issues of the *Yellow Journal*. Somebody painted a clenched fist on the Canadian flag that was draped on a wall. A *Vancouver Sun* columnist observed that an "accommodation problem has become a political problem ... The only losers are the kids without a place to sleep."[106] Nine hours after the standoff began, the decision arrived from Ottawa. The hostellers "threw open the doors" and ran outside shouting, "We've won!"[107]

Pelletier's office bowed to the hostellers' demands and extended the contract until October 2 on the condition that the "ragtag army" of 150 hostellers move to the Canadian Forces compound at the Jericho Beach garrison. The new hostel could accommodate three hundred men. It was located in Vancouver's middle-class Point Grey neighbourhood in the vicinity of some of the oldest and most expensive homes in Vancouver. The hostellers nicknamed the new hostel the "Jericho Hilton" and announced that all they wanted was to get off the front page and run a full-service hostel for kids in the community.[108] Campbell advised "everybody in Point Grey to bring in their lawnmowers and lock their doors" because they "put 300 hippies with nothing in their pockets and with no supervision in a residential area." Vancouver still had a problem. Campbell said, "They have moved the brothel to Point Grey."[109]

Pelletier's office hoped that a three-week extension would give the travellers a "cooling-off period" and permit local authorities to plan the next evacuation with as little "publicity as possible."[110] Over the next month, RCMP files grew fat with negative newspaper clippings. Journalists repeated the mayor's earlier prediction that hostels would become "immoral brothels" where "free love took place." Indeed, the first change that the hostellers made was to allow women to sleep in the Jericho hostel. By the second week of September, women constituted 30 percent of the 375 residents, and on September 21, 50 percent of the 160 residents were women.[111]

The Secretary of State heard reports of violence and civil disobedience at other federal hostels. An altercation between hippies and bikers outside Thunder Bay's youth hostel led to the accidental death of twenty-one-year-old Paul Marcino.[112] In Revelstoke a member of the Volunteer Fire Department threw a Molotov cocktail through the window of the youth hostel. When London hostellers heard about the occupation of the Beatty Street hostel, they tried to take over London's hostel and drop-in centre.[113] Up to that point, the City of London Police Department and local merchants had been delighted with the hostel and its adjoining drop-in centre because shoplifting and loitering in the downtown core had been greatly reduced; they agreed to allow the facility to remain open for two more weeks as a reward for good behaviour. Then, on September 12, a local motorcycle gang known as the Apocalypse, seeking revenge for a fight the night before, "swarmed the place and beat up everyone in sight ... They battered staff and centre-users with fists, boots and a ratchet wrench." The *London Free Press* reported, "It was nightmarish, one minute the old army headquarters' building was filled with hard rock and the next with the screams of frightened girls and the foul-mouthed cursing of the attackers."[114] Immediately after the fray, London's Department of Public Works cleared the building and nailed the front doors shut. Local teenager Carmen Hamilton admitted that the drop-in centre was a "human pigsty" and "a drug supermarket," but she said that it was "fun and interesting to hang out there," and her friends did so regularly.[115]

The new hostel at the Jericho Beach garrison continued to attract the attention of Vancouverites both in favour and against the hostellers. By all accounts, the hostellers were peaceful and committed to the countercultural value of making love, not war. They set up a communal leather shop and earned a bit of money selling coffee and rice in the kitchen.[116]

Seven simple rules captured their vision of "democratic control": "(1) don't tear up the rules, (2) no balling [sex], (3) no drugs inside, (4) no booze, (5) 16–25 age limit, (6) 11pm downstairs activity only, and (7) if any rule is broken you will be evicted."[117] The RCMP surveillance continued. Intelligence files indicate that the VLF stayed on hand to support the "Jericho People."[118]

An unexpected source of support came from the oldest labour organizations in Canada. The September 8 occupation of the Beatty Street hostel was on the monthly agendas of the Vancouver District Labour Council and the Longshoremen's Union Local 5000, which announced their support for the hostellers in the press and on radio call-in programs. They said, "These youths are not bums nor hippies, but Canadians, and as Canadians they have a right to travel any place, any time they wish across this country!" They are "under no obligation to get the consent ... to come and go!"[119]

Vocal opposition came from war veterans and young servicemen. Veterans heard about the youth hostels and went to see how the hostellers were treating the Beatty Street building. They were dismayed to discover that military medals were missing from the showcases.[120] The Jericho Beach garrison's quarters for married personnel were only 15 metres away from the youth hostel building.[121] Servicemen were "very upset with the prospect of hippies living in their compound." The *Vancouver Province* described how "close-cropped army men watched as the long-haired young men and a few girls loaded with duffle bags and bedrolls" moved in next door. A twenty-one-year-old serviceman threatened to put "a shot gun guard on his family's adjoining barracks home." A mother of three little girls said that she "had no idea these long-hairs were moving in" and wondered how she was supposed to raise her children "next to a barracks-room full of drug-taking hippies?"[122] Some of the tension was resolved after a metre-high barricade was erected between the properties and after a superior officer allegedly told the "army wives" to "shut up or move off the base."[123] Mayor Campbell made another angry speech: "This is what I predicted would happen ... The federal government hasn't considered the people of Vancouver in its decision. This is a *carte blanche;* travel on federal money and live on city money when they get here."[124]

The Battle of Jericho, October 15, 1970.
The transients blocked buses and traffic on 4th Avenue.
*Vancouver Sun Archives, byline Peter Hulbert,*
*Merlin ID 24003017, used with permission of Postmedia*

*Three Hours in Point Grey: The "Battle of Jericho"*
Critics of the National Hostel Task Force said that the Canadian Welfare Council had failed to understand the real needs of young people on the road. It had focused only on the needs of bored suburbanites and middle-class rebels, the majority of whom had dutifully returned home by September 30 when the hostellers moved to the Jericho Beach garrison. Late-summer task force surveys indicate that 50 percent of the hostellers were looking for work. In September, 90 percent of the residents at the

Jericho hostel were from outside of Vancouver, and 30 percent had been there less than a week. The Jericho hostel was scheduled to close October 2, so with nowhere else to go, the hostellers planned another peaceful sit-in, but the excitement was gone.[125]

On October 2 the police and military arrived to reclaim the building but found the hostellers barricaded inside. The *Vancouver Sun* ran the headline "Only the Deadline Passes: All Stands Still at Jericho."[126] The hostellers' demands included permission to stay until another residence was found, meal provision, and permission to continue working in the leather co-op. A part-time staffer told them to "remain cool and don't blow it." Another said, "The idea is not to call it an 'occupation' but to go on living as we normally would ... It will cost them more to put us on welfare than to let us stay here."[127]

A special issue of the *Georgia Straight* printed letters and poetry by the "Jericho People" that described how the world looked from behind the hostel walls; it was "not a happy place." On the door of the middle toilet in the men's washroom, someone had written, "One day this world will fucking end. And ours will take over. Peace is not giving a shit." One resident wrote a lengthy description of an evening at Jericho. Some residents watched a movie on a tiny portable television called *Loss of Innocence* (1961), directed by Lewis Gilbert, about the sexual awakening of a young girl played by Susannah York, while the "heads" and "bikers" watched a fourteen-year-old topless girl dance. One resident wrote,

> We people are not the government's summer students out to see the country so that they can relate to blindness. We're freaks ... orphans, smack freaks, love freaks, acid freaks, heavy freaks, stepped on, laughed at, spat on, shat on – the lost and the found ... It would be good to be able to rest here for a few months.[128]

A poem by Daniel Pfeiffer titled "How the People Feel," signed "A son from God, a flower for peace," appeared on the cover of the *Georgia Straight*'s special issue. Pfeiffer said, "We are God's children ... hiking day in day out to the mountains looking for help ... We are tired of hiking and looking ... Maybe 'God' will help you land at the foot of the mountains, take our hands and hold us up ... Maybe then the rain will come, the sun will shine, and you will watch us grow." A letter to Trudeau said, "If the purpose of the government is the welfare of the people ... then let's bring some purpose and meaning into our government. Otherwise it would be fairly dumb not to choose anarchy."[129] A traveller from Halifax wrote, "Jericho is a need; it should be kept open. Perhaps the Sociology Department of UBC [University of British Columbia] would like to dissect it."[130] The *Georgia Straight's* editors said, "It's IN this year to listen to problems and solutions of young people – it is not IN to do anything meaningful about problems or to respect any of the solutions."[131]

As days turned into weeks, the sit-in at the Jericho hostel gathered support from "defiant" youth and New Left students. The national media said that the occupation resembled "a mini rock festival."[132] The frustrated authorities had to face the fact that the hostellers were not going to quietly drift away. On October 8 the mayor ordered the city to shut off the water, heat, and power and to stop serving food. The hostellers fought back. They pulled a manhole cover off the sewer and erected an outhouse. Another group "tackled a fire hydrant with bare hands – unsuccessfully – in an attempt to get water." David Morgan, acting director of the city's Division of Environmental Health, denounced the city for cutting off the water because it was against the bylaws. He said, "No one is allowed to deprive anyone of the water supply ... This happens all the time with irate landlords of course."[133] Other hostellers stockpiled water by filling bottles from garden hoses in Point Grey backyards. Fearing an outbreak of hepatitis, Vancouver's Department of Health and Point Grey neighbours insisted that the city restore services. The Inner City Service Project refused to stop providing meals and treated the hostellers to a grand Thanksgiving dinner "with all the trimmings."[134] Two hundred "bearded youth and lank-haired girls" danced on the grass to a rock group called the Motherhood.[135] Behind the scenes, the hostellers stockpiled rice. According to RCMP intelligence, the VLF "was quite impressed by the militancy of the hostel group."[136]

Finally, on October 13, after weeks of national media scrutiny and passing the buck to avoid a "public relations nightmare, serious damage, or a riot,"[137] the attorney general of British Columbia instructed the

Department of National Defence to "evict the occupants" and board up the building. The question arose as to who was going to evict the hostellers – the army, the RCMP, or the city police? The army was the official landlord, and the hostellers were invited guests, so this was a civil, not criminal, situation.[138] The Vancouver City Police did not want to be involved with the eviction but were willing to be "immediately available to handle any breach of the peace." The Department of National Defence took charge of the eviction on October 15. Colonel C.L. Rippon, from the Judge Advocate General's Office in Esquimalt, arrived in civilian dress and read a proclamation announcing the department's intention to retake possession of the building. Behind him, one hundred Vancouver police officers in riot gear and some on horseback were ready to provide backup support when the RCMP moved in to secure the building.[139]

The national media camped outside the hostel and waited to report on the "Battle of Jericho." After Rippon's announcement, all but 42 of the 150 occupants had departed. The remaining hostellers and supporters filed onto West 4th Avenue, sat down, and "emphatically refused to leave." Chanting, dancing, and joining the protesters were hundreds of supporters from the University of British Columbia, the Youth International Party, the VLF, Cool Aid, Inner City Services, and the Jesus Army, as well as Hare Krishna monks with cymbals. A guitarist played "We Shall Overcome" while RCMP officers raided the building to look for drugs. All they found was a "nickel pack of marijuana, a pipe and several cubes of hashish."[140]

The *Vancouver Province, Vancouver Sun, Georgia Straight, Globe and Mail*, and television crews from CBC, CTV, and Channel 6 all reported similar accounts of what happened next. Motor traffic backed up on West 4th Avenue for several hours; the mood was jovial until 5:00 p.m. when Chief Constable Victor Lake declared the assembly "unlawful" and gave a five-minute warning. The crowd, which had been singing, "All we want is Love and Peace ... All we want is a Place to Sleep," stopped and began chanting, "Here come the Pigs ... You took our Home. You took our Home." Teddy Mahood said, "I got there about twenty minutes before the crush ... I am standing in the street between the kids and the policemen and I told the kids to get off the fucking road ... Before I knew it, I

The Battle of Jericho, October 15, 1970.
*Vancouver Sun Archives, byline Ken Oakes, Merlin ID 24003044,
used with permission of Postmedia*

was unconscious ... You just wake up and you spit your teeth out ... arm is broken."[141] The police reportedly removed their ID badges, took out their riot sticks, and shoved, jabbed, and booted the protesters. The hostellers returned the blows with rocks and punches.[142] Mahood said,

> The policemen were chasing kids across the lawn to the School for the Deaf. [They were] on horseback and whipping them ... They would knock them down, and they would get up again, and they would keep running ... I am covered in blood ... A little old lady ... driving a convertible was yelling, "Leave them alone! Leave them alone!" I got into her car ... We went around picking up people ... driving to UBC and dropping kids off.[143]

In the end, eight police officers and twenty-five hostellers and their supporters were injured in the fray, and seven hostellers were arrested.[144]

The mainstream press was stunned by the brutality but saluted all three levels of law enforcement for keeping the peace and restoring law and order to the city.

### Subculture: "Heads" versus "Straights"

The "Battle of Jericho" lasted only three hours, but it illustrates how the Canadian Welfare Council's construction of the transient youth movement became a framework for misunderstanding the conflicting needs of competing youth subcultures.[145] Not all youth declared themselves to be outside the mainstream or wanted to overthrow the establishment, even though they enjoyed the countercultural music, groovy clothes, and long hair.[146] Some youth agreed with Mayor Tom Campbell's complaint that hippies seemed to "want to take everything and give nothing ... Support should to go our good youth, our Boy Scouts ... the organizations in our town, the churches, the religious groups, the decent children."[147] Many conservative youth shared their parents' values. A teenager from a small town in Ontario said, "A person is considered to be of good character if he goes to church regularly, holds a job in the community, or gets high marks in school or is an athlete."[148] On the final day of the Sainte-Adèle consultation, one delegate noticed, "The life view of the 'heads' and the 'straights' didn't meet at all." A disapproving delegate remarked that the "heads" wanted only an "easy situation for drug taking, extramarital sexual relations and a non-working way of life."[149]

The problems Canadian youth faced in the late 1960s cannot be analyzed in isolation from factors such as youth employment, social class, expectations of race and gender, and regional disparities in opportunities for jobs and education. In high schools and on university campuses, the stereotype of the student radical conceals social, political, and status differences among young people and important cleavages in youth subcultures. Roberta Lexier argues that in the late 1960s university administrators responded to student protests by abandoning the traditional *loco parentis* role, which placed them in charge of the moral behaviour of students. A positive consequence was the "democratization" of decision making and the increased power of student clubs, student leaders, and student unions.[150] Some students enjoyed the newly found power, but nonactivist students and clubs decried protests, boycotts, and sit-ins as "disparaging Canadian values, norms and traditions."[151] Nonactivists did not want left-leaning leaders to force their own visions of the role of the university in society upon the entire student body. At the University of British Columbia, the Jericho Beach hostel's occupation exposed entrenched ideological divisions among students.

The unrest at the Jericho hostel was linked to disparities in opportunities for jobs, postsecondary education, and affordable student housing in the fall of 1970, when the university press called students the *nouveau poor*. The lack of affordable student accommodation and the limited space in residences were among the many problems at Canadian universities.[152] Students in Vancouver held "tent-ins" to protest the housing shortage, and the September issue of the University of British Columbia's student paper, *The Ubyssey*, informed students that they could "get a bed at the Youth Hostel in the old Jericho army barracks."[153] When classes began, the Vancouver Liberation Front asked the university's student society, called the Alma Mater Society (AMS), to support the next nonviolent sit-in if the Secretary of State declined to let them keep the hostel open year-round. The left-leaning AMS discussed the matter and voted nine to seven in favour of allowing the hostellers to move into the basement of the Student Union Building (SUB). A simpler decision was made at the University of Waterloo, where students "unofficially" invited fifty transients to move into the Campus Centre after Kitchener's youth hostel closed for the season.[154] The AMS also agreed to organize a series of consciousness-raising meetings on behalf of the "People of Jericho" with speakers from the VLF and to pay for four thousand copies of a special edition of the *The Ubyssey* to be distributed at Simon Fraser University and Vancouver Community College.[155]

Students in favour of sharing the SUB with the Jericho hostellers hoped "in a small way" to show that "the university is stepping down from its middle-class pedestal." They said, "We're all brothers under the skin."[156] Evert Hoogers, the graduate students' representative on the Student Council said, "The kids aren't the problem, the problem is a government that can't provide employment. Their problem is our problem."[157] Another student said, "We have let ourselves become the innocent dupes of Tom Campbell, Wacky Bennett and Pierre Trudeau. These people are the symptoms of our society." A member of the Anglican

Student Society pointed out, "The people in the Jericho hostel are our age ... By rights they should be in school too ... Since unemployment is on the rise we all could feel the pinch next summer."[158]

The announcement that the Alma Mater Society had offered accommodation to hostellers did not sit well with all members of the student body.[159] Subcultural rivalries have long reflected historically grounded class, race, and gender inequality, as described in Stanley Cohen's study of violent conflict between the middle-class mods and working-class rockers in the 1950s.[160] At UBC, intergenerational alliances proved to be shaky, and leadership both on and off campus fractured into various left, right, and centre camps.[161]

Vancouverite and history professor Lawrence Aronsen recalls that local "hoodlums" believed they "had some right to annoy and abuse hippies." He writes, "'Upper class frat boys' allied with 'lumpen-greaser' elements in a larger cultural rejection of hippies for their own reasons."[162] The police knew that gangs of greasers bullied and beat up long-haired freaks, and hippie girls complained that frat boys from UBC cruised West 4th Avenue to sexually harass them with "obscene remarks and propositions."[163] In the summer of 1970, young travellers faced hassles with "grease-balls" and "rednecks" who did not like their long hair. For years, anti-hippie pamphlets circulated in the Kitsilano neighbourhood. In response to the Alma Mater Society's vote to let the Jericho hostellers move onto campus, angry students in the "hard-hat" Faculty of Engineering and in others such as Agriculture, Education, and Home Economics expressed strong objections to "dirty hippies" moving into the Student Union Building. At a rally on September 29, engineering students shouted "anti-hippie rhetoric" and "pounded their desks and stamped their feet." Someone yelled, "The dirty long-hairs would depreciate our SUB."[164]

After two weeks of heated debate, the Alma Mater Society put the question to the entire student population on September 29, and the nays won. Four thousand students voted against allowing the Jericho hostellers to stay in the SUB.[165] Bob Smith was one of three members of the Student Council who were "pissed off," especially at students in the Faculty of Education, who voted four to one against the idea of "turning their (stress their and private property) SUB into a hostel." He said that "the decision" showed that UBC students "were trying for a place alongside

Campbell, among the gallery of City bigots."[166] Responding to the debate, a Jericho hosteller said, "We don't want your fucking SUB."[167] It should be noted that after the hostel was boarded up on October 15, about a hundred hostellers did spend the night in the Student Union Building. The next morning, a YMCA staff member quietly arrived to collect them. He warned them, "A few Engineers with some beers under their belts have no minds ... It was like running into a buzz saw."[168] Under the protective arm of the youth worker, the shaken-up and injured "People of Jericho" moved to the YMCA.

### Conclusion: Tolerance over Efficacy

In the late 1960s unprecedented intervention in youth travel affected the local gaze, and multigenerational anxiety about youth mobility played out in different ways.[169] The Canadian Welfare Council's proposition that kids travelled for "negative reasons" put the Secretary of State under the gun to provide sex-segregated sleeping accommodation "before *worse* movements flared up."[170] The CWC ignored Sainte-Adèle delegates' request for residential facilities resembling those run by Cool Aid, CRYPT, or the more ideologically conservative YMCA, YWCA, and Canadian Youth Hostels Association, which all had well-established community relationships.[171] When the task force hostels closed in September 1970, there were 75,000 travellers on the road looking for something to do and a place to go. A year later, in the third report of the transient youth inquiry, *Transient Youth, 70–71* (1970), Thomson admitted that due to the CWC's efforts to ally itself with countercultural values, the task force had hired youth hostel staff who could deal with "heads" but not straight youth, greasers, and bikers, who felt left out. "Freaks felt at home and straights didn't."[172] Moreover, the CWC had been so focused on creating educational experiences for middle class youth who "returned to their comfortable lives" that they overlooked those from broken families and victims of discrimination and racial prejudice without education, job skills, or a place to live – the kids who in former times would simply have been called "tramps."[173]

Hitchhikers and backpackers are not *flâneurs* who gaze, traverse, and wander freely "in a vacuum or a no-man's land."[174] When youth travel, they form friendly and cooperative relationships with some locals, but they may also feel cynical and exploited when they encounter hostility.[175] The morning after the Battle of Jericho, the Vancouver Liberation Front organized a public rally to renew support for the "People of Jericho." The date was October 16, and overnight Trudeau would invoke the War Measures Act in response to kidnappings in Quebec by the Front de Libération du Québec (FLQ). FLQ separatists had kidnapped British trade commissioner James Cross on October 5 and Quebec labour minister Pierre Laporte five days later. The federal government had to act decisively, so Trudeau declared the War Measures Act, and the nation was under martial law. In support of the FLQ, the Vancouver Liberation Front hastily added the statement "Smash the Police State" under the slogan "Return Jericho to the People." The VLF rally failed to ignite a "people's revolution." Only a few bruised and bedraggled Jericho hostellers turned up to listen to the speeches. They were disappointed. One hosteller said, "I don't want to blow up this town, I love this town, I just want a place to stay."[176]

Kids on the road are good and come from families of different races and breeds. They're getting a first-hand look at the country and at themselves, which will be an asset to them when they are ready to settle down in communities and raise children of their own. Hitchhiking is good education in the school of hard knocks.

— *David Black, letter to the editor,* Edmonton Journal *(1970)*

# 5
# Crash Pads
## Blue-Jean Bureaucrats versus
## the Canadian Youth Hostels Association

Elk Island hostel spring work party, 1974.
*Jasper Hostels Scrapbook, M7832, file 291, Canadian Youth
Hostels Association, Glenbow Museum Archives, Calgary*

**In the wake** of the October Crisis, when the country was still under martial law, most people would have applauded the government for getting out of the youth travel business, but Trudeaumania was crumbling and the Liberal Party was looking for innovative ways to affirm its commitment to the young in Canada. Unlike the Canadian Welfare Council, which did not fully trust the younger generation, the Secretary of State, through its Committee on Youth, decided to include the baby boom generation in policy making and program planning.[1] In the spring of 1971, Pierre Trudeau stood before the House of Commons and told the nation,

> The government believes ... that youth is sincere in its efforts to improve society ... We are saying, in effect, to the youth of Canada that we are impressed ... We have confidence in their value system ... We intend to challenge them to see if they have the stamina and self-discipline to follow through on their criticism and advice ... There is work to be done; there are tasks to be performed; there are experiences to be gained. There is a whole country to be explored. There is a generation desirous of improving the world in which it finds itself.[2]

By an order-in-council, Trudeau announced a new multi-million-dollar youth program.[3] A lesson the government had learned from conversations with policy makers and young people was that youth wanted to see themselves reflected in the social institutions that affected their lives. To that end, Secretary of State Gérard Pelletier said that, to "the greatest extent possible," the $67-million summer program for job training, travel, and youth hostels would be planned and implemented by the "hip new bureaucrats."[4]

In the mid-1960s, headlines in Canadian newspapers drifted away from the "scourge" of juvenile delinquency and crime and toward softer descriptions of dancing hippies, sit-ins and be-ins for peace, and psychedelic protests for love and understanding.[5] The tide also turned in professional social work when the baby boom generation entered the provincial and federal system. New professionals and young civil servants were concerned less with generational rebellion than with helping their generation to form new communities and cooperative alternative ways of living with people from all walks of life. The focus of this chapter is the relationship between the new "hassle-free" traditions of "open" youth hostels run by the Secretary of State's Opportunities for Youth program and Transient Youth Services and the older, members-only, European style of hostelling offered by the Canadian Youth Hostels Association, which had been serving the needs of transnational youth since 1933.[6] In the 1970s youth mobility continued to be a contested social problem, but for a time hitchhikers and hostellers ceased to be the "folk devil" of the Trans-Canada Highway and became transient roadside ambassadors for national unity.[7]

### The "Muk-Luk Mardi Gras": The Canadian Youth Hostels Association

Youth hostelling in Canada was an extension of the western European youth movement that grew out of late-Victorian private schools and poor children's charities, which recognized the value of fresh air and outdoor physical exercise for developing the minds and bodies of girls and boys. Temperance societies and Sunday schools sent poor children on fresh-air fortnights, and well-to-do English children joined the Boy Scouts and the Girl Guides. Pacifists and feminists created the youth organizations Woodcraft Folk and Kibbo Kift, which promoted anti-militarist, socialist comradeship for children. German youth had the Wandervogel (literally "wandering bird"), which celebrated class equality, the romantic image of the carefree medieval vagabond, and the innocent pleasures of overnight camping and hiking. It was said that an International Youth Hostel Federation membership offered its bearer a "passport throughout the free world."[8] While backpacking in Europe in the 1930s, two Calgary schoolteachers, sisters Mary and Catherine Barclay, fell under the influence of the international youth hostel movement and returned home to found the first branch of the Canadian Youth Hostels Association (CYHA).

The Barclay sisters put an anti-modernist, "city-to-country" philosophy at the centre of the CYHA's creed. They saw adolescence as a life stage for individual discovery and the chief source of spiritual renewal for the nation. At the core of Canadian hostelling was the message of international peace and understanding, captured by the maxim "It is better to build bridges of international understanding than to dig ditches of separation and hatred."⁹ More practically, youth hostelling promoted collective activity and physical fitness. Mary Barclay said, "We are all sitters today." She argued that "more social and athletic activities would help counteract the effects of too much movie-going and spectator sports ... I would prefer a society of 5,000 people participating in a game and 11 people looking on than the typical stadium scene of eleven participating and 5,000 looking on."¹⁰ This mission was still at the heart of youth hostelling in the 1960s. The CYHA's *Handbook* for 1961 said, "The spirit of adventure is as powerful today as it was in the days of our pioneers, for travel is a Canadian heritage." Hostelling "provides opportunities for our nation's youth to discover for themselves the magnificence of their own land ... Hostelling is Adventure, Safely Undertaken."¹¹

For European youth, membership in a youth hostel association was akin to membership in the Girl Guides, Boy Scouts, and YMCA or YWCA in Canada in terms of prestige and prominence. By the 1950s the CYHA was affiliated with the International Youth Hostel Federation and was registered as a nonprofit, educational, recreational, and charitable association.¹² The annual membership fee was $5 for junior members (under eighteen) and $10 for senior members. In the mid-1970s the average cost to stay in a hostel was $3. The national office in Ottawa dealt with matters concerning the Northwest Territories, Saskatchewan, and Manitoba. Six regional offices were divided between the Maritimes, the St. Lawrence River, the Great Lakes, the Mountains, the North West, and the Pacific, which were located in Halifax, Montreal, Toronto, Calgary, Edmonton, and Vancouver. CYHA hostels in Banff and Jasper National Parks were built with the cooperation of the National Parks Branch of the Department of Indian Affairs and Northern Development.¹³

In 1960 the CYHA had 10,000 members and fifty seasonal and year-round hostels. The number of hostels dropped to forty in 1965 and then started to climb rapidly after nine new "members-only" hostels opened in Ontario as part of the CYHA's Centennial project.¹⁴ After Expo 67 international membership increased by 42 percent, but the number of hostels remained at thirty-five. Most hostels were open year-round and catered to winter and summer activities and sports. Additional revenue for regional associations came from small provincial grants and by renting

Alberta Youth Hostels Association
Klondike Days parade float, Edmonton, n.d.
*Scrapbook 1953–1956, North West Region, Edmonton, M7832, file 289, Canadian*
*Youth Hostels Association, Glenbow Museum Archives, Calgary*

hostels to the Boy Scouts and the Girl Guides and to church and school groups. Active members volunteered as wilderness guides and instructors for special-interest programs in cycling, canoeing, skiing, sailing, orienteering, and rock climbing.

In 1970 there were about forty-two youth hostels roughly 320 kilometres apart along the Trans-Canada Highway between the Quebec and Manitoba borders.[15] Still, relatively few Canadians knew of the CYHA, which attributed low membership numbers to many features of life in Canada. First, the "great distances" between provinces and extreme weather made year-round hostelling difficult. Second, the spirit of Canadian hostelling was stifled by the "mentality" of working people. The "European thought" to take children from the city to the countryside was slow to catch on because the pursuit of pleasure during years when a young person should be earning a living was seen as a sign of weak moral character.[16] Third, the "idea of European travel" was a "terrifying thought" to recent immigrant families "who had fled Europe in the preceding decades."[17] For most of the century, inter-city and interprovincial travel for young people was quite exceptional, and worldwide travel was for wealthier families. Everyday Canadians failed to see how travel at home or abroad could be a form of self-education or be character building for young people.

CYHA membership recruitment was geared toward middle-class teenagers, university students, and young professionals who wished to "travel on their own steam" and to discover "out-of-the-way places" and who valued a warm welcome from the "youth-loving houseparents."[18] Membership privileges included the right to stay in all hostels affiliated with the International Youth Hostel Federation. Members were expected to do their own cooking and housekeeping and to abide by strictly enforced house rules. The bylaws stated that the omnipresent houseparents had the authority to confiscate membership cards for misbehaviour.[19] Active CYHA members were proud of their traditions and of the volunteerism that they promoted. For them, hiking and hostelling were more than hobbies but were identified with a private club's well-educated future professionals, who valued outdoor activities and fellowship with likeminded peers.

The basic physical design of a CYHA hostel included separate sleeping quarters for males and females and a communal living room, kitchen, and dining area. Volunteers donated their spare time to open, close, and renovate buildings and scouted out new hostel sites. Members transformed rustic little cabins into "homey places with individual character." At winter "wool bees" in the 1950s and 1960s, women members stitched curtains and quilts. In 1954 the CYHA's monthly publication the *Trailblazer* said that the quilts "are just beautiful, almost too good."[20] The Mountain region showcased its fine little hostels at the annual Muk-Luk Mardi Gras, and the Edmonton branch entered a float in the Klondike Days parade. The Great Lakes region had a booth at the Canadian National Exhibition. In 1965, in an article for *The Gateway* at the University of Alberta, a CYHA member wrote, "Hostellers are not an average breed ... What the hosteller looks for is a place where he can sit and enjoy the view without having to shout around a fat tourist with his camera, plus his wife, a few kids and the family dog."[21]

Annual reports, scrapbooks, and photograph albums show members happily shaking out blankets, moving beds, nailing down floorboards, sorting equipment, cooking over campfires, performing in costume at skit nights, kissing and cuddling, strumming guitars, and gluing postage stamps on issues of the *Trailblazer*. One weekend in 1960, after a night drinking "Fizzies," eating popcorn, and singing at the Kicking Horse Hostel in Yoho National Park, the hostellers set out for a day to explore the rock climbing and cliffs around Lake O'Hara. J.K. Alexander recalled,

> Four of the seven "going in" hitched to Lake Wapta, the rest followed in the Volks ... We took the path around the lake, stopping first at the Crystal Cave ... It was really quite cold that night ... Four brave girls took to the road to hitchhike into Lake Louise. Now some people have it and some don't ... With the flick of the thumb, they fulfilled a long-standing wish and got a ride in a 1960 white Pontiac convertible!"[22]

A CYHA scrapbook contains a photograph of members Ken and Herb in 1961 hitchhiking back to Edmonton after climbing to Morro Peak in Jasper National Park.[23] Jim Lothian saved a "thank you" letter from Judy Anderson of YHA Australia. Jim dropped her off on the highway to hitchhike to British Columbia. Judy said she and a friend stood with their backpacks in "the sweltering heat, thumbs extended," trying to get to Radium Hot Springs.[24] One CYHA member associated hostelling with "a spirit of the young in heart." It offered opportunities to find the fine qualities in people as "you trip or ski together," prepare meals, laugh, and sit around the stove or campfire. "Hostelling is educational in all its aspects. You are a participant not a spectator, and a hosteller gets by giving ... There is usually the thought, 'Does it have to end?' Each tripper had become a friend. THIS IS HOSTELLING."[25] The CYHA was proud of its charity status and opposed to "government-run structures" because they quickly developed an institutional quality, meaning that the "easy camaraderie of youth hostelling" would be in jeopardy.[26] However, the CYHA was not an entirely nonpolitical organization. In 1961 Edmonton member Denis Heney wrote a letter criticizing the Progressive Conservative government's plan to spend $5 million on amateur sports. He gave Prime

Minister John Diefenbaker a piece of advice about the "waste" of taxpayers' money on team sports:

> a) Amateur sport will encompass few players in relation to the total number of young people. b) There is little room ... (with exceptions such as tennis and basketball) for girls ... I feel that the Canadian Youth Hostels Association is an ideal organization to overcome these disadvantages, to promote physical fitness of Canadian Youth, and for personal experiences that are going to build their character and broaden their outlook.[27]

Heney added, "Affluence in other parts of the world, coupled with increasing interest in travel as an educational process, is increasing." He spoke for the whole CYHA when he told Diefenbaker, "We are on our own. No government or rich uncle will press a big cheque into our hand and tell us to get building." He enclosed several CYHA brochures and asked Diefenbaker to appoint a CYHA member to the National Advisory Council on Physical Fitness and Amateur Sport.[28]

As the ethos of youth activism spread in the late 1960s, the phenomenon of Trudeaumania drew the Canadian Youth Hostels Association into the transient youth movement.[29] Prime Minister Trudeau was cognizant of how to appeal to young people with his gunslinger style, dress, and hip rhetoric. He spoke of his own hitchhiking travels in Europe and the Middle East and encouraged young Canadians to follow in his footsteps and to learn about "Canada and the world."[30] As seen in Chapter 3, the business of youth hostelling changed dramatically in May 1968 after Trudeau appeared at the youth hostel in Jasper National Park dressed in "with it" shorts and hiking boots.[31] He followed up his visit with a bilingual memorandum addressed to the members of the CYHA, which was printed on the cover of its 1968–69 *Annual Report*. The memo said, "As one who has loved travel and enjoyed membership in the Youth Hostel Association, I am delighted to extend to you best wishes for continued success. Travel deepens understanding, provides fulfilment in adventure, and responds to a beckoning known to man since his beginning. What better way is there to promote national and international understanding than to know Canada and the world?"[32]

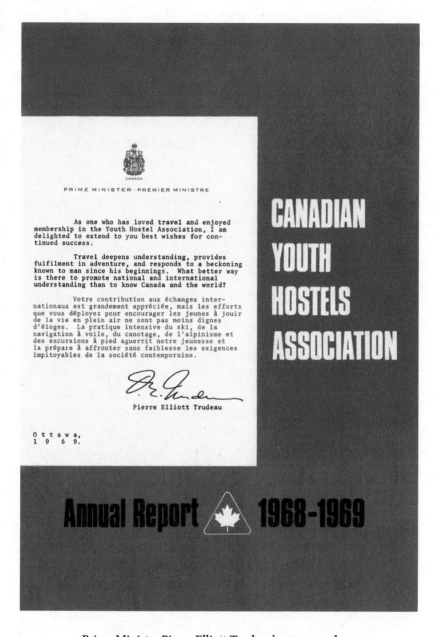

Prime Minister Pierre Elliott Trudeau's memorandum
to the Canadian Youth Hostels Association, 1969.
*Annual Reports 1965–1972, M7832, file 73, Canadian Youth Hostels Association,*
*Glenbow Museum Archives, Calgary*

Within months, the CYHA's membership had "quintupled."[33] The status of European-style hostelling was further enhanced when the CYHA was invited by the Secretary of State to submit a brief to the Committee on Youth in 1969. After that, the CYHA's national executive was invited to send a delegate to the Canadian Welfare Council's National Youth Consultation in Sainte-Adèle, Quebec, in order to advise on youth hostelling.[34] The national president, David Simonsen, was so "optimistic about future prospects" that he wrote, "Our growing pains are over."[35]

The excitement that characterized the 1970s youth scene was short-lived for the CYHA. Soon after the Sainte-Adèle consultation began, the delegates informally divided into opposing ideological camps, which they called "straights" and "heads." The CYHA delegate proudly took her place in the straight camp and promoted the "European hostelling" traditions. The "straights" were unimpressed when "youth participants" began "smoking grass" in the Hôtel Le Chantecler meeting rooms. This "polarizing" action sent a "clear" message that hostels were "where to go that's cool." Booze and drugs were not "where it's at" in CYHA hostels.[36] Since the 1930s the rules of conduct had been intended to meet the approval of parents, schools, and organized groups like the Boy Scouts and the Girl Guides. The CYHA was hoping the federal hostels would meet the same high standards as those of the International Youth Hostel Federation. However, for the time being, it was "straights against the heads" and unclear whether the CYHA's "outdoorsie people" would be able to find their groove in the "freak-oriented hostels" funded by the Canadian taxpayer.[37]

### Making Travel Work: Transient Youth Services' Hostel Program

The official connection between hitchhiking and youth hostels was the inquiry of the Canadian Welfare Council (CWC) on transient youth. However, behind the scenes, in the summer of 1969, Trudeau appointed a Committee on Youth to collect information and review the status of young people in the country. Following the Sainte-Adèle consultation, when the CWC approached the Secretary of State on behalf of the Hostel Task Force to request money for youth hostels, work on a highly "confidential" multi-million-dollar summer program for student employment was already well underway.[38] The sit-ins and violence at federal youth hostels in the summer of 1970 signified to many sectors of society that there were "much larger and deeper questions" about the position of youth that needed to be addressed.[39] The Committee on Youth's report, *It's Your Turn* (1971), was the largest study of youth in Canadian history. The 216-page report included surveys, public hearings, and questionnaires supplemented by 10,000 informal interviews with Canadian youth.[40] The committee looked at education, the transition from school to work, and new trends in leisure time, as well as listing numerous things the government could do for youth, including lowering the age of majority from twenty-one to eighteen. Drawing on new trends in recreation and travel, *It's Your Turn* said, "If we accept the premise that travel is a desirable and legitimate educational activity," a network of hostels was a "prerequisite."[41]

The federal government was under pressure to take action on behalf of young Canadians. Trudeaumania had faded in October 1970. Many believed that by imposing the War Measures Act, Trudeau had "exposed" himself "as fundamentally the defender of social order."[42] Following the announcement on March 16, 1971, of the Student Summer Employment Program, also called Summer '71, the federal government began to take direct control of youth policy. Trudeau believed that "social action" belonged with the Department of Citizenship, not the Department of Health and Welfare, and gave Summer '71 to Pelletier's office to manage.[43] To prevent the innovative program from being "obscured" by traditional youth service organizations, an early order of business was to ease the CWC out of the youth hostel business.

Months earlier, the CWC had applied for financial support for a follow-up to the Sainte-Adèle consultation. It wanted to use the meeting in order to launch its report *Transient Youth, 70–71* (1970) in a public forum, where it could plan hostel accommodation and related services for transient youth in 1971. After weeks of stalling, on February 25, 1971, Cabinet rejected the CWC's application. The official reason was the lack of "transient" participation and workshops. However, the agenda appeared too risky to a government trying to sell "a federal presence" and multi-million-dollar youth policy to Canadians.[44] Moving forward, Ottawa announced that it would give grants only to programs run by youth, meaning largely middle-class university students. Many CWC stakeholders and national voluntary organizations, including the Red Cross, the YMCA's and YWCA's leadership programs, group homes, and the members-only CYHA, were instructed to re-examine their programs if they wished to be eligible for federal grants.[45] The Canadian Welfare Council, now called the Canadian Council on Social Development, was furious about having been "kept in the dark." It shot back that thousands of Canadian youth would not be on the road if they could find jobs, declaring that "transients prefer work."[46] Lillian Thomson, the author of three reports for the Canadian Welfare Council's transient youth inquiry, acidly remarked that the "phenomenon of transient youth" had become the "catastrophe of youth unemployment."[47]

This was true. The Liberals were facing larger demographic, social, and economic problems. With an eye on youth unrest in Quebec, Europe, and the United States, and a wish to avoid a "long hot summer" in Canada, the prime minister's office was pressed to respond to the serious youth unemployment crisis facing the country. The largest cohort of baby boom children had come of age, and students were advancing on to postsecondary education in unprecedented numbers. In September 1971 there were 1,805,000 students returning to high school, college, or university. This was an increase of 96,000 over 1970 and 54,000 over 1969.[48] The urgency was exacerbated because there were no jobs, or at least not the type of jobs recent graduates expected to find. Female students in psychology and other humanities had the most difficult time. The *Edmonton Journal* said they "are being forced to take jobs as filing clerks."[49] Unemployment in Quebec was one-third higher than the national average.[50] The minister of manpower and immigration, Otto Lang, feared that the "release of students" posed more than a "statistical" problem; young people denied employment opportunities "by bureaucracy or neglect [were] liable to explode into demonstrative unrest."[51]

For the most part, student unemployment was a relatively new problem in Canada and a consequence of Prime Minister Lester B. Pearson's reforms to the student loan program before Trudeau was elected, the opening of seven new universities, and increasing numbers of youth from diverse backgrounds attending higher education. In the past, wealthy students read books and vacationed during the long holiday, and those who paid their own tuition worked on farms and for private local businesses. A limited number of summer jobs were created through Hire a Student programs in the private and government sectors. This was a suitable way to replace employees on summer vacations and to give students a brief apprenticeship prior to graduation.[52] In the late 1960s, with a hiring freeze, layoffs in the civil service, and less goodwill in the private sector, many outlets for student employment shrank. On January 28, 1971, an interdepartmental memo clarified that Summer '71 was a means of "attempting to keep 'idle hands busy.'"[53]

Gérard Pelletier kept his word. The Department of Citizenship took over Summer '71 and publicly passed the "youth welfare" torch over to a new generation of "hip new civil servants" in their twenties and early thirties, whom the press dubbed the "guerrilla bureaucracy."[54] The subcommittee in charge of youth hostels was Transient Youth Services, which overlapped with Opportunities for Youth. Notable consultants and evaluators included Andy Cohen of the Company of Young Canadians; Cam Mackie of the Department of Health and Welfare's Demonstration Grant Program; his twenty-three-year-old assistant, Rob Andras, of Opportunities for Youth; David Slipacoff, who was seconded from the Young Voyageurs to join the National Hostel Task Force during the Jericho Beach hostel's occupation; Brian Gilhuly, a twenty-five-year-old who in 1968 had been the residence manager at Rochdale College, an eighteen-storey, experimental, free university cooperative; and Byron Rogers, a twenty-five-year-old researcher on the federal government's Commission of Inquiry into the Non-Medical Use of Drugs, known as the Le Dain Commission.[55] These and other ""blue-jean bureaucrats" were hired or seconded from federal programs engaged in social action projects.[56]

Like the generation itself, former staff said that Summer '71 was innovative, fun, committed to new forms of communication, and "truly trying to figure things out." Cam Mackie said that many of the staff were still under the influence of 1967's Summer of Love. They shared their generation's belief that social institutions should reflect visionary ideals and a "new consciousness" of community development, as seen in initiatives such as grassroots urban and rural communes, housing and food co-ops, free schools, alternative media, and artists' collectives interested in new ways of living, with "youth involvement at every level." There was a great deal of excitement working in a bureaucracy that was willing to give "freedom and money with no fear of trying new things."[57] For Byron Rogers, it was exciting to try to change the system through radical instrumentalism from inside government, especially when youth hostels were a "political hot potato."[58] Brian Gilhuly recalled that the goal was a new community model of "client participation and youth involvement" and new institutional structures for the way "government should be run." It felt to him like youth had moved from the margins of a socially constructed problem to being full participants who were sharing in the goal of creating national unity.[59]

The first task of the Summer '71 committee was to assemble background information from the Canadian Welfare Council's *Transient Youth: Report of an Inquiry in the Summer of 1969* (1970) and the Secretary of State's *It's Your Turn* (1971), as well as from committee members' own hitching and hostelling adventures. The members were aware of the New Left position that youth should not be treated as a "class in itself." However, they disagreed with radicals like "Dollar Bill," who denounced Trudeau for trying to turn hitchhiking "into an institution" that "ultimately means control of people's minds."[60] The young liberals also rejected the conservative view of youth deviance, which saw nonconformity as an individual's failure to internalize the social rules of the normative culture. Unlike the Canadian Youth Hostels Association, which made a distinction between travelling CYHA members and transient and "disturbed youth" who needed "counselling,"[61] the Transient Youth Services committee did not want to treat some travellers as risky and others as at risk. Gilhuly recalled that they applied what they could remember from their courses at university and favoured the "social construction of reality" theory.[62] In 1966 sociologists like Peter Berger and Thomas Luckmann argued that social actors constructed society from moment to moment. Over time, through interactions, people would create a new social system.[63] Transient Youth Services wished to design a summer program that offered young Canadians productive "educational experiences" and an opportunity to test "radical ideas in real situations involving real people."[64] The new Trudeau hostels would be freely available to everyone, so a summer of hitching and hostelling would be a cheap holiday for all and a "means of developing national unity."[65]

More practically, Summer '71 was expected to solve the problem of youth unemployment. Federal statistics estimated that 200,000 young people travelled in the summer of 1970, and they forecast that between 300,000 and 400,000 students, workers, and unemployed persons from virtually all age groups would be on the road again in 1971 and possibly for years afterward. The Summer '71 staff were not in a position to intervene in the labour market, so they turned the Canadian Welfare Council's suggestion that kids travelled for negative reasons, such as a lack of alternative activities and unemployment, into a positive educational opportunity for English and French students and workers to travel united along the Trans-Canada Highway. Put sociologically, Summer '71 created the "functional equivalent" of paid work. Successful applicants received an honorarium rather than wages. The ideal candidate was a young man or woman with the cultural capital to understand the difference between monotonous and largely unproductive wage labour and spending "their holidays in a useful, productive way ... for which there will likely be little or no pay."[66]

Summer '71 had an initial budget of over $1.5 million, comprising $375,000 for hostels, $775,000 for kiosks, and $357,000 for buses,[67] and its short-term objectives were to distribute grants to local community hostels, create jobs for local students, meet the federal target of 300,000 bed nights, improve the safety and efficiency of hitchhiking as a means of travel, and establish a nationwide information network with up-to-date statistics on youth mobility. The long-term goals were to increase public acceptance and support for transients, create guidelines for the operation of youth hostels, and direct future youth travel policy. The budget was enough to provide three months of employment for three hundred students at up to twenty-five temporary facilities in Vancouver, Kamloops, Jasper, Banff, Edmonton, Calgary, Medicine Hat, Saskatoon, Regina, Winnipeg, Kenora, Thunder Bay, Sault Ste. Marie, Ottawa, Toronto, Rouyn-Noranda, Montreal, Sherbrooke, Quebec City, Rimouski, Fredericton, Charlottetown, Halifax, and St. John's.[68]

The guidelines they drew up said that accommodations and a small breakfast would be provided at no cost. Each hostel should have approximately one hundred beds, ample washroom facilities, one shower for every ten beds, gender-segregated sleeping accommodation, an office, a lounge, and workshops for handicrafts, music nights, coffeehouses, language courses, and a speakers' series. The carefully trained staff of the day and night shifts had to be students intending to return to university who were capable of enforcing the rules and willing to work with health and welfare departments, local police, and the Children's Aid Society.[69] The job entailed keeping accurate records of the names, ages, and destinations of hostellers, spotting travellers at risk, responding to medical problems and drug crises, and providing access to legal and psychological counselling services. The staff had to agree to foster communication between local businesses, community leaders, and the youth hostel. In an effort to avoid the violence and chaos of the previous summer, the public was assured that youth hostels would not be imposed upon municipalities that did not want them.[70]

Transient Youth Services thought that national unity "through citizenship development" would be strengthened "by giving participants the opportunity to establish a significant and personal rapport with other Canadians in other parts of the country."[71] So they decided to use their ample budget to link the network of hostels along the Trans-Canada Highway by means of a fleet of twenty transport buses and fifty hitchhikers' kiosks, thirty-five in English Canada and fifteen in Quebec. The kiosks and buses would "improve the efficiency of hitchhiking" whether done for pleasure or by young people seeking employment.[72] The kiosks would be "gaily-painted" with "striking and imaginative designs" and "flanked by visible signage of the federal presence," and the buses could be painted to "match the kiosks." They would ferry hostellers to hostels and between kiosks and provide six jobs for local students, Canadian Tourist Association staff, and volunteers. Local students could be employed as tour guides.[73] Most importantly, kiosks would serve as "safe pick-up" points for riders and motorists.[74] They would be equipped with phones, electricity, toilets, and running water, so hitchhikers could wait for a lift in the shade, go inside for a cool drink, use the phone and the washrooms, or ask for information about the next city or closest hostel.

The staff could collect information on the identity of drivers and hitch-hikers, record the destinations of both parties, and submit weekly reports on the numbers of people using the service, major traffic trends, and the public's response to the program as solicited from participants and the community. A hitchhiker database would "establish needed control of the rapidly growing transient phenomenon" and "afford protection to hitchhikers and drivers as well as giving reassurance to parents."[75]

The kiosk project went ahead, but when word got around Ottawa that Transient Youth Services was going to order a fleet of gaily painted buses for Summer '71, the Department of Manpower and Immigration was inundated with complaints from members of Parliament. Interviews with former staff of Transient Youth Services suggest that in the public's imagination, convoys of transient youth crossing the country in psychedelic school buses too closely resembled the Merry Pranksters' LSD-laced bus trip across America in the summer of 1964, journalist Tom Wolfe's semi-autobiographical *The Electric Kool-Aid Acid Test* (1968) about roadside encounters with counterculture guru Ken Kesey, the Hells Angels, beat generation poet Allen Ginsberg, and the music of the Grateful Dead. Certainly, Otto Lang's office was not willing to pay for magic buses, and Cabinet refused to sit back and watch the Trans-Canada Highway become a "hippie trail."[76]

The Kiosk Program encountered problems, too. Initially, the design of the hitchhiker kiosks was contracted by the Department of Public Works to the Fentiman design group, a specialist in patented "geodesic" structures, which had been seen, to great acclaim, at Expo 67 in Montreal and Expo 70 in Osaka. Regrettably, each cost over $4,000.[77] Rather than redirect money from the cancelled bus service, the department hired a theme coordinator, who submitted his own design for simpler "dismountable" tents that cost only $580 each. The designer said the teepees reflected the temporary choice of lifestyle and the earthy aesthetics of the transients. The distinctiveness of the 10-metre tents, which would be "the highest ever designed and constructed in Canada," would satisfy the desire for a visible "federal presence" in the youth scene.[78] Without consulting a structural engineer, the Public Works Department ordered forty-five chocolate-brown tepees printed with "Canada" in white, capitalized letters, which were unveiled on June 15, 1971.[79] Unfortunately, staff on the

"... no ... this is my house ... white man hitch-hiking kiosk down
highway nine hundred flaps of crow's wing ...," *Toronto Star,* May 24, 1971.
*Cartoon by Sid Barron, used with permission of Jessamine Barron,
Library and Archives Canada*

Prairies quickly discovered that the tents were "too weak" to withstand
winds of one hundred kilometres per hour. The manufacturer blamed
the "slipshod tent raising of the students." Strong winds also buckled the
main tent pole at the kiosk in Ottawa. Calgary's tent was stolen, and the
kiosk in Richmond Hill outside of Toronto was on the opposite side of
ongoing traffic. Garry Anka, the coordinator of the Kiosk Program, said
the kiosks were "a real headache."[80] The scheme was audacious enough
to catch the attention of political cartoonist Sid Barron. Halfway through
the summer, many were replaced by weather-resistant house-trailers.

For the next five summers, the federal government provided summer
jobs for returning students, it subsidized hostel accommodation, and it
communicated information to travellers via the press, university newspapers, and a switchboard number that travellers could call to speak with

a dispatcher about hostel addresses and advice. To improve hitchhiking safety, after the plans for buses and kiosks were cut, the Department of Health and Welfare published *On the Road: A Guide for Youth Travelling Canada* (1972). The thirty-one-page booklet included a map of the Trans-Canada Highway, advice on how to pack a backpack, prevent drowning, and give mouth-to-mouth resuscitation, tips on where to eat, and the addresses of every YMCA and YWCA.[81] Unfortunately, the numerous errors in the manual earned it the nickname "How to Get Lost." One hitchhiker called the "error-riddled road booklet" a "joke book." Worried parents called it "the apple with the worm in it" and feared that Ottawa had "handed out almost a million of them."[82] The Department of Health and Welfare immediately recalled *On the Road*, but only five thousand copies were actually taken off the market.

Despite bumbled bureaucratic interventions, each summer between 1971 and 1976 small, regional hostel associations formed to organize local hostels and lobby municipalities to improve services for travellers. Under the umbrella of the Independent Hostel Association, headed by Brian Gilhuly, the staff in regional federal hostels were proud of their hassle-free management style and their friendly little travel co-ops.

### Hitching and Hostelling on the Trans-Canada Highway: A Transitory Evil

There was nothing new in the travel traditions of young people. "In olden times the elegant and wealthy youth were given the Grand Tour of Europe and other fancy spas," the *Ottawa Journal* editorialized in 1970. "The intrepid, the adventurous, the disturbed, but rarely the timid" were travelling "the Canadian highways and byways ... They are often vilified, hated and discriminated against, in communities that pride themselves on their 'friendly little town.'"[83] Contemporary observations are good indicators of how the Liberal government's youth-centred policies were received by everyday Canadians. In its first twelve months, the Opportunities for Youth program was the subject of 2,587 press stories.[84] People wrote letters, signed petitions, and phoned radio call-in shows to express their opinions on hitchhikers, youth hostels, drop-in centres, and the general behaviour of the nation's young people. Fans called the philosophy of Opportunities for Youth "the future," and foes called the program a "larceny perpetrated with Canadian tax dollars."[85] Critics doubted that Ottawa had any idea what it was doing by turning a "make-work project" into a "lifestyle." A Londoner said, "Let's make these hippies get a bath and a job and stop wasting our money."[86] The *Winnipeg Free Press* called Pelletier the "high priest of the bizarre."[87] Penticton residents were "up in arms about Ottawa's idea" that "jobless youth would be transported across the country ... at government subsidies."[88] Two Charlottetown landlords who said that students left their rental houses in dreadful condition argued, "If that is a sample of what they do, I don't think we should give them hostels."[89] A University of Lethbridge student called Opportunities for Youth a government "pacification program."[90] A University of Ottawa student called it "gimmickry ... to keep Canada fairly quiet as student radicals were co-opted into the federal bureaucracy," predicting that "when middle-class university-educated students cannot find work, all hell is going to break loose."[91]

How any community responds to tourists and travellers is a function of how tourists and locals see each other. Whereas welcoming hosts may make efforts to meet travellers' demands helpfully and willingly, less welcoming hosts develop "veiled" forms of "resistance" to maintain boundaries between travellers and themselves. Entrepreneurial locals looking to make some money create phony attractions and "stage" culturally stereotyped performances enabling travellers to feel included in "authentic" cultural rituals. Darya Maoz says that young Israeli backpackers travelling in India are usually unaware of the staging efforts of "professional" locals who present themselves as Reiki teachers, babahs, gurus, and other self-appointed spiritual leaders. That these locals talk of love, friendship, and giving provides young Israelis with the "authentic" experience they seek.[92] This section shows that the absence of a welcome mat did not stop young people from travelling to regions where they were not invited. With the coast-to-coast battle over youth hostelling, rivalries and alliances developed among churches, the YMCA and YWCA, city councils, and groups that opposed hostelling and hitchhiking in Charlottetown, Montreal, Thunder Bay, London, Winnipeg, Saskatchewan, and Alberta.

There is no way of knowing how many young people hitchhiked across North America. The media estimated that between 50,000 and 100,000 hitchhikers would pass through Winnipeg every summer from 1970 to 1975. In 1970 readers of Canadian national and local newspapers were kept aware of the "summer army of hitchhikers" marching "across this land."[93] The *Montreal Gazette* said, "Thousands of youngsters will be on the road this summer."[94] In 1971, under the headline "Canada's Great Trek: 40,000 Transients Will Walk This Summer," the *Vancouver Province* proclaimed, "Hitchhiking has become a national phenomenon." The *Vancouver Sun* announced, "50,000 transients only the beginning."[95] In May 1972 the *Calgary Herald* told "taxpayers" to brace for transients because 50,000 hitchhikers had "passed through in '71." In June a *Winnipeg Free Press* headline read, "Army of Hitch-Hikers Already on the March."[96]

On Prince Edward Island, pristine beaches, a lobster fest, and Anne of Green Gables tours were an important sector of the summer tourism economy.[97] Locals discovered that the province's "clean, quiet, pastoral and unspoiled" image was also attractive to "hippies" from Canada, the United States, and Europe.[98] In 1970, when the hostel task force commandeered Brighton Compound C under the youth hostel program, it became know as the "Far East Hostel," which was still vilified when it closed in September.[99] The next summer, anti-hostel sentiments were reignited by the announcement that instead of continuing to use the Brighton armoury, a "tent city" for five hundred visitors would be erected in East Royalty. A resident threatened to "spread hog manure" on the site "if the province pursued the plan."[100] Neighbours started a petition after hearing that 5,000 to 6,000 hippies were headed to the island. The Community Improvement Committee of East Royalty circulated a petition addressed to the rest of Canada that said,

> [We] do hereby advise all levels of government that the citizens of this district have voted unanimously in disfavour of the establishment of any such tent city in this area ... This type of operation cannot be properly controlled due to poor cooperation of the type of youth who patronize these establishments ... [Mindful of] the safety of our youngsters including the availability of drugs, the immoral activities of young people connected with tent cities, [and] the spending of taxpayers money to promote idleness ... the people feel that this type of traveller does not help our island tourist trade.[101]

When the petition failed, thirty-six "housewives" and grandmothers erected a plywood and barbed-wire barrier around the youth hostel site. Two hundred onlookers witnessed "tears, shoving and hair pulling" when officers of the Royal Canadian Mounted Police escorted the mothers and grandmothers out of the pouring rain.[102] Concerned citizens turned to the Presbytery for advice. The religious leaders suggested that a chain of church-run youth hostels in local villages would be preferable to federal hostels.[103] When St. John's, Newfoundland, city councillor Brian Higgins said that he "didn't want bums coming into the city" and suggested that the city use its $20,000 grant from the Opportunities for Youth program to buy chains to put "across roads" to the city, students at Memorial University reacted by accusing him of "the kind of bigotry that has made Vancouver Mayor Tom Campbell hated by so many Canadians."[104]

Prince Edward Island's premier, Alex Campbell, said that the province's "hospitality cannot be limited to the wealthy tourist." He thought that it was "far better to build understanding between the generations than erect barriers of distrust and hostility."[105] To show "that he was pro-youth and that Prince Edward Island was not off limits to low-income, youthful tourists," Campbell slept at the tent hostel site with his wife and children on June 2, 1971.[106] Charlottetown mayor Dorothy Corrigan said that it was "unthinkable that any other areas of Canada, for instance, Toronto, would prevent islanders travelling there." She was "strenuously against a barrier to the free flow of goods between provinces ... Surely people are more important."[107] In 1972 the welfare ministers in Prince Edward Island, Nova Scotia, New Brunswick, and Newfoundland asked Ottawa for permanent funding for youth hostels. They agreed that "modest and well-managed hostels" for "normal and healthy" young travellers would be preferable to young people sleeping in parks and squares.[108] Youthful travellers were undeterred by the ambiguous welcome. Hitchhiking around the maritime provinces enabled them to share a "laid-back" way of life. As one enthusiastic hitchhiker said, "You don't find many 'plastic' people in Newfie."[109]

The "bohemian" community in Montreal was also attractive to Canadian and American travellers. In the early 1970s Saint Louis Square was the "meeting place of guitar strummers, motorcycle riders, panhandlers, runaways, revolutionaries, commune dwellers, crashers, the barefooted and the hairy-topped, a sprinkling of artists and intellectuals."[110] In 1971 Transient Youth Services gave a $15,000 grant for a "crash pad" in the private student residence called Co-op habitat étudiante de Durocher. Longueuil mayor Marcel Robidas was concerned about hostellers' use of drugs and their personal hygiene, and he wondered how the staff would keep the sexes separate because "modern boys and girls are often indistinguishable by hair length and dress."[111] Quebec faced one of the most serious youth unemployment problems in the country.[112] Transient youth were on the agenda at the Quebec meetings of the Canadian Catholic Conference and the Canadian Council of Churches. The interfaith position was that the churches did not "so much" want to "encourage" travel, yet neither did they condone giving the "cold shoulder" to travellers with little money.[113] They disapproved of the Vancouver mayor's "loudly" expressed protest and the recent rejection of a tent city in Toronto. Christian organizations asked the "adult world" to consider the needs of the travellers expected to "hit the open road." It was in the best interests of cultural exchange and interregional understanding "to acknowledge that they are here to stay."[114]

In Quebec a successful network of hostels was already set up due to the activities of the Quebec Youth Hostel Association. In preparation for Expo 67, a good system of rural youth hostels opened all over Quebec, especially the chain of hostels on the Gaspé Peninsula. In Montreal there were urban "emergency" shelters at the Community Switchboard for anglophones and at the Centre de Communications du Village Carré St. Louis for francophones. The staff provided meals, crash pads, legal advice, and medical referrals. In addition, Christian House operated a crash pad with an evangelical message.[115] In 1970 the National Hostel Task Force used the old B Squadron armoury of the Royal Canadian Hussars as a youth hostel.[116] In 1971 seven new hostels supplemented the eleven existing provincial youth hostels for travellers aged eighteen to thirty. Anxious taxpayers complained about "freeloading." For example, in a letter to the *Montreal Gazette,* an "infuriated" Montrealer wrote, "Where is the logic in my working so they can freeload and at the same time ridicule those who pay the freight? ... Everyone is afraid of youth these days ... afraid of being called 'square.' I am proud to be square in a world that kowtows to weak-willed kids who are spoiled rotten."[117] Young travellers were not deterred. In the summer of 1972, the five hostels in Montreal hosted 10,000 youth, 50 percent of whom were from the United States.[118] American hitchhikers compared Quebec to Europe. Paul DiMaggio called Montreal a "magnificent French-American city" with a lovely surrounding countryside.[119]

In the middle of June 1971, the number of youth on Ontario highways and street corners reached the thousands. The *Globe and Mail* said that the roads "look like a re-enactment of the Children's Crusade."[120] The Ontario Provincial Police printed 200,000 brochures warning hitchhikers of the areas along Ontario highways and parts of Quebec where hitchhiking was prohibited. The fine for hitchhiking was raised from $5 for a first offence to $50 for three or more offences. Nonetheless, drivers were still prepared to pick up hitchhikers, as shown by the fact that insurance companies issued automobile policies with no-fault coverage and benefits that protected drivers who had accidents that caused injury to hitchhiking passengers.[121]

The youth hostel question was a sensitive issue in northern and southern Ontario. Mickey Hennessy of the Centre for International Cooperation of Thunder Bay was furious that he could not receive a grant for homestays for participants from Canada World Youth because the money was going to the "non-C.Y.H.A. group" that operated the local federal hostel program. Hennessy said bitterly that adventurer accommodation should not be combined with welfare assistance. "The city might well give its full support" to "both men and women" at the Salvation Army.[122] The well-documented clashes between rival subcultures like hippies and bikers were used by mayors of other Canadian cities as examples of the violent consequences of youth unrest. In the 1960s Yorkville became a countercultural tourist attraction, drawing so many bikers, hippies, weekenders, and teenyboppers from around the country that middle-class motorists from suburbia drove in simply to "gawk at the hippies."[123]

Smaller cities along the Trans-Canada Highway found it more difficult to accommodate transient thumb-travellers than did urban centres. Contemporary reportage indicates that it was not unusual in the summer to see "a hundred young people at a time, with packsacks and sleeping gear, lining the roadside leading out of Thunder Bay."[124] Women in Dryden collected hundreds of signatures on a petition that said they "didn't want hitchhikers pushing drugs to their children."[125] In 1969, when the Board of Parks and Recreation in Fort William announced its intention to open a hostel for men and women, people circulated a petition against accommodating women travellers. It said, "We fail to see why the taxpayers of FW [Fort William] should provide a shelter or aid of this type to females who choose to travel through our city."[126] The Salvation Army began turning male travellers away because its Christian missionary work was not intended for middle-class, voluntary transients. The people of Fort William could not be talked into creating a youth hostel. They did not want their section of the city to become "another Yorkville."[127]

In southern Ontario, people in London formed the Committee Against Parasites and referred to hostellers as "pigs, freaks and kooks." It was the opinion of many that hostels and drop-in centres transformed girls and boys into "wandering scroungers."[128] A Londoner threatened to burn down the hostel and use shotguns to keep travellers away.[129] Joan Belford, the social worker in charge of the London hostel, said "people were so violently opposed to the hostel" that her "personal safety was threatened."[130] An unsigned letter to the editor of the *London Free Press* said, "On every street corner in the sleazier part of our cities, we see these vagabonds loitering and panhandling, their bodies unwashed, their garments bizarre and soiled ... whipper-snappers [without] taste or intellect, the drop-out dullards of society ... Living in these hostels and hitchhiking from one to another is tantamount to begging."[131]

Some Manitobans were open-minded about youth mobility, but not everyone was happy about the "cool community" reputation that Winnipeg developed among hitchhikers. Winnipeg's position roughly midway between Montreal and Vancouver astride the Trans-Canada Highway overloaded the city with travellers.[132] In 1970 the hostel at the HMCS Chippawa armoury accommodated 5,000 travellers over the summer; the projection for 1971 was 10,000 to 50,000 travellers.[133] This was far short of the "estimated five million young people" the *Winnipeg Free Press* said would be "crossing the country by thumb," but it reveals that when it came to transient youth, the press usually thought only in tens of thousands.[134] Winnipeg's deputy chief of police saw "nothing wrong with young people moving around the country." The police should "help them" whenever they can.[135] "Let's face it," Alderman Richard Willows said, "these kids are coming through ... At least they can be controlled in one location."[136] However, many city officials were afraid that liberal attitudes would make the city a "Mecca" for young people wanting handouts.[137]

The mayor of East Kildonan, Stanley Dowhan, did not want back-packers to "sleep in hobo parks," as was done in the 1930s.[138] In May 1971 the East Kildonan City Council voted down the request of the National Hostel Task Force to use the Memorial Arena as a youth hostel because the roof was poorly insulated.[139] A local church offered the top floor of St. Alphonse Parish Hall, but angry neighbours stormed the council meeting, protesting that the neighbourhood was already "too congested" by the church's bingos, baseball games, and Saturday night dances. The hostellers "playing on their guitars in the evening" would add to the noise and congestion of the neighbourhood.[140]

Transient youth crossing Saskatchewan had their opponents and their defenders. People in Saskatoon and Regina were "not disappointed" when young travellers showed no interest in sightseeing and city tours. The general feeling was that "the sooner they move on, the better."[141] In addition to the YMCA, YWCA, and Salvation Army, Saskatoon had a small hostel called the Gypsy Mattress. Regina's hostel consisted of 160 beds in an old theatre. Residents in Broadview and Moosomin said that "long-haired types" and "students out looking for work" came in waves heading to Ontario or British Columbia.[142] An article titled "Transient Youth Find Defender" quoted the chief of police in Medicine Hat, who stood up to local objections to a proposed youth hostel with six tents and a wash-trailer. "We had more trouble from thieves in motels than from youths," Chief Sam Drader said. Hitchhikers "don't wear horns, nor are they saints. They're no better, no worse than we are."[143] Farmers' pickup trucks were the chief mode of transportation. Riders perched in the open bed amused themselves "flashing peace signs at passing cars."[144]

It appeared to some people that hitchhikers had an easier time crossing the Prairies than in other parts of the country. They could be seen queuing up on the outskirts of Winnipeg, Regina, and Moose Jaw. The social significance and social effect of the massive westward flow of long-haired youngsters were just as worrisome in the West as in the East. An ex-hippie, John van der Raadt, ran a hostel in Moose Jaw called Cool-Aid. He could not understand kids in 1971 either. When he was on the road, he said, "he worked when he ran out of money and never relied on government hand-outs." The trouble with the new generation of "moneyless and aimless wandering youth" was that they "have come to expect service as a right." He complained that the kids refused to help with daily chores. "They figure we're here to serve them and that's really bad ... Hostels aren't the problem, people are."[145]

Moving farther west, Albertans were concerned about transients in the mid-1960s due to the volume of travellers who passed through Edmonton and Calgary on their way to the Rocky Mountains and to Banff and Jasper National Parks. In 1970 the Ortona armoury in Edmonton and "H" hut near the Mewata armoury in Calgary had about a hundred beds each. The *Edmonton Journal's* announcement that the city was "no utopia" for "junior tourists" did not stop students at the University of Alberta from starting a catering service that sold chili, stew, and chow mein dinners at the hostel for 40 cents.[146] In September 1972 the Calgary YMCA angered members when it offered drop-in space, recreation, and meals to young people. YMCA members thought the new "clients were not worthy of the organization's efforts."[147] In Banff and Jasper National Parks, "dirty" young people sleeping in picnic shelters antagonized officials and tourists, as well as business owners by shoplifting and stealing from cars. The police discovered that the young thieves often "have substantial sums of money with them – as much as $200 to $300 and yet they steal from grocery stores, clothing stores and cars."[148] After almost thirty years of cooperation, the Canadian Youth Hostels Association found its relationship with Parks Canada in jeopardy after the National Hostel Task Force was announced. The police and park wardens did not want crash pads; they liked how strictly the CYHA houseparents enforced their rules. Nonetheless, Parks Canada informed the CYHA that if it wished to keep its hostels in the parks, it had to relax its membership restrictions and declare "national parks a special area open to all reasonable types who want low cost accommodation during a recreational visit to the parks."[149]

The absence of a welcome mat did not stop young people from travelling to unfamiliar regions of Canada. Transients and hitchhikers received authentic welcomes from the staff at kiosks and federal hostels. Inside, the staff created an imagined countercultural world. There were chores for hostellers to do, underground film nights, macramé crafts, and musical entertainment in the lounges. Don Sanami Morrill of the Hostel Association of Nova Scotia said that a transient "should BE a traveller and not a local person hunting for a flop house after an argument with Dad"; however, the hostel facility should resemble travellers' co-ops so that guests could participate in the "community experience, such as gardening to assist providing for the hostels, laying trails, making maps or pottery."[150]

Federal youth hostel staff from every province formed the National Coalition of Provincial and Regional Hostelling Associations to act as a coordinating body that would lobby for year-round hostels and mediate conflicts between the needs of young travellers and the aims of neighbourhood associations, churches, the YMCA and YWCA, and city councils. In the spring of 1971 two young men in northern Ontario formed the Thunder Bay Travelling Youth Services Committee.[151] Darcy Moorey and Iain Angus wanted to teach their peers how to get support from town councils before they tried to set up youth hostels. They invited staff from Parks and Recreation, the Children's Aid Society, Lakehead University's Social Planning Council, mayors' offices, and interested youth from the region to attend a workshop that provided instruction on "how to present the problem of transient youth ... in a positive manner." They said, "To some people, a hitchhiker is a filthy animal involved in a not too respectable pastime." Locals were afraid of how "youth drifting through town" would affect "their own kids." Therefore, it was important to face this head-on and to present "a truthful picture."[152] Most importantly, youth hostel staff had to be willing to work with the police, enforce rules, prevent local kids from hanging around, never "take part in a mudslinging campaign either in the press or on the radio," and above all else, cooperate with the Children's Aid Society because if it was "not on your side (no matter how you feel about them personally), there would be problems."[153] Moorey and Angus offered the following advice:

Begin by showing that travel is a good thing ... The community should be directly involved in the process of social change, not have it thrust upon them by an outside group or agency ... Explain to them that a hostel will benefit them too ... Explain to them that the hostel will keep travelling youth away from their establishments and therefore will not "scare" business ... You must reach the Power Groups first ... we do not mean Mayor or Aldermen, MPP or MP ... The people to convince are the Chamber of Commerce ... It might be the owner of the highway restaurant or owner of the biggest car lot ... They can convince the rest of the community ... They have to be shown that it is not a zoo where wild animals live but a place where young people come to get a night's rest before they move on ... Transients must be established as People not as hippies or bums.[154]

The most pressing challenge for federal youth hostel staff was to get the government to commit to permanent funding for year-round "multi-service" hostels for travellers and low-income youth moving back and forth between cities regardless of the reason. In 1974 the British Columbia and southern Ontario hostel associations wanted year-round hostels where services could be extended to fruit pickers and temporary workers waiting for paycheques and to "Indian or French Canadians wanting to see the parts of Canada he [sic] knows nothing about." In Ontario, around Stratford, the Quebecois tobacco pickers needed cheap places to stay until they made "some quick money."[155] Ann McGougan, the director of the Association of British Columbia Hostels, said that the hostellers in her hostels could never afford to become members of an elite "Hostel Club" or afford the expensive ski boots worn by hostellers in the CYHA's "Hilton Hostels."[156] She doubted that the CYHA's executive of lawyers, doctors, and teachers had ever stayed in "a government-run, freak-oriented hostel."[157] Equally frustrating was the CYHA's "concept of a 'desirable hosteller' which excluded thousands of Canadians in the low-income bracket who wanted to travel for work, education or holiday."[158] The government's "temporary attitude" toward hostels restricted their use to summer travel and the provision of seasonal jobs for students. The clients of federal hostels – young workers, students, and travellers of

Youth hostel birthday party, Jasper hostel, 1975.
*Jasper Hostels Scrapbook, M7832, file 291, Canadian Youth Hostels Association,*
*Glenbow Museum Archives, Calgary*

every political stripe – were caught between multigenerational worldviews that kept youth in motion.

### Resistance to Cooperation: The Canadian Youth Hostels Association

The youth travel organization with the strongest opposition to the "Trudeau hostels" was the Canadian Youth Hostels Association. Since the 1930s, European-style hostelling, hiking, canoeing, fishing, horseback riding, and wilderness survival and discovery had been highly regarded as superior forms of international youth tourism, recreation, and fellowship. Generations of CYHA members had made long-term commitments to the fitness and moral development of Canada's youngsters. In the early 1970s the CYHA was proud of the houseparents who enforced the rules that kept their fifty-seven youth hostels from becoming "hangouts or crash pads for drifters."[159] In the early 1970s the CYHA flatly refused to compromise its vision of youth hostelling in order to meet the expectations of the equally idealistic leaders of the Independent Hostel Association. There was no place in the CYHA's cultural imagination for freak-oriented hostels.

Tension between the rivals was based on two opposing perceptions of youth-based travel subcultures. Clair Jeremiah, the national secretary of the CYHA, was sent to the consultation in Sainte-Adèle. It was obvious to her that the invitation to "sit in" had been a "very borderline case."[160] The few delegates who had heard of the CYHA criticized its curfews, "no long hair" philosophy, and membership fees.[161] Jeremiah wondered whether the CYHA would be included among the three hundred delegates at a follow-up National Youth Conference on Travel and Exchange at Algonquin College in Ottawa in September 1970. Once again, the CYHA felt out of touch with the "independents." Peter Watts of the British Columbia region said they were still "wearing their highway costumes, long hair and far-out clothes." He was baffled because the most important issues on the agenda, "charter flights and youth hostels," received the same scrutiny as "drugs and abortion."[162]

In unpublished letters and meeting correspondence, CYHA members referred to the federal hostels as "welfare hostels" and backpackers as the "weird types" who "frightened away members."[163] For the next five years the federal and CYHA staff enjoyed insulting each other. Staff in the "Trudeau hostels" ridiculed the "outdoorsie people" in the CYHA for their cold showers, fresh-air hikes, and "bland middle-class restrictions."[164] The CYHA retaliated by calling the "freak" hostels "missions for the destitute" and "'homes' for those needing counselling" and with "special social problems."[165] Lianne Gusway of the Saskatchewan office was disgusted when she arrived for a meeting with the executive director of the Independent Hostel Association, and "there he was with a friend, both with their bare feet on the desk."[166] Most seriously, for the CYHA, the real problem was that Transient Youth Services had appropriated the term "youth hostel," which the association believed its founders Richard Sherrman in Germany and Catherine and Mary Barclay in Canada had never intended for "crash pads," "hangouts," and "a place for drifters."[167] Incidentally, apart from the membership requirements, the day-to-day management of federal hostels was not so different from that of

CYHA hostels. This similarity irritated the CYHA because it had initially "shrugged off the transient phenomenon" as a fad and then found itself unable to apply for federal funding.[168]

In 1971 the CYHA had been in the "hostel business" for over forty years and was disturbed to learn that the Secretary of State's "counter-culture" hostel program had sidestepped it because it did not seem to be in a "position to quickly establish or operate hostels on a nation-wide basis."[169] President David Simonsen said,

> There is a great vitality in Canadian youth hostels today ... Hundreds of young people [are] setting up hostels and hostel organizations across the country; but few of these hostels are ours and most of the groups are not associated with or even aware of the CYHA. These are groups sponsored by the federal government through the Youth Hostel Program of the Secretary of State ... A diversity of aims in these non-CYHA groups is evident and they cannot all be characterized or shrugged off as transient social phenomena that will shortly disappear.[170]

While the CYHA pondered how to get back in step with modern youth, the YMCA, which faced the same challenge, decided to modernize. The study on youth leisure by the Secretary of State's Committee on Youth reported that Canadian youth had lost interest in highly structured activities. Baby boomers preferred unstructured activities that took place beyond the gaze of adults, as indicated by declining enrolment in the YMCA and YWCA, the Boy Scouts and Girl Guides, 4-H clubs, and the Air Cadets.[171] When the national director of the Canadian YMCA, Les Vipond, learned that the Secretary of State was funding hostels, he jumped at the opportunity to lead the YMCA into the modern age.[172] To solve its problem of "too conservative an image," which hindered the YMCA's credibility with the younger generation, Vipond committed his organization to the new model of youth participation in planning projects for youth by asking YMCAs and YWCAs to increase the number of nonmembership programs for youth, and drop-in centres and residences softened their Christian fellowship messages, relaxed their "high standards," and encouraged the staff to dress and talk hip.[173] On May 25,

1970, the *Regina Leader Post* announced that after "much arguing" three hundred delegates representing 125 YMCA and YWCAs had voted to permit youth to sit on the organization's Board of Directors and had deleted references to "sharing a common loyalty to Jesus Christ" from its forty-year-old statement of purpose.[174] In 1970 the "Vancouver Y" sent an article to the *Georgia Straight* titled "The Y – Get It On!" It said that the Vancouver YMCAs and YWCAs were into counterculture activities like batik, macramé, good semi-underground flicks, discothèques, rap sessions, hostelling, and "drop in centres." The article continued,

> Help us do what we want to do, not what some knitting circle patriots think is necessary to preserve our manifest destiny heritage of subservient defender of the faith (read: mother/pie democracy) ...
>
> We'd like to know if everybody in Van thinks the VLF [Vancouver Liberation Front] is the only viable alternative to the antiquated fear-and-hate politics of relics like Campbell ... We'd like to do more things. We'd like to do your things. If you want a legit foot, solid backing, or just ripped sidekicks, then bang, bark or fly in ... We're with you. Given time (and good dope) you might even be with us. There are too many groups with hatchets trying to split the movement.[175]

The Canadian Youth Hostels Association faced the same pressure to modernize or become redundant that the YMCA and YWCA faced. The executive invited members to consider whether the CYHA was really operating "for the benefit of the wishes and needs of today's youth or is it trying to impose an outdated concept on them? How much does it epitomize a system youth is increasingly rejecting?"[176] Dennis Lewis, the director of the national executive, said "history shows that movements" get "top heavy right after they have 'made it."[177] Traditionalists flatly refused to bend to the criticism that their hostels "epitomize a system youth is increasingly rejecting."[178] Rather than change, the CYHA decided to fight back and launched an aggressive public relations attack against the Secretary of State's "welfare hostels."

In 1973 the Canadian Youth Hostels Association sent a letter to the minister of culture, youth, and recreation outlining a series of complaints.

First, Lewis stated that the association was a private organization that could not "compete" with federally funded hostels. Second, in its opinion, there was a "moral danger" for "the future" of a government that provided "free lodging and free food for kids-on-the-road." Was this not just an "inexpensive form" of social assistance for unemployed hitchhikers?[179] Third, the CYHA could not understand why travellers should not pay for the pleasures they enjoyed. It had come to the CYHA's attention that "first-class transients" took Air Canada flights from Halifax to Vancouver and "then flopped around the hostels free of charge."[180] Next, the executive approached the leader of the Progressive Conservative Party, Robert Stanfield, to point out the contradiction between "so-called 'open' transient hostels and the CYHA 'closed' hostels." The executive said that it was the transient hostels that were "really 'closed'" to school children, families, youth groups, and individuals who "feel the need for a little more security and quality when travelling." The membership requirement "can be of tremendous comfort to parents and authorities when young children have left home and travelled by the transient hostel route. Lack of control ... is part of the reason for the public backlash against 'hostels.'"[181] The problems would be resolved by sticking with the membership-based, European-style hostelling tradition.

In Winnipeg social worker Grace Ivey was a strong proponent of the CYHA. She took it upon herself to lobby on its behalf, using the grand opening of the CYHA's jail hostel in Ottawa to praise its educational programs. In a letter to the Secretary of State, she stated,

> This was an historical building that might have been torn down had a use not been found for it. Now school groups, staying in the gaol, can tour the premises and learn a little of Canada's history. They will always remember where the last public hanging took place, when the man who murdered [Thomas] D'Arcy McGee was executed ... We feel that we are the answer to the current government program of transient hostels, which have received much criticism from both the public and local government across the country. Being members of the International Youth Hostel Federation, we have to maintain a standard of accommodation and rules of conduct that would meet with approval

from leaders of the church, school, Boy Scouts, and Girl Guide groups using the facilities.[182]

The CYHA escalated its attack on federal hostels by focusing on their problems housing travellers to the 1976 Olympic Games in Montreal and by continually jabbing at the unpopularity of transient, hippie-style hostelling, which they called bad for tourism and the image of the Liberal Party.[183]

From 1972 to 1973 the CYHA waited for the government to change hands or "to 'clean up' their hostel operations" by letting the CYHA give it "some air of respectability."[184] It was understood that permanent federal funding hinged on a merger of the National Coalition of Provincial and Regional Hostelling Associations with the Independent Hostel Association and the Canadian Youth Hostels Association. Toward this end, on May 24, 1973, the CYHA hosted a "planning and coordinating conference" in Banff, to which it had invited the Secretary of State's assistant national co-coordinator of the hostel program, David Smith, as well as members of the federal Department of Culture, Youth and Recreation, the provincial Departments of Special Development, the Alberta, British Columbia, and Saskatchewan Hostel Associations, the Youthful Touring Association, the Association of British Columbia Hostels, and the Independent Hostel Association. Some of the delegates created the slogan "Take hostels out of the welfare state" and wrote a position paper on "Canadian Hostel Development," which said that Canada needed one permanent youth hostel system with ancillary programs for foreign travellers.[185] With the backing of the Secretary of State, the second National Hostel Task Force was formed in April 1975. It was composed of the CYHA and the Independent Hostel Association. This time, the government's independent hostels were on the defensive. Representing the Independent Hostel Association, Ann McGougan said that all the task force personnel were CYHA-oriented, if not directly affiliated:

There is no one on the Task Force to speak for the majority of government-run, freak-oriented hostels ... They seem to be condescending toward some of our more "idealist" aims ... Most of the

directors have never stayed in a hostel, most of the members not for
several years ... There is no room for other kinds of individual difference or regional variations other than "tourist" variations ... All these
bland middle-class restrictions ... will kill hostelling, as we know it.
Perhaps it was inevitable to meet with institutionalism as we grew.[186]

In September 1976 the Secretary of State accepted the task force steering
committee's proposal to merge the federal and CYHA hostels. In May
1977 the inaugural meeting of the merged group was held at the opening
of the new sixty-four-bed Bragg Creek hostel, site of the first CYHA hostel
in Canada.[187] By 1977, after two years of meetings, the second task force's
work was done. The new Canadian Hostel Association was based on the
"city-to-country philosophy." There were two types of hostel: urban hostels to promote the "cultural life of the cities" by providing information
and guides for museums, theatres, and other forms of civic education;
and rural hostels for outdoor recreation, hiking and skiing, touring, and
foreign exchange. Membership cards were retained to "help" young people
"develop a sense of responsibility" and the "feeling that he is in a sense a
part-owner" of an association that valued active citizenship, voting in
elections, taking an interest "in improvements," and "promoting the
organization."[188] Nonmembers could pay a slightly higher nightly rate at
the door. Looking back on six years of struggle, on September 15, 1976,
Richard James and John Roberts, chairmen of the National Hostel Task
Force, told David Smith, "Canada has seen a growth in the use of hostels
that, at times, looked like a fad, at times resembled a counter-culture, at
times made opponents in individual communities, but at all times had
been an attempt by the late-adolescent age group to reach out for new
learning experiences."[189] Moving forward, youth hostelling in Canada
reiterated the CYHA's old motto from 1933. Hostelling would "promote
the education of all ... with no distinction of race, religion, class, political
opinion, sex or age."[190]

### Conclusion: Confusion and Consensus

In every generation, the youth scene is a historical phenomenon subject
to continual peer negotiation and change. In the early 1970s, turf wars
between hostile neighbours, police, biker gangs, self-styled freaks, and

curious onlookers dominated at many hostels from British Columbia to the East Coast. The freaks wanted local kids kicked out, local kids wanted greasers kicked out, and angry neighbours wanted everyone to just go home. A student at the University of Lethbridge thought that making "hitchhiking a sport" was silly and doubted that kiosks would make it "safer."[191] The *London Free Press* warned that hostels would "lead to the same outcome" as at Kent State University, where the Ohio National Guard had opened fire on antiwar protesters, killing four students.[192] Travellers who could afford the $5 membership fee avoided unpleasantness because houseparents enforced CYHA rules.[193]

The task forces of 1970 and 1975 fought over the issue of diversification in the youth scene so that freaks, bikers, and "outdoorsie people" could have a place to sleep, find friends, and feel at home. The typical youth leader changed. The scoutmaster "with a big tummy and a whistle around his neck" was replaced by the self-described "freak" who had training in psychological philosophy, sensitivity, situational actualities, and trust.[194] Youth workers learned that well-run hostels needed to employ a mixture of straight youth, hippies, and a sympathetic adult and that ID cards made it easier to enforce the rules. Anxious adults' initial uneasiness was calmed by the tourist dollars that youth hostellers brought into the community and by the "lack of fuss" with which most hostels operated.[195] Behind youth hostel walls, conservative youth "learned about troubled young people" and the importance of understanding the oppression they faced rather than "singling" them out "for the problems they caused."[196] Joan Belford said young people woke up "to the concept of Canada as an aggregate of equals rather than a mere collection of landscapes."[197] Criticism of youth on the road continued, but motorists were hesitant to exercise harsher authority or control. For a time, the young strangers became a familiar part of the landscape, and a few motorists "even caught themselves dreaming of an unattainable freedom somewhere out on the Canadian highway."[198]

"Hey! Did you hear about the hitchhiker who got stuck so long in Wawa he got married?"
"He got what?"
"He got married. He waited there a month and then he got married to a chick he met the second week he was there."

— "The Legend of the Wawa Hitchhiker," heard in 1971 in a youth hostel in Kamloops, British Columbia, and retold in numerous interviews

# 6
# Head Out on the Highway
## Stories from the Trans-Canada Highway

Toronto-bound hitchhikers from California, April 27, 1972.

*Photo by Jeff Debooy, Winnipeg Tribune Fonds, PC 18/3518/18–2747–015,*
*University of Manitoba Archives and Special Collections*

**In the early** 1970s tens of thousands of young travellers were on the road, sharing "the adventure and companionship of a travelling fraternity."[1] Prime Minister Pierre Elliott Trudeau gave them his blessing. He said, "National unity is a product of national understanding and national pride ... With or without help, young people will be traveling ... We should help make their experiences worthwhile."[2] The Secretary of State's youth hostel program, the YMCA and YWCA, the Canadian Youth Hostels Association, the Committee Representing Youth Problems Today (CRYPT), the Greater Vancouver Youth Communications Centre Society, or Cool Aid, and private citizens and agencies provided ways and means for hitchhiking and hostelling to become the fashionable young nation's contribution to the Age of Aquarius.

In 1970 the Trans-Canada Highway became Canada's "new main street" for hitchhikers.[3] Newfoundland premier Joseph Smallwood said that his province welcomed transient youth, "although I don't, in God's name, know what we're going to do with them when they get here."[4] Fredericton, New Brunswick, was at the crossroads of highways coming from the West and from the United States.[5] The most scenic and historically symbolic hostel was at La Petite Bastille, the old Quebec City jail located on the Plains of Abraham. The most easterly hostel was "The End of the World," in St John's, Newfoundland, and the most western place to crash was on the sand on Long Beach, Vancouver Island.[6] In northern Ontario, Sudbury constituted the funnel, and in the centre of Manitoba, Winnipeg, "the gateway to the West," was the watershed.[7] On a single day in the early summer of 1969, a motorist counted sixty hitchhikers on the 270-kilometre stretch between Sudbury and Sault Ste. Marie. For hitchhikers who made it out of Wawa, Ontario, the next hurdle was 1,144 kilometres later in Winnipeg. In the "windy city," hitchers did "the Winnipeg walkaround," hung out in Memorial Park, went to the feed-in at Augustine United Church, stocked up on bread and peanut butter, and tried to make it across the Prairies to Calgary or went north along the Yellowhead Highway to Edmonton.[8] Thumbers visited Banff and Jasper or stayed on the Trans-Canada Highway and joined the back of the long lines of hitchhikers around Kamloops heading westward to the "Mecca" of Vancouver, the hub of the Canadian youth scene and "the pot of gold sparkling at the end of a 3,000 mile rainbow." But the emperor had no clothes. Twenty-one-year-old Martin Dorrell was one of many wandering Canadians who marvelled at how little there was to do in Vancouver except hang around Stanley Park and Gastown. A hitchhiker with an extra $1.95 could take the ferry from Horseshoe Bay to Vancouver Island. All the same, the West Coast reunion with hitchhikers "met days and weeks before on the road" was like a homecoming.[9]

Young travellers taught each other the code of the road and became wanders, explorers, vagabonds, and outsiders in the world beyond the tourist bubble.[10] In the communitas stage of their rite of passage, travellers felt "untouchable" and free to ignore highway, vagrancy, and drug laws, majority-age restrictions, and puritanical sexual mores. On the journey, thumb-travellers passed time sharing heroic tales, quests, and feats of the longest wait, the nastiest meal, the biggest bugs, the dirtiest youth hostel, wild rides, dark nights, and ultimate rescues.[11] Battered cars, cruel weather, tough surroundings, harsh words, and insults were challenging parts of life on the road. Despite the tendency of travellers to exaggerate, Chandra Mukerji says that "road talk" is valuable because the pleasure of telling "scary bullshit" is just as important to the hitchhiker as the content of a road story.[12] This chapter examines what hitchhiking meant to travellers. The generations met each other across the dashboard of every type of automobile. Hostellers insisted the government's only role in youth travel should be to pay for it.[13] Without jobs, family obligations, or the scrutiny of their elders, hitchhikers created their own rituals, heroic mythology, and road stories.

### *"Thumbs Up": Road Codes and Etiquette*

Hitchhiking was prohibited on the 400-series highways in Ontario. In parts of the country, hitchhiking was permitted on municipal roadways provided that it was done safely from the shoulder. In the 1970s the maximum fine for hitchhiking in Prince Edward Island was one hundred dollars, but the Royal Canadian Mounted Police were too busy with other duties to bother with hitchhikers.[14] To "legally" hitchhike in Manitoba, the "Youthbeat" columnist for the *Winnipeg Free Press* said, "You must either stand on someone's property or hang out [of] a building ... You can be warned or ticketed for obstructing the flow of traffic if you stand in the middle of the road or have a particularly big thumb."[15] Hitchhiking was not an offence under the Alberta highway and traffic laws, but "stunt-ing" was, meaning "any act or stunt that would distract the attention of motorists."[16] In British Columbia the maximum fine for soliciting rides was $500 or six months in jail, but no member of the RCMP in Vancouver, Prince George, or Revelstoke could recall a case in which a hitchhiker had been arrested.[17] Overall, Canada's laissez-faire hitchhiking laws were vague and randomly applied, so they had never deterred car owners from offering rides to young people.

The hitchhiker's code of the road embodied great respect, apprecia-tion, expertise, and wonderment regarding automobile technology. Baby boom children absorbed from their parents' culture a preoccupation with consumerism. Tastes in subculture fashion, hairstyles, music, and cars expressed what a peer group thought of as "cool."[18] Each type of car sym-bolized a unique "cultural world" with its own form of specialist know-ledge, practices, and argot, which defined "in detail the car's anatomy, 'look,' style, image and ride."[19] Like other youth subcultures, transient youth deeply enjoyed riding in cars. Cars were their habitus, and the strangers driving them were an "imagined other."[20] Hitchhikers anthropo-morphized cars to match the physique, personality, and social status of the car's owner. University of Ottawa geography students Greg Ross and Hedley Swan had rides in "ancient cars," a battered '59 Chev, a farmer's son's '58 Ford, a Scottish chemistry professor's '62 Volvo, a '59 Stude-baker station wagon that a hippie had bought for one hundred dollars, a car in Edmonton that blared Ukrainian church music, a station wagon with "two chicks" in it, and a miner driving a battered, phosphorescent-orange Pontiac while playing a tape of the Beatles' 1969 album *Abbey Road* at full blast.[21] A University of Guelph student reported an amazing coincidence:

> One time, I ... stuck out my thumb and got a ride in a brand new 1967 Dodge. The driver let me off at the 401, where I instantly got a ride all the way to the Port Hope exit in another new '67 Dodge. As I was walking down the off ramp ... wait for it ... I was picked up by a third new Dodge. The guy was so amazed to hear my story that he drove me to my door.[22]

The design of cars in the 1970s was incorporated into the hitchhiking ritual. Ontario hitchhiker Keith Perkins said that cars in the 1970s were as "big as boats." The "great big front seats" improved hitchhiking safety. "You open the passenger door, push your pack in first, and it becomes a barrier between you and the driver and an arm rest." He continued,

> When they are travelling 60 miles per hour, what are they going to do? If they try anything, they will kill themselves, too ... The only weapons they have at that point are words, and you have words, too ... If you get in the backseat, the driver gets very worried ... The backseat is the power position for the hitchhiker ... You can grab them and do things they have no control over.[23]

The internal restrictions of automobile design were the focus of numerous accounts of hitchhikers' rides. An Edmonton hitchhiker said that once a "big boat of a car" had picked him up. The occupants "were passing around this big 40 [ouncer] of vodka ... I put my seatbelt on and took a swig of vodka, settled into the ride ... and hoped for the best."[24]

Hitchhiking was not just a mode of travel but also a ritual with its own theories, rules of exchange, and technologies of power. Michael O'Regan observes that modern backpackers produce their own system of inter-related manoeuvres, drills, guidebooks, routes, and "symbolic spaces of consumption."[25] Travel maps and guidebooks enable experienced travellers to pass on skills, knowledge, aesthetics, and cultural capital to future travellers.[26] As a mass means of mobility for young travellers in the Western world, hitchhiking was a vibrant part of youth culture in the twentieth century. *Let's Go* guidebooks captured the ethos, with its iconic "thumbs up" hitchhiker logo.[27] Canadian hitchhikers liked to share travel information. Bob Miller, a Grade 11 student at Elmira District Secondary School in Ontario, wrote "In Kanada by a Part-Time Transient" for the school paper in 1971. He warned his classmates that travelling would be harder in 1972 because more American youth would have heard "about free food and shelter provided for nothing by the Canadian govern-ment."[28] Ross and Swan published their travel diary, "Cross-Canada Jaunt," in several installments in the University of Ottawa's student paper, *The*

*Fulcrum.*[29] In their guidebook, *Handbook Canada: A Traveller's Manual* (1972), David Rideout and Ray Amiro remarked that a respectably dressed hitchhiker might get lifts more quickly, but they would be "less interesting ones."[30] In *The Hitchhiker's Field Manual* (1973), Paul DiMaggio advised travellers to budget $20 per week for living expenses, to bring maps and good identification, to use common sense, and not to carry dope because "cops love to search hitchhikers." He said never to "crash" in a public park. "If it is a big city you will be mugged, if it is a small city you will be busted."[31] The Department of Health and Welfare's brochure *On the Road: A Guide for Youth Travelling Canada* (1972) said, "Every year 5,000 Canadians die on the road ... Practice Safety ... Walk on the shoulder of the road facing oncoming traffic. Carry a sign if you are trying to flag someone down. Walk in a single file. Don't hitchhike on a bridge, at a junction, or on a curb ... It's illegal for motorists to stop there!"[32]

Travel narratives indicate hitchhikers' desire to be perceived by motorists and people back home as capable of living by their wits, outsmarting authority, and being helped by strangers, as well as clever enough to avoid real physical risk. One interviewee said that a genuine traveller flexed his "travel boner" telling heroic stories.[33] Perkins made up his own Boy Scout motto: "Be prepared ... be presentable, smile, carry a small pack ... and don't be stupid!"[34] Getting into a car was like going to work. A Vancouver hitchhiker said that the trick was to "make them trust you ... You feel responsible to tell the same story over and over again. It got to be wearing after a while ... it was good training for life."[35] Hitching a ride was a performance. Duncan McMonagle called it his "interested young traveller thing."[36] University of Victoria student Simon Gibson compared the "manners and poise" required of the successful hitchhiker to the advice that others gave on "how to be a good doorman."[37] Many men recalled that the hot topics of the 1970s were government insurance plans and hockey.

Some hitchhikers recommended using gimmicks to entice a car to stop. One Vancouver hitchhiker's "uniform" was a "tweed jacket with blue jeans." He said that he got picked up "regularly, and people said it was the jacket ... People said I look more interesting."[38] McMonagle said that in "extreme cases a striped shirt and tie ... is often enough to overcome the deficit of a beard and lots of hair."[39] DiMaggio was not convinced

Paul Orlowski hitchhiking from British Columbia
to Toronto for a Crosby, Stills, Nash & Young concert, 1974.
*Courtesy of Paul Orlowski*

that hair mattered anymore after 1973, but a hitchhiker in a hurry should "make a sign" and "comb" his hair.[40] A hitchhiker with a German shepherd said that the dog helped him to get rides: "Man, they just can't believe that a guy would be stupid enough to hitchhike with a dog so they pick me up and we rap about the dog and my stupidity all the way to the next town."[41] Rideout and Amiro's *Handbook Canada* recommended experimenting "10 minutes with, and 10 minutes without a sign." The old "'peace symbol' works sometimes." Rideout carried a guitar. It made a good place "on which to write (with white adhesive tape) your destination."[42] On the road, good manners and observing the "dos and don'ts" of road etiquette were the signs of a good hitchhiker.

### Sustenance: Greasy Spoons and Pea Water
Government and independent guidebooks offered basic advice on nutrition and how to eat healthily and cheaply. Despite criticism of the inaccurate maps in the Department of Health and Welfare's *On the Road,* the minister insisted that the thirty-one-page brochure contained valuable

Mealtime at the Winnipeg youth hostel with
L. Alfred Dubree and Sandi Ogden of Hamilton, July 24, 1972.
*Photo by Jim Walker, Winnipeg Tribune Fonds, PC 18/3561/18–2793–014,*
*University of Manitoba Archives and Special Collections*

advice.[43] It said to "guard that tummy," to keep perishable food out of the
sun, not to eat wild berries, and to wash and peel fruits and vegetables.
Nutritionists advised ordering toast and grilled-cheese sandwiches in
"greasy spoons." Powdered milk, hot dogs, and hamburgers were economical sources of protein "if supplemented with fruit and vegetable
snacks."[44] A McDonald's hamburger cost 19 cents in the United States
in 1970. DiMaggio's field manual had an "all-thumbs miniature cookbook"
with easy recipes, such as a crunchy granola called "n-r-g," which was a
mixture of "chocolate chips, raisins, peanuts and coconut," and "Stevey's
Peeny," which was a peanut butter, honey, and raisin spread that could
be eaten with fingers. DiMaggio wrote,

Your body will need a lot of protein and energy ... You will probably
consume more than your share of glutinous hamburgers and plastic

cheese amidst layers of accordion bread. Hopefully your rides will buy or give you food. When you must eat at a restaurant, eschew the fast food joints like Taco-Belle and Burger-King [sic]. Try to find a small, locally owned diner or restaurant. The food will usually be better and more nutritious. Even if it isn't, you will be exposed to local color you might otherwise miss.[45]

Federal youth hostel ledgers indicate that staffers dealt with travellers suffering from malnutrition, pneumonia, miscarriages, dental problems, broken bones, asthma, and "freak-outs" and with desperate parents and police looking for runaways.

Whether or not a hitchhiker's diet met the national food guide's requirements, road narratives included amusing tales of hard luck and near starvation. In 1966 seventeen-year-old Rod Willmot began a hitchhiking adventure from Ajax, Ontario, to British Columbia with $17 in his pocket.[46] Four sixteen-year-old Winnipeggers pooled their money and headed to British Columbia with $71.[47] In 1970 a twenty-one-year-old left Vancouver Island for New Brunswick with $40. Weeks later, she was completely broke. Then "something remarkable happened." She and her friend got up "really early" and headed to the highway to hitchhike to Quebec City. "This is absolutely true. We are walking across a playing field and there is not a person in sight ... and $20 flew through the air and plastered itself on my chest ... That was not nothing then! It was enough to get there ... [That] was a very strange highlight for me."[48] Douglas Williams "actually believed" that he would "attempt to eat once every two days in Europe."[49] Ross and Swan lived on Cheez Whiz sandwiches, youth hostel breakfasts, and pub suppers.[50] An English hitchhiker "lived on rice and soya sauce."[51] Two northern British Columbia women living the "hippie life" in Israel had to eat granola with sour cream instead of yogurt because they "couldn't read the label."[52] A prairie teenager forgot his canteen in a van, so he had to drink "pea water," which was "water from cans of peas."[53] Willmot went to the door of a farmhouse in Alberta to ask for directions. The farmer observed his "long bushy hair and a beard," gave him "this look," and returned with a baloney sandwich because "he assumed I was a poor person ... [and] he had to give me food."[54] Female hitchhikers said that many salesmen bought them meals and sometimes hotel rooms on their expense accounts. Many hitchhikers fondly remembered the diners at the Husky gas stations that dotted the landscape and the waitresses who gave them free chips and gravy. "To this day," a Saskatoon man said, "I can't pass a Husky without getting a warm-fuzzy feeling."[55]

Hitchhikers also survived by panhandling and busking. Two Ontario boys "hit the road" with a sleeping bag, a Second World War army surplus poncho to use as a tent, canned goods from the pantry, "a can of tobacco, rolling papers, and two bucks in cash." One recalled, "We lasted about six weeks ... and did a lot of panhandling."[56] Hitchhikers with guitars formed the aristocracy of the transient class, earning enough spare change from busking to haggle with local corner grocers for lower prices. Dorrell described a communal sidewalk supper that consisted of a group of hitchhikers dividing up a loaf of bread and coating it with peanut butter.[57] Communal meals in Banff National Park included "so many kids from all sorts of places ... buying and shoplifting for a feast every night."[58]

Following other hitchhikers' "dos and don'ts" enabled transient youth to ignore laws, social norms, and mainstream values. Some hitchhikers tested their luck at local welfare offices to see whether a soft-hearted social worker would give them a handout from some discretionary fund. One hitchhiker said, "It's beautiful, man ... They just laid some money onto our palms."[59] Canadians had to work at least eight weeks to collect insurance from the Canada Assistance Plan, and they could continue to collect as long as they were actively looking for work. Two British Columbia men quit their jobs to travel and collected unemployment insurance along the way. One said, "What we did was kind of illegal ... I used to get shit from my father. He said, 'You're living off the fat of the land' ... We wanted to keep collecting ... You had to declare it on a card every two weeks ... I just wrote, 'travelling and broadening my mind,' and they accepted it."[60] Others refused welfare on the principle that "we don't have any bread to speak of, but some people are in more desperate need than we are."[61]

### Dashboards, Ditches, Rat Pits, and "Trudeau Hostels"

The same esprit de corps that influenced life in the car influenced time off the road. Despite the hundreds of thousands of dollars that the federal

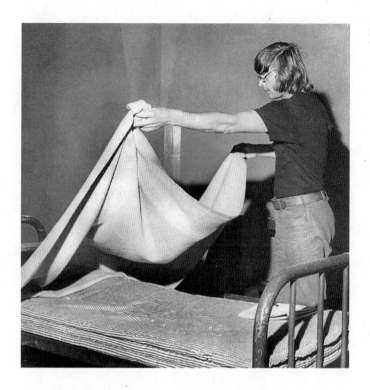

Bed and board, Winnipeg youth hostel, January 1, 1970.
*Winnipeg Tribune Fonds, PC 18/3561/18–2793–008,*
*University of Manitoba Archives and Special Collections*

government spent developing a network of summer youth hostels, finding a place to sleep was not a high priority for most travellers. Sleeping strategies ranged from knocking around the bush to tenting in ditches, using culverts, drive-in theatres, parking lots, sports fields, the cabs of transport trucks, or empty buses to sleep rough, and arriving in unfamiliar towns with only a scribbled address and being invited inside "to crash" by strangers who became instant new friends.

Travellers' tales of heroic homelessness were told with the same bravado as other stories. Bedtime rituals revealed the ability to charm, outwit, and evoke the help and kindness of strangers. One hitchhiker recalled a night in Deep River, Ontario. "Thirty or forty hitchhikers were preparing for a night in the ditch with the black flies." Suddenly, a "long row of cars came rolling out of the town of Deep River to where we were situated on

Men's section of Winnipeg youth hostel, July 19, 1974.
*Photo by Jeff Debooy, Winnipeg Tribune Fonds, PC 18/3561/18–2793–013,*
*University of Manitoba Archives and Special Collections*

the Trans-Canada Highway. We, of course, had visions of *Easy Rider* on our minds." In actor-director Dennis Hopper's 1969 road movie *Easy Rider*, hippies are brutally gunned down by hostile locals. The hitchhiker said, "We weren't sure what was coming." He continued,

> Well, much to our surprise, the convoy of cars was filled with towns-people ... They'd come out to see if we needed a place to sleep and a hot meal ... I asked a guy why they would pick up such a scruffy, dirty bunch of long-haired kids. He said, "We have kids of our own out on the road ... and we'd like to know that someone's treating them decently as well."[62]

Many hitchhikers found themselves hungry, cold, and lost in strange towns. In desperation, they showed up at police stations and county jails to ask for a place to sleep. One Christmas Eve two hitchhikers went to the Brockville County Jail to ask for a place to sleep. "The cops put us in the women's section ... We spent the night reading the lipstick messages" scrawled on the walls.[63] An Ottawa hitchhiker was stranded in Truro, Nova Scotia, on a Friday night. He had been unable to meet up with any kids his age, as he had done in other towns. With no place to sleep, he thought, "What the hell?" and went to the police station for help. He quickly found himself in a "genuine nineteenth-century jail." Referring to iconic films of the 1960s and 1970s, he said that it was "really really crude,"

> a real *Birdman of Alcatraz* jail ... with long keys on a big ring ... The drunk tank was down the hall ... I put my stuff down and paced my cell like Steve McQueen [in *The Great Escape* and *Papillon*] ... Hey, I'm in jail, I thought I was supposed to pace my cell ... The washbasin and a toilet were on the wall ... I slept terribly ... I was locked in.[64]

A teenager from Winnipeg admitted that her first hitchhiking adventure with three friends did not go well. She was barely sixteen years old and "encountering stuff" she was "not ready for yet." Two weeks into it, she had a fight with her boyfriend, packed up her stuff, and "left the whole gang behind." She decided to hitchhike home alone from the interior of British Columbia. When a trucker around Cornell Lake told her "he had not seen a woman in two months," she started to cry and made him drive her to the nearest RCMP station. Her parents had reported her missing. She said, "I turned myself in." The officers brought her food and magazines and "put me in jail until the bus came ... There was nobody else there ... I don't even think they closed the door."[65]

Youth hostels can be special locations specifically for performance, experience seeking, and communitas. Modern tourism researchers say that backpacker hostels may be travellers' ultimate destination, where they gain heightened perspectives on themselves, their relationships, and their social and cultural worlds.[66] This was clearly the original purpose of hostelling in Canada. The Canadian Youth Hostels Association's *Handbook* said, "Young people of all classes may come to know one another in a comradeship of common experience and common interest."[67]

In the late 1950s a hosteller wrote, "'Does it have to end?' Each tripper had become a friend. THIS IS HOSTELLING."[68] Stories about "Trudeau hostels" used similar tropes of adventure and finding one's worldly self. A hostel could be a drug-infested pit or a place where there was a healthy exchange of ideas and personal experiences. Student Ron Verzuh assured his peers at Simon Fraser University that "many a lifelong friendship has started in a youth hostel."[69] University of Saskatchewan student Myles Stasiuk loved how travellers in the federal hostels could "throw off their inhibitions" in a "family-like situation." He told his peers that activities in hostels happen because "people 'want' them to happen."[70] Two Saskatoon travellers said that the youth hostel in Kamloops was a big army tent that "really stunk."[71] A hitchhiker from British Columbia said that the hostel in downtown Toronto "was like a big jail ... You had to be in by 11:00 p.m." He and his friend had a "rift" because he was impressed with how clean it was and wanted to have a shower and turn in early, whereas his friend wanted to stay out late and check in at a place on Yonge Street that was filthy with rats.[72]

Two women from Vancouver Island said that the hostel at Dalhousie University "just looked horrible. People were doing a lot of drugs ... We were barricaded in our room."[73] In the summer of 1971, Thunder Bay's youth hostel was in a huge hockey arena. The lights were "almost blinding, music blared from the entertainment system, the mattresses sprawled over the floor and a curtain separated the sexes at night." A sign said, "No Booze, No Dope, No Sex," yet "the odour of marijuana was everywhere." The Secretary of State's guarantee to Thunder Bay parents that their children would not be permitted to hang around the youth hostel was not enforced. Local "teenyboppers paid a quarter to sit in the bleachers, smoke cigarettes and watch the out-of-town transients bed down for the night."[74]

Gender segregation and sexual abstinence were two rules that were difficult to enforce, widely criticized by travellers as hypocritical, and subject to the discretion of staff. A hosteller from Saskatchewan told the *Calgary Herald* that he thought buying a marriage licence made marriage "little more than legalized prostitution."[75] In 1971 the paper reported that boys were sneaking into the girls' quarters at hostels in Calgary and Ottawa. Even though hostel staff in Calgary denied that "couples have been zipping their sleeping bags together,"[76] the thought of unmarried transient youth couples cohabiting in federal hostels went against the dominant moral code of Canadian society and earned them the "brothel" moniker in Vancouver.[77]

Some rules are made to be broken; staff and hostellers at Carleton University's hostel fought the segregation rule on the grounds that "the government should not interfere with transients' moral standards."[78] In protest, they renamed the dorms. The men's sign said, "Male Chauvinists Here," and the women's sign said, "Feminists Here."[79] The Secretary of State ordered Brian Gilhuly, the director of transient services to investigate operations at Carleton University, and Canadian journalists took a look, too. To put the public's mind at ease, the *Ottawa Citizen* published a photograph of the rope separating the dormitories; the headline read, "The Hostellers Refusing to Segregate." Indeed, Carleton's Opportunities for Youth grant was in jeopardy. Gilhuly confirmed that the only boundary between the sexes was made of "yellow rope barriers and cardboard signs."[80] His forward-looking compromise was to set up three separate areas: one for men, one for women, and one for couples. The public was happy, and the system was copied in other hostels. In July 1971 the *Winnipeg Free Press* announced, "Hostel 'Cosy' Again," and Gilhuly received some "incredible fan mail from little old fascist ladies in tennis shoes."[81]

The Secretary of State's youth hostel program had much less to do with progressive education and youth empowerment rituals than with ensuring that political leaders maintained control and authority during a time of generational crisis. Therefore, it is unlikely that the majority of travellers noticed the behind-the-scenes staging of the youth hostel program.[82] The rhythms, rituals, and seemingly unstructured daily life in federal hostels gave middle-class travellers a taste of an imagined "hippie" experience, enabling them to broaden their own worldviews at a time of liminality.[83] Surveillance by young professionals behind the scenes, the three-day residence limit, curfews, frugal meals, assigned chores, and daytime closure kept travellers moving along in what George Orwell called "the tramp."[84] The "hip" and "drug savvy" staff worked in twenty-four-hour shift rotations, enforcing the rules in a democratic, nonconfrontational way and monitoring the coming and going of residents. A Toronto youth hostel supervisor said that his job was part camp counsellor, sorority den mother, and nightclub bouncer, "whatever the case demanded." The biggest problems came from local kids "who try to use the place to sell speed or dope."[85] In Calgary youth hostel director Brian Watt said, "Society seemed to go overboard helping out the kids on the road because everyone thought the kids must be screwed up. Most of the kids going through aren't screwed up at all."[86]

Travelling youth of all political creeds were looking for more than places to sleep. With or without adult-imposed structure and interference, travellers organized themselves according to their own distinctive subcultural styles, status, aspirations, and personal preferences. In 1974 federal hostels began to charge fees ranging from 50 cents to $200 a night. Brian Gilhuly said they had discovered that "most users were middle-class and could afford to pay," adding that staff at the door were unlikely to turn anyone away.[87] At one end of the subcultural spectrum, "purists" took their "outdoorsmanship straight" and stayed at the Canadian Youth Hostels Association's Maligne Canyon hostel. Those with consumerist predilections bought sophisticated equipment, aluminum packs, compact Primus stoves, and freeze-dried foods at Mountain Equipment Co-op. "Nature freaks" exchanged the "rigours of urban living" for "natural rigours" like a mountain hike at 3,650 metres and the "canoe-toting behaviour of voyageurs of old." At the other end of the spectrum, the freaks in Banff put up tents near Echo Creek on the Bow River and turned the scenic parkland into a "despoiled gypsy encampment" with nightly parties. "Fred the Cook," the "self-styled organizer" of the tent city at Echo Creek, asked, "Why shouldn't freaks ... have a chance for a vacation too?"[88] Many travellers said that the federal youth hostel experience was "great if you weren't looking for the Taj Mahal."[89]

*Drugs: Encounters with the Folk Devil*
Critics of youth hostels were correct when they said that they could become the locus of illegal drug use. Marcel Martel says that the operation files of the Royal Canadian Mounted Police exaggerate the hippie lifestyle, alleged immorality, and drug trafficking.[90] In the late 1960s, Canada's drug problem was no longer attributed to specific ethnic groups; the middle-class youth and hippies became "an identifiable" drug-using group.

Doug Owram says that adult hostility to the use of illegal drugs and harsh criminal penalties for the possession of small quantities of marijuana further "ingrained" the politicization of youth culture.[91] The Department of Health and Welfare's *On the Road* provided a list of "slang words for drugs," and undercover officers kept the comings and goings at youth hostels under surveillance.[92] Drug users and nonusers incorporated drug words into everyday speech, metaphors, and symbolism. The psychedelic drug culture elided travel and self-knowledge with the use of words like "tripping." In 1976 sociologist Jay Vogt said that, for wandering youth, travelling was like getting drunk or using LSD: "A 'trip' facilitates exploration of new realms of consciousness. These sometimes frightening exposures to unknown aspects of the self ... offer potential for personal growth. The wanderer also journeys ... into the unknown, often learning about himself and the world by taking risks."[93] Many hitchhikers believed that consuming mind-altering substances enhanced their lives on the road. A man from Montreal confessed, "I inhaled!"[94] A young woman from Montreal always carried a "bag of weed" in her pack "to share with drivers."[95] A hitchhiker recalled "the vivid colour" he perceived on LSD while watching film director Stanley Kubrick's *2001: A Space Odyssey* (1968).[96] Two northern British Columbia women went to Quebec and Amsterdam. They "hung out there and smoked drugs and partied." One said, "We were small-town girls out in the big wild world ... It was that whole hippie share-love thing ... We never worried about taking stuff from a stranger. We just thought, 'Wow, a new friend.'"[97] In 1979 "a couple of old hippies" gave Duff Sigurdson "some blotter acid." It was around the time that Disneyland opened the ride Thunder Mountain. He decided to "eat this acid" and go to Anaheim, California, and check it out. He "had the best day!"[98] A hitchhiker from England smoked pot for the first time and lost his virginity in a communal house in Winnipeg. He'd been "twice a virgin in the same night."[99]

Hitchhikers said that drugs were everywhere in hostels and communal houses and on campgrounds. Buying them could be a difficult and even terrifying experience for travellers. A couple of prairie teenagers wanted to buy pot in California. They "did the best" they could and "got ripped off a lot."[100] A traveller from Saskatchewan described the time she and her boyfriend got robbed buying dope in Colombia, South America:

We wandered all through this little town and finally scored some dope
... We [went] up to a hillside meadow to roll a joint, and some guys
who we had seen on the road came up ... Two came behind and put a
machete to our necks ... groping and grabbing and feeling and taking
... We had $2,000 in traveller's cheques, passports, immunization,
watches ... I was hysterical ... I said, "Don't fight these guys 'cause they
are the ones with the frickin' blades" ... [I thought] "Am I going to get
raped in broad daylight?"[101]

The "banditos" took off, and the couple made their way to the British
Embassy. The "really sad part," she said, "was meeting all the other hippie
kids who had also been ripped off."[102]

Not all drug experiences were pleasant. A woman said, "I remember
being so stoned on the Plains of Abraham" and thinking, "I should not
have ingested whatever this was."[103] Another woman said,

There was a lot of partying and dope smoking through that entire trip
... I'm not much of an alcohol drinker ... but did not pass up many joints
that came my way ... It's something you just laughed on and got the
munchies. It did not make you paranoid or psychotic ... but I did have
one episode ... seriously heavy dope. I could barely see ... I don't know
what it was.[104]

A prairie hitchhiker said that his "scariest time" was when he was "quite
stoned on LSD":

Got a ride with a drunk farmer in a pickup truck ... I thought I would
never escape the death trap of loud country music ... the images of road
signs and other cars bombarding me in a mélange of nightmarish and
desultory visual effects. Eventually he pulled into a small town local
bar ... I walked the mile or so back to the highway to resume hitchhiking,
which helped me come down and pull myself together.[105]

It was difficult to keep drugs out of youth hostels. Hostellers recalled
that people were always "freaking out." One said, "There'd be some young
woman screaming or crying, and her friends, the staff, or maybe a

volunteer would be with her trying to talk her down." Later, "someone would say she must have had that orange stuff ... It's not very good."[106] Teddy Mahood worked at the Beatty Street and Jericho Beach hostels. In 1969 he had been released from Oakalla Prison, where he had been from age fifteen to twenty-five. He went from jail to 4th Avenue and started volunteering with Cool Aid. He described himself as over six feet tall with Tsimshian First Nation heritage, a shaved head, and a giant mustache. "People thought I was a biker, but really ... I was a recovered addict who'd found Jesus." Hostellers called him "Holy Hood." He possessed an expertise at safely calming kids on bad drugs that could not be found in the Emergency Room of any city hospital. Mahood said, "I had roses and other instruments of beauty ... Kids on a bad trip are living on your words ... You talk them off their stone ... We had no problems. We did not phone the police once."[107] A bad drug trip was just one of the voluntary risks of life on the road.

It is equally important to point out that many travellers were "not attracted to drugs."[108] A teenage hitchhiker said that he did not thumb all the way from Saskatoon to Vancouver "just to be high all the time ... It wasn't a goal."[109] A Montrealer said that he "liked the freedom and the independent lifestyle ... [but] never did a lot of drugs."[110] A girl from Guelph left town to "get away from the stuff." After she met a Californian who told her, "I don't drink, I don't smoke, and I don't take drugs," she decided to quit all three.[111] Keith Perkins said that "there was still a lot of law" and that long-haired men were always being hassled by the police, so it would have been "stupid to travel with pot or hash in your sock." Paul DiMaggio "strongly advise[d]" travellers not to ask for trouble by carrying drugs since "you are committing a public crime (or even a quasi-crime) ... Someone will probably pick you up and turn you on anyway."[112] A member of the Canadian Youth Hostels Association told readers of *The Martlet* at the University of Victoria that when hitchhiking at the borders in Europe, where customs officers carried submachine guns, "Be polite, smile, and try not to be offended if they ask you to take your clothes off ... They are looking for dope so if you get caught carrying any make sure you have lots of books to read. You should be able to get through the complete works of Sir Walter Scott during your jail sentence."[113] Greg Ross and Hedley Swan declined the marijuana offered to them in a van full of hippies. They were amused to watch the Quebecois tripping on LSD. Their interest in mind-altering substances was confined to beer. In their travel diary, they recorded regional differences in beer-drinking rituals. For example, beer with tomato juice was called an "Alberta Red-Eye" in Edmonton and a "Calgary Red-Eye" in Calgary. One rainy night in Kamloops, they "got good and tight in the pub" and slept rough in the dugout at the baseball field. The sound of an elephant trumpeting at the travelling circus kept them awake all night. This was the extent of their deviance.[114]

### *"Mutual Gaze"*: The Rider-Driver Nexus

On the road, the thumb-traveller's universe was restricted to the self, the motorist, the automobile, and the landscape. In a "good" hitchhiking story, like a "fish story," the narrator constructed a heroic personage by exaggerating mundane or frustrating everyday inconveniences, such as a stranger asking to "borrow a toothbrush."[115] Good ride stories used humour to downplay danger and life-threatening activities like car accidents and crazy rides with intoxicated drivers. For example, a Vancouver hitchhiker recounted a story about a traveller named Rob who got dropped off on the side of the road late one night and headed 20 or 30 metres from the ditch to bed down for the night:

> So no sooner does he get into his sleeping bag and gets all comfortable than he hears this vehicle coming along – this is not a well-travelled road. Then he hears the vehicle stop, exactly where he just got let off, and then somebody gets out and starts moving toward him through the grass. Of course, his heart starts thumping. Well, the guy was actually only going to take a pee. And he would have peed on Rob, if Rob hadn't jumped out of the grass and scared the guy silly.[116]

Road stories about hitchhikers' encounters with locals illustrate the "mutual gaze," which is a term that Darya Maoz uses to include the images and stereotypes that tourists and locals have of each other.[117] In contemporary writing and oral narratives, hitchhikers recalling their youth used hegemonic and derogatory terms like "Newfie," "redneck," "Indian," "freak-haters," "drunks," "pill-poppers," "truckers," "bikers," "weirdos," "creepy guys," and "perverts." Some commented on cowboy hats, slimy teeth, and body odour. They also appreciated the generosity of the people whom their parents' generation had warned them against. Their resistance to the cultural prejudices of their class, gender, and generation was revealed through their willingness to embrace intimate cross-class encounters and to tell stories about good rides.

Liminality and vulnerability in road narratives went hand in hand. Tough terrain and bad rides, called "bummers," formed the basis of numerous road stories. Narrative plot twists minimized the genuine risks of life on the road. With bummers, the familiar became frightening due to loss of control, accidents, recklessness, insults, and assaults by drivers. In most cases, motorists have their own psychological reasons for picking up hitchhikers. DiMaggio called hitchhikers a "ready people-bank" for lonely, sad, frightened, or sleepy motorists, who expected the hitchhiker to help them stay awake. He said that there were two types of most irritating ride. The first was with teenagers who picked up hitchhikers so that they would have someone to talk to about the "good dope they've been smoking." The second was with anxious and nagging parents, who always started the conversation by "asking you why you are the way you are." Their "riff" continued, "Boy, when I see someone like you I'd really like to kick his ass," and it ended, "Why don't you go back where you came from?"[118]

Before the growth of discourses that were opposed to impaired driving, the emergence of lobby groups like Mothers Against Drunk Driving (MADD), and the implementation in 1976 of new offences related to drunk driving and higher minimum penalties for operating a vehicle under the influence of alcohol, hitchhikers affirmed that drunk driving was a bigger social problem than pot smoking. Hitchhikers talked openly about feeling trapped in cars with intoxicated drivers. Perkins made it a priority to poke his head in the window, "like a cop," to see "how much booze is on their breath."[119] A road reality was that many tired, hungry, and cold hitchhikers risked their personal safety. One said, "You get into a spot where you'll take anything." He was stuck outside of Kamloops on a cold, dark night when a trucker stopped to pick him up. He said, "I was really tired ... He was drinking Scotch and popping [Benzedrine] ... Anyway, I kept nodding off, and every time I did, he'd jerk the steering wheel. He said, 'I didn't pick you up so you could sleep. I picked you up so you could keep me company.'"[120] One hitchhiker recalled getting a lift on the outskirts of Moncton in a "fabulous Mercedes-Benz" full of intoxicated fruit pickers. They were "all drunk as a skunk, weaving all over ... and running out of gas ... They started planning to rob a liquor store ... I don't want to be in a robbery ... I have a couple of bucks on me ... I say, 'Here's a couple of bucks. Let me buy some gas for you.'"[121] Two prairie teenagers said their "worst ride" was with an old drunk guy in a motorhome. "His wife left him ... He was can't-hold-his-eyes-open drunk."[122]

Long hair and backpacks were supposed to magically enable suburban boys and girls to become drifters and wanderers. Rod Willmot said that a beard and long hair "were like a litmus test on the people." Motorists were either "fearful, judgmental, dismissive or, on the contrary, accepting, sympathetic, even admiring."[123] Backpacks and a good performance did not always help them to pass the informal legitimacy test for nomadic liminality. The reaction to young men with backpacks and long hair revealed that one's lifestyle choice could lead to physical and emotional conflict. Ross and Swan described themselves as "relatively clean-cut" geography students. They had their backpacks and "a sheet of newsprint with all the addresses of all the hostels in Canada." They were planning to take advantage of the federally funded shuttle buses and to stay in as many free government hostels as they could find. Before leaving Ottawa, they made a sign that said, "B.C. PLEASE." Motorists picked them up because they did not look like hippies. They found it hurtful when, outside of Sudbury, a man with New Jersey licence plates slowed down and yelled, "Bunch of goddamn hippies, why don't you get a job?" and then sped away, spraying a whole line of hitchhikers with shoulder gravel.[124] When an American customs officer at Detroit interrogated a Canadian hitchhiker who was "wearing a ski jacket" and had "long curly hair and a scruffy beard," neither his nomadic image nor the "cans of food, plenty of matches, and a big hunting knife and sleeping bag" that he was packing impressed the officer. He told the hitchhiker that if he did not "come back with a round-trip bus ticket, he would be put in jail."[125]

Hitchhiking is a gendered ritual. The dramaturgical statements by young male hitchhikers, especially those from materially comfortable families, reveal a tension between their achieved self-image and their ascribed class, gender, and sexual status. Their dress, unemployment, and behaviour transgressed the Protestant work ethic and traditional codes of successful masculinity, material acquisitions, and power. Simon Gibson told readers of *The Martlet* at the University of Victoria to "leave the sunglasses at home ... Never just sit on the side of the road with a casual arm out or stand out on the road, because it would attract the attention of the police."[126] An Edmontonian's advice was "to avoid looking like a guy who did not have it together enough to own a car." He said, "Don't stand with your hands in your pockets ... stand straight up. All these trivial things might make the difference ... when people are driving along and they think, 'Should I pick him up or not?'"[127]

On the patriarchal highways, female mobility and feminine respectability were evaluated on the basis of how far a woman appeared to be transgressing prescribed gender norms. In the 1930s and 1940s, there was no reason why, as an act of chivalry, a gentleman motorist should not offer a lift to a hitchhiking waitress or factory girl, or to a schoolgirl with an armload of books, or to a mother burdened with heavy grocery bags. As discussed in Chapter 7, women were conscious that motorists, other travellers, and even hitchhiker guidebooks regarded their bodies as a form of currency. The sex and gender politics of hitchhiking meant that women encountered unequal power relations, conflicting gazes, stereotypes, physical obstacles, and danger. A woman from Prince Edward Island hitchhiked back and forth between Aulac, New Brunswick, and her home wearing her uniform for the "PEI Tourist Information Center." She said, "It didn't take long to get a ride ... In my uniform, I would not infrequently get couples ... I think the women probably felt safer with the uniform."[128] A Vancouver Island woman travelled with a friend who had long brown hair and was "voluptuous ... She looked like a real hippie." She noticed that they got rides instantly "because of who we were."[129]

The impact of second-wave feminism was undeniably shaping a new feminist aesthetic. Young women exploring feminism rejected conventional makeup and hairstyles, shaving and plucking body hair, and most notably wearing brassieres, which women's liberationists saw as oppressive. A nursing student described her hitchhiking persona of the late 1960s, recalling that she did not wear a bra but "still covered up ... relatively modestly" and did not let herself get "really dirty" when she was on the road.[130] A Montreal hitchhiker described her "long, dark hair ... elephant pants, and probably a see-through shirt or little, cotton, gauzy top, a backpack, and a bag of weed."[131] Two northern British Columbia hitchers quit their jobs in Kitimat to travel. One said that the funniest thing her friend packed was a long flannel nightgown.[132] Two sisters from Montreal also quit their factory jobs. They identified themselves as hippies, by which they meant that they "smoked pot." Each packed "basic clothes and a light dress" that she could "roll up ... for a big night" when they got to San Francisco.

Many women admitted to feeling vulnerable to what Sandra Lee Bartky calls the "panoptical male connoisseur." The power that men have over women on the road lies in the fact that, as Michel Foucault writes, "There is no need for arms, physical violence, material constraints. Just a gaze. An inspecting gaze, a gaze which each individual under its weight will end by interiorising."[133] In reaction, women became their own overseers and had to censor themselves. Some women dressed androgynously in the overalls and T-shirts that were in style at the time. A woman from Moose Jaw wore a "unisex" kibbutz jacket and pants.[134] The double standard was frustrating and offensive. A Windsor woman said, "I was a good girl – I wasn't promiscuous in any way. I wanted to see the world. I had the book called *Hitchhiker's Guide to Canada*."[135] Like all dutiful daughters of patriarchal culture, female hitchhikers were expected to perform what Kristine Alexander calls "emotion work," which includes "producing happiness in others."[136] The dullest rides for women on the road were with bored parents who expected them to play with their kids.

### Going My Way: "The Entrepreneurial Self"[137]

Rite of passage travel at a liminal stage in the transition between adolescence and adulthood caused many everyday Canadians to worry that young transients would become stuck in liminality and never resettle and that their futures would be ruined. Hitchhikers were highly self-conscious of the local gaze and realized that their "weirdo-hair," beards, and blue jeans were off-putting to drivers. They enjoyed playing up how "worldly" they had become and their outlaw status.[138] The best stories used humour and exaggeration to make motorists look ridiculous. A Newfoundlander

Kel Ziolkoski in the Fraser Valley on a
hitchhiking trip from Saskatoon to Vancouver, 1976.
*Photo by Ken Zakreski, courtesy of Kel Ziolkoski*

wrote a parody of the difficulties of hitchhiking in his conservative province. He said that Roche's Line to Conception Bay was "one of the hardest places in the world to get a ride." Imitating the local dialect, he wrote,

> Drivers are suspicious about hitchhikers ... I once noticed a car pulled
> over to the side of the road. The middle-aged man had rolled down his
> window and was looking me over ... and said, 'aven't got [your] gun on
> ya 'ave ya! Well, I said, "No Sir, no I never carry guns although I should
> to protect myself from moose during mating season and bull-dozer
> drivers during election campaigns."[139]

A photograph of him shows a pleasant-looking young man with earlobe-length hair, a neatly trimmed beard, flared trousers, a blazer, and a backpack. He said that the best way to get a ride in Conception Bay was to wear a "clergyman's collar" and "kneel down on the shoulder of the T.C.H., join your thumbs and extend them in the direction of your destination, with eyes extended towards the clouds offering up prayer to St. Christopher or Jude."[140]

Hitchhikers' days began when they joined the string of other hitch-hikers out along the highway. They might stand for hours and hours, flipping peace signs to the passing middle-aged motorists in the pour-ing rain or with burning feet and mounting exhaustion. After a thumb-traveller accepted a lift, it became the driver's prerogative to praise or criticize the hitchhiker's hair, clothes, attitude, and lifestyle. Ironically, hitchhikers' stories reveal a counternarrative reflecting the intimacy of the rider-driver nexus, which evoked their compassion, fear, and pity. In the privacy of their automobiles, family men and "squares" confessed that they envied the freedom of the youth. An official of the Provincial Control Board in British Columbia said that he was planning to quit his job in five years and move to his cabin in the rolling country north of Kamloops in order to become "a nature freak."[141]

Hitchhikers enjoyed both natural and human-made landscapes. Travellers agreed that the best way to see the country was from the back of a pickup truck. One hitchhiker said,

> You'd literally be huddled behind your pack, taking it all in ... It was fabulous to go through the Rockies and through the Prairies that way ... I travelled in the back of a lot of pickup trucks ... wrapped in a sleeping bag or top sheet ... [with] buckets of rain and sheets of light-ening ... sleeping in mud all night long.[142]

Ross and Swan were excited to stand on Canada's windiest corner at Portage Avenue and Main Street in Winnipeg. Swan wrote, "I was eagerly anticipating the sensation of being whisked off my feet 'Peter-Pan like' above the traffic, but nothing happened." They remarked that the trees around Sudbury looked unhealthy and that the birches were stunted and had wilted leaves due to Inco Limited's multitudes of slag heaps and belching smoke stacks.[143]

The unique character of weather on the Prairies enhanced the feel-ing of communitas among travellers. Somewhere around the Alberta-Saskatchewan border, a traveller from Surrey discovered the "magic" of thunderstorms on the "the bald prairie ... There were seven or eight of us. We set up our tents ... No one wanted to sleep ... You could smell the rain coming."[144] An Ontario hitchhiker described the beauty of the interior of British Columbia, the rugged mountains along the Alberta border, and the dams of the Columbia River. Premier W.A.C. Bennett had built so many dams that people were calling "the 'preem' Dam Bennett."[145] The discovery that travellers had so much in common with people from other provinces further created communitas. A dairy farmer's daughter "loved being by the ocean in Conche," Newfoundland, and noticed that the fishermen were similar to the farmers in Ontario. They were "honest, hardworking, and quiet-natured."[146] Travellers enjoyed the different regional accents and quaint expressions. Ross and Swan said that in Alberta the "old timers" still referred to the "bus lines as stageliners." They thought the Rocky Mountains at Edson looked like "grey teeth on the horizon." Jasper was such an "awe-inspiring sight" that it led to a "photographic orgy." Everybody told them "go to Vancouver," but people never said where to go or what to see. They wandered around Georgia Street, Gastown, English Bay, and Stanley Park. They took a bus tour to Capilano Canyon and appreciated the Western red cedars, Douglas firs, and "cornucopia of young women." In Victoria they visited the waterfront and were delighted to come across the marker for mile-zero of the Trans-Canada Highway at Dallas Road and Douglas Street.[147]

Communitas is the space where honesty and openness are sought and valued, where co-ritualists share the secrets and traditions of their culture.[148] For some, "the best parts were the times we walked between rides along the Trans-Canada Highway."[149] Leaders emerged from the ranks of the army of summer travellers. Two southern Ontario girls' first hitchhiking experience was in the Alberta Rockies, around Maligne Lake, and they were nervous until they met Gus. He drove them to a former Second World War internment camp that had become the Jasper Free Camp. The girls said that it was a "giant hippie camp" and that Gus was "like the mayor." He introduced them around, helped them to set up their tent, and showed them how to clap sticks together to frighten away bears.[150] A British Columbia hitchhiker recalled being let off at a roundabout on that "classic" Route 66. He was alarmed because there were already about sixty hitchers standing there, and he thought, "We're in trouble here, man!" He said,

Nobody's got water or anything ... I held a meeting of hitchhikers, and I made sure everybody came. We've got to get more people off this corner. If somebody stops, ask them, 'Can you take another person?' So, in about three hours, we had the corner cleared ... I thought organizing the hitchhikers was a good job for that day.[151]

Being a young traveller with a backpack enabled hitchhikers to cross geographical barriers and to enter communities outside of the "tourism bubble."[152] From "Barbie to the World Series," baby boomers grew up "in the shadow" of the United States, and all across Canada the influence of American popular culture was strong.[153] A teenager from Saskatchewan said that in the late 1970s, "California was the nexus for all that was happening in our little world [and] we wanted to go down and check it out."[154] Late boomers were more sensitive to the deterioration of the image of the United States than were the early boomers.[155] A Toronto teenager thumbing around Fort Lauderdale, Florida, walked out to the ramp where the highway started and was alarmed to see a huge billboard

with a picture of a guy all slumped over in his car, and there's a hoodlum running off in the distance. Underneath it says, "Don't Pick Up Hitchhikers." I'm looking at the sign wondering if I am ever going to get a ride ... This is a place where people have guns in the back of their trucks and bumper stickers that say, "God, Guns and Guts Made America Free. Keep All Three and Free We'll Be."[156]

Two Saskatoon teenagers in Los Angeles bought some black hash and tickets to a Commodores concert. They noticed that everyone was staring at them. Then they noticed all the "afros and the picks." They were "the only white boys in the whole place. It didn't make any difference to us."[157] In 1979 two Vancouverites wanted to check out the Haight-Ashbury neighbourhood of San Francisco. The hippie heyday had ended there in the 1960s, but they were curious:

We got there and it's really depressing, windows boarded up and everything. We were really naive ... We had cameras and were taking pictures ... in an area that is all blacks and pretty rough, and then this little girl comes up and looks us right in the eye and says, "White motherfuckas." She couldn't have been more than ten ... We just kept walking. She really freaked us out, and we realized how stupid we were.[158]

National flags had long been popular backpack accessories for international hitchhikers. Richard Ivan Jobs notes that badges, pins, and flags conveyed personal narratives.[159] Hitchhikers hoped that motorists and other travellers would respond favourably to their flags. After 1965 Canadians had the new Maple Leaf flag on their backpacks, and many interviewees said that Americans sewed Canadian flags onto their backpacks, too.[160] Hitchhikers in Nicaragua in the mid-1970s said, "It was beneficial to be Canadian." They "had big red backpacks with Canada flags."[161] When a young man from England planned his trip to Canada, he followed his father's "great idea" and sewed the Union Jack onto his carry-all. His father assured him that Canadian servicemen would spot the Royal Union flag of Great Britain and happily pick him up. However, when a bunch of "hippies and draft dodgers" in a rainbow-coloured Volkswagen Microbus picked him up, they asked him, "What the fuck's on your bag?" He replied, "It's the Union Jack, so if a serviceman sees me, he'll pick me up." A hippie replied, "Well, if we'd seen that, we wouldn't have picked you up." He realized that many North Americans believed that "any Limey was pro-Vietnam" because Britain and the United States had been allies in other wars. After that, when hitchhiking, he concealed his flag.[162]

The Canadian flag was no guarantee of a ride for young men with long hair hitchhiking in the United States, especially during the Vietnam draft. Those years could be dangerous for Canadian men, who feared being mistaken for "draft dodgers." In 1971 two twenty-one-year-olds hitchhiking in the United States sewed Canadian flags onto their backpacks and pointed them in the direction of oncoming traffic, but the flags did not prevent them from being jeered at when they thumbed past a boot camp in Washington State. The hitchhiker said, "We knew they were going to Vietnam, and they were probably thinking, 'Who the hell are those guys?' ... My buddy pointed to the Canada flags we sewed onto our packs."[163] Many hitchhikers would probably agree with a seventeen-year-old's explanation that "not understanding was the thing that kept me safe. I would walk into places, and people would look at me like, 'What the fuck are you doing in here?' ... I could feel the tension mounting up, but I was proud of that!"[164]

During roadside encounters, hitchhikers told each other where to go, what to see, and where to stay. "Dwelling in mobility" enabled them to feel at home in strange towns and cities and with motorists in cars, and it created communitas between the strangers with whom they shared tents, beds, and ditches, musical instruments for busking, details about good and bad drug trips, panhandling rations, sex, and love.[165] After months on the road, Rod Willmot recalled:

> As my ride brought me back into Montreal, the dark snowy street was lined with spiral staircases that seemed incredibly delicate and exotic, unutterably different from English Canada. That visual memory has never left me, and it still comes back now and then in my explorations of what is now my home city. Similar things must surely be true of a great many people whose real lives began when they took to the road in the sixties and seventies.[166]

### Conclusion: "Tits Up on the Pavement"

In 1972 the Canadian rock band Crowbar captured the living folklore of life on the road in its song "Tits Up on the Pavement," which is a dirge about the blues of hitchhiking in Wawa, northern Ontario: "Anytime you go across this country, you have to go through Wawa, Ontario. Cars are going by at 85 miles an hour with nobody in 'em. The longer you stand there, the longer your hair gets. The longer your hair gets, the less your chance of getting a ride."[167] Today, Wawa residents still tell "horror stories" about the "big headache" caused by "thousands and thousands" of hitchhikers stranded for days, weeks, and months on the outskirts of town.[168] Soldiers stationed with Wawa's 49th Field Regiment used to put hitchers in army trucks and drive them "off to Sudbury."[169] Tall tales of thumbers stranded in Wawa passed from hitchhiker to hitchhiker and across the Atlantic Ocean. A Canadian in Europe said, "People asked me if it was true."[170] The longevity of these stories about Wawa hitchhikers was not solely due to Wawa's position on the shore of Lake Superior, which made getting a ride around it "notoriously" difficult, but also due to their status as urban legends, the telling of which was an essential part of the pleasure of travel, communitas, performance, and play.[171]

In the late twentieth century, thousands of young Canadians became tourists, drifters, and wanderers in their own regions and provinces and across the continent, where they put a new twist on coming of age. By conspicuously adorning themselves with Canadian flags, weirdo hair, and cardboard peace signs, baby boom youth reinvented the old wandering-vagabond traditions of bygone days for their generation. The summer after Grade 11, two boys found an old book on how to hitchhike. They followed the advice, made eye contact with the drivers, "never had problems getting rides" to Victoria, and returned to Saskatoon with grand stories to tell.[172] "It felt great," a young woman said. "I loved the freedom of having everything on your back ... We could go somewhere we didn't expect to go ... I just remember it feeling fun and really light."[173] A Wawa boy and a neighbour girl hitched all the way to Montreal for Expo 67 but did not go in because they "didn't give a damn!"[174] It was the trip, not the destination, that defined the experience.

Hitchhikers did not see themselves as dropping out of society but as opting in by embracing experience, personal growth, and self-awareness. Once they were ready to leave the road, the temporal and spatial communitas became less clear. Their tourist gaze shifted away from the romance and freedom that wanderers covet and back to the "familiarity, convenience, and guidance" of family, friends, and home.[175] After spending most of 1972 on the road, Tony Bonnici remembered this dissonant moment clearly. He said, "It was the Thursday before Thanksgiving," and he and his girlfriend, Vicki, were "sitting on the curb in Gastown" reading Richard Bach's *Jonathan Livingston Seagull* (1970). "We are getting really inspired" by the message to find the freedom to be your true self. "I started thinking how nice it would be back in Ontario ... All the kids got together up at our Muskoka cottage for Thanksgiving weekend." He asked Vicki, "Why don't we just go home?"[176]

I am one of the generation of hitchhikers ...
In 1972 I hitchhiked everywhere ... The reason
for my letter was Ingrid Bauer, a beautiful,
fourteen-year-old young woman who went
missing from Kleinburg that summer ... It is a
frightening story, and I am sure it has stayed
with all of us who knew her ... When it
happened, we were just standing in the local
store, and then on the radio we heard Ingrid
was missing. Just missing at that point ... I just
thought, "Okay, she's gonna turn up." We'd
never heard of anyone who went missing ...
It was something we really never thought
about ... They never found her body.

— *Ingrid's friend, interview with author, 2013*

# 7

## Car Sick

### Hitchhiking Dos and Don'ts

"One of 42 billboard crews across Canada pastes
a sign seeking 14-year-old Ingrid Bauer ... Her mother,
Mrs. Gisela Bauer, watches workmen finishing off a billboard ...
Ingrid walked out of her home about 9:40 p.m. to hitchhike
to visit her boyfriend about 4½ miles away and hasn't
been seen since." *Toronto Star,* August 6, 1972.
*Photo by Fred Ross via Getty Images/*Toronto Star

**In the 1970s** there was nothing about hitchhiking that should have
threatened social order more than it had when practised by other generations of thumb-travellers. Hitchhiking became a youth travel tradition
in the 1920s. In the 1930s the "classic" legend of the vanishing hitchhiker
appeared in popular culture. Folklorists say that the allure of the phantom
hitchhiker story reflects North America's worship of the car, coming of
age rituals, and "a Romance of the Open Road."[1] Teenagers still relish
telling the urban legend about a ghostly girl who appears on the road on
the anniversary of her death to foretell catastrophes and then disappears
without explanation. The "truth value of the legend" is that she never
vanishes without leaving something behind as "proof."[2] Hitchhiking
was funny in *The Three Stooges* movies of the 1930s through the 1960s.
Squeaky-clean girl next door Sandra Dee hitched home from college
with her goat in film director Harry Keller's *Tammy Tell Me True* (1961).[3]
In 1963 singer-songwriter Marvin Gaye sparked an international dance
craze when he performed the "hitchhike" song and dance moves on
the television show *American Bandstand*.[4] In 1974 the *Globe and Mail*
editorialized, "We must be into the second generation of knapsacked
young Canadians on their quest to see their country on thumb-power."[5]
Today, baby boomers say that it was the ideal way to get to sports fields,
after-school jobs, parties, and dances. It was "fun to see who might pick
you up."[6]

In the early 1970s, the final cohort of baby boomers came of age
and followed "the romantic waves of hitchhikers before them along the
Trans-Canada Highway."[7] A typical thumb-traveller was Melissa Rehorek
of Windsor, Ontario. In high school, she worked as a cashier at a grocery
store. Melissa used to say, "Oh, I rang up on my till $4.01 again!" Her best
friend recalled that for Melissa "it wasn't a fluke" but a "sign that the 401
Highway was calling out to her." To heed the call, she and Melissa hitchhiked around Ontario and Quebec on weekends and across Canada a
couple of times.[8] In the summer of 1976, when Melissa was twenty years
old, she was working in Calgary as a chambermaid and saving money to
go to Sir Sandford Fleming College in Ontario, but Melissa never went
to college.[9] On September 16 the Royal Canadian Mounted Police found
her strangled body on a lonely road near the Trans-Canada Highway
just west of Calgary. There was five dollars in her wallet, and her body

showed signs of a struggle. RCMP investigators told her friend, "She fought for her life."[10] This was not a fictional story. Melissa Rehorek, fourteen-year-old Ingrid Bauer, and an untold number of other "vanishing hitchhikers" are part of Canadian highway lore.[11]

The vanishing hitchhiker reminds us that there is always some risk and uncertainty surrounding thumb-travel. In the early 1970s national newspaper readers noticed that "with every summer of hitchhiking" came more lurid accounts of criminal assaults done to young women on the road.[12] This chapter focuses on the dark side of hitchhiking. The common-sense assumption that rituals are shared suggests compatibility between people's imaginary worlds, but in the case of hitchhiking, this was impossible. In expert discourse and public opinion, women are seen to have a different relationship to cars and roads than do men, which suggests why women and girls pay a high "social cost" for hitchhiking.[13] The gender politics of hitchhiking indicate that thumb-travellers encountered unequal power relations, conflicting gazes, sex and gender stereotypes, physical obstacles, and danger. In Canada, in the mid-1970s, the police, city councillors, feminists, and civil libertarians responded to hitchhiking-related crime and violence with safety information that reflected adult-driven agendas for coming of age, gender socialization, and youth cultural boundaries that reduced mobility for girls and young women.

### Sex Brats and Hitch-Hooker: *The Vanishing Hitchhiker in Popular Culture*

About 500,000 young people passed through federal hostels in 1973.[14] When youth workers and police got to know them, they began talking about a new type of liberated female traveller whose attitudes and behaviour were out of step with conventional notions of femininity. The Canadian Welfare Council's first publication on the subject, *Transient Youth: Report of an Inquiry in the Summer of 1969* (1970), said that "transient girls" were lonely and displayed a strong need for affection. They were also ambivalent toward marriage but had a disturbingly high attachment to the "idea of raising children." When boys were ready to "return to a settled and ordinary life," they could do it easily, whereas "in many cases a girl's whole chance of happiness is destroyed."[15] The federal government ignored the report's concerns. Rather than shutting hitch-hiking down through aggressive law enforcement or creating safer alternatives like the transport buses suggested by Transient Youth Services, the Secretary of State opened a network of youth hostels, leaving Canadian girls to take "their liberation out to the highways."[16]

So-called transient girls became a frequent sight in youth hostels, on the highways, in magazine photographs and articles, and as characters on television. In 1973 Lester David wrote "Hitchhiking: The Deadly New Odds" for *Good Housekeeping* magazine, and *Reader's Digest* published Nathan Adams's "Hitchhiking – Too Often the Last Ride." Two decades earlier, Don Wharton's lengthy *Reader's Digest* article "Thumbs Down on Hitchhikers! Too Many Rob and Kill" had summarized twenty years of hitchhiking-related crimes and murders but had made scant reference to the danger of thumb-travel for girls or women,[17] whereas Adams focused exclusively on "abduction, rape, murder," and the unwillingness of girls to admit that it could happen to them.[18] Similarly, David said, "Once an almost solely male practice ... thumbing a ride is now common among girls," who regard "the very act of hitchhiking" as "a kind of excitement. She may not be able to verbalize it, but they are getting kicks by flirting with risks ... [and] shrug off the dangers." The consequence was that "female hitchhikers practically invite rape."[19] Adams provided a detailed account of numerous "Jekyll-and-Hyde" hitchhiker murders and quoted senior crime scene investigators who said that "most hitchhike-rapists remain undetected because only one of every five girls assaulted by a motorist is likely to report it. Many young victims are embarrassed ... and if not injured they prefer to avoid lengthy questions and trial publicity ... Most juries figure that if the kid puts out her thumb, she was asking for it."[20] Psychologists, parents, and police wondered why girls were not getting the message not to hitchhike. David and Adams agreed that, "like a broken record," the victims of hitchhiker rapes said, "I knew that things happened, I just didn't believe it would happen to me."[21]

Wandering girls became important fictional characters on television shows and in movies, novels, and AM radio songs. Like the vanishing hitchhiker narrative, stock plot lines about wandering girls may be read as counterparts to boys' narratives about sexual rites of passage in automobiles, where "the car represents a potential mobile bedroom."[22] Anonymous sexual encounters in cars were the subject of numerous male-fantasy pop songs, notable examples being chart hits like "Chevy Van" (1975) by Sammy Johns about a suntanned hitchhiker who "took him by the hand" and "made love" to him in his van. In the more sexually explicit "Sweet Hitch-Hiker" (1971), by Creedence Clearwater Revival, John Fogerty sings, "Do you want to ... would you care ... Won't you ride on my fast machine?"[23] Automobiles are not gender-neutral spaces, so the sense of adventure, freedom, and romance of the open road rooted in the lyrics repeated the double-standard assumption that motor vehicles provided a ready locus for sexual rites of passage for young men. Carol Sanger notes that cars do not always represent freedom for women.[24]

In 1979 the *Globe and Mail* called "the runaway teenager" the decade's "newest of film stereotypes."[25] The image of the teenage girl on the side of the road was a stock character in situation comedies like the episode of *The Partridge Family* called "Road Song" (1971) and in serious "lost-girl" films like director Martin Scorsese's *Taxi Driver* (1976) about a runaway from a good family who became a teenage prostitute.[26] Numerous made-for-television movies like *Little Ladies of the Night* (1977), *Born Innocent* (1974), *Dawn: Portrait of a Teenage Runaway* (1976), and the quasi documentary *Diary of a Teenage Hitchhiker* (1979) portrayed defiant teenagers who thumbed rides for kicks and equated hitchhiking with sex work.

The sexually liberated female hitchhiker was also a figure in adolescent literature. American youth counsellor Beatrice Sparks anonymously published her bestselling novel *Go Ask Alice* in 1971, which became a film in 1973. Her teenage audience believed that they were reading the authentic diary of a fifteen-year-old girl from a good family who got mixed up with a hippie crowd, stole money, exchanged sex for drugs, hitchhiked to California, and died of an overdose. One undated diary entry began with "another day, another blow job" and ended with "I've got to get out of this shit hole."[27] In Canada, in 1970, the *Edmonton Journal* said that fifteen of the thirty-nine women found penniless and wandering in the city were "Indian Canadians." Motorists, YMCA staff, Greyhound bus drivers, police, and staff of the Department of Indian Affairs often made requests to the Department of Health and Welfare on behalf of young women encountered on the road.[28] In the years to follow, the symbolic moral of the urban legend of the vanishing hitchhiker was repeated in diverse forms of adult-produced media to warn teenagers that a girl who allowed herself to be "picked up" was inadvertently consenting to a sexual encounter in a stranger's car.[29] The connection between hitchhiking and the sex trade devalued the lives of women on the road. This would have fatal implications for cases of missing women and girls, especially those from northern and First Nations communities.[30]

*The Flower Child and the Professor: Hitchhiking in Social Theory*
In the early 1970s the disturbing figure of the hitchhiker became the subject of academic discourse and studies of female behaviour in the United States, Britain, and Canada. American sociologists James Greenley and David Rice said, "In the eyes of many US citizens, hitchhiking by females is viewed as a morally questionable behaviour that may serve to impugn the reputation of the hitchhiker."[31] To discover why college girls were unconcerned about their reputations, Greenley and Rice gave questionnaires to 428 women students at the University of Wisconsin that asked them about their hitchhiking habits. The socio-economic profile that they drew was of an upper-middle-class, suburban, "non-conventional," liberal arts major with weak religious affiliation. Alarmingly, 87 percent admitted that they had heard of hitchhikers being sexually assaulted, robbed, or involved in automobile accidents. Twenty-seven percent said that they had been sexually "approached" by motorists. Nevertheless, they chose to overlook risks because thumbing was convenient and free and because they liked doing it.[32] One hitchhiker said,

> A fair amount of cautiousness is reasonable with hitchhiking, [but] I do not feel it to be dangerous when done with caution; it is dangerous with perverts, horny old men, even horny young men. Also a hassle with cops. I still hitchhike because I'm selective of who I ride with, [and] my standards have proven reliable; the situation always has a potential for danger, but in most instances I feel I can handle it.[33]

Female hitchhikers with dog, July 21, 1971.
*Photo by Jim Walker, Winnipeg Tribune Fonds, PC 18/3518/18–2747–003,*
*University of Manitoba Archives and Special Collections*

Greenley and Rice concluded that hitchhiking, "in the face of recogniz-able danger," was how young women expressed their desire to "run" their own lives. In their opinion, by entering a stranger's car, a female hitchhiker was consenting to "weird things."[34]

Rather than develop new frameworks for understanding new cultural influences on young women in the 1970s, sociologist Abraham Miller drew upon the sexual double standard inherent in patriarchal psychoanaly-sis. Miller surmised that running away from home was simultaneously a "death fantasy" and a normal "puberty ritual" for girls and boys. The action told parents, "Now that I'm gone, you'll learn how much you miss me." It also said, "I can get along without you. I'm more self-reliant than you give me credit for."[35] The gender difference was that boys left home with a rational plan of action and some idea of "how to survive." The life histories of men on the road showed that they made the self-conscious decision to be "outsiders" and deliberately sought "roles that the larger adult social order had not approved."[36] All the while, they were confident that in the future when their period of masculine rebellion ended, they would be able to rejoin mainstream society with options awaiting them.

Miller constructed young women's lives on the road differently. He said that the road symbolized a "therapeutic alternative" for girls and women; running away was an unstable female's emotional response to a broken heart or her attempt to "heal personal wounds."[37] Young women left home irrationally, impulsively, and ill-equipped for the journey. Their lives on the road were "simultaneously more difficult and easier."[38] On the one hand, they faced the constant threat of assault, but on the other hand, rides, shelter, and food were more accessible. Discussing a hitch-hiker named Mary, Miller wrote,

> She feels that rape is an ever-present possibility, but any woman who is going to travel alone had better accept the possibility without concern ... She adds, with the confidence of experience, the cold resignation of the response [she gives to sexual advances], "really turns men off." Mary acknowledges ... that having affairs along the road is part of the fun and adventure of being on the road, and adds ... "Promiscuity is not a big idea ... Choice is."[39]

In Britain female hitchhiking was also a controversial subject. In 1974 Mario Rinvolucri wrote a 50,000-word book called *Hitch-Hiking*, in which he drew upon Freudian psychology to equate female hitchhiking with casual prostitution.[40] Citing a 1966 article in the *Evening Standard* of London, he wrote, "Awareness of sexual display is strong among female hitchers." Uninhibited women exploited their "visual sex appeal" because "it gets them lifts quick." He quoted a sixteen-year-old "school girl" who said, "I find it rather exciting to see how soon a car stops. I think it easier to hitch when one is female (preferably wearing a miniskirt)." An American hitcher told him, "When I show my hair to let people know I'm a girl, I get rides faster than if I put it behind my head." In contrast, sexually "up-tight" hitchhikers deliberately minimized their "sexual display." He quoted a student nurse who said, "Any girl who goes hitching on her own in a mini skirt ... is just asking for trouble ... When I hitch I like to wear trousers." Drawing upon numerous cases before the British courts, Rinvolucri said that the "errant" girl or woman "deeply desires ... what she horribly dreads in the lift situation." Consequently, the trend of young women falsely reporting sexual assaults to the police had made motorists afraid to pick up girls for fear of "a false accusation" and "sexual blackmail."[41]

In 1978 psychologists Robert Johnson and James Johnson decided to test how female hitchhikers ranked on Richard I. Lanyon's Psychological Screening Inventory of 1970, which was a diagnostic tool to screen prison inmates for indicators of "severe psychiatric difficulty" and "social pathology." Lanyon's "social nonconformity scale" was also used to find out which students would be most likely to use LSD or to join radical organizations like the Weather Underground, Black Panthers, and Students for a Democratic Society. In the Johnsons' study, "nonconformist" girls were described as "independent, free thinking and free acting." They tested forty-nine middle-class high school and college girls and discovered that those who hitchhiked alone, weekly, and for long distances scored significantly higher on the social nonconformity scale than did "socially conforming" nonhitchhikers and "less deviant" girls who only occasionally hitchhiked. According to Lanyon's inventory, "less deviant nonconformists" were also expected to be "law-breakers."[42] By 1970 it appeared to college professors that their female students were using hitchhiking to defy patriarchal codes for female behaviour.

### Queering Youth Mobility: "John Q. Public's Secret Lusts"
The social reconstruction of the hitchhiking ritual that reached the status of common knowledge in literature, songs, television, scholarly studies, and police reports was that hitchhiking girls were "flirting with trouble."[43] In the 1930s and 1940s, thumb-travel tales about the pleasures of hitching and hostelling were pitted against the remote danger of

encountering homicidal maniacs and Hollywood's femme fatales. Elise Chenier argues that in the 1950s and 1960s, anxious adults replaced fear of the 1930s sexual psychopath with fear of gay and straight "sex deviates" and hebephiles, who had an insatiable and uncontrollable sexual attraction to teenagers.[44] Male hitchhikers said that they had to keep an eye on the conversation because drivers "want to see what your interest in sex is."[45] A male teenager described being picked up by an older man:

> He did not say anything, but I could hear this kind of whispering like the radio was on really low. I thought, "Why don't you just turn the radio up?" But then I realized it was him. Rubbing the front of his pants with his finger ... He was saying, "I want you to suck my cock, want you to suck my cock – and he is stroking the front of his pants ... I leaned my foot up and yelled, "Stop the car, just stop the car. Stop the car ..." Finally, he did. I grabbed my stuff ... I was so mad.[46]

A sixteen-year-old boy travelling from Ontario said, "I was pretty innocent, [but] there was a lot of solicitation ... I met a fellow [and] he told me this truck driver guy ... tried to fiddle with him."[47]

After 1967's Summer of Love, anxiety about girls thumbing rides symbolized a variety of white, middle-class, patriarchal, adult problems. Karen Staller notes that the old assumption that the young runaway would return home tired and hungry was "undermined" in public opinion by the opening of urban youth hostels by meddling counterculturalists who offered runaways crash pads, free food, a shoulder to cry on, and the promise not to turn unwilling minors over to the Children's Aid Society.[48] It was easier to believe the claim by mainstream social work agencies that bad adults, hippies, pimps, pornographers, drug dealers, and sex deviates lured teenagers from good homes than to admit that boys and girls were indeed on the run from domestic violence and sexual abuse. Nervous parents pressured local police forces to raid gay bars, cruising spots, and parks looking for known sex deviates and child molesters.[49] The Canadian Welfare Council's transient youth inquiry was emphatic that Salvation Army men's hostels were bad environments for teenage boys due to the "disturbed and disturbing older men."[50] Municipalities, the police, and politicians in cities like Toronto, Montreal, and Vancouver were determined to "demonize the gay community" in their efforts to clean up inner-city "strips." The appearance of hippie-run headshops, crash pads, and youth hostels on the same streets as massage parlours, adult bookstores, and "grindhouses" in older "flophouse" districts contradicted "upright" family values in cities and towns all over the country.[51] Explicit talk of homosexuality was still a taboo in the mainstream media, but the insinuation could be easily softened by the androgynous image of sweet hitchhikers, for whom the real or imagined ending was a last-minute rescue "from her [or his] life of hell," or not.[52]

Even though they were powerless to change it, hitchhikers were contemptuous of sexism. In *The Hitchhiker's Field Manual* (1973), twenty-one-year-old Paul DiMaggio said that the fantasy of a hitchhiker "with nymphomaniac tendencies" was still the "kind of mythology [that] is rampant in the slicker men's magazines and in the bars and locker rooms," but he added that a new, equally disturbing, "milder stereotype is the Adventurous Hippie Chick," who was "also fair game for John Q. Public's secret lusts."[53] It is not without irony that on the Prairies, the summer hit among soft-porn movies of 1974 was the double bill *Sex Brats* and *Hitch-Hooker*. The movie section of the *Winnipeg Free Press* showed a poster of four women wearing miniskirts, leather boots, crop-tops, and see-through negligees. The caption said, "Again, Again, Again ... the erotic adventures of a call-girl on the move."[54] In 1972 the Department of Health and Welfare's brochure *On the Road: A Guide for Youth Travelling Canada* also indulged male fantasies of sexually liberated hippie girls and hitchhikers. The largest pictures in the free publication were drawings of pretty girls with flowing blond hair and bright yellow dresses.[55] The commentary surrounding one illustration said, "VD is on the increase ... Many women do not notice anything at all ... Hence the woman becomes the silent carrier."[56]

Androgynous hitchhikers were a temptation, a danger to themselves, and whether male or female, open to blame if attacked, but it was troublesome female (auto)mobility that became the subject both of journalism and of academic and popular psychology.[57] Commentators on popular culture, esteemed professors, youth workers, experts, and bystanders promoted "the truth" that the men who picked up hitchhiking girls should be seen as victims and the female hitchhikers as vamps. Little was made of a study on hitchhiking by psychologist Sheldon Geller of Seneca College in Toronto, who argued that hitchhiking created the locus of the crime but did not create the rapist. In 1977 Geller used a thirty-three-day strike by the Toronto Transit Commission to study reported instances of sexual assault. He hypothesized that if women were "innocent victims," the number of hitching-related sexual assaults should rise, whereas the number of assaults against the general population should remain the same. During the strike, he found that the overall number of assaults remained the same but that women were nine times more likely to be assaulted when hitchhiking. Therefore, the rapists had been there all along.[58]

### Anti-Thumb Propagandists

Before the Second World War, child psychologist John B. Watson encouraged childhood independence by instructing parents not to tell children stories about the bogeyman and not to tell them to fear strangers when there was likely nothing to be afraid of.[59] Pediatrician Benjamin Spock's *The Common Sense Book of Baby and Child Care* (1946) supported behaviourist warnings against adults excessively frightening children. Tamara Myers notes that the exception to this directive was road safety. In the 1950s and 1960s the police were permitted to use frightening images and films with chilling depictions of "real life" car crashes in order to impress upon children the need to modify their behaviour around motor vehicles.[60] Through successful techniques of behaviour modification, children learned to obey road safety rules, to never play in traffic, and to look out for each other.[61] In the mid-1970s, baby boom parents, the police, and city councillors used similar scare tactics in printed anti-hitchhiking literature and educational films. Anti-hitchhiking educational material incorporated statistics on hitchhiking-related rapes and deaths and provided detailed "dos and don'ts" in order to encourage youth, notably girls, to stop hitchhiking.

The most gruesome anti-hitchhiking information was on the front pages of Canadian newspapers. Ontario newspapers printed headlines like "Death Threat Makes Girls Leap from Car," "Guilty of Raping Hitchhiker," "Toronto Hitchhikers: 3 Raped at Knifepoint," and "Hand of Death."[62] In 1970 the *Globe and Mail* and the *Montreal Gazette* reported that two California college girls had leapt out of a moving car during an

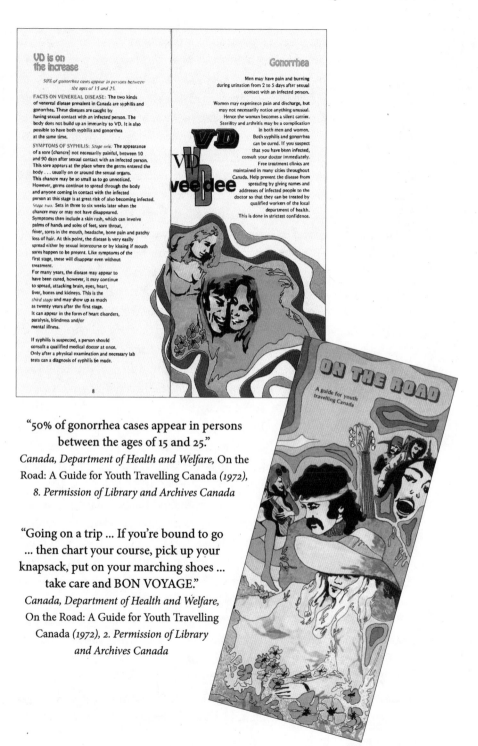

"50% of gonorrhea cases appear in persons between the ages of 15 and 25."
*Canada, Department of Health and Welfare,* On the Road: A Guide for Youth Travelling Canada *(1972), 8. Permission of Library and Archives Canada*

"Going on a trip ... If you're bound to go ... then chart your course, pick up your knapsack, put on your marching shoes ... take care and BON VOYAGE."
*Canada, Department of Health and Welfare,* On the Road: A Guide for Youth Travelling Canada *(1972), 2. Permission of Library and Archives Canada*

attack by the driver. One was killed and the other badly injured.[63] A month later, a Quebec City student hitchhiked out West. Her partly decomposed body was found by some berry pickers about 15 kilometres from Hudson's Hope, British Columbia. Her father said that she had left home without telling anyone.[64] In 1972, under the headline "Rape and Robbery: Hitchers Attract Crime," the *Ottawa Citizen* tallied three rapes, two armed robberies, and "dozens" of assaults connected with hitchhiking.[65] In 1973 the *Edmonton Journal* counted three sexual assaults of young women who had "paid dearly" for hitchhiking.[66] In 1974 two nineteen-year-old Kamloops girls, Pamela Darlington and Gale Weys, "hitchhiked to death." Their parents told the *Edmonton Journal* they didn't like their daughters thumbing. They offered to pay for bus and cab fare or pick them up in the family car. Gale's mother said, "I think Gale was in the wrong place at the wrong time."[67] The *Winnipeg Free Press* reported that 40 percent of all sex crimes were committed by or against hitchhikers. The chief of psychiatry at North York General Hospital said that three-quarters of the rapists in his practice chose "hitchhikers as victims."[68]

In the early 1970s, police departments published anti-hitchhiking "dos and don'ts" that focused on scare tactics directed at girls. In 1972 Lieutenant Joe Penkala of the Morality Division of the Saskatoon Police Department said, "Men giving rides to young girls should consider the possibility of sex charges being laid against them ... Women giving rides to men make themselves vulnerable to assaults, car theft, or robbery." Saskatoon's police chief, James G. Kettles, urged all three levels of government to make hitchhiking an offence.[69] In 1972 sixteen-year-old Christine Walkowiak's murder became the fifth unsolved hitchhiking-related case in Ontario. Coroner Roger Hughes demanded "a vigorous program of education" on the dangers of hitchhiking for school officials, police personnel, and parents.[70] To assist with this campaign, Toronto filmmaker Ralf Tillack collected seventy letters from "adventurous youngsters." Ninety percent of them described sexual attacks, threats with broken bottles, or nightmarish rides at breakneck speeds, and one told of a motorist who had pulled up without a stitch of clothing on.[71]

The anti-hitchhiking advice of police was directed at school children and motorists, but the main message pressed upon girls was never to get into cars with strangers. A pamphlet by the Community Services Branch of the Ontario Provincial Police called "BE AWARE ... ATTENTION!" urged parents to talk to their children about how to avoid "child molesters." The opening statement said, "Remember, a child molester doesn't have to look like a disreputable degenerate with dark clothing. They generally look like you or I." The first piece of advice for children said, "Never hitchhike or accept a ride from a stranger." Women were told that "if they must hitch a ride, they should do it with a friend. In daylight. And avoid getting into the backseat of a two-door car."[72] Detective Herman Meyer said, "If a girl gets into the backseat of a two-door car and it turns out the man wants to rape her, she has no escape. If she's in the front, she has a chance at least."[73] In 1977 the Peel Police Department's "dos and don'ts" warned hitchhikers not to get into a car with a motorist who "looks or acts strange or appears impaired," not to "ride in the back of an open truck," to get a licence number, and to report "anything untoward."[74] The Edmonton police coached girls to "never hitchhike alone. Even if there are two [girls], don't get in a car with three or four men."[75] After three girls aged thirteen, fourteen, and fifteen were raped when hitchhiking from Toronto to Orangeville, the Rape Crisis Centre contradicted the police by advising girls who hitchhiked to sit in the backseat. The *Toronto Sun* said, "Police are advising women of any age not to hitchhike."[76]

The mayors of many Canadian cities were also considering ways to impose hitchhiking bans. In 1974 North York's mayor, Mel Lastman, cited cases where six teenage girls were murdered in the Metropolitan Toronto area. He wanted to ban girls from hitching and to impose a $50 fine for motorists who picked them up. Lastman's statistics showed that 10 in 102 cases of rape and assault in the area were connected with hitchhiking. He added, "We have got perverts prowling our streets, no matter how much you want to believe Metro Toronto is a little village. You ask a girl why she's hitchhiking, and she says she's looking for a friendly face. Well, some of the friendliest faces in the world are sex maniacs."[77] In support, Staff Superintendent James Morgan of the Metro Toronto Technical Traffic Committee, said, "I always shudder ... when I see young girls – 13 or 14 years old – standing on the street corner."[78]

Syndicated advice columnists used the teenage survivors of sexual assault to drive home anti-hitchhiking messages. Ann Landers, Abigail

Van Buren ("Dear Abby"), and the *Globe and Mail*'s Elizabeth Thompson published letters from girls, wives, and mothers asking them to warn of the dangers of hitchhiking.[79] A letter to Ann Landers from "Exhibit A" said, "I know you've printed several letters in your column on this subject, but mine might make a stronger impression than most because I can tell them first hand what it's like to be raped."[80] In 1973 Van Buren published a letter from "WORRIED FOR MY HUSBAND." The writer said that girls who hitchhiked were "begging for trouble." She asked Van Buren's readers to consider the point of view of the driver's family:

> My husband has a problem he has been trying [with psychiatric treatment] to overcome for six years. It's a compulsion to expose himself to young women. He's not a rapist, he only does this for a thrill from their reaction ... One of these girls reported him to the police and he's facing the possibility of having to leave me and our three small children for a jail term ... Abby please ask girls not to hitchhike ... They may be giving someone who is trying to go straight an opportunity to stray again.[81]

In 1974 "Jenny's Mom" asked Thompson what to do about her fifteen-year-old daughter. Respectable neighbours had seen Jenny hitchhiking. Jenny had been grounded and now felt like a prisoner who said that "we've made the home a jail." She's "storming and screaming ... saying we're mean, unreasonable parents who don't know what it is like to be stuck in a dump like this with a bunch of dumb brothers." Jenny would rather hitch to the restaurant up the highway, where she liked "hanging around with a bunch of young punks." Thompson advised all Canadian mothers with devious, sulky, and angry daughters to contact the YWCA for information about summer camps, swimming, canoeing, music, art, or dancing lessons, horseback riding, or drama. In any case, girls must be prohibited from "hitchhiking at night ... because the number of teen-age girls who have been murdered after hitchhiking in this country is growing alarmingly."[82]

Helen Benedict argues that myths about rape are perpetrated by journalists, judges, police, and medical experts who hold the view that young women who are assaulted at parties, in bars, while hitchhiking, wearing miniskirts, or in places where "good girls" are not supposed to be are "asking for it."[83] Today, the official testimonies of professionals and experts under oath and judicial verdicts are criticized for perpetuating misconceptions about sexual assault and what we now call "rape culture." In the 1970s the Canadian judicial system endorsed the belief that girls who hitchhiked were asking for trouble. In 1972 a rape charge against a twenty-eight-year-old married motorist was dismissed. In his instructions to the court, the judge said that all young women who hitchhiked, including the seventeen-year-old victim, "were inviting motorists to believe their purpose is not entirely innocent." He said, "The real victim of this episode was the girl's mother."[84] In 1976 Judge Harry Waisberg found a North York man guilty of choking a teenage hitchhiker into sexual submission. Before he sentenced the twenty-five-year-old man, Waisberg said that "rape is an assault of a particularly hideous nature" but added that "the victim contributed to the circumstances by hitchhiking."[85] Double standards and stereotypes made it more difficult for female and male victims to complain after assaults.

As the link between sexual assault and hitchhiking grew in the minds of the public, stop-hitchhiking campaigns became more explicit. In 1974 the Ontario Provincial Police collaborated on an anti-hitchhiking film for younger viewers called *Hitch-Hiking*. Promotional material was sent to youth organizations, including the Canadian Youth Hostels Association. The poster showed a girl in pigtails hitchhiking and a car with two men in sunglasses slowing down to pick her up. She was wearing shorts and a tank top and was carrying a backpack.[86] The film featured dramatized assault survivors' stories and an interview with Gisela Bauer, whose fourteen-year-old daughter had gone missing in Kleinburg, Ontario. Ingrid Bauer was last seen hitchhiking at 10:00 p.m. on August 16, 1972. Her mother assured the police that her daughter had not run away. Ingrid "didn't have any problems." She was a school leader and a fashion model. The Bauers "never let her hitchhike at night," but Ingrid caught them "off guard" and got her father's permission.[87] The Bauers told the *Globe and Mail*, "There's no way we can stop them hitchhiking completely."[88] During the weeks immediately following Ingrid's disappearance, there was a nationwide search and a $1,000 reward for information. Two years later, in the film *Hitch-Hiking*, the Bauers pleaded for Ingrid's return. Tragically, she was never found.

Inherent in the construction of anti-hitchhiking campaigns is Michel Foucault's concept of "biopower," which in the case of adolescent risk taking focuses on the regulation of the individual self and on disciplining bodies.[89] In 1977 this idea was illustrated in the Ontario Provincial Police's poster contest, which offered a $200 scholarship to the student who designed the best poster that illustrated the dangers of hitchhiking. Detective Herman Meyer of the Community Services Branch in Toronto believed that "in order to draw a poster depicting the danger," the artist would have to "think about what those dangers were" and imagine living through them.[90] The most frequent message of the two hundred submissions was "Don't," followed by the advice that "if you must hitchhike, then be selective about the rides ... and never hitchhike alone, especially at night."[91] Five judges unanimously awarded first prize to Kenneth Herman of Thunder Bay. The Grade 11 student's design, called "The Hand of Death," depicted a skeletal, hitchhiking hand flanked by the bilingual slogan "Going my way? Tu me prends?" The Ontario Provincial Police printed 5,000 postcards for distribution in schools and erected sixty giant billboards.[92] The police force was satisfied that the message was clear in French and English: "You court death when you hitchhike."[93]

By 1978 the Ontario Provincial Police had assembled a number of Canadian and American rape-prevention films with anti-hitchhiking messages and had appointed community liaison officers to show them in high schools and public libraries. One film they rated as a "Good Film" was *Rape: A Preventative Inquiry* (1974), whose promotion material said that it had won the American Film Festival's Red Ribbon Award. This documentary's intention was to "emotionally involve" viewers so that they could identify with rape victims.[94] The film had interviews with tough-talking cops who said that "mobility and visibility" caused rape. The voiceover began, "More and more nowadays, girls are using hitchhiking as a mode of travel ... For today's women to understand the rapist, she must first understand the man." Next, a police officer said, "Quite a few of our rape-homicides start out as hitchhikers ... The victim ends up in a canyon somewhere or at a deserted warehouse, and she is a victim for the homicide team ... When a girl gets into a car, she has no control of the situation once the car takes off." The film featured an interview with "Nancy," a college student who had survived a hitchhiking assault. Nancy said, "At the time he had the knife at my throat ... I thought back over my whole life ... and I thought, 'I don't care how expensive it is or how much of a hassle ... I'm not going to hitchhike again.'" Nancy's interview was followed by interviews with teachers in a women's self-defence class. The feminist martial arts instructor said, "Last year there were about twenty movies where women were raped ... In *Deliverance* [1972] when some guy is getting raped, people are shocked." The maker of the documentary then spoke to three men serving life sentences related to sexual offences. From their prison cells, they described the role that hitchhiking had played in the selection of victims. One said, "A lot of the rapes I committed I probably wouldn't have ... if those girls weren't out there hitchhiking." The convicts agreed that self-defence classes would not have helped their victims. A man said, "The average girl on the street who's hitchhiking says it couldn't happen to me ... A self-defence course wouldn't help her, man! ... When I've got a knife against your throat, I don't care what you know ... A self-defence course could get her killed ... The woman I was with, she fought back and she is dead."[95]

Anti-hitchhiking information was clear, contradictory, and in line with the myths and stereotypes of police, scholars, and judicial rulings, such as the "truth" that girls on the road were maladjusted and getting their kicks, so they would not strongly object to or report unwanted sexual encounters in a stranger's car. In 1969, when Flora Grace Elk froze to death on the road while hitchhiking home to Griswold, Manitoba, after being released from the Prince Albert Correctional Centre in Saskatchewan, the Department of Indian Affairs faced charges for "contributing to her death by failing to insure her transportation home from the centre." Indian Affairs staff said they were "blameless" and denied knowing anything about the incident.[96] In 1977 Detective Randy Warden of the Peel Police Department said that it should be "common sense not to hitchhike, or pick up a hitchhiker," but if "they haven't learned by now, they're never going to."[97]

### Backlash: "Stand Up for Equal Rights!"

Throughout the twentieth century, hitchhiking had been a longstanding coming of age ritual for girls and boys.[98] In the final decades of the century, second-wave feminists challenged women's lack of access to the public sphere. The visibility of women's liberationists caused problems for male professors, crime-stopping professionals, and commentators who scrambled to make sense of the new liberated girl. Feminists were accused of guiding girls to abandon "fear of potential sexual threat or assault." Greenley and Rice attributed girl hitchhikers' "quasi-deviant" behaviour to pressure from the movement.[99] Most notorious, in their opinion, was Kate Millett's *Sexual Politics* (1970), which sold 80,000 copies and put Millett's picture on the cover of *Time* magazine. Greenley and Rice were told by "younger liberated co-eds" that they had the same prerogatives as men, namely "the right to take a walk at night, to thumb a ride, to have freedom of access and movement at any time and in any place."[100] The more positive hitchhiking experiences a woman had, the more "strongly" she believed that "she could handle a dangerous situation."[101]

Oral history and autobiography show that women of the baby boom generation were engaged in consciousness raising and standing up for their rights. Understanding the impact of feminist ideas on their lives requires recognition of the intersection of history and biography – the interplay between self, society, and evolving ideas about gender roles, marriage, family, education, careers, and interpersonal networks – which contemporary feminists popularly phrase as "the personal is political."[102] Journalist Myrna Kostash was a graduate student at the University of Toronto in the late 1960s. She recalls her delight after reading Betty Friedan's *The Feminine Mystique* (1963), Sojourner Truth's "Ain't I a Woman" (1851), and Simone de Beauvoir's *The Second Sex* (1949) with the other members of her women's liberation group. None of them believed they would end up like Friedan's "defeated women in the suburbs." They wanted an education, careers, adventures, and travel experiences before they made babies and peanut butter sandwiches.[103] It was natural for late baby boomers interested in gender equality to hang out at feminist bookstores, go to women's studies lectures, participate in Take Back the Night and pro-choice marches, volunteer at the Women's Centre, and protest against sexism in the workplace and in the sections of the Criminal Code

"Typical of the hitchhikers passing through Toronto on their way east or west were Carole Lebrec and Monique Fouquet, both of Quebec City, spotted on Highway 401 ... The two girls were unable to find summer jobs this year and decided to travel instead ... 'You get a strange feeling when you are on the road,' said Carole. 'You meet so many different people and do so many different things' ... They had no major problems ... 'On warm nights we'd just sleep in the park, nobody minded.'" *Toronto Star,* August 1, 1970.

*Photo by Boris Spremeo via Getty Images/* Toronto Star

of Canada that controlled access to contraception and abortion. A student at Simon Fraser University said that in her women's studies course she had learned that "there had been a double standard."[104]

Central to the feminist critique of patriarchy was the societal belief that women needed special laws to protect them.[105] Feminists in women's shelters and anti-rape lobbyists challenged misinformation about rape, including its link to hitchhiking bans that denied women's right to mobility. For some, the right to hitchhike was central to "taking back the streets" because it put feminist theory into spatial practice.[106] Geller's study of rape during the 1977 strike by the Toronto Transit Commission showed that hitchhiking did not create "the rapist," so hitchhikers were not "temptresses" to otherwise honourable men.[107] Women's groups objected to the link between rape and hitchhiking. The rape crisis groups that accepted invitations from the Ontario Provincial Police to preview twenty-eight 16-millimetre films about rape prevention, including *Rape: A Preventative Inquiry*, said that the convicted rapists in the film were "not typical." They said that the film was "fear-producing" and "left a message to submit." They favoured positive messages that promoted self-protection, self-defence, and saying "no."[108] The feminist goal was to stop rape, not to stop hitchhiking. Toronto alderwoman Betty Sutherland summed up both sides of the debate when she said that if a way could be found to "ban hitchhiking for girls without causing a big outcry, that would be hitting it on the spot."[109]

Young men were aware of sexism and how the women's liberation movement was changing the beliefs and behaviour of their sisters and female friends. Duncan McMonagle met "women's libbers" in youth hostels during his hitchhiking travels in 1971. In his travel diary, he described a conversation with a woman who told him that she "preferred men who did not put across male chauvinist attitudes." He described a "Women's Lib" poster on the wall "by the can" in a communal house: "Two guys are standing in front of a urinal with a girl standing in front of the urinal in between them." The wall was emblazoned with the appropriate slogan: "Stand Up for Equal Rights!"[110] DiMaggio met feminists on the road who said that they hitchhiked because it enabled them to "prove that they are the equals of men." He suspected that "feminism" had become "a kind of counter-*machismo* – self-definition on other people's terms." He thought that hitchhiking for "political reasons" was "less a step towards liberation than a closing of the eyes to the imperfect nature of society."[111]

What was being articulated was women's rejection of the patriarchal misunderstanding of rape. The "rape myth" made several general assertions: rape is sex, assault is motivated by lust, assailants are perverted or crazy, assailants are of the lower class or racially motivated, women provoke rape, women deserve rape, only "loose" women are victims, a sexual attack sullies the victim, rape is punishment for past deeds, and women cry rape for revenge.[112] Twenty-two-year-old York University students Elizabeth Cull and Anne Scotten formed a "right to hitchhike" group in 1974. Cull had been hitching for five years and had taken at least 200 rides "with all sorts of folks." She had never had a bad experience, "not even so much as a mugging." Her two precautions were to "never get into a car with more than one man" and to "never hitch after dark." Cull opposed hitchhiking bans because "to teach people to anticipate violence and to induce unnecessary fear of violence is to encourage violence."[113] Scotten was the president of York University's Federation of Students. She was not a hitchhiker herself, but she asserted that "it would be stupid to make it illegal." For her, it was "a pretty stupid thing to say" that hitchhiking girls were looking for trouble; "most of those who hitchhike are looking for a ride."[114] Connie Russell of the National Organization for Women, who was a rape crisis volunteer at Cedars-Sinai Medical Center in Los Angeles, agreed that "if women refrained from hitchhiking they would only maintain the sexist convention that women were seen by men as victims."[115]

Debatably, the principle of freedom of movement is upheld as a democratic right in Canada. Civil libertarians challenged the official statistics on hitchhiking-related crime on the grounds that Statistics Canada did not ask police forces to collect or record them. Moreover, they called scare tactics an irrational deterrent when thousands of people hitchhiked safely every day.[116] University of Toronto law student Alex Sweezey pointed out the "absurd" philosophical weakness in Mel Lastman's proposed total hitchhiking ban. Sweezey said that such legislation was discriminatory, "*ultra vires* the Government of Ontario and outside the power of any municipality." He asked, "What about the male hitchhiker who is unlikely to be raped? Should he be forbidden to hitch as well?"[117] That hitchhiking had been a part of Canadian highway culture since the 1920s may be attributed to the long-held belief that Canada was a tolerant and trustworthy society. Despite mounting evidence to the contrary, many people were still reluctant to admit that these values might be an artefact of bygone days.

The reaction of pro-hitchhiking commentators to the Ontario Provincial Police's billboards was negative. Herman's bilingual billboard design with a skeletal hitchhiking thumb was called tasteless, excessive, ridiculous, and depressing.[118] A veteran hitchhiker of more than 11,260 kilometres called it "ridiculous" to tarnish motorists and hitchhikers as "synonymous with death." Another transatlantic thumb-traveller said that the hitchhiker's "milieu was not a milieu of maniacs and the criminally insane, but a random sample of society on the move ... Of course ... there *are* frightened, freaked and frantic people about, but erecting billboards that pander to them will not make society a better place."[119] Ontario resident Mark Cairenius said, "The message is depressing and shows bad taste." He asked the Brampton police to "please take the dead man down from the billboard and bury him."[120] The *Globe and Mail* printed a petition signed by five "shocked" people who wanted the provincial police to remove the "offensive" and "horrid" image of "a very true-to-life skeleton hand." The petitioners said that if the intention

> is to discourage hitchhiking, then why is it necessary to do so by instilling fear in all of us? ... Fear breeds mistrust, which in turn breeds more fear. Such a situation can only bring out the worst in people ... These scare tactics encourage violence ... The OPP has no right to use public funds to inflict their views upon us.[121]

Veteran hitchhikers, civil libertarians, and motorists who wished to share their cars thought that anti-hitchhiking messages would cause "fellow Canadians" to distrust strangers, friends, and neighbours.[122] Nevertheless, civil society's anxiety about the counterculture, sexual deviates, and women's liberation cast a dark shadow over women's mobility and hitchhiking.

### "Mr. Wandering Hands": Resistance and Efficacy

The rituals of youth subcultures make sense to those who choose to engage in them, so youth behaviour is best understood when interpreted in light of the meaning and value that youngsters of a certain generation give to these rituals. Belonging to rebellious subcultures frequently requires the ritualist to embrace risk-taking activities, codes of behaviour, and dress styles that display their symbolic disdain for, and mutiny against, parental values, school, and the status quo. Modern psychologists argue that a "negative identity" such as greaser, punk, or slut at a critical stage of adolescent development may be unpleasant but not altogether "undesirable" for a teenager.[123] In her study of girls in Toronto family court after the Second World War, Franca Iacovetta notes that many middle-class and working-class girls relished their image as "bad girls" and "gave lip" to the authorities.[124] For them, negative identities offered relief from invisibility and highly sought social capital among peers.

Like earlier generations of travelling youth, hitchhikers were not a homogeneous group. Some were conservative and conforming, whereas others consciously defied parental authority and patriarchal codes of behaviour and relished the "freak" and "flower child" image. The 1960s unarguably emerged as a more sexually permissive era, but interviews with baby boom hitchhikers show that at the time they travelled, most had very narrow and negative information about human sexuality, which explains why some appeared to be willing to put up with unwelcome sexual advances and molestation by motorists and adults in general.[125] Following Foucault's assertion that the history of sexuality has been limited by contemporary discourses about sex theory and practice, anti-hitchhiking messages were likely defeated from the outset because parents in Cold War Canada preferred the discursive construction of "youthful innocence" over forthright and frank information about sexual behaviour, erotic variation, and "deviance."[126]

In 1948 a new description of "criminal sexual psychopath" was added to the Criminal Code of Canada, which defined the psychopath as "a person who by course of misconduct in sexual matters has evidenced a lack of power to control his sexual impulses."[127] Chenier notes that everyday citizens began to think of sexual behaviour in terms of a mental health disorder rather than offences against religious doctrine. To protect the sanctimonious image of the "traditional," heterosexual, nuclear family as a haven in a heartless world, "sex deviates," child molesters, and hebephiles were marginalized, and "nuisance-type" sex-fetishists, Peeping Toms, and flashers were treated as "failed men," regarded as silly and sick, snickered at in popular culture, such as jokes in *Playboy* magazine, and confined to the outer limits of social respectability, thereby maintaining the fiction of the family as a refuge from sexual danger. Thus the rhetoric of "stranger danger" was born.[128]

In the 1970s the postwar homosexual panic was gradually superseded by the discovery of sexual assaults against children by pedophiles, strangers, and dirty old men.[129] Nevertheless, teachers and parents confined the curriculum on sex education and family life to heterosexuality and "feeling good" about growing up.[130] Anxious baby boom parents hoped that teenagers would confine their corporeal heterosexual exploration to holding hands, modest kissing, and light petting and that they would heed the police's warning not to get into cars with strangers. Cold War social anxieties about child molesters made "sex deviants" into the "folk devil" of the day, but factual information and biological evidence were unfit for the ears of innocent children and therefore de-emphasized in the "hitchhiker BEWARE!" pamphlets.[131]

Hitchhikers ignored parental warnings. Armed with contradictory and confusing information about human sexuality, they had difficulty interpreting cross-generational sexual encounters in cars. In interviews and contemporary writing, hitchhikers spoke openly about sexual harassment and unpleasant encounters with voyeurs, fetishists, and exhibitionists who trolled roads looking for someone to shock.[132] Ontario hitchhiker Keith Perkins said,

> All the kids in Barry's Bay knew about the guy who drove back and forth from Ottawa picking up hitchers. He was very nice ... no fear ... but conversation. He liked to talk about black guys' penis size ... Every ride was the same. He just wants to talk ... To get his thrill this way ... After a while, I knew it verbatim.[133]

Hitchhikers in Vancouver called a local man "Mr. Wandering Hands." They were not afraid of him, but neither did they want to have sex with him.[134] A twenty-year-old hitchhiker said that she was picked up by "a perv." She "looked over and saw that he's playing with himself ... I was so pissed off and disgusted ... The light turned red ... [so] I flung open the door and cursed at him."[135] Two teenage boys were picked up by one of "those guys who wants to tell you about the chicks he screwed right before ... A kind of a weirdo ... We doubted it."[136] A male hitchhiker took a ride from an older man who "started talking about the strip club ... There are certainly sexually suggestive things that you don't tell to a young man." He felt that "the guy could pull out a knife or a gun. You never know what they are going to do." At a junction, he opened the door and said, "'I am getting out' ... He was just hoping to get lucky."[137] Perkins once took a lift from a "highway surveyor," who told him,

> I am going to have to stop and check the surveyor's tape... He would lean over me and look out the window ... Each time he did this, he was getting closer and closer. The last time, he put his hands between my open legs to support himself ... Then I realized he was smelling me ... I cut him off that time ... I just told him I had to get out. He didn't have a gun or say, "I want to fuck little boys" ... He was a smeller ... He let me out. Just getting a thrill.[138]

A hitchhiker said, "Looking back, I am surprised my parents let me ... There were a couple of drivers I wished I hadn't gotten into the car with, but at that age you don't feel vulnerable."[139] A thirteen-year-old boy from the East Coast "was raped by a male." He said, "Suddenly, we are travelling on a dirt road, and we are taking his 'short cut,' and you get molested."[140] The dominant assumption that only girls could be victims of sexual assault was contradicted by these interviewees and the convicted rapists in *Rape: A Preventative Inquiry*. In the film, these men were emphatic that rape was about degradation and humiliation, not sex. One man gestured to the inmate beside him and said, "When he needed it, there was a woman present, so he raped her ... When he needed it, there was a man present, so he raped him."[141] This information would have been valuable to Canadian high school students. For many generations, misjudgments in the sexual education of children produced unequal relations of power, leaving them vulnerable to abuse, fearful, and ashamed.[142]

A seventeen-year-old girl described a fun ride with a nice family. She played with the kids in the backseat. When it was time for her to go, everyone was standing beside the car. As she said goodbye to the father, he hugged her and discreetly "put his hands inside my sweater and squeezed my breasts." She was shocked and disappointed, but like many youth of this generation, she said nothing.[143] A possible explanation for survivors not reporting sexual assault by family members or strangers was the socialization of children, especially girls, to accept their role as "priceless" protectors of the sacred ideal of the nuclear family. In the 1980s feminist scholars began to argue that the myth of the safe patriarchal family depended on the victim's silence.[144]

Some hitchhikers refused to remain silent. Their responses to sexual assault show that they followed safety information or adapted it in order to avert dangerous situations whenever they could. A woman said that when she thumbed alone, she made it clear that she did not want to "screw around ... I babbled like a little brook ... My brother this, and my brother that." She thought that "it was good to let them know that someone knew me, so don't try anything ... There will be retaliation."[145] A man in a van picked up a female hitchhiker from Guelph who said that "the scariest experience of my life" was when he suddenly pulled over at a gas station. She noticed the passenger door did not have a handle. "Coincidentally enough," she had just read "an article on dangerous hitchhiking scenarios ... One red flag was filling the tank with gas, indicating a long journey without the need to stop." The article advised hitchhikers to "personalize yourself ... make yourself a real human being." She said,

> When he got back in the van, I asked why there was no door handle. He gave me a lame explanation ... I started talking like a mad woman about my brother, my parents, my dog, my inane self ... We were just under the overpass ... I cried out ... [He] then suddenly pulled over, ran out, and opened my door, telling me to get out now.[146]

The police and media were incorrect to assert that hitchhikers would not report "pervy" motorists to the police. A Vancouver hitchhiker asked a driver to let her off at the main gate to Jericho Beach, but he did not stop. "He got me into the forest ... He tried to pull my shirt out," which was tucked into her pants. She hit him and reported the assault to the Vancouver City Police.[147] In 1976 a motorist on parole for "attempted rape and kidnapping" attacked a twenty-year-old hitchhiker in Boston. She recalled knowing instantly that something was wrong:

> I thought, "This guy is creepy" ... He must have been talking about bizarre things ... He put his hand on my breast. He is feeling me up and still driving ... I'm thinking, "Is this how I want to go?" It was a

moment when you have to think clearly. I pressed my back on the door and just started kicking. I didn't care if we hit someone ... He burned me with his cigarette ... I said, "Let me out of this fucking car!" ... He said, "You are crazy, you are crazy." I said, "You're damned right I am crazy" ... I grabbed the keys out of the ignition ... I called the police ... I called my parents and they got a lawyer. I remember the lawyer asking, "What were you wearing?" I said, "What the fuck does it matter what I was wearing?" ... He got ten years for me and the other girls, on top of what he was doing ... I was so pissed off at the other girls for not reporting it.[148]

One night, a young waitress at a national park resort finished cashing out, locked up, and headed up the hill to thumb home. She recalled,

There was another couple hitching, and I walked further up the road ... The first vehicle that came along did not pick them up ... It picked me up instead ... I was just chatting away ... He asked if I wanted a cigarette ... He was reaching into the glove compartment ... Suddenly, I heard the guy say, "Sorry I have to do this to you" ... He was holding a hunting knife out at me ... It all happened pretty fast ... He said, "I am not fooling around."

She remembered something from a sociology class about "trying to humanize myself," but it was not working. "So I opened the door and jumped out ... I severed two ligaments and a bone in this leg [which had a long scar] and broke this foot in three places." She described the local police department's reaction to the incident. The police made a composite sketch and then broke their promise of confidentiality and released her name and location in the hospital to the press. She suspected that the authorities would have taken the incident more seriously if she had been raped or killed.[149]

Some hitchhikers in trouble turned to strangers for help. A young woman travelling from Calgary to Saskatoon was picked up in Stettler, Alberta. Without warning, the driver pulled off the main highway to "show me some cows." She knew she "was in a bad spot and started panicking

... I just got lucky. He just stopped and let me out." She was unaware that another motorist had seen her get into the car and had followed them. He told the frightened young woman, "I watched you get picked up back there, and I was just making sure that you were okay."[150] The trip ended safely. He drove her directly to her parents' house in Saskatoon.

Hitchhiker Vanessa Veselka observes that during her time on the road in the mid-1980s, society "collectively decided" that hitchhiking stories should be told as morality tales "that exist only in the shadow of a predator."[151] In this research, I have noted that male and female hitchhikers often made "jokes" about troubling encounters. Psychological studies of post-traumatic stress suggest that people tend to minimize the extent of fear and danger so as not to seem lacking in courage. Humour was one of the many defence mechanisms that hitchhikers used to normalize bad behaviour, defend the ride-sharing ritual, and deny fear. Jokes about "Mr. Wandering Hands" and drunk drivers were a significant part of interviews and contemporary writing, and they were repeated in the newspapers of the day. Simon Fraser University student Ron Verzuh said, "Roman hands and Russian fingers ... were normal encounters for girls."[152] The *Edmonton Journal* quoted a young woman in 1971 who announced, "After four days hitchhiking on my own ... I'm unmolested."[153] The *Globe and Mail* mentioned a sign designed by two frustrated young men stranded around Espanola in northern Ontario that said, "Will Accept Deviants."[154] Post-traumatic stress research also suggests that trauma continues after the objective danger has disappeared.[155] A young woman who had been raped at knifepoint said, "The first time I hitchhiked after it happened, I was okay ... The second time, I had a very hard time with it ... Then I just couldn't do it anymore."[156]

Information on hitchhiking safety was not the first instruction in traffic safety that baby boom children received. Tamara Myers shows that in the 1950s and 1960s, Elmer the Safety Elephant and traffic safety patrols instructed Canadian children about the importance of looking both ways before crossing the street and watching out for younger pedestrians.[157] Following the message that they should look out for each other, hitchhikers produced their own hitchhiking safety "dos and don'ts" that embodied the communal notion of taking responsibility for others.

Canadian university newspapers telegraphed warnings to local hitch-hikers about bad drivers. In 1975 a twenty-two-year-old female student at the University of Waterloo sent a long letter to *The Chevron* after a hitchhike attack by a policeman. She wrote,

> Tonight I sit angry and repulsed by the obvious hypocrisy of one who is supposed to be a figure of justice, a defender (not an attacker) of the people, one who is to be treated with respect ... Due to my desire to put myself through university ... I have had to depend mainly on hitchhiking as a means of transportation. I do recognize the risks as well as the benefits ... I realize when I am hitchhiking that I am taking a certain risk, that no driver "owes" me a ride, but if he should decide to stop, I offer in exchange congenial company and polite conversation ... and that is all! ... I was hitchhiking ... The driver who stopped for me assumed the exchange to be of a different nature ... He was a member of the police force! ... I marvelled at the contradiction between his actions and his role as a policeman ... There will probably always be people like this fellow who unfairly assume that any young woman hitchhiker is a whore of some order.[158]

Students at Simon Fraser University organized a "pervert patrol" and sent descriptions of a local "jack-off artist" to *The Peak*. One warning said, "Girls hitchhiking down the mountain – Don't accept a ride from a single guy in a small green sports car ... deeply tanned, and medium length curly dark brown hair ... Don't get in the car!"[159] Another warning said, "This guy picks up hitchhiking chic[k]s ... No one really believes in perverts until they meet one."[160] In October 1969, under the "thumb-name" Wanda Lust, a student wrote an article for *The Ubyssey* called "Drivers Bare Balls, Hearts to Hitchhiking Chick." The article said, "There's a man in Vancouver who does nothing but drive around picking up girl hitchhikers and pulling his wire."[161]

In *The Hitchhiker's Field Manual*, DiMaggio told hitchers that they might "occasionally encounter homosexual drivers." He said that if hitchhikers were not interested in sex, they should "firmly but civilly refuse their advances." He argued that homosexuals "may be sufficiently grateful to be treated like human beings (as opposed to being stomped or condemned) to go out of their way for you."[162] The staff at many federal youth hostels encountered victims of sexual assault. According to a founding member of the Greater Vancouver Youth Communications Centre Society, or Cool Aid, "Very quickly, we realized that a lot of women were being raped ... and we began to put up notices: 'Don't Hitchhike Alone' and 'Hitchhike with a Male' ... Word was getting out."[163] Many of the assault survivors just wanted to go home.

The purpose of schoolroom lessons on road safety was to get children to take responsibility for their own safety and the safety of others. David Rideout and Ray Amiro adapted this message to hitchhiking. They said that the safest way to travel was in small groups and with other hitchhikers. Women were "not an accessory, but a great advantage whether you are a guy or a woman yourself ... One guy alone is not too bad. A woman alone should be careful. Never hitch with more than two or three at most, unless of course you're all girls."[164] Youth hostel bulletin boards were plastered with notices from hitchhikers seeking partners.[165] When rides were tough to get and on busy highways, boys hid in ditches while girls thumbed for rides. Once, two boys from Edmonton and three girls from Cold Lake made it all the way to Kenora as a group of five, but their luck ran out at a truck stop at 2:00 a.m. To get a ride, "the plan" was to "put all the bags in the ditch, and my buddy and I lay in the ditch while the girls hitched."[166] By following the advice of more experienced hitchhikers, heeding schoolroom lessons on road safety, and looking after each other, generations of hitchhikers have tried to behave responsibly and to demonstrate citizenship values the best they could.[167]

### Conclusion: Ambiguity and Ritual

In fact and fiction, hitchhiking was an "ambiguous ritual" that reproduced the moral dilemmas and sexual violence inherent in everyday life. The truth of hitchhiking was that one never knew the true identity of a hitchhiker or the true motives of a motorist. Adam Seligman and colleagues would argue that hitchhikers therefore naively behaved as though the "social order" that was produced was a real one. In actuality, the world that rituals create is imperfect, temporary, make-believe, and risky.[168]

Female and male hitchhikers talked openly about sexual harassment and violence in cars with motorists. They knew that bad rides and risks were inherent parts of any journey. Jeremy Packer argues that many hitchhikers embraced the danger in order to prove that it was harmless.[169] A hitcher told me that his mother used to pull out the *Ottawa Citizen* and show him a statistic about "a hitchhiker whenever something bad happened." He would reply to her, "One hundred thousand trips went on, [and] you are going to show me one statistic?"[170]

In the mid-1970s the focus of the Canadian media shifted toward reports of sex crimes against hitchhikers and away from the exciting adventure stories of those who had survived the trip through Wawa in northern Ontario and discovered prairie thunderstorms and the beauty of the Rocky Mountains. At the same time, the adult world indulged a wider range of adolescent risk-taking behaviour than had earlier generations of parents, including looser dress codes, "the pill" for birth control, and soft drugs.[171] The Department of Health and Welfare's brochure *On the Road* told kids where to go. Inevitably, thumb-travellers received mixed messages. The police "frowned" on hitchhiking, but nobody in charge had any firm plans to make it illegal.[172] Statistics Canada did not collect data to show how many assaults, rapes, molestations, robberies, or killings began "innocently with a wagging thumb."[173]

The idea that sexual assault happened only to girls has never been supported by the evidence. Within the (hetero)normative construction of sexuality, boys' and men's bodies were also desired, fantasized about, and sexualized as they paraded and performed. One traveller told the *Winnipeg Free Press* that it did not matter whether a hitchhiker was "a delectable young thing in a mini-skirt or a long-haired youth ... There is a distinct chance the person will not reach his destination safely."[174] As a popular bumper sticker in the mid-1970s said, "Gas, Grass or Ass – Nobody Rides for Free." The "rules of the hitchhiking game" are such that sooner or later the hitchhiker will come to harm.[175] In 2014 I interviewed three women who had hitchhiked in the late 1970s. One said that the "coolest thing" about hitchhiking had been "that total sense of freedom." Another added, "You could literally just walk onto the road and get yourself anywhere in North America that you wanted to go." Her travelling companion said, "You never knew what sort of vehicle or driver was going to drive up." We all agreed that "it could be some beater truck, or a hot car, or a Mercedes, or it could be some bloody pervert."[176] Then and now, in the pages of Canada's newspapers, hitchhikers appear as dreamy ghosts whose message from beyond the grave is, "Don't hitchhike."[177]

# Conclusion
## The Vanishing Hitchhiker Eulogy

The world's hope lies in youth, Trudeau ...
told 400 delegates to a Canada World Youth
gathering [and] reminisced on his own youthful
days hitchhiking around the globe with a
packsack.

 – Globe and Mail *(1981)*

Times change. As one person said, "Kids
aren't travelling anymore because the right
songs aren't being sung."

 – *David Smith, "Hostelling Canada" (1976)*

**On July 27, 2014**, a child-sized robot named HitchBOT began a hitch-hiking adventure in Halifax; by the time it arrived in Victoria a month later, its global-positioning system indicated that it had hitchhiked 10,000 kilometres.[1] The next summer, it thumbed through Germany and the Netherlands.[2] By all accounts, motorists loved HitchBOT. They escorted it to art galleries, rock concerts, weddings, Brandenburg Gate, Neuschwanstein Castle, and a First Nations pow wow.[3] HitchBOT chatted with motorists, charming and engaging them with its knowledge of the entire *Wikipedia* library.[4] In July 2016 HitchBOT set out to discover

America, but sadly, a month later, its broken body was found in Philadelphia, pummelled, vandalized, and damaged beyond repair.[5]

HitchBOT was created by a team led by Professor David Smith of McMaster University in Hamilton. In a CBC interview, Smith said he had hitchhiked across the country several times in his youth. "For young people it used to be almost a rite of passage."[6] During HitchBOT's time on the road, its website was flooded with blogs from hitchhikers and motorists who shared their own road stories, nostalgia, self-reflection, tips, and wishes for a safe journey.[7] The outpouring of grief on social media following HitchBOT's violent demise lasted for weeks.[8] Nevertheless, HitchBOT's foes said that it was a "foolish experiment," with one headline reading, "HitchBOT Was a Literal Pile of Trash and Got What It Deserved."[9] For Smith and his colleagues, HitchBOT was a nostalgic social experiment: "Unfortunately ... sometimes bad things happen to good robots."[10] HitchBOT reminded its fans and foes of the legend of the vanishing hitchhiker and the darker side of sharing a ride.[11] Risk is an inherent part of every journey.[12]

Historical forms of youth mobility have included the tramp travel of preindustrial apprentices, the elite Grand Tours of Europe, "slumming" in late-Victorian cities, "tramping" in the countryside, the 1960s "Hippie Trail" crossings of South Asia, Pakistan, India, and Nepal, and Prince William's and Prince Harry's "gap year" volunteering adventures, as covered by social media.[13] In Canada the road stories of the 1930s and 1940s told by young people of many different social backgrounds contain accounts of sleeping in barns, haystacks, hedges, and hostels, not eating for days, wiring parents for money, and arriving home with "thin shoes and empty pockets" that are similar to the stories collected in my interviews with travellers of the baby boom era.[14] Depression-era prime minister R.B. Bennett was not the only leader of the country to give young hitchhikers his blessing. One of the most prominent hitchhiking role models was Pierre Elliott Trudeau. In the late 1960s he harnessed the enthusiasm of media-literate baby boomers with his vision of a "Just Society" and "participatory democracy."[15] A northern Ontario boy captured the excitement of Trudeaumania when he recalled, "Trudeau was our man ... We heard he liked canoeing and the outdoors. He was like us!"[16] For every generation, it was a lark to get from one place to another by begging rides, whether the transport was a wagon, railcar, motor vehicle, boat, or airplane. In 1970 the annual "communal pilgrimage" of freaks and lank-haired girls in blue jeans and backpacks became a fad and the focus of media attention and community intervention.[17] That hitchhiking continued to exist was a tribute to many Canadians' belief that mobility was a democratic right and that if a car owner freely consented to give a footloose traveller a lift, it was no business of the police or an insurance company.[18]

In tourism research, members of the hippie generation are called the "pioneers of alternative tourism."[19] The iconic image of the hippie hitchhiker resonates with modern backpackers and trekkers who wear the same hairstyles, tie-dyes, sandals, and knapsacks that their parents' and grandparents' generations wore.[20] Twenty-first-century "global nomads" are surprised to hear that only a couple of generations ago, their elders believed that taking a year off after high school or during college to travel was called dropping out or drifting around; it was the unorthodox behaviour of an alienated individual with "crazy hippie" ideas. Today, diverse forms of youth travel are encouraged for personal growth, self-enhancement, and the development of global consciousness.[21] "Gap years" are "self-imposed rites of passage" and excellent opportunities for young "pillars of society, on temporary leave from affluence," to accumulate cultural capital for future careers in the global marketplace.[22]

Cynthia Comacchio observes that the leisure time of youth tends to remain their own "only until some of its pieces are broken off and reintegrated into mainstream popular culture."[23] The idea of hitchhiking kiosks and free youth hostels sounds as good today as it must have in 1970. A federal youth travel program to strengthen "national unity through citizenship development" would be an excellent program for young people of any generation.[24] In this book, public concerns about the mobility of baby boom youth, skirmishes with neighbours, and the occupation of the Jericho Beach hostel have enabled us to see policy on youth leisure in action. In the 1970s youth mobility was promoted by federal travel programs as an ad hoc response to the problem of student unemployment and the inability of adults to provide real opportunities for youth.[25] The government assumed that middle-class youth had the cultural capital to appreciate cheap travel as the functional equivalent to real employment opportunities. Middle-class youth were offered heavily subsidized tuition, lucrative grants from the Opportunities for Youth program, and the chance to work and stay in the Independent Hostel Association's federally funded hostels.[26] Certainly, young people appreciated the government-funded lodgings, emergency medical services, legal advice, and hot meals provided to them at a time when hostelling and hitchhiking were their chosen lifestyle.[27]

In 1970 unprecedented intervention in youth travel affected the local gaze, and multigenerational anxiety about youth mobility played out in different ways. Texts that focus solely on youth resistance may be exciting to read because they enable us to applaud the actions of unique members of a generation, but Mona Gleason argues that this "agency trap" obscures our understanding of conforming and compliant youth, such as those students at the University of British Columbia and those hostellers who did not support the "People of Jericho."[28] Rebellious, revolutionary, and conservative youth subcultures arise when teenagers experience a contradiction between the society they discover and the one they were "led to believe" they would find.[29] The federal hostel program had numerous critics from across the political spectrum. Delegates at the National Youth Consultation in Sainte-Adèle, Quebec, in May 1970 were quick to point out that the paternalistic federal program reminded them of "the way the average North American father attempts to solve the conflict with his son by offering the car or tuition for yet another year of university."[30] A student at McGill University wondered whether the term "rip-off" had made its way into the Secretary of State's "groovy" new vernacular.[31] A student at Trent University said that the "ruling class" was using Opportunities for Youth to "capitalize on the new individualism" and to transform "middle-class youth into a subculture of freeloaders." Capitalists knew that there was nothing working people hated more "than a freeloader."[32] In the summer of 1970 at the University of British Columbia, many conservative and nonactivist students got caught up in a left-wing leaders' protest movement, and they protested against it. In the third report of the transient youth inquiry, *Transient Youth, 70–71* (1970), Lillian Thomson admitted that due to pressure to conform to countercultural values, the task force had hired youth hostel staff who could deal with "heads" but not "delinquents and greasers." Straight youth, greasers, and bikers felt left out completely, and federal hostels became perceived by mainstream travellers as places where "freaks felt at home and straights didn't."[33] The whole time, the "outdoorsie people" in the Canadian Youth Hostels Association thought that federal intervention was dubious, threatening, and unfair. A motorist dismayed by the "hairy-and-ragged cult" of hitchhikers who "look as if they had crawled out from under the nearest rock," asked fellow readers of the *Edmonton Journal*, "How does one sort out the PhD candidate from the Pothead?"[34]

In the youth tourism industry, alternative tourists, like backpackers, have a history of causing varying degrees of conflict within host communities. Darya Maoz's study of Israeli backpackers in India shows that in the "local eyes," backpackers embody "the most negative characteristics of Western culture" because they congregate in enclaves and engage in free and permissive behaviour, including experimentation with drugs and sexual freedom. Maoz identifies conscious and unconscious ways that tourists and locals maintain boundaries and negotiate the tourist experience, including "open resistance," which consists of protests, violence, and aggression by locals, and "veiled resistance," where locals manipulate and "stage authenticity," thereby selling the image of the culture that the young tourists expect to see.[35] In the late 1960s hitchhiking and hostelling caused a clash between the conservative mainstream "establishment" and "transient" youth. From the Atlantic to the Pacific, motorists and taxpayers complained about hitchhikers' panhandling, sleeping in parks and ditches, rock music, and indecent and illegal activity. The state used the hitchhiking fad for its own political gain and curried political capital among some young people, but manufacturing youth hostels instead of opportunities increased risk exposure for teenagers and young adults, who were encouraged to equate travelling with independence and enhanced life choices. In 1970 federal youth hostels were in effect staged "receiving centres" where a new generation of civil servants and youth workers could refer hostellers to job banks, education programs, family counselling, venereal disease clinics, psychiatric centres, and the police. The ultimate goal was to ease the transition of "all youth" – weekend hippies, teenyboppers, draft dodgers, black-leather-jacket types, and student radicals – back into society when they were ready to leave the road. The liberal tolerance inherent in these programs was directed largely at conservative ends, as seen in 1976 with the Secretary of State's merger of the hostels of the Independent Hostel Association and the Canadian Youth Hostels Association, which was constructed as the victorious return of order, structure, and discipline to youth culture.

In this book, the emphasis on the long sixties has introduced new figures into the historical study of baby boom youth. To understand what was happening in the lives of baby boomers, we need to be cognizant that the term "teenager" originally described a "white, Anglo-Saxon-Protestant, urban or suburban, male youth."[36] By the 1970s the good kid, who was "a compliant, gendered, heterosexual, middle-class ... contributor to society," could no longer be easily separated out from bad kids, radicals, idealists, delinquents, and dropouts.[37] Barbara Jane Brickman's work on the pathologization of the teen girl argues that it is no coincidence that in popular culture a "new adolescent" emerged as a disturber of the status quo; teenage girls asserted their disturbing potential, power, androgyny, and independence, which titillated, destabilized, and queered the stereotypes, fantasy, and nostalgia of adolescence.[38] The terminology of the day referred derogatively to "freaks," "heads," "nature freaks," "teenyboppers," "granola munchers," "hardhats," and "students." Elise Chenier argues that today in Canada, in their everyday efforts to preserve the ideal of the white, middle-class, traditional, heterosexual family as "the site for the production and reproduction of social and political norms," anxious parents, medical and legal experts, and politicians, fearful of a more sexually permissive culture, focus on dangerous strangers with an "insatiable sexual desire for young people."[39] Fear of strangers, dirty old men, and johns serves to bind children closer to home and places them under patriarchal authority and discipline. In Canada in the 1970s, the period of childhood innocence was extended to the age of eighteen and in some cases to twenty-five.[40] By the middle of the decade, police were warning motorists not to pick up hitchhikers, and locals condemned them, especially female hitchers, for tempting predatory adults.[41] The continuous sight of youth on the road reinforced the stereotype that teenagers were inherently lazy, unstable, immoral, and dangerous, which further institutionalized what Bernard Schissel calls the "politics of fear and hatred" and the "xenophobia collectively felt towards young people" in Canada that dominated in the late twentieth century.[42]

A nuanced understanding of agency enables us to see why rituals of youth subcultures make sense to those who choose to participate in them. For example, teenage drinking and driving, drug taking, unsafe sex, and school truancy are best interpreted in light of the meaning and value that young people give to them. With hindsight, we can see how the youth-transition theories of the 1960s and 1970s that predicted which youth were "at risk" reveal more about the "taken-for-granted prerequisites for adult achievement" than about the real lived experience of adolescence.[43] Peter Kelly uses the concept of "the entrepreneurial self," instead of the negative youth-at-risk discourse, because it is a productive, positive way to see how young people participate in their own socialization and identity construction.[44] In this research, hitchhikers did not see themselves as dropping out of society but as opting in – by embracing experience, personal autonomy, and self-awareness. For them, hitchhiking was not part of a deviant career but was an optimistic, participatory, physical experience that would improve the unity of mind and body and create a union of peers across the country.

Mona Gleason argues that "empathetic inference" enables scholars to imagine how conservative, radical, and rebellious youth subcultures perceive and reward risk.[45] When valorizing and applauding hitchhiking trips, we must be mindful of teenagers' naive belief in their power and capacity to control unpredictability and danger.[46] Conservative subcultures may use prejudice and negative behavioural labels drawn from their moral ideologies to justify their non-risk-taking activities, whereas rebellious subcultures embrace risky practices by describing them as self-affirming, playful, spontaneous, experimental, adventurous, communal, powerful, and transformative.[47] Tracing the codes and conventions that structured the telling of hitchhiking tales and ghostly folk narratives, as well as the conventions of standard journalism, shows that the teenage body was both the currency and at stake in processes by which bodies, mobilities, spaces, and nationalism – seeing the country – were made and remade. In the 1970s androgynous backpacks and hairstyles along with unisex blue jeans and T-shirts gave rise to the often-repeated phrase, "You can't tell the boys from the girls," which made both male and female hitchhikers fair game for the sexual perusal of passing motorists. The other side of the story is the judgments that adults make about youth risk taking.[48] Whether or not adults praised or condemned youth mobility as a fad, craze, or pointless rebellion, when the hitchhiking ritual failed and violence and abuse occurred, experts were called in to verify the traveller's inability to rationally recognize risk. Victims of bad rides faced further victimization by adults through disciplinary phrases like "I told you so" or "She'll never learn," which kept many silent.[49]

Any history of youth culture must confront the many moral panics linking youth to social problems, but the concept of a media-generated moral panic makes it difficult to see the real risks that kids faced on the road and the ability of young people with divergent values and opinions to overcome their own struggles and try to shape their own lives.[50] Children and youth of any generation have a right to expect to be able to count on their parents, teachers, and authority figures to guide them and to teach them the best way to conform to existing norms so that they can grow up safe and healthy. Academic scholarship on children's agency that applauds actions of resistance and rebellion against the status quo may unwittingly betray and fail to protect children's rights. Both Kristine Alexander and Mona Gleason have called for greater nuance in scholarly approaches to understanding agency.[51] David Lancy goes so far as to say that "work which wears, prominently, the 'Children's Agency' label" may be counterproductive to the best interests of the child and to genuine efficacy on behalf of young people and may not promote children's rights. Lancy asks, "If the essential ingredient in a campaign to extend agency to at-risk youth is enhanced choice and respect for their decisions and views, how do we respond when they cho[o]se to use drugs, steal, prostitute themselves or join gangs?"[52] For Lancy, "efficacy" can occur only when "someone older pays attention and responds to the child's needs" so as to elevate the child's "social position and power."[53] In the era of the "priceless" child, youth-friendly policies and hip jargon laid out the expectation for travellers to perform what Alexander calls "emotion work" for adults.[54] Hitchhiking guidebooks told travellers to perform for the delight of passing motorists: "Smile. Wave your arm. Look into the driver's eyes. Make yourself noticeable. Keep working ... Keep smiling and look like you are having a good time, dance and play, that's OK."[55] Cultural scripts such as this one tell children what is expected to please adults, especially men. It is difficult to talk about hitchhikers' choices and risk taking without falling into the agency trap.[56] Today, scholars like Elaine Sharland argue that it is time for us to step back and dissect what neoliberal – and, I suggest, neoconservative – adults, politicians, and policy makers in postmodern culture conceive of as acceptable and unacceptable levels of youth risk taking and what they regard as clearly "beyond the pale."[57]

Urban legends about ghostly, vanishing hitchhikers and classic "thumbsploitation" movies like *Thumb Tripping* (1972) and *The Texas Chain Saw Massacre* (1974) where innocent hitchhikers and unsuspecting motorists are humiliated, terrorized, or chopped up are a product of modernity.[58] Unlike other collective folklore, ghoulish highway tales could flourish only in a culture that saw nothing strange or exotic about long automobile trips, roadside pickups, and casual intimacy between friends and strangers met on the road.[59] Hitchhiking has been pronounced dead many times. In 1943 folklorists noticed that the legend of the vanishing hitchhiker was rarely told anymore.[60] In 1958 historian John T. Schlebecker said that the art of hitchhiking was practically dead.[61] In 2008 Jeremy Packer said "hitchhiking died in the mid-seventies" due to the "generation of fear, the application of surveillance, and a governmental appropriation."[62] The legend of the vanishing hitchhiker did not die. Folklorists assert that, "no matter how brief its popularity, nor how trivial its theme long after its disappearance ... it may emerge to give rise to a quite altered story."[63] In the 1970s the legend of the vanishing hitchhiker reappeared in popular culture to warn another generation about the dangers of hitchhiking. The moral of the story was still the same. A girl who compromised her "chastity" by hitchhiking was "punished for all eternity by trying desperately though to no avail to return to the sanctity of home."[64] Twenty-first-century hitchhiker Vanessa Veselka says the people she met on the road thought "I was either 'lucky to be alive' or so abysmally stupid for hitchhiking in the first place that I deserved to be dead."[65] Statistically and in the popular imagination, something terrible always happens to girls on the road. In 2004 the FBI started the Highway Serial Killers Initiative to attempt to account for girls and women who had gone missing.[66] The Royal Canadian Mounted Police are currently presumed to be investigating over five hundred unsolved highway murders, thirty-three of which, including Melissa Rehorek's, occurred between 1973 and 1981 on the Trans-Canada Highway and on Highway 16 between Prince Rupert and Prince George.[67] An investigation called the "Highway of Tears" is also focused on the disappearance and murders of mainly Aboriginal women and girls since 1969.[68]

Canada's latest hitchhiking "craze" ended in the late 1970s due to pressure on provincial and federal police to enforce restrictions against hitchhiking on highways and due to new municipal bylaws that banned hitchhiking in towns and cities. The commercial tourism sector increased the number of cheap alternatives for young passengers through student discounts and standby tickets on buses, trains, and airplanes. New ten-speed bicycles facilitated cycling across the country, and a new rite of passage and form of youth mobility was born. A positive legacy of the transient youth subculture has been the acceptance of the value of travel for young people, as evidenced by the institutionalization of the "gap year" between high school and university or college, semesters abroad, and travel experiences through volunteering. Modern studies of young tourists' perceptions of fear show that they deliberately seek out risky activities to enrich the experience, thrill, and excitement of travel.[69] Whether travelling alone or as the member of a school, church group, or youth club, young travellers return home with good and bad stories to tell.

In the late twentieth century, thousands of young Canadians became tourists, drifters, and wanderers in their own regions, provinces, and across the continent, where they put a new twist on coming of age through travel. Whether self-consciously adorning themselves with beads, feathers, Canadian flags, and long, bushy hair or flipping a peace sign to oncoming traffic, they performed symbolic rituals of a romantic subculture. The Canadian government's direct involvement in hitchhiking came to an end in 1977 with the announcement of a new youth program called Katimavik, meaning "meeting place." Katimavik is a six-month volunteer-work-travel program for English and French Canadians aged seventeen to twenty-one. Katimavik started with three simple rules: no sex, no drugs, and no hitchhiking.[70]

# Notes

## Chapter 1: Get Your Motor Running

1 Gary Barclay, "Hitch Bitch," *Georgia Straight* (Vancouver), July 29, 1970. See also "Province-Wide Hitch-Hike Ban Fails, Motion Called 'Absurd,' 'Idiotic,'" *The Martlet* (University of Victoria), September 23, 1971.

2 Letter from Rik Morgan, Faro, Northwest Territories, to Mayor Tom Campbell, Vancouver, August 22, 1970, City of Vancouver Public Records, 45-E-5, file 32, City of Vancouver Archives.

3 Ibid. At its height, in the early 1970s, *Mad* magazine had a circulation of over 2 million. See Jamie Lutton, "What, Me Worry? The Legacy of MAD Magazine," *Capitol Hill Times* (Seattle), September 11, 2013.

4 Paul DiMaggio, *The Hitchhiker's Field Manual* (London: Macmillan, 1973), 9.

5 Joel Finsel, "Set Forth," *Oxford American*, June 13, 2017, http://www.oxfordamerican. org/magazine/item/1245-set-forth.

6 Doug Owram, *Born at the Right Time: A History of the Baby-Boom Generation* (Toronto: University of Toronto Press, 1996), 181; Crystal Luxmore, "Vice, Vagabonds, and VD: The Skyrocketing Popularity of Hitchhiking during the Sixties and Seventies Led to a Generation of 'Modern Nomads,'" *The Walrus*, July 2008.

7 John T. Schlebecker, "An Informal History of Hitchhiking," *Historian* 20, 3 (1958): 311.

8 "Hitch-Hikes across Huron to Save Farm," *Toronto Globe*, January 30, 1935; "Hitch-Hikers – Even the Baby," *Globe and Mail*, August 1, 1938.

9 Jeremy Packer, *Mobility without Mayhem: Safety, Cars, and Citizenship* (Durham, NC: Duke University Press, 2008), 91. See also Lawrence Aronsen, *City of Love and Revolution: Vancouver in the Sixties* (Vancouver: New Star Books, 2010), 18; and Luxmore, "Vice, Vagabonds, and VD."

10 Barclay, "Hitch Bitch." Tom Campbell said, "If people haven't got money, they should stay home. Travelling is a luxury." See "Vancouver May Ban Hitchhiking," *Edmonton Journal*, July 18, 1970.

11 The term "transient youth" was coined during the National Youth Consultation in Sainte-Adèle, Quebec, in May 1970. See Canadian Welfare Council, *Transient Youth: Report of an Inquiry in the Summer of 1969* (Ottawa: Canadian Welfare Council, 1970), 5, 9–10.

12  Neil Sutherland, *Children in English-Canadian Society: Framing the Twentieth-Century Consensus* (Waterloo, ON: Wilfrid Laurier University Press, 2000), 4–7. See also Susan E. Houston, "The 'Waifs and Strays' of a Late-Victorian City: Juvenile Delinquents in Toronto," in *Childhood and Family in Canadian History*, ed. Joy Parr (Toronto: McClelland and Stewart, 1982), 130–34.

13  Lisa Colletta, "Introduction," in *The Legacy of the Grand Tour: New Essays on Travel, Literature, and Culture*, ed. Lisa Colletta (Madison, NJ: Fairleigh Dickinson University Press, 2015), x; John Towner, "The Grand Tour: A Key Phase in the History of Tourism," *Annals of Tourism Research* 12, 3 (1985): 297–333.

14  John Gillis, *Youth and History: Tradition and Change in European Age Relations, 1770–Present* (New York: Academic, 1974), 23–24.

15  Judith Adler, "Youth on the Road: Reflections on the History of Tramping," *Annals of Tourism Research* 12, 3 (1985): 339.

16  Ibid., 348. Youth in the 1960s did the same thing. Erik Cohen, "Nomads from Affluence: Notes on the Phenomenon of Drifter-Tourism," *International Journal of Comparative Sociology* 14, 1–2 (1973): 91.

17  Seth Koven, *Slumming: Sexual and Social Politics in Victorian London* (Princeton, NJ: Princeton University Press, 2004), 204. Seth Koven notes that, for some, slumming was a social experiment, an erotic expression of creativity, and the fulfillment of a desire for personal liberation, self-realization, and freedom. Ibid., 8, 149, 187. Ellen Ross argues that social work in slums provided women with freedom, duty, and gender autonomy. Ellen Ross, "Introduction: Adventures among the Poor," in *Slum Travelers: Ladies and London Poverty, 1860–1920*, ed. Ellen Ross (Berkeley: University of California Press, 2007), 16–17.

18  George Orwell, *The Road to Wigan Pier* (New York: Harcourt, Brace and Co., 1958), 185, quoted in Adler, "Youth on the Road," 350.

19  Quoted in Koven, *Slumming*, 148–49.

20  Ross, "Introduction," 26.

21  Linda Mahood, *Feminism and Voluntary Action: Eglantyne Jebb and Save the Children, 1876–1928* (London: Palgrave MacMillan, 2009), 120.

22  D. Owen Corrigan, *Juvenile Delinquency in Canada: A History* (Toronto: Irwin, 1998), 3–5, 61, 82. See also Ivy Pinchbeck and Margaret Hewitt, *Children in English Society*, vol. 2, *From the Eighteenth Century to the Children Act 1948* (London: Routledge and Kegan Paul, 1969).

23  Sarah Carter, *Aboriginal People and Colonizers of Western Canada to 1900* (1999; reprint, Toronto: University of Toronto Press, 2003), 164.

24  Adler, "Youth on the Road," 341, 342.

25  G. Stanley Hall, *Adolescence: Its Psychology and Its Relations to Physiology, Anthropology, Sociology, Sex, Crime, Religion and Education* (1904; reprint, New York: D. Appleton and Company, 1924), vol. 2, 377.

26  Gillis, *Youth and History*, 133; Cynthia Comacchio, *The Infinite Bonds of Family: Domesticity in Canada, 1850–1940* (Toronto: University of Toronto Press, 1999), 56.

27  Rolf E. Muuss, *Theories of Adolescence* (New York: Random House, 1964), 56–57.

28  Cited in Linda Mahood, *Policing Gender, Class and Family: Britain, 1850–1940* (London: UCL Press, 1995), 3–5.

29 Skott-Myhre describes "modern youth work" as a field that is "deeply shaped by the development and construction of ideas and 'truths' about youth or adolescents ... These ideas have not only shaped the world of adolescence, but also the world of the youth worker." Hans Arthur Skott-Myhre, *Youth and Subculture as Creative Force: Creating New Spaces for Radical Youth Work* (Toronto: University of Toronto Press, 2008), 124.

30 Marcel Danesi, *Geeks, Goths, and Gangstas: Youth Culture and the Evolution of Modern Society* (Toronto: Canadian Scholars' Press, 2010), 15; Elaine Sharland, "Young People, Risk Taking and Risk Making: Some Thoughts for Social Work," *Forum: Qualitative Social Research* 7, 1 (2006): 2, http://www.qualitative-research.net/index.php/fqs/article/view/56/116; David Dobbs, "Beautiful Teen Brains," *National Geographic*, October 2011.

31 Peter Stearns and Timothy Haggerty, "The Role of Fear: Transitions in American Emotional Standards for Children, 1850–1950," *American Historical Review* 96, 1 (1991): 66. As early as 1831, abolitionist and suffragist Lydia Child offered mothers this advice: "A child made afraid of spider bites may get bitten just as easily as a child who had not been warned, while at the same time bites are not nearly as bad as a fear that troubles one all life long. Still more obvious, the temptation to use dire warning about old men prowling about to steal infants, however well intentioned by a mother concerned about safety, must be resisted, for they might embitter the whole existence of her offspring." Ibid.

32 Deborah Gorham, *The Victorian Girl and the Feminine Ideal* (London: Croom Helm, 1982), 97, 112–13. See also Carol Dyhouse, *Girls Growing Up in Late Victorian and Edwardian England* (London: Routledge, 1981).

33 Gillis, *Youth and History*, 141.

34 Erik Erikson, *Childhood and Society* (New York: Norton, 1963), 262; Erik Erikson, *Identity: Youth and Crisis* (New York: Norton, 1968), 172, 174.

35 Cynthia Comacchio, *The Dominion of Youth: Adolescence and the Making of Modern Canada, 1920 to 1950* (Waterloo, ON: Wilfrid Laurier University Press, 2006), 32.

36 Ann Hulbert, *Raising America: Experts, Parents and a Century of Advice about Children* (New York: Vintage Books, 2004), 14 (quote), 227–29.

37 Veronica Strong-Boag, *The New Day Recalled: Lives of Girls and Women in English Canada, 1919–1939* (Toronto: Copp-Clark, 1993), 28. Following the First World War, touring in open spaces of "free nature" was experienced through groups such as the German Wandervogel (literally "wandering bird"), the Boy Scouts, and the Girl Guides. Cohen, "Nomads from Affluence," 91.

38 Stanley Cohen, *Folk Devils and Moral Panics: The Creation of the Mods and Rockers* (1972; reprint, London: Routledge, 2002), 2.

39 David Fowler, *Youth Culture in Modern Britain, c. 1920–c. 1970: From Ivory Tower to Global Movement – A New History* (London: Palgrave Macmillan, 2008), 4. See also Hulbert, *Raising America*, 227–29.

40 Cynthia Comacchio, "Dancing to Perdition: Adolescence and Leisure in Interwar English Canada," *Journal of Canadian Studies* 32, 3 (1997): 4.

41 David Monaghan, *Canada's "New Main Street": The Trans-Canada Highway as Ideal and Reality, 1912–1956* (Ottawa: Canadian Science and Technology Museum, 2002),

40, 76, 80; Mathieu Turgeon and François Vaillancourt, "The Provision of Highways in Canada and the Federal Government," *Publius* 32, 1 (2002): 163.

42  Monaghan, *Canada's "New Main Street,"* 44, 48; Turgeon and Vaillancourt, "Provision of Highways," 164.

43  Murray Milner Jr., *Freaks, Geeks and Cool Kids: American Teenagers, Schools, and the Culture of Consumption* (New York: Routledge, 2004), 4. Murray Milner Jr. adds that although adults may complain about teenagers' materialism and consumerism, they are hesitant to exercise control or authority over the way young people organize their lives.

44  Tamara Myers, "Didactic Sudden Death: Children, Police, and Teaching Citizenship in the Age of Automobility," *Journal of the History of Childhood and Youth* 8, 3 (2015): 451. See also James J. Flink, *The Automobile Age* (Cambridge, MA: MIT Press, 1990), 1–55; Rudi Volti, "A Century of Automobility," *Technology and Culture* 37, 4 (1996): 663–85.

45  Mimi Sheller, "Automotive Emotions: Feeling the Car," *Theory, Culture and Society* 21, 4–5 (2004): 211.

46  June Edmunds and Bryan S. Turner, "Introduction," in *Generational Consciousness, Narrative, and Politics,* ed. June Edmunds and Bryan S. Turner (Lanham, MD: Rowman and Littlefield, 2002), 6.

47  Mike Brake, *Comparative Youth Culture: The Sociology of Youth Cultures and Youth Subcultures in America, Britain and Canada* (New York: Routledge, 1985), 18.

48  Sheller, "Automotive Emotions," 221.

49  "Youth Going Nowhere in Search of Adventure," *Globe and Mail,* July 18, 1970; "Thousands of Youngsters Will Be on the Road This Summer," *Montreal Gazette,* August 25, 1970; Martin Dorrell, "A Really Big Bedroom," *Globe and Mail,* June 14, 1971; "City Braced for Transients," *Calgary Herald,* May 17, 1972; "Army of Hitch-Hikers Already on the March," *Globe and Mail,* June 22, 1972.

50  "Hostel Program Remains," *Penticton Herald,* May 21, 1971, News Clippings, British Columbia, 1967, 1970–1971, 1977, M7832, file 268, Canadian Youth Hostels Association, Glenbow Museum Archives, Calgary (hereafter CYHA-GMA). For many, the Mecca of their journey was "Canada's Los Angeles, the almost sunny city of Vancouver." "The Hitchhikers," *Globe and Mail,* August 10, 1970.

51  Owram, *Born at the Right Time.*

52  "Canada's Great Trek: 40,000 Transients Will Walk This Summer," *Vancouver Province,* April 6, 1971, News Clippings, British Columbia, 1967, 1970–1971, 1977, M7832, file 268, CYHA-GMA.

53  Canadian Council on Social Development, *Transient Youth, 70–71: Report of an Inquiry about Programs in 1970, and Plans for 1971* (Ottawa: Department of Health and Welfare, 1970); Matt Cavers, "Dollars for 'Deadbeats': Opportunities for Youth Grants and the Back-to-the-Land Movement on British Columbia's Sunshine Coast," in *Canadian Countercultures and the Environment,* ed. Colin M. Coates (Calgary: University of Calgary Press, 2016), 179–81.

54  Quoted in Jane Desmond, *Staging Tourism: Bodies on Display from Waikiki to Sea World* (Chicago: University of Chicago Press, 1999), xx. John Urry's concept of the

"tourist gaze" is developed in Phil Macnaghten and John Urry, eds., *Bodies of Nature* (London: Sage, 2001).

55 Desmond, *Staging Tourism*, xx.

56 Ibid. David Crouch and Luke Desforges say "sensuous" tourist encounters include metaphors, performance, the encounter, dwelling, embodiment, and negotiation with the unexpected. David Crouch and Luke Desforges, "The Sensuous in the Tourist Encounter," *Tourist Studies* 3, 1 (2003): 7, 10.

57 John Urry, *The Tourist Gaze: Leisure and Travel in Contemporary Societies* (London: Sage, 2002). The individual, solitary gaze is the romantic gaze, and the collective gaze is levelled at sights and events where crowds of fellow gazers add to the experience. Erving Goffman, *The Presentation of Self in Everyday Life* (New York: Doubleday, 1961).

58 Victor Turner, *The Ritual Process: Structure and Anti-Structure* (1969; reprint, New Brunswick, NJ: Transaction, 2008), 95.

59 Cohen, "Nomads from Affluence," 93. Dean MacCannell defines "contrived authenticity" as what host communities choose to show to travellers. Dean MacCannell, "Staged Authenticity: Arrangements of Social Space in Tourist Settings," *American Journal of Sociology* 79, 3 (1973): 593. In 1973 MacCannell observed that in the industrial West commercial establishments "went hippie" to prepare for the influx of hip young tourists seeking natural experiences. Ibid., 597.

60 Amie Matthews, "Young Backpackers and the Rite of Passage of Travel: Examining the Transformative Effects of Liminality," in *Travel and Transformation*, ed. Garth Lean, Russell Staiff, and Emma Waterton (Surrey, UK: Ashgate, 2014), 160. Chandra Mukerji links hitchhiking adventures and telling road stories to performance and play. Chandra Mukerji, "Bullshitting: Road Lore among Hitchhikers," *Social Problems* 25, 3 (1978): 242–43.

61 Chaim Noy, "Performing Identity: Touristic Narratives of Self-Change," *Text and Performance Quarterly* 24, 2 (2004): 146.

62 Richard Ivan Jobs, *Backpack Ambassadors: How Youth Travel Integrated Europe* (Chicago: University of Chicago Press, 2017), 184.

63 Torun Elsrud, "Risk Creation in Travelling: Backpacker Adventure Narration," *Annals of Tourism Research* 28, 3 (2001): 598, 599–600.

64 Darya Maoz, "The Mutual Gaze," *Annals of Tourism Research* 33, 1 (2005): 229. See also Darya Maoz, "The Conquerors and the Settlers: Two Groups of Young Israeli Backpackers in India," in *The Global Nomad: Backpacker Travel in Theory and Practice*, ed. Greg Richards and Julie Wilson (Clevedon, UK: Channel View, 2004), 115–16.

65 Maoz, "Mutual Gaze," 222, 225.

66 Greg Richards and Julie Wilson, "Drifting towards the Global Nomad," in *The Global Nomad: Backpacker Travel in Theory and Practice*, ed. Greg Richards and Julie Wilson (Clevedon, UK: Channel View, 2004), 6; Anders Sørensen, "Backpacker Ethnography," *Annals of Tourism Research* 30, 4 (2003): 853; Kate Simpson, "Dropping Out or Signing Up? The Professionalization of Youth Travel," *Antipode* 37, 3 (2005): 448.

67 Sharland, "Young People," 3.

68 Comacchio, *Dominion of Youth*, viii, 216.

69 The research for this book included a content analysis of hitchhiking and youth-hostelling stories published in the *Toronto Star, Globe and Mail, Montreal Gazette, Vancouver Province, Vancouver Sun, Calgary Herald, Winnipeg Free Press, Winnipeg Tribune, Edmonton Journal, London Free Press, Windsor Star, Saskatoon Star Phoenix, Regina Leader-Post, Charlottetown Guardian, Penticton Morning Star,* and popular American and Canadian magazines like *Reader's Digest, Good Housekeeping, Saturday Night,* and *Maclean's.*

70 Julian A. Compagni Portis, "Thumbs Down: America and the Decline of Hitchhiking" (Honor's thesis, Wesleyan University, 2015), 16, http://wesscholar.wesleyan.edu/etd_hon_theses/1427.

71 James Pitsula, *New World Dawning: The Sixties at Regina Campus* (Regina: University of Regina Press, 2008), 3. See also Cyril Levitt, *Children of Privilege: Student Revolt in the Sixties: A Study of Student Movements in Canada, the United States, and West Germany* (Toronto: University of Toronto Press, 1984), 3–4.

72 Charles Levi, "Sex, Drugs, Rock & Roll, and the University College Lit: The University of Toronto Festivals, 1965–69," *Historical Studies in Education* 18, 2 (2006): 163–64. See also Michiel Horn, "Students and Academic Freedom in Canada," *Historical Studies in Education* 11, 1 (1999): 5.

73 "Universities Form Own Press Service," *Montreal Gazette,* January 17, 1938. Campus newspapers include *The Gateway* (University of Alberta), *The Gauntlet* (University of Calgary), *The Meliorist* (University of Lethbridge), *The Ubyssey* (University of British Columbia), *The Peak* (Simon Fraser University), *The Manitoban* (University of Manitoba), *The Muse* (Memorial University), *The Dalhousie Gazette* (Dalhousie University), *The Charlatan* (Carleton University), *The Sheaf* (University of Saskatchewan), *The Chevron* (University of Waterloo), *The Martlet* (University of Victoria), and *The Projector* (Red River College). Finally, Vancouver's alternative weekly, the *Georgia Straight,* contained extensive coverage of the occupation at the Jericho Beach youth hostel and posted messages from friends and families searching for missing persons and runaways.

74 For example, see DiMaggio, *Hitchhiker's Field Manual;* and David Rideout and Ray Amiro, *Handbook Canada: A Traveller's Manual* (Toronto: Transglobular Functions, 1972).

75 Stanley Cohen, *Visions of Social Control: Crime, Punishment and Classification* (Cambridge, UK: Polity, 1985), 40, 41.

76 Canadian Welfare Council, *Transient Youth;* Canadian Council on Social Development, *More about Transient Youth* (Ottawa: Canadian Council on Social Development, 1970); Canadian Council on Social Development, *Transient Youth, 70–71;* Canadian Council on Social Development, *Youth '71: An Inquiry into the Transient Youth and Opportunities for Youth Programs in the Summer of 1971* (Ottawa: Department of Health and Welfare, 1972).

77 Canada, Secretary of State, Committee on Youth, *It's Your Turn: A Report to the Secretary of State by the Committee on Youth* (Ottawa: Information Canada, 1971); Canada, Department of Health and Welfare, *On the Road: A Guide for Youth Travelling Canada* (Ottawa: Department of Health and Welfare, 1972).

78  RCMP, "National Hostel Task Force, Vancouver, B.C.," September 30, 1970, National Force, Correspondence etc., 70HQ, 559-E-4, provided to Patrick Esmonde-White under the Access to Information Act.

79  Lynn Abrams, *Oral History Theory* (London: Routledge, 2010); Donald Richie, *Doing Oral History: A Practical Guide* (New York: Oxford University Press, 2003); Anna Sheftel and Stacey Zembrzycki, eds., *Oral History Off the Record: Toward an Ethnography of Practice* (New York: Palgrave Macmillan, 2013).

80  Stuart Henderson writes that "media construct events and frame them ... not from scratch but out of ideologies interconnected with the general common sense of the society in which they are based." Stuart Henderson, *Making the Scene: Yorkville and Hip Toronto in the 1960s* (Toronto: University of Toronto Press, 2011), 25.

81  Schlebecker, "Informal History," 306; Packer, *Mobility without Mayhem*, 110.

82  Stephen Davis, "'Reckless Walking Must Be Discouraged': The Automobile Revolution and the Shaping of Modern Urban Canada to 1930," *Urban History Review/Revue d'histoire urbaine* 18, 2 (1989): 123–24, 134.

83  In many cultures, the "thumbs up" gesture does not mean "okay" but is considered an obscene sexual insult. One book advised Western hitchhikers to carefully investigate local hitchhiking culture, noting that outside the West, most hitchhikers loosely wave a hand or use a flat hand gesture when hailing a ride. Desmond Morris, Peter Collett, Peter Marsh, and Marie O'Shaughnessy, *Gestures: Their Origin and Meanings* (London: Jonathan Cape, 1979), http://lecschool.com.br/v1/biblioteca/EDUGesturesTheirOrigin andMeanings.pdf.

84  Graeme Chesters and David Smith, "The Neglected Art of Hitch-Hiking: Risk, Trust and Sustainability," *Sociological Research Online* 6, 3 (2001): sec. 1.2; Cohen, "Nomads from Affluence," 90.

85  As Tim Edensor notes: "This praxis emerged out of an eighteenth-century European romanticism which reacted against the first signs of industrialisation and chose as its object that which was, by contrast, conceived as natural, traditional and authentic. This anti-modern sentiment was inspired by the classical and renaissance sights of the Grand Tour, the sublime and pantheistic realm of 'nature,' and the figure of the 'noble savage.'" For Romantic poets such as William Wordsworth, memories of nature made "the clamour and chaos of the modern world" survivable. *Tourists at the Taj: Performance and Meaning at a Symbolic Site* (London: Routledge, 1998), 136–37.

86  Michael O'Regan, "Alternative Mobility Cultures and the Resurgence of Hitch-Hiking," in *Slow Tourism: Experiences and Mobilities*, ed. Simone Fullagar, Kevin Markwell, and Erica Wilson, 128–42 (Bristol, UK: Channel View, 2012).

87  Nelson Graburn, "The Anthropology of Tourism," *Annals of Tourism Research* 10, 1 (1983): 11.

88  Camille Caprioglio O'Reilly, "From Drifter to Gap Year Tourist: Mainstreaming Backpacker Travel," *Annals of Tourism Research* 33, 4 (2006): 1003.

89  Mukerji, "Bullshitting," 250. Elsrud states that although risks in travelling are at times true, "mythology is vital to narrative survival ... Risk taking can be a device to construct a story." Elsrud, "Risk Creation," 599–600.

90  Packer, *Mobility without Mayhem*, 90.

91  Chaim Noy, "Travelling for Masculinity: The Construction of Bodies/Spaces in Israeli Backpackers' Narratives," in *Tourism and Gender: Embodiment, Sensuality and Experience*, ed. Annette Pritchard, Nigel Morgan, Irena Ateljevic, and Candice Harris (Wallingford, UK: CABI, 2007), 67.

92  Mimi Sheller and John Urry, "The City and the Car," *International Journal of Urban and Regional Research* 24, 4 (2000): 748.

93  Elsrud, "Risk Creation," 602.

94  Vanessa Veselka, "Green Screen: The Lack of Female Road Narratives and Why It Matters," *American Reader* 1, 4 (2012): 9–10. For girls, there was no sowing wild oats or coming of age "narrative outside of victimization and violence." Ibid., 13.

95  Leslie Paris reminds us of the fluidity of age itself by defining it as a "historically contingent system of power relations and cultural expectations." Leslie Paris, "Through the Looking Glass: Age, Stages, and Historical Analysis," *Journal of the History of Childhood and Youth* 1, 1 (2008): 107. Lesley Anders and Joanne Wynn argue that historical events shape adolescence, making youth an artefact of government policies intended to monitor and smooth the transition of young people from education to employment so that each generation can contribute to Canada's economic growth. Lesley Anders and Joanne Wynn, *The Making of a Generation: The Children of the 1970s in Adulthood* (Toronto: University of Toronto Press), 30.

96  Paul Bennett, "Campus Life in Canada's 1960s: Reflections on the 'Radical Campus' in Recent Historical Writing," *Acadiensis* 42, 2 (2013): 1. For a focus on leisure rather than political engagement, see Arthur Marwick, *The Sixties: Cultural Revolution in Britain, France, Italy and the United States, c. 1958–c. 1974* (Oxford: Oxford University Press, 1998); and Pitsula, *New World Dawning*, 1–131.

97  Lara Campbell, Dominique Clément, and Gregory S. Kealey, eds., *Debating Dissent: Canada and the 1960s* (Toronto: University of Toronto Press, 2012), 6–7, original emphasis.

98  Thomas Hine, *The Rise and Fall of the American Teenager* (New York: Harper Perennial, 2000). Crime and recidivism rates for people born in 1958 show that they were 80 percent more likely than previous generations of convicts to commit multiple crimes, and 80 percent more likely to send their victim to the hospital or morgue. William Strauss and Neil Howe, *Generations: The History of America's Future, 1584–2069* (New York: William Morrow, 1991), 305–6, 310–11.

99  Canadian Welfare Council, *Transient Youth*, 5.

100  Bryan D. Palmer, *Canada's 1960s: The Ironies of Identity in a Rebellious Era* (Toronto: University of Toronto Press, 2009), 304–5.

101  Henderson, *Making the Scene*, 216.

102  "Youth Going Nowhere in Search of Adventure," *Globe and Mail*, July 18, 1970.

103  Sociologist Cyril Levitt has challenged the popular stereotype of the 1960s radical as the product of a collective neurosis of baby boom youth. Instead, he situates the movement in the broader economic and social contexts as "a revolt of privilege against privilege," a battle "for privilege in a society in which the character of privilege had been changing." Levitt, *Children of Privilege*, 4.

04  Strauss and Howe, *Generations*, 311. Psychologists of aging Abigail Stewart and Cynthia Torges note that the dramatic social events of the 1960s and 1970s were the context for the development of the future expectations of late boomers, whereas for early boomers these events contributed to their identity and consequently helped them to form their political commitments. Stewart and Torges also stress that the late boomers were "engaged observers" of the Vietnam War and the civil rights movement. They were interested, concerned, and attentive but were too young to have been active or mobilized like the early boomers. Abigail Stewart and Cynthia Torges, "Social, Historical, and Developmental Influences on the Psychology of the Baby Boom at Midlife," in *The Baby Boomers Grow Up: Contemporary Perspectives on Midlife*, ed. Susan Krauss Whitbourne and Sherry Willis (Mahwah, NJ: Lawrence Erlbaum Associates, 2006), 27–28, 32. See also Karen Fingerman and Megan Dolbin-MacNab, "The Baby Boomers and Their Parents: Cohort Influences and Intergenerational Ties," in *The Baby Boomers Grow Up: Contemporary Perspectives on Midlife*, ed. Susan Krauss Whitbourne and Sherry Willis (Mahwah, NJ: Lawrence Erlbaum Associates, 2006), 237–60.

5  Canada, Secretary of State, Committee on Youth, *It's Your Turn*, 7. The Canadian Welfare Council's inquiry on transient youth described the youth in question as between thirteen and twenty-two years of age. Canadian Welfare Council, *Transient Youth*, 1.

6  Samuel Zeidman, "Thumb Fun!" *Review of Reviews* 95 (April 1937): 55–56.

7  Canadian Welfare Council, *Transient Youth*.

### Chapter 2: Thumb Wars

1  "Boys' Journey to Florida Ends: Three from Port Erie Are Returned to Their Homes," *Globe and Mail*, March 8, 1937.

2  Studies of runaway children in the Depression and war years show that in well-adjusted children, "runaway behaviour was relatively benign." Robert Shellow, Juliana Schamp, Elliot Liebow, and Elizabeth Unger, "Suburban Runaways of the 1960s," *Monographs of the Society for Research in Child Development* 32, 3 (1967): 3. See also Karen Staller, "Constructing the Runaway Youth Problem: Boy Adventurers to Girl Prostitutes, 1960–1978," *Journal of Communication* 53, 2 (2003): 331.

3  John T. Schlebecker, "An Informal History of Hitchhiking," *Historian* 20, 3 (1958): 331.

4  "Just Kids Safety Club: Here's Where We Meet," *Toronto Globe*, July 9, 1932.

5  Under the federal Juvenile Delinquents Act (1908), a child or young person could be legally censured for noncriminal behaviours such as truancy, wandering, and loitering, as well as for engaging in "adult" practices, particularly gambling, drinking, smoking, and sex. Cynthia Comacchio, *The Infinite Bonds of Family: Domesticity in Canada, 1850–1940* (Toronto: University of Toronto Press, 1999), 29.

6  Alan Gordon, *Time Travel: Tourism and the Rise of the Living History Museum in Mid-Twentieth-Century Canada* (Vancouver: UBC Press, 2016), 83; Donald F. Davis, "Dependent Motorization: Canada and the Automobile to the 1930s," *Journal of Canadian Studies* 21, 3 (1986): 122; Stephen Davis, "'Reckless Walking Must Be

Discouraged': The Automobile Revolution and the Shaping of Modern Urban Canada to 1930," *Urban History Review/Revue d'histoire urbaine* 18, 2 (1989): 133.

7   Mathieu Turgeon and François Vaillancourt, "The Provision of Highways in Canada and the Federal Government," *Journal of Federalism* 32, 1 (2002): 162; David Monaghan, *Canada's "New Main Street": The Trans-Canada Highway as Ideal and Reality, 1912–1956* (Ottawa: Canadian Science and Technology Museum, 2002), 7–11.

8   Monaghan, *Canada's "New Main Street,"* 48.

9   Turgeon and Vaillancourt, "Provision of Highways," 163; Monaghan, *Canada's "New Main Street,"* 15–16, 50.

10   Turgeon and Vaillancourt, "Provision of Highways," 164.

11   Gordon, *Time Travel,* 83.

12   Alisa Apostle, "The Display of a Tourist Nation: Canada in Government Film, 1945–1959," *Journal of the Canadian Historical Association* 12, 1 (2001): 180–81. See also Michael Dawson, "A Civilizing Industry: Leo Dolan, Canadian Tourism Promotion, and the Celebration of Mass Culture," *American Review of Canadian Studies* 41, 4 (2011): 440.

13   Monaghan, *Canada's "New Main Street,"* 40, 76, 80; Turgeon and Vaillancourt, "Provision of Highways," 163.

14   In the 1940s everyone emphasized the tourism potential of Canada's "new main street." Revenue from increased tourism traffic in 1948–49 from American tourists was $450 million, making tourism one of Canada's primary export industries. Monaghan, *Canada's "New Main Street,"* 49.

15   "Scouting and Hitch-Hiking," *Toronto Globe,* July 5, 1935.

16   Davis, "Dependent Motorization," 127.

17   Davis, "'Reckless Walking,'" 124.

18   Jane Nicholas, *The Modern Girl: Feminine Modernities, the Body, and Commodities in the 1920s* (Toronto: University of Toronto Press, 2015), 185.

19   Quoted in Davis, "'Reckless Walking,'" 129.

20   Quoted in Tamara Myers, "Didactic Sudden Death: Children, Police, and Teaching Citizenship in the Age of Automobility," *Journal of the History of Childhood and Youth* 8, 3 (2015): 456.

21   Comacchio, *Infinite Bonds of Family,* 163.

22   Mimi Sheller and John Urry, "The City and the Car," *International Journal of Urban and Regional Research* 24, 4 (2000): 747.

23   Mike Featherstone, "Automobiles: An Introduction," *Theory, Culture and Society* 21, 4–5 (2004): 13–14; Sheller and Urry, "City and the Car," 743, 749.

24   Davis, "'Reckless Walking,'" 134.

25   Quoted in Myers, "Didactic Sudden Death," 456.

26   Lara Campbell, *Respectable Citizens: Gender, Family, and Unemployment in Ontario's Great Depression* (Toronto: University of Toronto Press, 2009), 115. Lara Campbell adds, "In the 1930s the growth and development of mass culture in its various forms coexisted with local or familial-based culture and leisure, and this was especially so at a time when money was tight ... Both grassroots and local culture, along with mass culture, played a role in shaping the lives of youth in this period."

7   Erik Cohen, "Nomads from Affluence: Notes on the Phenomenon of Drifter-Tourism," *International Journal of Comparative Sociology* 14, 1–2 (1973): 91.

8   "A Canadian's Journey: Hitch-Hiking Round the World," *Scotsman* (Edinburgh), September 14, 1928.

9   Edward Jewitt Wheeler, "A Studious Hitch-Hiker Looks at Hitch-Hiking," *Literary Digest*, May 16, 1931, 43, 44.

0   H.L. Verry, "Hitch-Hiking in England: Good-Humored British Motorists Carry Scores of Youths along Open Road," *New York Times*, July 23, 1939, 29.

1   Richard Ivan Jobs, *Backpack Ambassadors: How Youth Travel Integrated Europe* (Chicago: University of Chicago Press, 2017), 15–18; Anton Grassl and Graham Heath, *The Magic Triangle: A Short History of the World Youth Hostel Movement* (Welwyn Garden City, UK: International Youth Hostel Federation, 1982).

2   Verry, "Hitch-Hiking in England," 29.

3   "Young Hitch-Hikers Have Bennett's Blessing," *Toronto Globe*, July 27, 1934, 18.

4   "Young Hikers Reach Pacific," *Globe and Mail*, July 26, 1937, 11.

5   "Hitchhiking Is a Risky Job: Globe-Trotting 'Knight of the Road' Tells of Many Hazards," *Globe and Mail*, August 31, 1937, 10.

6   "Travels 40,000 Miles, But Pays Nothing: Gananoque Youth, Who Has Seen Many Countries, Returns to Home of His Parents," *Globe and Mail*, February 28, 1938, 4.

7   "Around the World Hitchhiking," *Stouffville Tribune*, April 30, 1936, 1; "Hitchhiking Round the World: The Toll Brothers," *Toronto Globe*, April 15, 1936, 2; "A Wonderful Travelogue," *Kingsville Reporter*, October 15, 1936, 1.

8   Heidi MacDonald, "Being in Your Twenties, in the Thirties: Liminality and Masculinity during the Great Depression," in *Bringing Children and Youth into Canadian History*, ed. Mona Gleason and Tamara Myers (Toronto: Oxford University Press, 2017), 156.

9   Vanessa Veselka, "Green Screen: The Lack of Female Road Narratives and Why It Matters," *American Reader* 1, 4 (2012): 1–3.

0   Schlebecker, "Informal History," 306, 310. For example, nineteen-year-old Linda Folkard of Toronto was crowned "Miss Hitchhiker of 1946." Ibid., 320.

1   "Runaway-Girl Total in City High This Year: 76 under 16 Years and Double This Number over Age 16," *Globe and Mail*, August 25, 1938, 15.

2   Quoted in Carol Sanger, "Girls and the Getaway: Cars, Culture, and the Predicament of Gendered Space," *University of Pennsylvania Law Review* 144, 2 (1995): 712.

3   Ibid.

4   "Adventurous Trip Hiking across Persia Described by Woman: Miss Lillian Schroedler Startled the Natives by Driving Own Car," *Toronto Globe*, February 4, 1930, 16.

5   "'L.A.' Was the Cry of Two Hiking Vancouver Girls," *Vancouver Sun*, September 1, 1924, in Henrietta Lethbridge Watson Nickel, "Scrapbook," in private possession of the Bohun family, Calgary and Nanoose Bay, Vancouver Island.

6   Katharine Götsch-Trevelyan, *Unharboured Heaths* (London: Selwyn and Blount, 1934), 10. See also "Hon. Katharine Trevelyan Hitchhiking across Canada," *Toronto Globe*, May 10, 1930.

7   Götsch-Trevelyan, *Unharboured Heaths*, 164.

8   Ibid., 88.

49  Sheller and Urry, "City and the Car," 749.

50  "23-Year-Old Girl Reaches Montreal after Hitchhiking from Victoria," *Globe and Mail*, August 30, 1939.

51  "Travelling via Thumb, Joyce Hill on West Coast," *Newmarket Era and Express*, August 23, 1945, 1; "Girl Hiker Returns from Trip to West," *Newmarket Era and Express*, September 27, 1945, 1; Samuel Zeidman, "Thumb Fun!" *Review of Reviews* 95 (April 1937): 56.

52  Wheeler, "Studious Hitch-Hiker," 44. See also Loring A. Schuler, "He Thumbed His Way through College," *Reader's Digest*, June 1941.

53  "Travelling via Thumb, Joyce Hill On West Coast," *Newmarket Era and Express*, August 23, 1945, 1.

54  Lenny Burton and Johnny Cochrane, "Our Passport Was a Dishrag," *Maclean's*, May 1, 1952, 22–23, 31–32.

55  Ibid., 30–31.

56  Ruth Latta, *They Tried: The Story of the Canadian Youth Congress* (Ottawa: Ruth Latta, 2006), 1, 64.

57  "Any Mode of Travel Welcome as Youth Head for Congress," *Globe and Mail*, June 22, 1939.

58  Ibid.

59  Cited in Latta, *They Tried*, 88.

60  "Toronto Youth Thumbs in 8 Days Way to Edmonton," *Globe and Mail*, July 17, 1938.

61  Other items on the agenda were trade unions and the United Nations. "Hitchhiking CCF Youth Will Talk in $$ Billions at Winnipeg Session," *Globe and Mail*, August 12, 1948, 15.

62  "Undergrads Hitch-Hike with Protest Petitions," *Globe and Mail*, April 15, 1939.

63  Judith Adler, "Youth on the Road: Reflections on the History of Tramping," *Annals of Tourism Research* 12, 3 (1985): 337.

64  Moreover, this fear "betrays a failure to remember that mobility is ... a democratic 'right.'" Sheller and Urry, "City and the Car," 741.

65  Bill Waiser, *All Hell Can't Stop Us: The On-to-Ottawa Trek and Regina Riot* (Calgary: Fifth House, 2003), 2.

66  Wayne Roberts, "Hobos and Songsters: Working Class Culture," *Oral History Forum/ Forum d'histoire orale* 7 (1984): 24–36.

67  John Stewart, "The Hobo Jungle in Kamloops," City of Kamloops, History Archive, http://www.kamloops.ca; Edmund Francis, "Why? The Diary of a Camp Striker: A Year of a Young British Columbian's Life in Canada's Relief Compounds," 1935, quoted in James Struthers, *No Fault of Their Own: Unemployment and the Canadian Welfare State, 1914–1941* (Toronto: University of Toronto Press, 1983), 100.

68  Cynthia Comacchio, *The Dominion of Youth: Adolescence and the Making of Modern Canada, 1920 to 1950* (Waterloo, ON: Wilfrid Laurier University Press, 2006), 15–16.

69  "Police Halt First Truck with Strikers: Mounted Police Execute Federal Government Edict, Appeal to Premier," *Toronto Globe*, June 28, 1935, 1.

70  Waiser, *All Hell*; Laurel Sefton MacDowell, "Relief Camp Workers in Ontario during the Great Depression of the 1930s," *Canadian Historical Review* 76, 2 (1995): 205–28;

Lorne Brown, *When Freedom Was Lost: The Unemployed, the Agitator, and the State* (Montreal: Black Rose Books, 1987).

71  Comacchio, *Dominion of Youth*, 189.

72  David Fowler, *Youth Culture in Modern Britain, c. 1920–c. 1970: From Ivory Tower to Global Movement – A New History* (London: Palgrave Macmillan, 2008), 38.

73  Rolf E. Muuss, *Theories of Adolescence* (New York: Random House, 1964), 56–57.

74  Jobs, *Backpack Ambassadors*, 13.

75  Ibid., 14.

76  Quoted in ibid., 17.

77  "Calgary School Teachers Made Hostel Dream Come True," *Calgary Herald Magazine*, June 21, 1958, Youth Hostels, M7832, file 74, Canadian Youth Hostels Association, Glenbow Museum Archives, Calgary (hereafter CYHA-GMA); "Fresh Trails, Fields Afar Opened by Youth Hostels, *Toronto Star Weekly*, July 30, 1938; "Hostel Movement Promotes Fellowship," *Calgary Herald Magazine*, June 21, 1958, Youth Hostels, M7832, file 74, CYHA-GMA. While studying for a doctorate at the University of Chicago, Mary Barclay was introduced to the ideals of John Dewey through a group of under-privileged children from one of the poorer Chicago school districts, whose teacher had arranged an outdoor hiking program as a means of reaching children who knew nothing but poor homes and city streets. Catherine Barclay was a French teacher and interested in mental and physical fitness for young Canadians as important for re-inforcing ideas about the body as well as citizenship goals.

78  Comacchio, *Dominion of Youth*, 163–64. Cynthia Comacchio writes, "Modern youth was conceptualised and institutionalised as both positive and negative outcomes of modernity, and as an instrument for attaining the best that the modern represented." The "adventurous instinct" intrinsic to adolescence was proclaimed to be the same "spirit that grips the heart and soul in passionate devotion to the national ideal." Cynthia Comacchio, "Dancing to Perdition: Adolescence and Leisure in Interwar English Canada," *Journal of Canadian Studies* 32, 3 (1997): 9.

79  "Calgary School Teachers Made Hostel Dream Come True," *Calgary Herald Magazine*, June 21, 1958, Youth Hostels, M7832, file 74, CYHA-GMA. Fifty hostels in Canada had joined their group.

80  Quoted in Katherine Arnup, *Education for Motherhood: Advice to Mothers in Twentieth-Century Canada* (Toronto: University of Toronto Press, 1994), 87. This overprotect-iveness would give way in the 1950s to pediatrician Benjamin Spock's more permissive approach.

81  Harriet Mitchell, "A Letter from a Parent of a Youth Hitchhiker," in Canadian Youth Hostels Association, *Hostel Trails in Nouvelle France* (1935), 4–5, Canadian Youth Hostels Association Handbook/Hostel Trails of Canada, 1939–1940, 1942, 1945–1946, M2169, file 11, CYHA-GMA.

82  H.J. Cody, "Foreword," in Canadian Youth Hostels Association, *Handbook* (1939–40), 4, Canadian Youth Hostels Association Handbook/Hostel Trails of Canada, 1939–1940, 1942, 1945–1946, M2169, file 11, CYHA-GMA.

83  Canadian Youth Hostels Association, *Handbook* (1971), 14, M7832, file 131, CYHA-GMA.

84  "Recall Thrills of Hitch-Hiking across Europe Last Summer," *Edmonton Journal,* November 15, 1954, Scrapbook 1953–1956, North West Region, Edmonton, M7832, file 289, CYHA-GMA.

85  Alcohol was prohibited and cigarette smoking confined to designated areas. In the early 1950s Canadian hostels were chaperoned by houseparents responsible for collecting nightly fees, distributing the housekeeping duties of hostellers, and seeing that the rules were obeyed. It was a two-week commitment, and "previous experience with young people" was preferred. "Youth Hostellers Planning Big Year of Summer Travel," n.d., Scrapbook 1953–1956, North West Region, Edmonton, M7832, file 289, CYHA-GMA.

86  "Two City Hostellers Claim Canadians Liked in Europe," n.d., Scrapbook 1953–1956, North West Region, Edmonton, M7832, file 289, CYHA-GMA.

87  On September 8, 1951, the *Edmonton Journal* announced that Valeen's parents had received word that their daughter had won a Ministry of Education scholarship valued at $800. "Hitchhike across Europe Adventure for Miss Pon," *Edmonton Journal,* n.d., Scrapbook 1953–1956, North West Region, Edmonton, M7832, file 289, CYHA-GMA.

88  Mike Brake, *Comparative Youth Culture: The Sociology of Youth Cultures and Youth Subcultures in America, Britain and Canada* (New York: Routledge, 1985), 147.

89  Mariana Valverde, *The Age of Light, Soap, and Water: Moral Reform in English Canada, 1885–1925* (Toronto: McClelland and Stewart, 1991), 44–47, 50–52. Lara Campbell argues that in the 1930s "clothing was more than just simple material: it reflected one's status within the community ... To have visibly worn clothes or hand-me-downs could be a source of shame, especially for children. Worn and poor quality clothing was a very public marker of poverty and unemployment." Campbell, *Respectable Citizens,* 35.

90  Mike Brake writes that because "work is an important means to the respectable life," failure to work is associated with personal failure, not the failure of the system. He notes that "for older established Canadians" – but not new immigrants and First Nations people – "this means a generational rise in the standard of living," which leads to "a subdued conservatism." Brake, *Comparative Youth Culture,* 149. See also James Pitsula, "The Treatment of Tramps in Late Nineteenth-Century Toronto," *Historical Papers* 15, 1 (1980): 116–32.

91  Cohen, "Nomads from Affluence," 91; Barbara Ehrenreich, *Fear of Falling: The Inner Life of the Middle Class* (New York: Harper Perennial, 1989), 12; Laurie Loker-Murphy and Philip Pearce, "Young Budget Travelers: Backpackers in Australia," *Annals of Tourism Research* 22, 4 (1995): 819–23.

92  Jeremy Packer, *Mobility without Mayhem: Safety, Cars and Citizenship* (Durham, NC: Duke University Press, 2008), 81.

93  Cited in Latta, *They Tried,* 26.

94  Lloyd Mitton, email to author, January 2, 2012.

95  Jewison was shocked to see the way that white people treated African Americans. Years later, he said that his "intense hitchhiking journey" had led him to make films such as *In the Heat of the Night* (1967) and *The Hurricane* (1999), which emphasize themes of racism in America. Norman Jewison, *This Terrible Business Has Been Good to Me* (Toronto: Key Porter Books, 2004), 27, 31. See also Latta, *They Tried,* 29.

96 Zeidman, "Thumb Fun!" 56.

97 "Hitchhiking Round the World: The Toll Brothers," *Toronto Globe,* April 15, 1936. The brothers gave their travelogue in Toronto's Eaton Auditorium and in churches and high school auditoriums in Brampton, Stratford, St. Mary's, Exeter, Paris, Port Credit, Greenbank, Cannington, King, Stouffville, Norval, Keswick, Claremont, Guelph, Fergus, and Beamsville.

98 Katherine Adams, Michael Keene, and Melanie McKay, *Controlling Representations: Depictions of Women in a Mainstream Newspaper, 1900–1950* (Cresskill, NJ: Hampton, 2009), 117.

99 Jane Nicholas, *The Modern Girl: Feminine Modernities, the Body, and Commodities in the 1920s* (Toronto: University of Toronto Press, 2015), 184. Nicholas writes, "Bobbed hair was one of the most dramatic and problematic symbols of the Modern Girl ... Long hair was powerful because it could seduce or charm, while cutting one's hair could be seen as an act of defacement, a renunciation of (hetero)sexuality, or even a violation." Ibid., 48, 49. For a discussion of women's clothing and late-Victorian unconventional travellers see Tim Cresswell, "Embodiment, Power and the Politics of Mobility: The Case of Female Tramps and Hobos," *Transactions of the Institute of British Geographers* 24, 2 (1999): 179.

00 Quoted in Götsch-Trevelyan, *Unharboured Heaths,* 10.

01 Götsch-Trevelyan, *Unharboured Heaths,* 46–47, original emphasis.

02 Ibid., 47.

03 "Recall the Thrills of Hitchhiking across Europe Last Summer," *Edmonton Journal,* November 15, 1954, Scrapbook 1953–1956, North West Region, Edmonton, M7832, file 289, CYHA-GMA. In her study of women and leisure travel, Jennie Small argues that the special clothing women pack for holidays makes them feel more confident and affirmed in their identity, which "enables them to resist oppression in all aspects of their lives." On holiday, women experience emotions that they cannot experience at home. They feel "pleasure and satisfaction in the aestheticizing of one's own body" on holiday. Jennie Small, "The Emergence of the Body in the Holiday Accounts of Women and Girls," in *Tourism and Gender: Embodiment, Sensuality and Experience,* ed. Annette Pritchard, Nigel Morgan, Irena Ateljevic, and Candice Harris (Wallingford, UK: CABI, 2007), 73, 85.

04 "Young Hostellers Planning Big Year This Summer," n.d., Scrapbook 1953–1956, North West Region, Edmonton, M7832, file 289, CYHA-GMA.

05 "Hitchhike across Europe Adventure of Miss Pon," *Edmonton Journal,* n.d., Scrapbook 1953–1956, North West Region, Edmonton, M7832, file 289, CYHA-GMA.

06 Burton and Cochrane, "Our Passport Was a Dishrag," 32.

07 Sanger, "Girls and the Getaway," 715; Alexandra Ganser, "On the Asphalt Frontier: American Women's Road Narratives, Spatiality, and Transgression," *Journal of International Women's Studies* 7, 4 (2006): 155.

08 "Hitch-Hikers – Even the Baby," *Globe and Mail,* August 1, 1938, with photograph of the Cooper family of Von Koughnet, Ontario, including three women, two girls, and an eight-month-old baby.

09 "Emily Post Gives the Nod to Hitch-Hiking and Frames Rules for 'Defense Debutantes,'" *New York Times,* December 23, 1942.

110  Mary Louise Adams, *The Trouble with Normal: Postwar Youth and the Making of Heterosexuality* (Toronto: University of Toronto Press, 1997), 50, 51. Adams writes, "The prolonging of childhood was one of the distinctive markers of the postwar world, a signal that grown-up worries could be kept at bay for a good part of life ... Teens were seen to have greater freedom than their parents had had. That young people were permitted to choose their own courses at school, to date without chaperones, to drive cars, and keep pocket money frequently obscured the fact that, as not-quite-adults, they had little real power in their lives." Ibid., 51.

111  "Traveling via Thumb, Joyce Hill on West Coast," *Newmarket Era and Express*, August 23, 1945.

112  Burton and Cochrane, "Our Passport Was a Dishrag," 32. See also "Bit-Time Hitch-hikers: Blue Jeans Only Outfit for 21,000 Miles," *Globe and Mail*, January 17, 1952.

113  "Hitchhike across Europe Adventure for Miss Pon," *Edmonton Journal*, n.d., Scrapbook 1953–1956, North West Region, Edmonton, M7832, file 289, CYHA-GMA.

114  Veselka, "Green Screen," 9.

115  "Hitch-Hiking Past Jobs on Farms, Say Police," *Toronto Globe*, July 10, 1935, 1; "Notes and Comments," *Toronto Globe*, July 11, 1935, 4.

116  "Hitchhiking a Punishable Offence," *Stouffville Tribune*, June 9, 1938, 2.

117  Pitsula, "Treatment of Tramps," 117. In the early twentieth century, "tramp menace" symbolized the supposed rejection of the work ethic and middle-class values. Ibid., 116.

118  "Hitch-Hiking Past Jobs on Farms, Say Police," *Toronto Globe*, July 10, 1935, 1.

119  "Hitchhiking a Punishable Offence," *Stouffville Tribune*, June 9, 1938, 2; "Injury Peril Grows with Hitch-Hiking among Students," *Toronto Globe*, December 12, 1935, 11; "Not All Hitchhikers Deserving," *Globe and Mail*, July 26, 1943, 6; Lex Shrag, "Mortgage Manor: Neat Priority List Set for Hitchhiking Artists," *Globe and Mail*, August 14, 1953, 7.

120  Quoted in Davis, "Dependent Motorization," 124. Historian Donald Davis adds that by the mid-1920s all provinces had excellent highways connecting them with the United States, yet it would not be until 1945 that the first car was able to cross Canada entirely by road without the occasional detour into the United States or drive down the railway tracks.

121  Ibid., 124.

122  Ibid., 122, 124.

123  G. Stanley Hall, *Adolescence: Its Psychology and Its Relations to Physiology, Anthropology, Sociology, Sex, Crime, Religion and Education* (1904; reprint, New York: D. Appleton and Company, 1924), 349.

124  Quoted in Shellow et al., "Suburban Runaways of the 1960s," 3. See also "Hitchhiker Called a Growing Menace," *New York Times*, August 25, 1935, N2.

125  Robert E. Park, "Community Organization and Juvenile Delinquency," in *The City: Suggestions for Investigation of Human Behavior in the Urban Environment*, ed. Robert E. Park, Ernest W. Burgess, and Roderick D. McKenzie (Chicago: University of Chicago Press, 1925), 159.

126  Comacchio, *Dominion of Youth*, 15–16. See also Thomas Minehan, *Boy and Girl Tramps of America* (New York: Farrar and Rinehart, 1934), 13.

7  Cyril Burt, cited in Shellow et al., "Suburban Runaways of the 1960s," 2; "The Hitch-Hiker's Ranks Grow Thin: New Troubles Beset the Dusty Ride-Thumber Victim of Misfortune," *New York Times*, July 25, 1937, 141; "Hitchhiker Called a Growing Menace," *New York Times*, August 25, 1935, N2.

8  Minehan, *Boy and Girl Tramps*, 136–37. See also Struthers, *No Fault of Their Own*, 83; Bryan D. Palmer, *Working-Class Experience: Rethinking the History of Canadian Labor, 1800-1991* (Toronto: McClelland and Stewart, 1992); and Campbell, *Respectable Citizens*, 139–42.

9  "Youth Project Stresses Jobs, Official Holds," *Globe and Mail*, February 28, 1939; "Unhappy Homes Drive Out Boys," *Toronto Globe*, December 27, 1935, 1. The circumstances of "girl hobos" were not widely discussed in the press. Comacchio, *Dominion of Youth*, 37.

0  Minehan, *Boy and Girl Tramps*, 136–37.

1  "Youth Project Stresses Jobs, Official Holds," *Globe and Mail*, February 28, 1939.

2  "Injury Peril Grows with Hitch-Hiking among Students," *Toronto Globe*, December 12, 1935, 11.

3  "Roadside Beggars," *New York Times*, October 12, 1925, 20.

4  "Parental Neglect," *New York Times*, October 12, 1925.

5  "Advises Walking for Motor-Ride Beggars," *New York Times*, June 21, 1925, 22.

6  "Injury Peril Grows with Hitch-Hiking among Students," *Toronto Globe*, December 12, 1935, 11.

7  Ibid.

8  "Hitchhikers Not Liked by This Driver," *Globe and Mail*, December 1, 1936, 7.

9  "Injury Peril Grows with Hitch-Hiking among Students," *Toronto Globe*, December 12, 1935, 11.

0  Lara Campbell writes that in Canadian author "Pierre Berton's popular history of the Great Depression, riding the trains was an 'adventure,' particularly for young men ... In the symbolism of 'the road,' it is the men who walked, travelled, and organized, and the women who offered support and dealt with the economic consequences of being left behind." Campbell, *Respectable Citizens*, 79–80. See also Christopher Greig, *Ontario Boys: Masculinity and the Idea of Boyhood in Postwar Ontario, 1945–1960* (Waterloo, ON: Wilfrid Laurier University Press, 2014), 19.

1  MacDonald, "Being in Your Twenties," 157.

2  Rebellious youth cultures began to make the news, and juvenile delinquency, teenage mothers, gang violence, comic books, venereal disease, and a lack of patriotism were on the list of "respectable fears." Jonathan Swainger, "Teen Trouble and Community Identity in Post–Second World War Northern British Columbia," *Journal of Canadian Studies* 47, 2 (2013): 162.

3  "Along Boy Scout Trails: Scouting and Hitch-Hiking," *Toronto Globe*, July 5, 1935; Greig, *Ontario Boys*, xix.

4  "Along Boy Scout Trails: Discourage Hitch-Hiking," *Toronto Globe*, December 10, 1932, 15.

5  "Along Boy Scout Trails: Hitch-Hiking Taboo," *Toronto Globe*, June 3, 1933, 13.

6  "Along Boy Scout Trails: Discourage Hitch-Hiking," *Toronto Globe*, December 10, 1932, 15; "Along Boy Scout Trails: Hitch-Hiking Taboo," *Toronto Globe*, June 3, 1933, 13;

"Along Boy Scout Trails: Scouting and Hitch-Hiking," *Toronto Globe,* July 5, 1935; "Along Boy Scout Trails: Not Hitch-Hiking," *Toronto Globe,* September 25, 1936, 16.

147 Jeffrey Keshen, *Saints, Sinners, and Soldiers: Canada's Second World War* (Vancouver: UBC Press, 2004), 41. Geoffrey Hayes and Kirk Goodlet, "Exploring Masculinity in the Canadian Army Officer Corps, 1939–45," *Journal of Canadian Studies* 48, 2 (2014): 41.

148 When asked his age, Cyples said he was nineteen years old. He supposed he was "tall for his age." "Canadian Soldiers Recall Service on the Front Lines," *Lunenburg County Progress Bulletin,* November 6, 2013, A15. See also "Soldier Fast Hitchhiker," *Globe and Mail,* October 25, 1941, 23.

149 Swainger, "Teen Trouble," 162, 163.

150 Ibid., 162; Comacchio, *Infinite Bonds of Family,* 183–84; Adams, *Trouble with Normal,* 71–72.

151 Swainger, "Teen Trouble," 161, 171.

152 "Hitchhikers in Khaki," *Globe and Mail,* August 20, 1940, 6. See also Keshen, *Saints, Sinners, and Soldiers,* 284–86.

153 Hayes and Goodlet, "Exploring Masculinity," 41. See also Keshen, *Saints, Sinners, and Soldiers,* 41.

154 Hayes and Goodlet, "Exploring Masculinity," 41; Keshen, *Saints, Sinners, and Soldiers,* 43.

155 Hayes and Goodlet, "Exploring Masculinity," 41, 45; Keshen, *Saints, Sinners, and Soldiers;* Greig, *Ontario Boys,* 19.

156 Hayes and Goodlet, "Exploring Masculinity," 41, 44.

157 Mario Rinvolucri, "The Hitch-Hiking Revolution 1939–45," in *Hitch-Hiking,* ch. 10 (London: Mario Rinvolucri, 1974), https://prino.neocities.org/Mario%20Rinvolucri/chapter10.html.

158 "Hitchhikers in Khaki," *Globe and Mail,* August 20, 1940, 6.

159 This phrase references film director William Wellman's *Wild Boys of the Road* (1933), which tells a story about teenage boys and girls who ride the rails and become hobos. A middle-class boy has to sell his beloved car after he learns that his father's business has been ruined.

160 "The Soldier's Version," *Globe and Mail,* September 9, 1941, 6; "Hitchhiking Is Preferred by Soldiers, H.Q. States," *Globe and Mail,* August 28, 1940, 4; "Amend Motion for Free Rides: Cheaper Transportation for Soldiers Is Urged," *Globe and Mail,* August 22, 1941, 4.

161 "Hitchhiking CWACs [Canadian Women's Army Corps] Thumb Way to California in 7 Days," *Globe and Mail,* September 1, 1945, 5.

162 "Rides for Soldiers," *Globe and Mail,* November 18, 1940.

163 "Soldier Hitchhiker Jailed for Assault," *Globe and Mail,* September 30, 1942, 2; "Two Soldiers Rob, Assault Trucker; Were Hitchhikers," *Globe and Mail,* June 12, 1950, 9; "Not All Hitchhikers Deserving," *Globe and Mail,* July 26, 1943, 6.

164 "Hunt for Fugitive Nazis Moves to United States," *Globe and Mail,* May 7, 1942, 1.

165 Richard K. Beardsley and Rosalie Hankey, "History of the Vanishing Hitchhiker," *California Folklore Quarterly* 2, 1 (1943): 16. See also Ernest W. Baughman, "The Hitchhiking Ghost," *Hoosier Folklore* 6, 2 (1947): 77–78.

56  Ganser, "On the Asphalt Frontier," 162. See also Cresswell, "Embodiment, Power," 179–81; and Sanger, "Girls and the Getaway," 715.

57  Sheller and Urry, "City and the Car," 748.

58  Torun Elsrud, "Risk Creation in Travelling: Backpacker Adventure Narration," *Annals of Tourism Research* 28, 3 (2001): 614.

59  Veselka, "Green Screen," 9–10, 13.

70  Franca Iacovetta, "Gossip, Contest, and Power in the Making of Suburban Bad Girls: Toronto, 1945–60," *Canadian Historical Review* 80, 4 (1999): 594.

71  Zeidman, "Thumb Fun!" 56.

72  Schuler, "He Thumbed His Way," 77.

73  "'L.A.' Was the Cry of Two Hiking Vancouver Girls," *Vancouver Sun*, September 1, 1924, in Henrietta Lethbridge Watson Nickel, "Scrapbook," in private possession of the Bohun family, Calgary and Nanoose Bay, Vancouver Island.

74  "Runaway-Girl Total in City High This Year: 76 under 16 Years and Double This Number over Age 16," *Globe and Mail*, August 25, 1938, 15.

75  "Emily Post Gives the Nod to Hitch-Hiking and Frames Rules for 'Defense Debutantes,'" *New York Times*, December 23, 1942.

76  Elsrud, "Risk Creation," 611.

77  Referring to a 1934 study by American social workers Sheldon Glueck and Eleanor Glueck, Joan Sangster writes, "Old-fashioned and superior moralism permeated their conclusions: with 'this swarm of defective, diseased, anti-social misfits,' the Gluecks concluded, it is a 'miracle' the proportion 'we do rehabilitate.'" Joan Sangster, *Regulating Girls and Women: Sexuality, Family, and the Law in Ontario, 1920–1960* (Don Mills, ON: Oxford University Press, 2001), 89.

78  "Forced to Submit: Three Hitchhiking Girls Overcome Male Driver," *Globe and Mail*, May 12, 1951, 8.

79  David Bright, "Loafers Are Not Going to Subsist upon Public Credulence: Vagrancy and the Law in Calgary, 1900–1914," *Labour/Le Travail* 36 (1995): 39.

80  Sangster, *Regulating Girls and Women*, 138, 152–53, 193.

81  "Girls Tour on $2.50: Hitchhike from Bay State to Carolinas and Back Here," *New York Times*, February 15, 1933, 23; "Runaway-Girl Total in City High This Year," *Globe and Mail*, August 25, 1938, 15; "Girl Hikers March on the City Now," *New York Times*, July 18, 1926, E18; Veronica Strong-Boag, *The New Day Recalled: Lives of Girls and Women in English Canada, 1919–1939* (Toronto: Copp Clark Pitman, 1988), 22–23.

82  "Question 2 Men in 1,500-Mile Hike by Toronto Girl," *Globe and Mail*, March 14, 1949, 2.

83  "Girl Hitchhikers Going Home," *Globe and Mail*, January 22, 1948.

84  Paul DiMaggio, *The Hitchhiker's Field Manual* (London: Macmillan, 1973), 10. DiMaggio adds, "The 'mad hitchhiker of Oklahoma' murdered five people before a sheriff gunned him down. The outcry was so great that one town built a monument to one of his victims with the inscription: 'A Martyr to Hitchhiking.'"

85  "War Is Declared on Hitch-Hikers: 'Thumbing a Ride' Is Banned by Law in New Jersey," *Toronto Globe*, September 29, 1928, 8.

86  "Hitchhiker Called a Growing Menace: Police of Nation Point to a Rising Toll of Murders by Youths on Highways," *New York Times*, August 25, 1935, N2; "The Hitch-

Hiker's Ranks Grow Thin: New Troubles Beset the Dusty Ride-Thumber Victim of Misfortune," *New York Times,* July 25, 1937, 141.

187   Quoted in "Hitchhiker Risk Cited: J.E. Hoover Issues Warning to Nation's Motorists," *New York Times,* July 4, 1957, 15. See also DiMaggio, *Hitchhiker's Field Manual,* 13.

188   "Doomed to Death Sticks Out Tongue," *Globe and Mail,* December 2, 1943.

189   Don Wharton, "Thumbs Down on Hitchhikers! Too Many Rob and Kill," *Reader's Digest,* April 1950, 21–25. See also a special ad for this issue of the *Reader's Digest* in the *Globe and Mail,* May 30, 1950. Tamara Myers says that Canadians trusted *Reader's Digest* to deliver the truth about car safety, untrustworthy drivers, and accidents. Myers, "Didactic Sudden Death," 463.

190   "Family of Five Feared Victims of Hitchhiker," *Globe and Mail,* January 4, 1951, 7.

191   "Hitchhiker Slew Farmer, Police Think," *Globe and Mail,* November 16, 1938, 17.

192   "Motive Lacking in Murder, Young Hitchhiker Charged," *Globe and Mail,* December 15, 1944, 15.

193   "Sex, Identity a Mystery: Find Pieces of Hacked Body in 3 Sacks on B.C. Trail," *Globe and Mail,* March 25, 1963, 1.

194   "Hitchhiking Risky Job," *Globe and Mail,* August 31, 1937.

195   "Not All Hitchhikers Deserving," *Globe and Mail,* July 26, 1943. See also "Girl Hitch-Hiker Killed," *Globe and Mail,* July 13, 1945.

196   Elise Chenier writes, "The crimes covered by sex psychopath laws generally included the full spectrum of sex-related offences from sexual assault against children to sex between two consenting male adults. Sexual assault against adult females was not often included under criminal sexual psychopath law since the object of the perpetrator's desire – an adult female – was not seen as abnormal or 'deviant' and therefore was simply a violent assault and not the product of a mental defect." Elise Chenier, "The Criminal Sexual Psychopath in Canada: Sex, Psychiatry and the Law at Mid-Century," *Canadian Bulletin of Medical History* 20, 1 (2003): 78–79.

197   Quoted in Graeme Chesters and David Smith, "The Neglected Art of Hitch-Hiking: Risk, Trust and Sustainability," *Sociological Research Online* 6, 3 (2001): sec. 4.1.

198   Gary Kinsman, *The Regulation of Desire: Homo and Hetero Sexualities* (Montreal: Black Rose Books, 1996), 129–31.

199   Quoted in Roger Ebert, "Detour," film review, RogerEbert.com, June 7, 1998, http://www.rogerebert.com/reviews/great-movie-detour-1945. In the film *Detour,* regarded today as a film noir classic, a down-on-his-luck piano player hitchhikes to California. On the way, he becomes implicated in the death of a bookie, who has given him a ride. He steals the man's car and picks up a woman hitchhiker, who learns of the death and blackmails him into helping her with a criminal scheme. Jeremy Packer argues that the femme fatale "manifested the fears of returning servicemen unable to cope with changed gender norms" and new roles for women. Packer, *Mobility without Mayhem,* 86.

200   "Television Guide for Next Week: Dragnet," *Globe and Mail,* August 13, 1955, 31.

201   "Not All Hitchhikers Deserving," *Globe and Mail,* July 26, 1943, 6.

202   "Motorists Take Chances in Picking up Hitchhikers," *Stouffville Tribune,* September 22, 1938, 2.

03  "Hitchhikers Can Be Bad Business," *Stouffville Tribune,* August 20, 1964; "Facts Are Startling on Hitchhike Menace," *Newmarket Era and Express,* August 20, 1964.

04  "Facts Are Startling." See also "Hitchhikers Can Be Bad Business."

05  Sheller and Urry, "City and the Car," 749.

06  Adler, "Youth on the Road," 341.

07  John Steinbeck, *The Grapes of Wrath* (London, UK: Penguin, 2006), 7. Jason Spangler says that "dustbowler" Tom Joad in Steinbeck's book and "hobo-tramp hipster[s]" Sal Paradise and Dean Moriarty in Jack Kerouac's novel *On the Road* (1957) have a great deal in common. They all find themselves "suddenly rising and roaming America, serious, curious, bumming and hitchhiking everywhere, ragged, beatific, beautiful in an ugly graceful new way." Jack Kerouac, "About the Beat Generation," in *The Portable Jack Kerouac,* ed. Ann Charters (New York: Penguin, 1995), 559. Quoted in Jason Spangler, "We're on a Road to Nowhere: Steinbeck, Kerouac, and the Legacy of the Great Depression," *Studies in the Novel* 40, 3 (2008): 311–12.

08  Packer, *Mobility without Mayhem,* 86. For a detailed discussion of *The Hitch-Hiker,* see Therese Grisham and Julie Grossman, *Ida Lupino, Director: Her Art and Resilience in Times of Transition* (New Brunswick, NJ: Rutgers University Press, 2017), 23–28.

09  "Thumbs Down on Hitchhikers," *Acton Free Press,* July 22, 1948. "Pass Up Hitch-Hikers," *Kingsville Reporter,* August 23, 1966. Canadians responding to the 1950 *Reader's Digest* article discussed above said that they "hate to see the disappearance of Good Samaritans off the road." "In the Editor's Mail Box," *Stouffville Tribune,* August 31, 1950. See also "You Take a Chance," *Acton Free Press,* June 23, 1950.

10  "Lenient Attitude to Hitch-Hikers," *Regina Leader Post,* August 1, 1970.

### Chapter 3: Rucksack Revolution

1  Interviewee 87, Salt Spring Island, BC, June 15, 2011.

2  Tarah Brookfield, *Cold War Comforts: Canadian Women, Child Safety, and Global Insecurity* (Waterloo, ON: Wilfrid Laurier University Press, 2012), 12, 60.

3  Jay Vogt, "Wandering: Youth and Travel Behavior," *Annals of Tourism Research* 4, 1 (1976): 26–27, 33. See also Erik Cohen, "Nomads from Affluence: Notes on the Phenomenon of Drifter-Tourism," *International Journal of Comparative Studies* 14, 1–2 (1973): 89–103.

4  Brookfield, *Cold War Comforts,* 12, 60.

5  Mavis Reimer, "Homing and Unhoming: The Ideological Work of Canadian Children's Literature," in *Home Words: Discourses of Children's Literature in Canada,* ed. Mavis Reimer (Waterloo, ON: Wilfrid Laurier University Press, 2008), 10.

6  "Ca-na-da," also called "The Centennial Song," was recorded by the Young Canada Singers, a choir consisting of French and English ten year olds. Raymond Berthiaume conducted the francophone group in Montreal, and Laurie Bower conducted the anglophone group in Toronto. The song became the most popular Canadian single of 1967. It set a record for a Canadian recording at that time, with over 270,000 singles sold. See http://www.thecanadianencyclopedia.com/en/article/ca-na-da.

7  Reimer, "Homing and Unhoming," 10.

8  Spock's radical opinions were viewed suspiciously, and Canadian schools ignored him. Brookfield, *Cold War Comforts,* 45.

9   "There's Plenty at the Party – and a Fine, Fat Future," *Toronto Daily Star,* July 1, 1967, 4.
10  Ibid.
11  Paul Litt, "The Massey Commission, Americanization, and Canadian Cultural Nationalism," *Queen's Quarterly* 98, 2 (1991): 48.
12  Doug Owram, *Born at the Right Time: A History of the Baby Boom Generation* (Toronto: University of Toronto Press, 1997), 72. David Lancy argues that the consumerism inherent in motor "holidays" enabled parents to give their offspring a temporary "false sense of agency in return for conceding" to high parental expectations the rest of the year. David F. Lancy, "Unmasking Children's Agency," *Sociology, Social Work and Anthropology Faculty Publications* (Utah State University), paper 277 (2012): 13, http://digitalcommons.usu.edu/sswa_facpubs/277.
13  Email correspondent 44, December 22, 2011.
14  Email correspondent 19, December 21, 2011.
15  Richard Ivan Jobs, *Backpack Ambassadors: How Youth Travel Integrated Europe* (Chicago: University of Chicago Press, 2017), 187.
16  Interviewee 88, Vancouver, June 22, 2011.
17  Interviewee 63, Ladysmith, BC, February 17, 2012.
18  Email correspondent 74, Rod Willmot, December 23, 2011.
19  Interviewee 12, Saskatoon, September 12, 2012.
20  Judith Adler, "Youth on the Road: Reflections on the History of Tramping," *Annals of Tourism Research* 12, 3 (1985): 341, 342; Ellen Ross, "Introduction: Adventures among the Poor," in *Slum Travelers: Ladies and London Poverty, 1890–1920,* ed. Ellen Ross, 1–39 (Berkeley: University of California Press, 2007).
21  Cohen, "Nomads from Affluence," 92. For details of the international phenomenon, see Jobs, *Backpack Ambassadors.*
22  Vogt, "Wandering," 25, 28, 39.
23  Brookfield, *Cold War Comforts,* 12, 103.
24  Stuart Henderson, *Making the Scene: Yorkville and Hip Toronto in the 1960s* (Toronto: University of Toronto Press, 2011), 9.
25  Cyril Levett, *Children of Privilege: Student Revolt in the Sixties: A Study of Student Movements in Canada, the United States, and West Germany* (Toronto: University of Toronto Press, 1984), 14.
26  Brookfield, *Cold War Comforts,* 125; Kenneth Westhues, "Inter-Generational Conflict in the Sixties," in *Prophecy and Protest: Social Movements in Twentieth-Century Canada,* ed. Samuel Clark, J. Paul Grayson, and Linda Grayson, 387–408 (Toronto: Gage, 1975).
27  Ron Verzuh, "Trip Tips," *The Peak* (Simon Fraser University), May 20, 1970, 6.
28  Mike Brake, *Comparative Youth Culture: The Sociology of Youth Cultures and Youth Subcultures in America, Britain and Canada* (New York: Routledge, 1985), 27.
29  Mimi Sheller and John Urry argue that due to "the discovery" of crash culture and car sex, "various 'coming-of-age' rituals revolve around the car." Mimi Sheller and John Urry, "The City and the Car," *International Journal of Urban and Regional Research* 24, 4 (2000): 747.
30  Owram, *Born at the Right Time,* 187–89.

31 Marcel Danesi argues that cars were a "sign of both maturity and independence." Marcel Danesi, *Geeks, Goths, and Gangstas: Youth Culture and the Evolution of Modern Society* (Toronto: Canadian Scholars' Press, 2010), 69.

32 Pitsula, *New World Dawning*, 72.

33 "Ian and Sylvia," *The Meliorist* (University of Lethbridge), February 1, 1968, 3.

34 Verzuh, "Trip Tips," May 20, 1970, 6.

35 Interviewee 27, Montreal, June 28, 2011. Other songs with hitchhiking themes were Simon & Garfunkel's "America" (1968), Kris Kristofferson's "Me and Bobby McGee" (1969), the Doors' "The Hitchhiker" (1969), and Creedence Clearwater Revival's "Sweet Hitch-Hiker" (1971).

36 Interviewee 5, Barrie, Ontario, May 29, 2016.

37 Joanne Will, "Thumbs Up or Down for Hitchhikers?" *Globe and Mail*, July 12, 2012.

38 Canada, Secretary of State, Committee on Youth, *It's Your Turn: A Report to the Secretary of State by the Committee on Youth* (Ottawa: Information Canada, 1971), 43, 64–65.

39 Vogt, "Wandering," 33.

40 Canada, Secretary of State, Committee on Youth, *It's Your Turn*, 43. "The young feel that pop festivals were one of the greatest things happening to them, and view their active discouragement ... as another instance of anti-youth discrimination." Ibid., 47.

41 Ibid., 43.

42 Ibid., 64.

43 Lawrence Aronsen, *City of Love and Revolution: Vancouver in the Sixties* (Vancouver: New Star Books, 2010), 47; Owram, *Born at the Right Time*, 284–85, 206.

44 Greg Marquis, "Uptight Little Island: The Junction '71 Affair," *The Island*, Fall–Winter 2002, 10–11, http://vre2.upei.ca/islandmagazine/fedora/repository/vre%3Aislemag -batch2-669.

45 Ibid., 12.

46 Canada, Secretary of State, Committee on Youth, *It's Your Turn*, 43.

47 Email correspondent 45, January 1, 2012.

48 Katharine Whitehorn, "The Hallelujah of Being a Hitchhiker," *Globe and Mail*, July 28, 1964, 9.

49 Ibid.

50 Westhues, "Inter-Generational Conflict," 399–400; Owram, *Born at the Right Time*, 306.

51 Stewart Gooding, "The Rights of Youth in Canada," printed in Canadian Welfare Council, *Report of the Canadian Committee of the International Council on Social Welfare for the 14th International Conference on Social Welfare, May 1968* (Ottawa: Canadian Welfare Council, 1968), 13.

52 Cyril Levitt, *Children of Privilege: Student Revolt in the Sixties: A Study of Student Movements in Canada, the United States, and West Germany* (Toronto: University of Toronto Press, 1984), 21.

53 Jim Harding, "Youth Crisis Next Summer," *The Chevron* (University of Waterloo), September 11, 1970, 3.

54  Harding, who caused some consternation at Simon Fraser University by kissing the chancellor's feet after receiving a doctoral degree, saw modern hitchhiking by high school and university students as developing a communal spirit similar to the one that had developed among workers in the 1930s. Harding, "Youth Crisis Next Summer," 3.

55  Gary Barclay, "Hitch Bitch," *Georgia Straight* (Vancouver), July 29, 1970. Tom Campbell said, "If people haven't got money, they should stay home... Travelling is a luxury." "Vancouver May Ban Hitchhiking," *Edmonton Journal*, July 18, 1970.

56  Whitehorn, "Hallelujah," 9.

57  "Wild Wacky BC, an Eastern View," *The Chevron* (University of Waterloo), August 17, 1972, 3.

58  Abigail Stewart and Cynthia Torges say that late baby boomers were engaged and concerned observers of the Vietnam War and the civil rights movement, but they were too young to have been active or mobilized like the early boomers. Abigail Stewart and Cynthia Torges, "Social, Historical, and Developmental Influences on the Psychology of the Baby Boom at Midlife," in *The Baby Boomers Grow Up: Contemporary Perspectives on Midlife*, ed. Susan Krauss Whitbourne and Sherry Willis (Mahwah, NJ: Lawrence Erlbaum Associates, 2006), 32.

59  Interviewee 80, Salt Spring Island, BC, June 27, 2011.

60  Interviewee 56, Vancouver, June 23, 2011.

61  "Long, Hot Summer ahead for Students," *The Martlet* (University of Victoria), January 28, 1971, 3. See also "Transient Youth Leave the Driving to Us," *The Manitoban* (University of Manitoba), January 21, 1971.

62  Ian Milligan, *Rebel Youth: 1960s Labour Unrest, Young Workers, and New Leftists in English Canada* (Vancouver: UBC Press, 2014), 12–13.

63  Canada, Secretary of State, Committee on Youth, *It's Your Turn*, 26–27.

64  Milligan, *Rebel Youth*, 12–13.

65  Interviewee 23, Erin, Ontario, March 7, 2013.

66  Douglas Williams, *Promised Lands: Growing Up Absurd in the 1950s and '60s* (Kingston, ON: Michael Grass House, 2012), 11.

67  Interviewee 63, Ladysmith, BC, February 17, 2012.

68  Interviewee 88, Toronto, June 22, 2011.

69  Interviewee 30, Tony Bonnici, Vancouver, March 1, 2012.

70  Peter Kelly, "The Entrepreneurial Self and 'Youth-at-Risk': Exploring the Horizons of Identity in the Twenty-First Century," *Journal of Youth Studies* 9, 1 (2006): 27. See also Vogt, "Wandering," 33.

71  Williams, *Promised Lands*, 16–17, original emphasis.

72  "Really Living," letter to the editor, *The Meliorist* (University of Lethbridge), March 14, 1968, 4.

73  Interviewee 22, Toronto, June 22, 2011.

74  Brake, *Comparative Youth Culture*, 150, 161.

75  Canada, Secretary of State, Committee on Youth, *It's Your Turn*, 54, 57.

76  Quoted in Celia Haig-Brown, *Resistance and Renewal: Surviving the Indian Residential School* (1988; reprint, Vancouver: Arsenal Pulp Press, 2006), 27.

77   Bryan D. Palmer, *Canada's 1960s: The Ironies of Identity in a Rebellious Era* (Toronto: University of Toronto Press, 2009), 121.

78   Quoted in Palmer, *Canada's 1960s*, 378.

79   Ibid.

80   Jeannette Armstrong, herself a veteran of the Red Power movement, tells stories that capture the restless mood of Aboriginal youth and their emerging will for liberation and self-determination through the actions of the character Thomas Kelasket, his friends, and other wandering heroes who travel Canada and the United States assessing the assault of colonialism. Jeannette Armstrong, *Slash* (Penticton, BC: Theytus Books, 1985).

81   Canada, Secretary of State, Committee on Youth, *It's Your Turn*, 52.

82   Bryan D. Palmer, "'Indians of All Tribes': The Birth of Red Power," in *Debating Dissent: Canada and the 1960s*, ed. Lara Campbell, Dominique Clément, and Gregory Kealey (Toronto: University of Toronto Press, 2012), 197.

83   Canadian Welfare Council, *Transient Youth: Report of an Inquiry in the Summer of 1969* (Ottawa: Canadian Welfare Council, 1970), 7.

84   Bernelda Wheeler, "Our Native Land: On the Pow Wow Trail," *CBC Radio*, July 13, 1974, http://www.cbc.ca/archives/entry/our-native-land-on-the-pow-wow-trail. See also Brian Maracle, "Our Native Land: Rise of the Native Rights Movement," *CBC Radio*, February 4, 1984, http://www.cbc.ca/archives/entry/our-native-land-rise-of -the-native-rights-movement.

85   Wheeler, "Our Native Land." See also Palmer, *Canada's 1960s*, 387.

86   Wheeler, "Our Native Land."

87   Ibid.

88   Palmer, *Canada's 1960s*, 368.

89   Wheeler, "Our Native Land."

90   Centre for Indigenous Scholars, "History of the Indian Ecumenical Conference and the Centre for Indigenous Scholars," n.d., http://www.ciscentral.com/history1.htm.

91   Wheeler, "Our Native Land."

92   Ibid.

93   Palmer, *Canada's 1960s*, 385.

94   Wheeler, "Our Native Land."

95   Colin M. Coates, "Canadian Countercultures and Their Environments, 1960s–1980s," in *Canadian Countercultures and the Environment*, ed. Colin M. Coates (Calgary: University of Calgary Press, 2016), 9.

96   Sharon Weaver, "Back-to-the-Land Environmentalism and Small Island Ecology: Denman Island, BC, 1974–1979," in *Canadian Countercultures and the Environment*, ed. Colin M. Coates, 29–54 (Calgary: University of Calgary Press, 2016).

97   Mimi Sheller, "Automotive Emotions: Feeling the Car," *Theory, Culture and Society* 21, 4–5 (2004): 236.

98   Joseph Heath and Andrew Potter, *Nation of Rebels: Why Counterculture Became Consumer Culture* (New York: HarperCollins, 2004), 3.

99   "Get Your Shit Together with Good Food," *The Martlet* (University of Victoria), December 3, 1970, 6. See also "To Whom It May Concern," letter to the editor, *The*

*Martlet* (University of Victoria), March 11, 1971, 15; "Manual Mobilization Day, March 22, Take a Car, Fill It with Hitchhikers," announcement, *The Martlet* (University of Victoria), March 19, 1971; and "Drivers Don't Forget Hitchhikers," cartoon, *The Martlet* (University of Victoria), March 19, 1971.

100  Simon Gibson, "Hitchhiking," *The Martlet* (University of Victoria), December 5, 1973, 12.

101  Lorna Rasmussen, "Thumbs Up," letter to the editor, *The Meliorist* (University of Lethbridge), January 29, 1970, 2.

102  "Help Yourself: Help Save the Environment," *The Martlet* (University of Victoria), February 18, 1971, 8–9.

103  Marcel Dansi points out that before the Second World War, "jazz was *hot*, fast and passionate." In the 1940s Charlie Parker's softer jazz style caught on. It was described as "cool." The term "cool" entered teen jargon in the 1950s to indicate an attractiveness. "You were either cool or you were not ... The term allowed teens to make up their own minds as to the social qualities of their peers." In the 1960s and 1970s, being cool extended to the hippie worldview, which was characterized by a "new philosophical stoicism and behavioural nonchalance with respect to mainstream culture." Dansi, *Geeks, Goths and Gangstas*, 13, original emphasis.

104  Brake, *Comparative Youth Culture*, 68. See also Samuel Clark, "Movements of Protest in Post-War Canadian Society," in *Prophecy and Protest: Social Movements in Twentieth-Century Canada*, ed. Samuel Clark, J. Paul Grayson, and Linda Grayson (Toronto: Gage, 1975), 416–17.

105  Torun Elsrud notes that for modern backpackers dressing properly means dressing down rather than up. Worn, ripped clothes tell a story of "rough" living and "adventure." Torun Elsrud, "Risk Creation in Travelling: Backpacker Adventure Narration," *Annals of Tourism Research* 28, 3 (2001): 611. See also Brake, *Comparative Youth Culture*, 12–16.

106  Canadian Council on Social Development, *More about Transient Youth* (Ottawa: Canadian Council on Social Development, 1970), 6.

107  Bennett Berger, "Hippie Morality – More Old Than New," *Transaction*, December 1967, 20.

108  Quoted in Brake, *Comparative Youth Culture*, 13–14.

109  Owram, *Born at the Right Time*, 204. Doug Owram adds that by about 1967 "the counter-culture was a political movement expressed through non-political means – music, style, language, drugs ... This was a movement that really did run 'counter' to many of the prevalent trends of the day."

110  Berger, "Hippie Morality," 22.

111  Canadian Welfare Council, *Transient Youth*, 10.

112  Canadian Council on Social Development, *Transient Youth, 70–71: Report of an Inquiry about Programs in 1970, and Plans for 1971* (Ottawa: Department of Health and Welfare, 1970), 6–7.

113  Henderson, *Making the Scene*, 48.

114  Quoted in ibid.

5   Michael O'Regan, "Backpacker Hostels: Place and Performance," in *Beyond Back-packer Tourism: Mobilities and Experiences*, ed. Kevin Hannam and Anya Diekmann (Bristol, UK: Channel View, 2010), 86–87.

6   Phil Macnaghten and John Urry, "Bodies of Nature: Introduction," in *Bodies of Nature*, ed. Phil Macnaghten and John Urry (London: Sage, 2001), 2.

7   Interviewee 77, Vancouver, June 28, 2011.

8   Interviewee 3, Edinburgh, Scotland, October 11, 2012.

9   Interviewee 83, Saskatoon, March 8, 2012. See also Macnaghten and Urry, "Bodies of Nature," 3.

0   Williams, *Promised Lands*, 14.

1   Brake, *Comparative Youth Culture*, 151.

2   John T. Schlebecker, "An Informal History of Hitchhiking," *Historian* 20, 3 (1958): 325; Edward Jewitt Wheeler, "A Studious Hitch-Hiker Looks at Hitch-Hiking," *Literary Digest*, May 16, 1931, 44.

3   Rod Willmot, email to author, December 23, 2001.

4   Interviewee 85, Salt Spring Island, BC, June 29, 2011.

5   Interviewee 46, Vancouver, June 22, 2011.

6   "Road Sign," *Montreal Gazette*, August 7, 1971. The fifteen-year-old boy was on his way to Niagara Falls when he was interviewed by the Montreal paper.

7   Robert Shellow, Juliana Schamp, Elliot Liebow, and Elizabeth Unger, "Suburban Runaways of the 1960s," *Monographs of the Society for Research in Child Development* 32, 3 (1967): 14.

8   Jennie Small, "The Emergence of the Body in the Holiday Accounts of Women and Girls," in *Tourism and Gender: Embodiment, Sensuality and Experience*, ed. Annette Pritchard, Nigel Morgan, Irena Ateljevic, and Candice Harris (Wallingford, UK: CABI, 2007), 83–84.

9   Interviewee 80, Salt Spring Island, BC, June 27, 2011.

0   Interviewee 61, Toronto, May 5, 2013.

1   Verzuh, "Trip Tips," May 20, 1970, 6.

2   Marilyn Dawson, "Book Publishers Discover Canadian Young People on the Move," *Globe and Mail*, June 17, 1972, 38.

3   Canada, Secretary of State, Committee on Youth, *It's Your Turn*, 66.

4   "To remain in the lower depths of the work force, or among the unemployed, is seen as surrendering respectability ... Those who fail deserve to be losers." Brake, *Comparative Youth Culture*, 151. It was a father's responsibility to advance his son's social status. Robert Griswold, *Fatherhood in America: A History* (New York: Basic Books, 1993), 201.

5   Quoted in Meg Luxton, *More Than a Labour of Love: Three Generations of Women's Work in the Home* (Toronto: Women's Education Press, 1980), 88–89.

6   Rolf E. Muuss, *Theories of Adolescence* (New York: Random House, 1964), 34–35. Erik Erikson wrote, "Many a sick or desperate late adolescent, if faced with continuing conflict, would rather be nobody or somebody totally bad or, indeed, dead – and this by free choice – than be not-quite-somebody." Quoted in Paulo Jesus, Maria

Formosinho, and Maria Helena Damião, "Risk-Taking in Youth Culture as a Ritual Process," *International Journal of Developmental and Educational Psychology* 5, 1 (2011): 453.

137  Milligan, *Rebel Youth*, 14; Brookfield, *Cold War Comforts*, 166.

138  "Roots of Discontent: Young People Wonder Just Who and What They Are," *Winnipeg Free Press*, August 4, 1971.

139  "Hostel Program Remains," *Penticton Herald*, May 21, 1971, News Clippings, British Columbia, 1967, 1970–1971, 1977, M7832, file 268, Canadian Youth Hostels Association, Glenbow Museum Archives, Calgary (hereafter CYHA-GMA).

140  Canadian Welfare Council, *Transient Youth*, 83–84.

141  Ibid., 87–88.

142  Interviewee 92, Vancouver, June 22, 2011.

143  Interviewee 56, Vancouver, June 23, 2011.

144  Interviewee 30, Tony Bonnici, Vancouver, March 1, 2012.

145  Interviewees 32a and 32b, Gabriola Island, BC, February 22, 2012.

146  Interviewees 81a and 81b, Vancouver, June 23, 2011.

147  Interviewee 86, Salt Spring Island, BC, March 4, 2012.

148  Email correspondent 25, June 29, 2011.

149  Interviewee 94, Vancouver, June 22, 2011.

150  Henderson, *Making the Scene*, 5. Joanna Davis uses the term "scene" instead of "subculture" to create a space where cultures come together. The concept of scene enables us to theorize how aging members of society negotiate identity in relation to youth. Joanna R. Davis, "Punk, Ageing and the Expectations of Adult Life," in *Ageing and Youth Cultures: Music, Style and Identity*, ed. Andy Bennett and Paul Hodkinson (London: Berg, 2012), 106.

151  Brake, *Comparative Youth Culture*, 10, 150–51; David Matza and Gresham Sykes, "Juvenile Delinquency and Subterranean Values," *American Sociological Review* 26, 5 (1961): 712–19.

152  Betty Friedan, *The Feminine Mystique* (New York: Dell, 1974), 224.

153  Naomi Wolf, *Promiscuities: The Secret Struggle for Womanhood* (Toronto: Random House, 1997), 19. Wolf says that kids in the 1970s "got the sense that, though our parents loved us, a part of them wanted to be free of us. In the erosion of the emotional contract, the modern 'kid' was born. Many of us responded to that elemental, if unspoken, rejection by acting out the wish to be free of our parents." Ibid., 22.

154  Canadian Welfare Council, *Transient Youth*, 115.

155  Elizabeth Thompson, "Mother Is Told to Let Boy Try Hitchhiking," *Globe and Mail*, July 20, 1971.

156  Email correspondent 45, January 1, 2012.

157  Quoted in Richard Needham, "Something to Do, Nothing to Do," *Globe and Mail*, September 13, 1966.

158  Email correspondent 2, January 1, 2011.

159  Email correspondent 74, Rod Willmot, December 23, 2011.

160  Interviewee 78, Salt Spring Island, BC, June 27, 2011.

161  Canadian Welfare Council, *Transient Youth*, 88.

62  Victor Turner, "Betwixt and Between: The Liminal Period in *Rites de Passage*," in *The Forest of Symbols: Aspects of Ndembu Ritual* (Ithaca, NY: Cornell University Press, 1967), 93. See also Amie Matthews, "Young Backpackers and the Rite of Passage of Travel: Examining the Transformative Effects of Liminality," in *Travel and Transformation*, ed. Garth Lean, Russell Staiff, and Emma Waterton (Surrey, UK: Ashgate, 2014), 160. Jay Vogt says that if travellers' parents accompany them, their "independence will be reduced and consequently the amount of social prestige." Vogt, "Wandering," 28.

63  Macnaghten and Urry, "Bodies of Nature," 2. Macnaghten and Urry argue that "affordances do not cause behaviour but constrain it along certain possibilities." Ibid., 9.

64  Dean MacCannell, "Staged Authenticity: Arrangements of Social Space in Tourist Settings," *American Journal of Sociology* 79, 3 (1973): 597; Vogt, "Wandering," 28. See also Jobs, *Backpack Ambassadors*, 185.

65  Jack Kerouac, *The Dharma Bums* (1958; reprint, New York: Penguin, 2006), 83, 58.

66  Macnaghten and Urry, "Bodies of Nature," 3. See also O'Regan, "Backpacker Hostels," 88; and Camille Caprioglio O'Reilly, "From Drifter to Gap Year Tourist: Mainstreaming Backpacker Travel," *Annals of Tourism Research* 33, 4 (2006): 1003.

67  Interviewee 12, Saskatoon, September 12, 2012. The Obernkirchen Children's Choir, from Obernkirchen in north Germany, was founded in 1949 by Edith Möller. In 1953 BBC Radio aired the choir's performance of the song, which made the choir an international phenomenon, and it was invited to sing all around the world. See "The Happy Wanderer by the Obernkirchen Children's Choir," Songfacts, n.d., http://www.songfacts.com/detail.php?id=7983.

68  Email correspondent 47, January 19, 2011.

69  Interviewee 96, Vancouver, June 23, 2011.

70  Interviewee 23, Erin, Ontario, March 7, 2013.

71  Williams, *Promised Lands*, 1.

72  Dawson, "Reviews."

73  "Ontario Warns Hitchhikers," *Globe and Mail*, June 17, 1971.

74  The series, titled "Going Down the Road," began on May 31, with Dorrell taking it over on June 8. Martin Dorrell, "From North Bay to Sudbury, Two Rides and Peanut Butter," *Globe and Mail*, June 8, 1971.

75  Duncan McMonagle, "Hitchhiker Should Plan," *Winnipeg Free Press*, August 25, 1971; Interviewee 98, Duncan McMonagle, Winnipeg, August 24, 2012.

76  Canada, Department of Health and Welfare, *On the Road: A Guide for Youth Travelling Canada* (Ottawa: Department of Health and Welfare, 1972), 1.

77  David Rideout and Ray Amiro, *Handbook Canada: A Traveller's Manual* (Toronto: Transglobular Functions, 1972), 11. See also Dawson, "Reviews."

78  Rideout and Amiro, *Handbook Canada*, 9.

79  Ibid.

80  DiMaggio, *Hitchhiker's Field Manual*, 28.

81  David Crouch and Luke Desforges, "The Sensuous in the Tourist Encounter," *Tourist Studies* 3, 1 (2003): 5.

82  Verzuh, "Trip Tips," May 20, 1970, 6, and June 17, 1970, 7.

183  "The Complete Youth Hosteller: Being Some Advice on Student Travel in Europe,"
     *The Martlet* (University of Victoria), July 20, 1972, 4, 8.
184  "Wild Wacky BC, an Eastern View," *The Chevron* (University of Waterloo), August
     17, 1972, 3.
185  "Got Them Old Half-Way between Carbonear and St. John's Blues Again," *The
     Muse* (Memorial University), June 9, 1972.
186  "Cross Canada Hitchhiker Warns Fellow Travellers," *The Chevron* (University of
     Waterloo), July 10, 1970, 8.
187  Martin Dorrell, "A Really Big Bedroom," *Globe and Mail*, June 14, 1971.
188  Myles Stasiuk, "Travelling and Living in Canada '73," *The Sheaf* (University of Sas-
     katchewan), February 27, 1973, 4–5.
189  Jack English, "No 'Charge,'" editorial, *The Martlet* (University of Victoria), March 1,
     1973, 4–5.
190  Quoted in Canadian Youth Hostels Association, *Annual Report 1968–1969* (1969),
     Annual Reports 1965–1972, M7832, file 73, CYHA-GMA.
191  Cohen, "Nomads from Affluence," 93; Stephen Wearing, Deborah Stevenson, and
     Tamara Young, *Tourist Cultures: Identity, Place and the Traveller* (London: Sage, 2010),
     103; Brake, *Comparative Youth Culture*, 18.
192  Patrick Esmonde-White, "The Trudeaumaniac: The Summer of 1970," 10, unpublished,
     quoted with author's permission.
193  Canada, Secretary of State, Committee on Youth, *It's Your Turn*, 63.
194  "Roots of Discontent: Young People Wonder Just Who and What They Are," *Winnipeg
     Free Press*, August 4, 1971.
195  "Government Hostels and Ease of Registering on the Welfare Rolls Make a Lack of
     Money No Deterrent," *Winnipeg Free Press*, August 7, 1971.
196  Aronsen, *City of Love*, 18.

### Chapter 4: Cool Aid

  1  RCMP, "Memorandum File, Vancouver Liberation Front," September 17, 1970, provided
     to Patrick Esmonde-White under the Access to Information Act (hereafter PEW);
     "After the Battle of Jericho," *Vancouver Province*, October 17, 1970; "Chronology of
     Confrontation," *Globe and Mail*, October 17, 1970; "150 Police Drive out Rebels at
     Jericho," *Vancouver Sun*, October 17, 1970; "Jericho Hostel Crisis 'Avoidable,'" *Vancouver
     Sun*, October 30, 1970.
  2  "Military Building Opened for Hitchhiking Youth," *Globe and Mail*, July 9, 1970;
     "Transients Seize Vancouver Hostel, Win Right to Remain," *Globe and Mail*, Septem-
     ber 9, 1970.
  3  Canadian Council on Social Development, *More about Transient Youth* (Ottawa:
     Canadian Council on Social Development, 1970), 31.
  4  Darya Maoz reports that in India today locals pass themselves off as self-appointed
     spiritual leaders, gurus, and Reiki teachers to give Israeli backpackers the idealized
     image of India that they seek. Darya Maoz, "The Mutual Gaze," *Annals of Tourism
     Research* 33, 1 (2006): 229.
  5  Quoted in Donald F. Davis, "Dependent Motorization: Canada and the Automobile
     to the 1930s," *Journal of Canadian Studies* 21, 3 (1986): 124.

6  Alisa Apostle refers to "the much-fetishized 'tourist dollar.'" Alisa Apostle, "The Display of a Tourist Nation: Canada in Government Film, 1945–1959," *Journal of the Canadian Historical Association* 12, 1 (2001): 188.

7  Ibid., 186.

8  "Centre Provides Stop-Overs for Canadian Transient Youth," *Winnipeg Free Press*, July 8, 1970, 21. This article reported, "Young strangers ... are a source of worry in many towns ... They are not indigent vagrants in the traditional sense ... Many are middle class, could work, but see no reason why they should."

9  Judith Adler, "Youth on the Road: Reflections on the History of Tramping," *Annals of Tourism Research* 12, 3 (1985): 341. See also "The Hitchhikers," *Globe and Mail*, August 10, 1970, 7.

10  Canadian Welfare Council, *Transient Youth: Report of an Inquiry in the Summer of 1969* (Ottawa: Canadian Welfare Council, 1970), 10–11.

11  Douglas Millroy, "Youth Going Nowhere in Search of Adventure," *Globe and Mail*, July 18, 1970, 8.

12  "Centre Provides Stop-Overs for Canadian Transient Youth," *Winnipeg Free Press*, July 8, 1970, 21. See also Canadian Welfare Council, *Transient Youth*, 60; and Canadian Council on Social Development, *Youth '71: An Inquiry into the Transient Youth and Opportunities for Youth Programs in the Summer of 1971* (Ottawa: Department of Health and Welfare, 1972), 34.

13  Jonathan Swainger, "Teen Trouble and Community Identity in Post–Second World War Northern British Columbia," *Journal of Canadian Studies* 47, 2 (2013): 162.

14  Quoted in Richard Needham, "Something to Do, Nothing to Do," *Globe and Mail*, September 13, 1966, 6.

15  Quoted in Canadian Welfare Council, *Transient Youth*, 9–10.

16  "Could Hostel Be Spelled 'Hostile'?" *Georgia Straight* (Vancouver), July 29, 1970.

17  Cited in Hans Arthur Skott-Myhre, *Youth and Subculture as Creative Force: Creating New Spaces for Radical Youth Work* (Toronto: University of Toronto Press, 2008), 124. See also Canada, Secretary of State, Committee on Youth, *It's Your Turn: A Report to the Secretary of State by the Committee on Youth* (Ottawa: Information Canada, 1971), 7.

18  Quoted in Skott-Myhre, *Youth and Subculture*, 124.

19  Cynthia Comacchio, *The Infinite Bonds of Family: Domesticity in Canada, 1850–1940* (Toronto: University of Toronto Press, 1999), 161.

20  Franca Iacovetta, "Gossip, Contest, and Power in the Making of Suburban Bad Girls: Toronto, 1945–60," *Canadian Historical Review* 80, 4 (1999): 596.

21  Ibid., 594.

22  Nancy Christie, *Engendering the State: Family, Work, and Welfare in Canada* (Toronto: University of Toronto Press, 2000), 12, 168.

23  Stanley Cohen, *Visions of Social Control: Crime, Punishment and Classification* (Cambridge, UK: Polity, 1985), 167.

24  Canadian Welfare Council, *Transient Youth*, 2.

25  Byron Rogers, "Addendum: Role of the Canadian Council on Social Development," 1971, 1, 2, unpublished, quoted with author's permission. See also Canadian Welfare Council, *Transient Youth*, 15.

26  Canadian Welfare Council, *Transient Youth*, 50.

27  Ibid., 1.

28  Ibid., 2.

29  Ibid., 50; Ken Rubin, telephone interview with author, March 16, 2016. A student at the University of Manitoba and later Carleton University, as well as a youth worker, Rubin also recalled, "We were the token youth ... going across the country. They said the youth 'are freaking us out.'" The campus paper at the University of Waterloo wrote that staff of the Canadian Welfare Council thought of themselves as "enlightened bureaucrats." Rubin said the CWC wanted more money for the welfare system "to calm things." "Stop Mind Control in the 1970s," *The Chevron* (University of Waterloo), May 22, 1970, 23.

30  On-the-spot interviews were done in French or English. Canadian Welfare Council, *Transient Youth*, 90.

31  CWC data indicated that 23 percent of the Canadian population were considered to be "managerial or professional and technical." Ibid., 83.

32  Ibid., 89.

33  Ibid., 92, 93.

34  Rogers, "Addendum," 13.

35  Canada, Secretary of State, Committee on Youth, *It's Your Turn*, 149.

36  Rogers, "Addendum," i.

37  Ibid.

38  Canadian Welfare Council, *Transient Youth*, 76.

39  Cohen, *Visions of Social Control*, 161.

40  Ibid., 40–43.

41  The "Boom Generation," born 1943–60, had what chronicler Landon Jones described as "Great Expectations." Quoted in William Strauss and Neil Howe, *Generations: The History of America's Future, 1584–2069* (New York: William Morrow, 1991), 299. The new youth-operated groups "wanted to be free of the rigidities of older organizations." Canadian Welfare Council, *Transient Youth*, 51.

42  Floyd Dale, Robert Haubrich, and Robert Herchak, "A Research Report on the Outcome of Transient Youth Referrals Made by CRYPT to Three Social Service and Medical Agencies in Metropolitan Winnipeg from June 1, 1970 to September 30, 1970," School of Social Work, University of Manitoba, April 30, 1971, 12, https://mspace.lib. umanitoba.ca/handle/1993/29826. See also Canadian Welfare Council, *Transient Youth*, 68.

43  "Victoria's Cool Aid Assists Transients," *Winnipeg Free Press*, June 6, 1970, 11.

44  Rubin added that the whole purpose of CRYPT was to relate to and communicate with youth. Quoted in Richard Epp, "CRYPT Communicates – But Not to Police," *The Manitoban* (University of Manitoba), October 28, 1968, 3.

45  S.N. Eisenstadt, "Archetypal Patterns of Youth," in *The Challenge of Youth*, ed. Erik Erikson (Garden City, NY: Anchor Books and Doubleday, 1965), 33; Erik Erikson, "Youth: Fidelity and Diversity," in *The Challenge of Youth*, ed. Erik Erikson (Garden City, NY: Anchor Books and Doubleday, 1965), 11.

46  Cited in Madeleine Gauthier and Diane Pacom, *Spotlight On – Canadian Youth Research* (Sainte-Foy, QC: Editions de l'IQRC, 2001), 102–3.

47 John Byles, "Introduction," in *Alienation, Deviance and Social Control: A Study of Adolescents in Metropolitan Toronto* (Toronto: Interim Research Project on Unreached Youth, 1969), 5–12. See also Canadian Welfare Council, *Transient Youth*, 32.

48 "Recommendations for the Benefit of Severely Troubled Youth," in Canadian Welfare Council, *Transient Youth*, v.

49 Canadian Welfare Council, *Transient Youth*, 5.

50 Canadian Council on Social Development, *More about Transient Youth*, iv–v.

51 Canadian Welfare Council, *Transient Youth*, 7.

52 Ibid., 5.

53 Canadian Council on Social Development, *More about Transient Youth*, iv–v, 9, 14. See also Daniel Ross, "Panic on Love Street: Citizens and Local Government Respond to Vancouver's Hippie Problem, 1967–68," *BC Studies*, 180 (Winter 2013–14): 34.

54 Canadian Welfare Council, *Transient Youth*, 14.

55 Ibid., 9.

56 Epp, "CRYPT Communicates," 3.

57 "On the Road," *Ottawa Journal*, March 23, 1970.

58 Canada Welfare Council, *Transient Youth*, 93.

59 Adler, "Youth on the Road," 341.

60 Canadian Welfare Council, *Transient Youth*, 86.

61 Ibid., 60.

62 Ibid., 116.

63 Stuart Henderson, *Making the Scene: Yorkville and Hip Toronto in the 1960s* (Toronto: University of Toronto Press, 2011), 15.

64 Canadian Welfare Council, *Transient Youth*, 68; Rogers, "Addendum," i.

65 Quoted in Canadian Council on Social Development, *More about Transient Youth*, i.

66 Sixty-four percent of the delegates were between the ages of sixteen and thirty. Ibid., 46.

67 Ibid., 6, 14. The report of the federal government's Commission of Inquiry into the Non-Medical Use of Drugs, or the Le Dain Commission, established in 1969, would be published on June 19, 1970. Ibid., 16.

68 Ibid., 2.

69 Ibid., 11.

70 Ibid., 7, 31.

71 "Victoria's Cool Aid Assists Transients," *Winnipeg Free Press*, June 6, 1970, 11.

72 Canadian Council on Social Development, *More about Transient Youth*, 11.

73 Ibid., 27, 23.

74 Andy Cohen and Vince Kelly were members of the Committee on Youth, Department of Secretary of State. Ibid., 41–42.

75 "Hostel Funds Allocated," *Winnipeg Free Press*, July 9, 1970, 22.

76 Ibid.

77 Interview with Patrick Esmond-White, Ottawa, December 5, 2012; Patrick Esmonde-White, "The Trudeaumaniac: The Summer of 1970," 7–8, unpublished, quoted with author's permission.

78 Canadian Council on Social Development, *More about Transient Youth*, 14.

79  Clyde Sanger, "2,000 Hostel Beds in 12 Cities: Military Building Opened for Hitch-hiking Youth," *Globe and Mail*, July 9, 1970, 1. See also "Hippie Menace on Sunshine Coast?" *Georgia Straight* (Vancouver), May 5–11, 1971, 5.

80  Interviewee 29, Ottawa, December 5, 2012, and March 23, 2013.

81  "Tent City Is Approved," *Charlottetown Guardian*, May 15, 1971, PEI Scrapbook: Information Gathered Summer of 1981, by Atula Joshi, M7832, file 292, Canadian Youth Hostels Association, Glenbow Museum Archives, Calgary (hereafter CYHA-GMA). The criticism of the government program was that "the youth hostel was put into the community instead of growing out of the community." Canadian Council on Social Development, *Transient Youth, 70–71: Report of an Inquiry about Programs in 1970, and Plans for 1971* (Ottawa: Department of Health and Welfare, 1970), 14.

82  Numerous letters and petitions with hundreds of signatures from members of the Kitsilano Ratepayers' Association against hippie businesses and activities are in Special Committee on Hippies, 1968, 79B-5, files 11 and 15, City of Vancouver Archives.

83  Ross, "Panic on Love Street," 17.

84  Ibid., 18; Letter from Chief Constable of the Vancouver Police Department to the Mayor/City Council, March 23, 1967, Complaints: Beatnik Establishments in 2000, 2100, 2200 Blocks West 4th Avenue, Special Committee on Hippies, COV-S450, City of Vancouver Archives. See also Letter from Chief Constable of the Vancouver Police Department to the Mayor/City Council, April 26, 1967, Complaints: Beatnik Estab-lishments in 2000, 2100, 2200 Blocks West 4th Avenue, Special Committee on Hippies, COV-S450, City of Vancouver Archives.

85  Lawrence Aronsen, *City of Love and Revolution: Vancouver in the Sixties* (Vancouver: New Star Books, 2010), 15–18, 25; Ross, "Panic on Love Street," 12.

86  "Calder Raps Hostels Stand," *Vancouver Province*, July 24, 1970.

87  "Federal Hostels Hippie Havens," *Vancouver Province*, July 10, 1970; "Probes City Armoury Hostel: Mayor Fears Draft Dodger 'Haven,'" *Vancouver Sun*, July 10, 1970.

88  These hostels admitted travellers and runaways aged thirteen to twenty-one. "Some Are in Turn Rejected," *Vancouver Sun*, November 27, 1970.

89  Bob Quintrell, "Vancouver Politicians Averse to Hippies," *CBC Television*, March 18, 1968, http://www.cbc.ca/archives/entry/vancouver-politicians-averse-to-hippies. See also Ross, "Panic on Love Street," 33.

90  Michael Barnholden, *Reading the Riot Act: A Brief History of Rioting in Vancouver* (Vancouver: Anvil, 2005), 89.

91  "Federal Hostels Hippie Havens," *Vancouver Province*, July 10, 1970; "Probes City Armoury Hostel: Mayor Fears Draft Dodger 'Haven,'" *Vancouver Sun*, July 10, 1970.

92  "Probes City Armoury Hostel: Mayor Fears Draft Dodger 'Haven,'" *Vancouver Sun*, July 10, 1970. This article reported that the Beatty Street hostel was one of four hostels in Vancouver that summer. The YMCA (50 beds), the YWCA (80 beds), and Alexandra House (50 beds) served a total of 12,500 youth, of whom 60 percent were from out of province, 15 percent from the United States, and 5 percent from Europe.

93  Marcel Martel, "'They Smell Bad, Have Diseases, and Are Lazy': RCMP Officers Re-porting on Hippies in the Late Sixties," *Canadian Historical Review* 90, 2 (2009): 245.

)4  Patrick Esmonde-White, "Concept Paper: The Battle of Jericho Beach," March 21, 2014, unpublished, quoted with author's permission.

)5  M. Athena Palaeologu, ed., *The Sixties in Canada: A Turbulent and Creative Decade* (Montreal: Black Rose Books, 2009).

)6  Aronsen, *City of Love*, 108.

)7  Barnholden, *Reading the Riot Act*, 89.

)8  Maoz, "Mutual Gaze," 222–23.

)9  "After the Battle of Jericho," *Vancouver Province*, October 17, 1970.

)0  RCMP, "Memorandum File, Vancouver Liberation Front," September 17, 1970, PEW; "Director of Security and Intelligence to Secretary of Security," September 17, 1970, PEW.

)1  Special Committee on Transient and Alienated Youth, "Evaluation of Hostel Facilities Provided for Transient Youth during the Summer of 1970," September 1970, Special Committee on Hippies, COV-S450, City of Vancouver Archives.

)2  Teddy Mahood, interview with author, Turtle Valley, BC, August 7, 2013.

)3  "Ottawa Axes Hostel Use at Jericho," *Vancouver Sun*, September 16, 1970; RCMP, "Operations Records, 1997–98/582, ESI (E) – 108 re: VLF," PEW; "Military Convoy Called Back: Transients Seize Vancouver Hostel, Win Right to Remain," *Globe and Mail*, September 9, 1970, 1.

)4  "Inmates Occupy Armoury Hostel," *Vancouver Province*, September 8, 1970.

)5  "Ottawa Bows to Transients," *Vancouver Province*, September 9, 1970; "Officials Back Down: Youth Win Hostel Fight," *Vancouver Sun*, September 11, 1970.

)6  Alan Fotheringham, *Vancouver Sun*, September 10, 1970.

)7  "Hostel – Occupation a Success," *Georgia Straight* (Vancouver), September 9, 1970, 12–13, 21.

)8  "Jericho Hilton to Close," *Vancouver Sun*, September 16, 1970.

)9  "Tom Terrifically Outraged at Transients and Ottawa," *Vancouver Province*, September 12, 1970.

·0  RCMP, "National Hostel Task Force, Vancouver, B.C.," September 30, 1970, National Force, Correspondence etc., 70HQ, 559-E-4, PEW.

1  "Tom Terrifically Outraged at Transients and Ottawa," *Vancouver Province*, September 12, 1970; RCMP, "Operations Records, 1995–96/691, Memorandum from DSI to 'D' Branch," October 8, 1970, PEW.

2  "Thunder Bay Row Leads to Death," *Winnipeg Free Press*, August 28, 1970.

3  Esmonde-White, "Trudeaumaniac," 21; "Emergency Committee Seeks to Keep Drop-In Centre Open," *London Free Press*, September 15, 1970.

4  "Youth Centre Hopes Crushed under Boots of Raiding Gang," *London Free Press*, September 16, 1970.

5  Carmen Hamilton, "Human Pigsty," letter to the editor, *London Free Press*, October 6, 1970.

6  "Chow Time at Jericho," *Vancouver Province*, September 15, 1970.

7  "Movement for Democratic Control of the Hostel Started with the Occupation of Beatty Street: JERICHO! Caught in Between," *Georgia Straight* (Vancouver), September 16, 1970, 2.

118 RCMP, "Operations Records, 1995–96/691, Memorandum," October 5, 1970, PEW; RCMP, "National Hostel Task Force, Vancouver, B.C.," September 30, 1970, National Force, Correspondence etc., 70HQ, 559-E-4, PEW.

119 "By Labour 'Hard-Hat' Rejected," *Vancouver Sun*, September 16, 1970.

120 "Veteran Flays Hostellers," *Vancouver Province*, September 10, 1970; "Armoury Hostel a Mess," *Vancouver Province*, September 10, 1970; "Shut Hostel, Perrault Urges," *Vancouver Province*, September 10, 1970; RCMP, "National Hostel Task Force, Vancouver, B.C.," September 30, 1970, National Force, Correspondence etc., 70HQ, 559-E-4, PEW.

121 RCMP, "Operations Records, 1995–96/691, Intelligence, 'Secret,'" September 11, 1970, PEW; RCMP, "National Hostel Task Force, Vancouver, B.C.," September 30, 1970, National Force, Correspondence etc., 70HQ, 559-E-4, PEW.

122 "Tom Terrifically Outraged at Transients and Ottawa," *Vancouver Province*, September 12, 1970.

123 "Transients Like Jericho Home," *Vancouver Province*, September 14, 1970.

124 "An Invitation to Disaster," *Vancouver Province*, September 9, 1970.

125 Marcus Zeir, "Help Out Jericho People," *Georgia Straight* (Vancouver), October 7–14, 1970, 2; Coordinating Committee on Hostels and Other Services for Transient Youth, "Proposal Related to the Needs of Youth," October 9, 1970, Transient Youth, 618-A-7, file 9, City of Vancouver Archives.

126 "Only the Deadline Passes: All Stands Still at Jericho," *Vancouver Sun*, October 3, 1970. See also Ken Romain, "Jericho Army Base Stays Occupied as Youngsters Defy Orders to Quit," *Globe and Mail*, October 3, 1970.

127 "How the Battle of Jericho Was Fought," *Vancouver Sun*, October 16, 1970, 15; Zeir, "Help Out Jericho People."

128 Zeir, "Help Out Jericho People."

129 Ibid.

130 "C.F.M. Halifax," *Georgia Straight* (Vancouver), October 21, 1970.

131 "The Streets," *Georgia Straight* (Vancouver), October 7, 1970.

132 "Rebels at Vancouver: Youngsters Defy Order to Quit Jericho Base," *Globe and Mail*, October 3, 1970.

133 "Let There Be Light at Jericho-City," *Vancouver Province*, October 9, 1970.

134 Ibid.

135 "Rebels at Vancouver: Youngsters Defy Order to Quit Jericho Base," *Globe and Mail*, October 3, 1970.

136 RCMP, "Operations Records, 1995–96/691, Memorandum from DSI to 'D' Branch," October 8, 1970, PEW; RCMP, "National Hostel Task Force, Vancouver, B.C.," October 10, 19, and 30, 1970, National Force, Correspondence etc., 70HQ, 599-E-4, PEW.

137 Ibid.

138 Zeir, "Help Out Jericho People."

139 The RCMP reported that "a good number of photographs were taken during the operation by our Identification Section." RCMP, "Operations Records, 1995–96/691, Solicitor General's Office, Minutes of Meeting," October 8–10, 1970, PEW; RCMP, "National Hostel Task Force, Vancouver, B.C.," October 10, 19, and 30, 1970, National Force, Correspondence etc., 70HQ, 599-E-4, PEW.

40 RCMP, "Sit-in at Bldg. #47, Jericho CFB, Known as the Jericho Hostel, Defence Establishment Trespass Regulations," sec. 9, October 15, 1970, in "National Hostel Task Force, Vancouver, B.C.," October 10, 19, and 30, 1970, National Force, Correspondence etc., 70HQ, 599-E-4, PEW.

41 Teddy Mahood, interview with author, Turtle Valley, BC, August 7, 2013.

42 "Chronology of Confrontation: How the Battle of Jericho Was Fought," *Vancouver Sun*, October 16, 1970; "Riot Sticks Help Clear Way for Traffic," *Vancouver Province*, October 16, 1970; Lorne Parton, *Vancouver Province*, October 16, 1970; "From Idle Jeering to Sharp Violence," *Vancouver Sun*, October 16, 1970; "After the Battle," *Vancouver Province*, October 17, 1970; Ken Romain, "Rally Proves Flop: Vancouver Separatists Win Few Supporters," *Globe and Mail*, October 19, 1970, 4; RCMP, "National Hostel Task Force, Vancouver, B.C.," October 10, 19, and 30, 1970, National Force, Correspondence etc., 70HQ, 599-E-4, PEW.

43 Teddy Mahood, interview with author, Turtle Valley, BC, August 7, 2013.

44 Ken Romain, "Beds Being Found for Transients," *Globe and Mail*, October 17, 1970, 3; "Evicted Transients Billeted in City," *Vancouver Sun*, October 19, 1970.

45 Canada, Secretary of State, Committee on Youth, *It's Your Turn*; Swainger, "Teen Trouble," 162.

46 Marcel Danesi, *Geeks, Goths, and Gangstas: Youth Culture and the Evolution of Modern Society* (Toronto: Canadian Scholars' Press, 2010), 85. Darya Maoz notes that in cases of unwanted tourist encounters between hosts and young travellers, "mutual gazes can result in cynical exploitation, mutual suspicion and even hatred." Maoz, "Mutual Gaze," 235.

47 Quintrell, "Vancouver Politicians."

48 Quoted in Needham, "Something to Do," 6.

49 Canadian Council on Social Development, *More about Transient Youth*, 32.

50 Roberta Lexier, "To Struggle Together or Fracture Apart: The Sixties Student Movements at English-Canadian Universities," in *Debating Dissent: Canada and the 1960s*, ed. Lara Campbell, Dominique Clément, and Gregory Kealey (Toronto: University of Toronto Press, 2012), 84–88.

51 Danesi, *Geeks, Goths, and Gangstas*, 85.

52 Marcel Martel, "'Riot' at Sir George Williams: Giving Meaning to Student Dissent," in *Debating Dissent: Canada and the 1960s*, ed. Lara Campbell, Dominique Clément, and Gregory Kealey (Toronto: University of Toronto Press, 2012), 105; Susan Reisler, "It Ain't Heavy, It's My Unemployment Insurance," *The Meliorist* (University of Lethbridge), January 22, 1971, 4; "Long Hot Summer ahead for Students," *The Martlet* (University of Victoria), January 28, 1971, 3; Lynn Atkins, "Will You Find a Job in the Summer?" *The Peak* (Simon Fraser University), March 11, 1970, 16.

53 "Where to Live," *The Ubyssey* (University of British Columbia), September 8, 1970, 21.

54 "UBC Rejects Plea to Turn SUB into Hostel," *The Charlatan* (Carleton University), October 2, 1970.

55 It was decided that people from Cool Aid would act as "buffers between the 'pigs' and the hostel people." RCMP, Directorate of Security and Intelligence, D Branch, Memorandum, in "National Hostel Task Force, Vancouver, B.C.," October 1, 1970, National Force, Correspondence etc., 70HQ, 599-E-4, PEW.

156  "16-Hour SUB Occupation Had Tense Moments," *UBC Report,* October 22, 1970, 1–2. See also Jack Wasserman, *Vancouver Sun,* October 6, 1970.

157  "UBC Rejects Plea to Turn SUB into Hostel," *The Charlatan* (Carleton University), October 2, 1970.

158  Both quoted in Jim Scott, "The Hostel Issue: More Yet," *The Ubyssey* (University of British Columbia), September 24, 1970, 4–5.

159  "Transients UBC Bound," *Vancouver Province,* September 29, 1970, 4.

160  Mike Brake, *Comparative Youth Culture: The Sociology of Youth Cultures and Youth Subcultures in America, Britain and Canada* (New York: Routledge, 1985), 64. See also Stanley Cohen, *Folk Devils and Moral Panics: The Creation of the Mods and the Rockers* (1972; reprint, London: Routledge, 2002).

161  Lexier, "To Struggle Together," 93.

162  Aronsen, *City of Love,* 24. See also "The Hate-4th Scene," *Georgia Straight* (Vancouver), June 28, 1967, 3.

163  Letter to Kitsilano Ratepayers' Association, August 11, 1967, Transient Youth, 618-A-7, file 69, City of Vancouver Archives.

164  Quoted in Scott, "Hostel Issue," 4–5.

165  Ginny Galt, "Split Council Approves Hostel in Wednesday Vote," *The Ubyssey* (University of British Columbia), September 24, 1970, 3; "To the Rear, March," *The Ubyssey* (University of British Columbia), September 24, 1970, 4.

166  "U.B.C. Rejects Pleas to Turn SUB into Hostel," *The Charlatan* (Carleton University), October 2, 1970.

167  "Students Vote to Keep Out 'Green Saliva,'" *The Ubyssey* (University of British Columbia), October 2, 1970, 2.

168  "YMCA Aids Jericho Family," *Vancouver Province,* October 17, 1970.

169  Greg Marquis, "Uptight Little Island: The Junction '71 Affair," *The Island,* Fall–Winter 2002, 10–14, http://vre2.upei.ca/islandmagazine/fedora/repository/vre%3Aislemag -batch2-669.

170  Canadian Council on Social Development, *More about Transient Youth,* iv–v, 9, 14, emphasis added.

171  "Centre Provides Stop-Overs for Canadian Transient Youth," *Winnipeg Free Press,* July 8, 1970.

172  Canadian Council on Social Development, *Transient Youth,* 70–71, 21.

173  Canadian Welfare Council, *Transient Youth,* 65. See also "Higgins's Remarks Irresponsible," *The Muse* (Memorial University), May 25, 1971.

174  Maoz, "Mutual Gaze," 235.

175  Ibid.

176  Quoted in Romain, "Rally Proves Flop," 4. See also "Help Out Jericho People," *Georgia Straight* (Vancouver), October 21, 1970.

### Chapter 5: Crash Pads

1  Byron Rogers, "Background Study on Hostel and Kiosk Program Summer '71," September 5–8, 1971, 2, unpublished, cited with author's permission. See also Canada, Secretary of State, Committee on Youth, *It's Your Turn: A Report to the Secretary of State by the Committee on Youth* (Ottawa: Information Canada, 1971), 147.

2  Trudeau's speech to the House of Commons on March 16, 1971, was printed in Tony Di Franco, "OFY: Showcase Participation," *The Chevron* (University of Waterloo), November 10, 1972; and in "Opportunities for Youth," *McGill Daily* (McGill University), September 20, 1971. See also Pierre Elliott Trudeau, "Announcement of Summer Student Employment and Activities Program," March 16, 1971, https://www.lipad.ca/full/1971/03/16/1.

3  Sandra Gwyn, "The Great Ottawa Grand Boom," *Saturday Night,* October 1972, 22.

4  Of the $67.8 million initially allocated, approximately $25 million was for the Opportunities for Youth program. "Canada's Young Get Busy as Politicians Complain," *Toronto Daily Star,* June 26, 1971.

5  Bryan D. Palmer, *Canada's 1960s: The Ironies of Identity in a Rebellious Era* (Toronto: University of Toronto Press, 2009), 204, 208–9. Countercultural values and ideologies promote arduous intellectual discussions, poetry, music, exploring nature, touring, and "peace and love." The marriage of high culture and low culture would lead to "new ways of living." David Fowler, *Youth Culture in Modern Britain, c. 1920–c. 1970: From Ivory Tower to Global Movement – A New History* (London: Palgrave Macmillan, 2008); Marcel Danesi, *Why It Sells: Decoding the Meanings of Brand Names, Logos, Ads, and Other Marketing and Advertising Ploys* (Lanham, MD: Rowman and Littlefield, 2008), 39.

6  Members had access to 4,700 youth hostels around the world. "Youth Hostels Merge, Form National Group," *Globe and Mail,* December 1, 1976. The Canadian Youth Hostels Association reported, "In 1970 it had in operation 42 youth hostels. A trans-Canada network of youth hostels is still the CYHA's ultimate goal." Canadian Youth Hostels Association, National Office, "Submission to the Committee on Youth," April 16, 1970, 2, National Executive Council Meeting, 1970, M7832, file 64, Canadian Youth Hostels Association, Glenbow Museum Archives, Calgary (hereafter CYHA-GMA).

7  Stanley Cohen says, "In the gallery of types society erects to show its members which roles should be avoided ... folk devils [are] reminders of what we should not be." These "social types" are usually adolescents, regarded as "public property," and commented upon as such. Stanley Cohen, *Folk Devils and Moral Panics: The Creation of the Mods and the Rockers* (1972; reprint, London: Routledge, 2002), 2.

8  Canadian Youth Hostels Association, *Handbook* (1961), 1, M7832, file 290, CYHA-GMA. For a discussion of international youth clubs, see John Gillis, *Youth and History: Tradition and Change in European Age Relations, 1770–Present* (London: Academic, 1981), 148–49.

9  H.J. Cody, "Foreword," in Canadian Youth Hostels Association, *Handbook* (1939–40), 3, Canadian Youth Hostels Association Handbook/Hostel Trails of Canada, 1939–1940, 1942, 1945–1946, M2169, file 11, CYHA-GMA. The Canadian Youth Hostels Association stated that one of its objectives was "to help all, but especially young people, to a greater knowledge, care and love of the countryside." Canadian Youth Hostels Association, National Office, "Submission to the Committee on Youth," April 16, 1970, 1, National Executive Council Meeting, 1970, M7832, file 64, CYHA-GMA.

0  "City Teachers Build Hostel Movement Here," *Calgary Herald,* n.d., Scrapbook 1953–1956, North West Region, Edmonton, M7832, file 289, CYHA-GMA; "Calgary School Teachers Made Hostel Dream Come True," *Calgary Herald Magazine,* June 21, 1958, Youth Hostels, M7832, file 74, CYHA-GMA.

11  Canadian Youth Hostels Association, *Handbook* (1961), 1–2, M7832, file 290, CYHA-GMA. In Europe and Canada, hostels were chaperoned by houseparents, who in the early 1950s were responsible for collecting nightly fees, distributing the housekeeping duties of hostellers, and seeing that the rules were obeyed. It was a two-week commitment, and "previous experience with young people" was preferred. "Youth Hostellers Discuss Banff-Jasper Facilities," circa 1954, Scrapbook 1953–1956, North West Region, Edmonton, M7832, file 289, CYHA-GMA.

12  The Canadian Youth Hostels Association stated that it "had no political, religious or ethnic ties and does not discriminate in any way against race, creed or religion." In 1937, with fewer than one hundred members and a total of ten hostels, it became the twentieth member of the International Youth Hostel Federation. Canadian Youth Hostels Association, National Office, "Submission to the Committee on Youth," April 16, 1970, 2–3, National Executive Council Meeting, 1970, M7832, file 64, CYHA-GMA.

13  Canadian Youth Hostels Association, "President's Report, 1970," Annual Reports 1965–1972, M7832, file 64, CYHA-GMA.

14  "Hostels Open in '67," *The Chevron* (University of Waterloo), May 27, 1966.

15  Ibid.

16  Richard James and John Roberts, "Hosteling in Canada," September 15, 1976, 1, National Task Force 1974–1976, drafts and proposals, M7832, file 108, CYHA-GMA.

17  Canadian Youth Hostels Association, *Hostelling in Canada* (1974), 2, National Task Force 1974–1976, drafts and proposals, M7832, file 108, CYHA-GMA.

18  Canadian Youth Hostels Association, "Houseparents' Responsibilities," 1968, 9, Publications December 1965–1968, M7832, file 140, CYHA-GMA. See also Canadian Youth Hostels Association, *Houseparent's Manual* (1974), Publications 1974, M7832, file 140, CYHA-GMA.

19  Canadian Youth Hostels Association, *Handbook* (1961), 9, Scrapbook 1959–1966, North West Region, Edmonton, M7832, file 290, CYHA-GMA.

20  Canadian Youth Hostels Association, Mountain Region, *Trailblazer,* May 1954, Scrapbook 1953–1956, North West Region, Edmonton, M7832, file 289, CYHA-GMA.

21  Bryan Campbell, "Canadian Youth Hostels: The Answer to a Tired Hiker's Dream," *The Gateway* (University of Alberta), October 29, 1965, 9.

22  J.K. Anderson, "A Visit to Yoho National Park," July 1, 1960, Scrapbook 1959–1960, North West Region, Edmonton, M7832, file 290, CYHA-GMA.

23  See the photo on page 25.

24  "Dear Everyone," letter from Judy Anderson, quoted in *Pathfinder,* September–October 1961, Scrapbook 1959–1966, North West Region, Edmonton, M7832, file 290, CYHA-GMA.

25  "What Is Hostelling?" Scrapbook, 1959–1966, North West Region, Edmonton, M7832, file 296, CYHA-GMA.

26  Canadian Youth Hostels Association, "President's Report, 1968," Annual Reports 1965–1972, M7832, file 73, CYHA-GMA.

27  Letter from Denis Heney, Edmonton, to Prime Minister John Diefenbaker, September 11, 1961, Scrapbook 1959–1966, North West Region, Edmonton, M7832, file 290, CYHA-GMA.

28  Ibid. The CYHA was frustrated because it wanted to showcase Canada to travelling youth from around the world. It reported, "In Austria, one in 47 of the population is a Youth Hostel member; in Sweden one in 67; in Germany one in 180; in Japan one in 249; in Canada one in 2,690; [and] in the USA one in 7,226." Canadian Youth Hostels Association, "President's Report, 1965," Annual Reports 1965–1972, M7832, file 73, CYHA-GMA.

29  Liberal leadership convention polls showed that young Canadians overwhelmingly preferred Trudeau. A youth said that Trudeau was "the most exciting single thing that could happen to this country." See Doug Owram, *Born at the Right Time: A History of the Baby-Boom Generation* (Toronto: University of Toronto Press, 1996), 201.

30  Canadian Youth Hostels Association, *Annual Report, 1968–1969* (1969), front cover, Annual Reports 1965–1972, M7832, file 73, CYHA-GMA.

31  Canadian Youth Hostels Association, "President's Message," *Pathfinder,* September 1968, 1, Pathfinder December 1965–November 1968, M7832, file 167, CYHA-GMA.

32  Canadian Youth Hostels Association, *Annual Report 1968–1969* (1969), front cover, Annual Reports 1965–1972, M7832, file 73, CYHA-GMA.

33  Canadian Youth Hostels Association, "President's Report, 1968–1969," 3, Annual Reports 1965–1972, M7832, file 64, CYHA-GMA.

34  Canadian Youth Hostels Association, National Office, "Submission to the Committee on Youth," April 16, 1970, National Executive Council Meeting, 1970, M7832, file 64, CYHA-GMA; Canadian Welfare Council, "Report on National Consultation on Transient Youth," May 2–4, 1970, Circulars to Regions, M7832, file 113, CYHA-GMA; David Simonsen, "The President's Report, October 1969–September 1970," in Canadian Youth Hostels Association, "Annual General Meeting," May 1, 1971, Circulars to Regions, M7832, file 113, CYHA-GMA.

35  Speech by National President David Simonsen, National Executive Meeting, in Canadian Youth Hostels Association, *Annual Report 1969–1970* (1970), Annual Reports 1965–1972, M7832, file 64, CYHA-GMA.

36  Canadian Council on Social Development, *More about Transient Youth* (Ottawa: Canadian Council on Social Development, 1970), 31–32.

37  Canadian Youth Hostels Association, "Task Force Visit, Vancouver," August 18, 1975, National Task Force 1974–1976, M7832, file 107, CYHA-GMA.

38  Notes from interview with Andy Cohen, Interim Co-coordinator, National Hostel Task Force, April 1970, Sainte-Adèle, Quebec, cited in B. Rogers and A. Arda, "Background Study: Development of Summer '71, Goals, Objectives and Criteria of Opportunities for Youth," September 27, 1971, unpublished, cited with authors' permission.

39  Canadian Council on Social Development, *More about Transient Youth,* 31.

40  Canada, Secretary of State, Committee on Youth, *It's Your Turn,* 1–2.

41  Ibid., 147.

42  Kenneth Westhues, "Inter-Generational Conflict in the Sixties," in *Prophecy and Protest: Social Movements in Twentieth-Century Canada,* ed. Samuel Clark, J. Paul Grayson, and Linda Grayson (Toronto: Gage, 1975), 403.

43  The Department of Citizenship was created by Prime Minister William Lyon Mackenzie King in 1941 as a "wartime propaganda agency" to keep an eye on "putative aliens,

Canadianize new immigrants, and provide grant money to the Boy Scouts." Gwyn, "Great Ottawa Grand Boom," 23.

44 Rogers and Arda, "Background Study"; Byron Rogers, "Addendum: Role of the Canadian Council on Social Development," 1971, 7–8, unpublished, cited with author's permission; Canada, Secretary of State, Committee on Youth, *It's Your Turn*, 147.

45 Rogers and Arda, "Background Study," 4–5.

46 "'Transients Prefer Work': Job Lack Criticized in Report on Youth," *Globe and Mail*, March 5, 1971, 3.

47 Quoted in ibid. See also Canadian Council on Social Development, *Youth '71: An Inquiry into the Transient Youth and Opportunities for Youth Programs in the Summer of 1971* (Ottawa: Department of Health and Welfare, 1972), 7.

48 Canada, "Report of the Interdepartmental Committee on the Program for Student Summer Employment and Activities," January 28, 1971, 1–2, in private possession of Byron Rogers.

49 "A 'Long Hot Summer' for Young Workers," *Edmonton Journal*, May 29, 1970, 13.

50 Rogers and Arda, "Background Study," 9.

51 Quoted in Canada, "A Plan for Student Summer Employment and Activity," December 15, 1970, in private possession of Byron Rogers.

52 The number of unemployed in July 1970 was 283,000, an increase of 87,000 over 1969. The projection for 1971 was 316,000 unemployed students aged fourteen to twenty-four. Quebec had the worst youth unemployment problem, at 21 percent, which was one-third higher than the national average. The Prairies fared better with 13 percent student unemployment, as did Ontario (10.2%), the Pacific (14.4%), and the Atlantic (14.4%). Rogers and Arda, "Background Study," 9.

53 Quoted in Canada, "Plan for Student Summer."·

54 Di Franco, "OFY: Showcase Participation," 14. See also Tony Di Franco, "Opportunities for Youth," *The Martlet* (University of Victoria), February 1, 1973, 6.

55 Rob Andras was appointed regional director for Ontario, and Brian Gilhuly was appointed director of hostels and kiosks. In October 1970 a subcommittee under the Department of Manpower and Immigration began to look into student summer unemployment and openings for youth programs and activities. Rogers and Arda, "Background Study," 9.

56 Matt Cavers, "Dollars for 'Deadbeats': Opportunities for Youth Grants and the Back-to-the-Land Movement on British Columbia's Sunshine Coast," in *Canadian Counter Cultures and the Environment*, ed. Colin M. Coates (Calgary: University of Calgary Press, 2016), 179–80.

57 Cam Mackie, interview with author, London, Ontario, June 20, 2014.

58 Rogers, "Addendum," 12.

59 Brian Gilhuly, telephone interview with author, March 2, 2017.

60 Quoted in "Anyone Can Ride the 'Road Toad,'" *Winnipeg Free Press*, June 28, 1971, 14. See also "Opportunities for Youth," *The Fulcrum* (University of Ottawa), October 21, 1971, 12; Di Franco, "OFY: Showcase Participation."

61 Canadian Youth Hostels Association, "Annual General Meeting," May 2, 1970, 17, Executive Meeting Toronto, M7832, file 64, CYHA-GMA.

52 Brian Gilhuly, telephone interview with author, March 2, 2017. See also Di Franco, "OFY: Showcase Participation."

53 Peter Berger and Thomas Luckmann, *The Social Construction of Reality: A Treatise in the Sociology of Knowledge* (New York: Doubleday, 1966).

54 Rogers and Arda, "Background Study," 48. See also "Canada's Young Get Busy as Politicians Complain," *Toronto Daily Star,* June 26, 1971.

55 Ibid.

56 Canada, "Report of the Interdepartmental Committee," 28. See also Judith Sanderbrook, "Youth and Work," May 1970, 200–2, copy provided by Byron Rogers.

57 After the "scuttling of the buses" by Cabinet, "the kiosks lost much of their original raison d'être." Rogers, "Background Study on Hostel and Kiosk Program," 15.

58 Canada, "Report of the Interdepartmental Committee," 29.

59 Michael Wheeler of the Canadian Welfare Council said, "Private crash pads are dangerous for everyone, youth and host." Quoted in "On the Road," *Ottawa Journal,* March 23, 1971.

70 "No Hostel without Local Okay," *Winnipeg Free Press,* June 8, 1971.

71 "Youths Get Hostels, 50 Kiosks," *Edmonton Journal,* May 31, 1971.

72 Rogers, "Background Study on Hostel and Kiosk Program," 12.

73 Ibid., 13–14.

74 Ibid., 8.

75 The ideas of Andy Cohen and David Slipacoff are summarized in ibid.

76 Richard Gregory, "A Brief History of the Hippie Trail," 2015, https://www.richard gregory.org.uk/history/hippie-trail.htm.

77 Rogers, "Background Study on Hostel and Kiosk Program," 16.

78 Ibid., 15.

79 "Information Kiosks for Hitchhikers Open Here Soon," *Winnipeg Free Press,* June 25, 1971.

80 "Tent Kiosk Program Blowing in the Wind," *Globe and Mail,* July 23, 1971, 7. See also "The Opening of Winnipeg's 2 Kiosks Delayed," *Winnipeg Free Press,* June 25, 1971; and "Ottawa Folds Its Tents," *Winnipeg Free Press,* July 23, 1971.

81 Canada, Department of Health and Welfare, *On the Road: A Guide for Youth Travelling Canada* (Ottawa: Department of Health and Welfare, 1972). See also Canadian Council on Social Development, *Transient Youth, 70–71: Report of an Inquiry about Programs in 1970, and Plans for 1971* (Ottawa: Department of Health and Welfare, 1970), 67.

82 Michael Moore, "The New Ottawa Booklet That's Bound to Lead Youth Astray," *Globe and Mail,* June 17, 1972.

83 "Federal Transient Program," *Ottawa Journal,* March 23, 1970.

84 Gwyn, "Great Ottawa Grand Boom," 22. See also Jennifer Keck and Wayne Fulks, "Meaningful Work and Community Betterment: The Case of Opportunities for Youth and Local Initiatives Program, 1971–1973," in *Community Organizing: Canadian Experiences,* ed. Brian Wharf and Michael Clague, 113–36 (Toronto: Oxford University Press, 1997).

85 Gwyn, "Great Ottawa Grand Boom," 22.

86  "Drop-In Drop-Outs Doing Own Thing for Teens," *London Free Press*, August 19, 1970; "Two London Teen-Agers Claim That the City's Drop-In Centres Are for Only One Type of Youth," *London Free Press*, July 26, 1970.

87  "The Theme Is Youth: The Recommendations Are Bizarre," *Winnipeg Free Press*, July 7, 1971.

88  "A Way Out Is Wanted," *Penticton Herald*, May 5, 1971, News Clippings, British Columbia, 1967, 1970–71, 1977, M7832, file 268, CYHA-GMA.

89  "Islanders Threaten to Spread Hog Manure beside PEI Tent City for Hippies," *Globe and Mail*, June 2, 1971.

90  "Gov't Reveals Pacification Program," *The Meliorist* (University of Lethbridge), March 26, 1971, 4.

91  "Opportunities for Youth," *The Fulcrum* (University of Ottawa), October 21, 1971.

92  Ironically, because these tourist attractions are staged, travellers appear to locals as "suckers and shallow." Darya Maoz, "The Mutual Gaze," *Annals of Tourism Research* 33, 1 (2006): 230.

93  "Youth Going Nowhere in Search of Adventure," *Globe and Mail*, July 18, 1970.

94  "Thousands of Youngsters Will Be on the Road This Summer," *Montreal Gazette*, August 25, 1970.

95  "Canada's Great Trek: 40,000 Transients Will Walk This Summer," *Vancouver Province*, April 6, 1971; "50,000 Transients Only the Beginning," *Vancouver Sun*, February 5, 1971.

96  "City Braced for Transients," *Calgary Herald*, May 17, 1972, News Clippings, Alberta, 1970–1980, M7832, file 268, CYHA-GMA; "Army of Hitch-Hikers Already on the March," *Winnipeg Free Press*, June 22, 1972, 3.

97  Greg Marquis, "Uptight Little Island: The Junction '71 Affair," *The Island*, Fall–Winter 2002, 10, http://vre2.upei.ca/islandmagazine/fedora/repository/vre%3Aislemag -batch2-669.

98  Ibid., 13–14.

99  "Tent City Is Approved," *Charlottetown Guardian*, May 15, 1971, PEI Scrapbook: Information Gathered Summer of 1981, by Atula Joshi, M7832, file 292, CYHA- GMA. The criticism of the government program was that "the youth hostel was put into the community instead of growing out of the community." Canadian Council on Social Development, *Transient Youth, 70–71*, 14.

100  "Islanders Threaten to Spread Hog Manure beside PEI Tent City for Hippies," *Globe and Mail*, June 2, 1971; "Hostel Site Set at East Royalty," *Charlottetown Guardian*, May 20, 1971, PEI Scrapbook: Information Gathered Summer of 1981, by Atula Joshi, M7832, file 292, CYHA-GMA.

101  "Legal Action Voted by Area Residents," *Charlottetown Guardian*, June 1, 1971; "Court Action Is Considered in East Royalty Tent Hostel," *Charlottetown Guardian*, June 1, 1971; "East Royalty Planning to Continue to Fight," *Charlottetown Guardian*, June 4, 1971, all in PEI Scrapbook: Information Gathered Summer of 1981, by Atula Joshi, M7832, file 292, CYHA-GMA.

102  "Women Hold Position along Hostel Barrier," *Charlottetown Guardian*, June 8, 1971; "Way Is Cleared for Start of Youth Hostel Project," *Charlottetown Guardian*, n.d., both

in PEI Scrapbook: Information Gathered Summer of 1981, by Atula Joshi, M7832, file 292, CYHA-GMA.

03  "PEI Youth Hostel Question Discussed by Presbytery," *Charlottetown Guardian,* July 3, 1970, PEI Scrapbook: Information Gathered Summer of 1981, by Atula Joshi, M7832, file 292, CYHA-GMA.

04  "Higgins's Remarks Irresponsible," *The Muse* (Memorial University), May 25, 1971. See also "Newfoundland Wondering What Can Be Done: Quarters for Youth Hostels Hard to Find," *Globe and Mail,* May 31, 1971; and "Postpone Action on Hostel Plan," *Charlottetown Guardian,* May 28, 1971, PEI Scrapbook: Information Gathered Summer of 1981, by Atula Joshi, M7832, file 292, CYHA-GMA.

05  "Islanders Threaten to Spread Hog Manure beside PEI Tent City for Hippies," *Globe and Mail,* June 2, 1971. See also "No Tent Hostel Problem Anticipated by City Mayor," *Charlottetown Guardian,* June 1, 1971, PEI Scrapbook: Information Gathered Summer of 1981, by Atula Joshi, M7832, file 292, CYHA-GMA. "Newfoundland Wondering What Can Be Done: Quarters for Youth Hostels Hard to Find," *Globe and Mail,* May 31, 1971.

06  Marquis, "Uptight Little Island," 14. See also "Army of Hitch-Hikers Already on the March," *Winnipeg Free Press,* June 22, 1972.

07  "Postpone Action on Hostel Plan," *Charlottetown Guardian,* May 28, 1971, PEI Scrapbook: Information Gathered Summer of 1981, by Atula Joshi, M7832, file 292, CYHA-GMA.

08  "National Hostels Urged," *The Muse* (Memorial University), August 21, 1971. See also "Travelling Youths Rely on Hostels," *Winnipeg Free Press,* August 9, 1971.

09  "Newfoundland Wondering What Can Be Done: Quarters for Youth Hostels Hard to Find," *Globe and Mail,* May 31, 1971.

10  "Signs Point to Good Reception at Quebec Hostel for Canada's Wandering People," *Globe and Mail,* June 7, 1971. See also Canada, Secretary of State, Committee on Youth, *It's Your Turn,* 41.

11  "Longueuil Leery of Hostel Plan," *Montreal Gazette,* June 17, 1971, 33. See also "Nomad Youth Get 'Crash Pad,'" *Montreal Gazette,* June 30, 1971, 3.

12  A Montreal Manpower survey indicated that in the city there were at least 64,000 high school, college, and university students seeking summer work in 1971. This was up by 6,000 from 1969. There were only 50,000 jobs available in 1970. L.G. Smith, "Hitchhikers Freeloading," letter to the editor, *Montreal Gazette,* July 22, 1971.

13  "'Give Action Form to Virtue of Love': Churches Ask 'Spirit of Openness' Be Shown Summer Travellers," *Montreal Gazette,* June 12, 1971, 39. A joint statement of the Canadian Catholic Conference and the Canadian Council of Churches was published in "4 Youth Hostels Are Open Here for Transients," *Winnipeg Free Press,* July 6, 1971.

14  "'Give Action Form to Virtue of Love': Churches Ask 'Spirit of Openness' Be Shown Summer Travellers," *Montreal Gazette,* June 12, 1971, 39.

15  "Thousand of Youngsters on the Road This Summer," *Montreal Gazette,* August 25, 1970; "Mayor Worries about Summer Hippie Invasion," *Montreal Gazette,* May 22, 1970.

16  Canadian Council on Social Development, *Transient Youth,* 70–71, 25.

117  Smith, "Hitchhikers Freeloading."
118  "Life Insight for Wanderers Provided by Youth Hostels: Thousands Here," *Montreal Gazette*, July 25, 1972.
119  Paul DiMaggio, *The Hitchhiker's Field Manual* (London: Macmillan, 1973), 291.
120  Martin Dorell, "A Really Big Bedroom," *Globe and Mail*, June 14, 1971.
121  Ibid.
122  Lloyd Jones, Director, Centre for Hostelling Plans, "National Task Force Correspondence 1973," National Correspondence 1972–1975, M7832, file 105, CYHA-GMA.
123  Stuart Henderson, *Making the Scene: Yorkville and Hip Toronto in the 1960s* (Toronto: University of Toronto Press, 2011).
124  "Hitch-Hikers Increase Adds to Road Problems," *Port Arthur News-Chronicle*, April 16, 1971, Thunder Bay Youth Clippings, Thunder Bay Public Library.
125  "A Lonely Christening for the Upsala Hostel," *Globe and Mail*, June 16, 1971. See also "Even the Bad Days Have Satisfactions," *Globe and Mail*, June 16, 1971.
126  Fort William, "Petition," July 18, 1969, and "Memo from Parks and Recreation to E.C. Reid, City Administrator," July 21, 1969, Relief, Youth Hostel, 1969, Thunder Bay City Archives.
127  Fort William, "Petition," July 18, 1969.
128  "Threats Only Slightly Better Than Bullets," *London Free Press*, July 2, 1971.
129  Patrick Esmonde-White, National Coordinator, National Youth Hostel Task Force, 1970, interview with author, December 5, 2012; "Threats Only Slightly Better Than Bullets," *London Free Press*, July 2, 1971.
130  Joan Belford, "Summer Youth Hostel, London," 1971, 23, doc. r362.B411su, Public Library, London City Archives.
131  Letter to the editor, *London Free Press*, July 29, 1974.
132  Canadian Welfare Council, *Transient Youth: Report of an Inquiry in the Summer of 1969* (Ottawa: Canadian Welfare Council, 1970), 27.
133  Canadian Council on Social Development, *Transient Youth, 70–71*, 25; "Center Provides Stopovers for Canada's Transient Youth," *Winnipeg Free Press*, July 8, 1970.
134  "Hitchhiking Rides Dangerous," *Winnipeg Free Press*, May 9, 1970.
135  "Winnipeg Is the Midway Stop for Canada's Youth," *Globe and Mail*, June 1, 1971.
136  Quoted in "Youth Hostel Needed," *Winnipeg Free Press*, May 26, 1970.
137  "Hostel Okayed For Woodlawn," *Winnipeg Free Press*, June 8, 1971; Canadian Welfare Council, *Transient Youth*, 28.
138  In East Kildonan 100 percent of the residents between Brazier Street and Rich Street signed a petition. "Angry 9 Object to Youth Hostel in East Kildonan," *Winnipeg Free Press*, June 22, 1971.
139  "Hostel Plan Refused," *Winnipeg Free Press*, May 26, 1971.
140  "Angry 9 Object to Youth Hostel in East Kildonan," *Winnipeg Free Press*, June 22, 1971.
141  "Hitchers Have Better Time on Prairies," *Winnipeg Free Press*, August 7, 1971.
142  Canadian Welfare Council, *Transient Youth*, 25, 26.
143  "Transient Youth Find Defender," *Winnipeg Free Press*, May 4, 1971.
144  "Hitchers Have Better Time on Prairies," *Winnipeg Free Press*, August 7, 1971.

5  Ibid.

6  "Edmonton Plans No Utopia for Transients, but There'll Be Some Help for Young People," *Globe and Mail*, June 3, 1971; "Government Help Urged for Youth," *Edmonton Journal*, May 9, 1970.

7  "It's Wall to Wall Bodies: Hostel Space in Short Supply," *Calgary Herald*, June 23, 1972.

8  The CWC stated that a segment of young travellers did not use the parks responsibly. They "do not seem to really enjoy the park but hang around, causing disturbances ... and want to form 'colonies'" similar to "the hippie communities in rural or forest areas in the United States." Canadian Welfare Council, *Transient Youth*, 21. See also "Banff Unprepared for Youth Onslaught," *Edmonton Journal*, July 4, 1970.

9  Memo to Lorne Hurst, Edmonton, and Don Campbell, Calgary, from Dennis Lewis, "Re: Open Hostels and Memberships," November 30, 1972, 2, National Correspondence 1972–1975, M7832, file 76, CYHA-GMA.

0  Letter to Dick James from Don Sanami Morrill, Hostel Association of Nova Scotia, September 6, 1974, National Task Force 1974–1976, M7832, file 107, CYHA-GMA.

1  Thunder Bay Travelling Youth Services Committee, "Minutes," April 13, 1971, Parks and Recreation, PR 8.25, Thunder Bay City Archives; Letter from Donna Crocker, Parks and Recreation, to E.C. Reid, City Administrator, March 3, 1971, Hostel, Travelling Youth, PR 8.25, Thunder Bay City Archives.

2  Darcy Moorey and Iain Angus, "Report of the North Western Ontario Workshop on Transient Youth Services, January 8–10, 1971," 5, Hostel, Travelling Youth, PR 8.25, Thunder Bay City Archives.

3  Ibid.

4  Ibid., 4–5.

5  Ron Bradley, Hostel Association of South Western Ontario, "Response to Drafting Committee's First Paper," 1974, 3, National Task Force 1974–1976, M7832, file 107, CYHA-GMA.

6  Ann McGougan suspected the CYHA wanted "to get their hands on a possible twenty million dollars to build Hilton Hostels in various parts of the country." Quoted in Canadian Youth Hostels Association, "Task Force Visit, Vancouver," August 18, 1975, 1, National Task Force 1974–1976, M7832, file 107, CYHA-GMA.

7  Letter from Ann McGougan to Ron Bradley, Hostel Association of South Western Ontario, August 8, 1974, National Task Force 1974–1976, M7832, file 107, CYHA-GMA.

8  Quoted in Canadian Youth Hostels Association, "Task Force Visit, Vancouver," August 18, 1975, National Task Force 1974–1976, M7832, file 107, CYHA-GMA.

9  Canadian Youth Hostels Association, "Submission to the Honorable Robert Stanfield, Head of the Progressive Party of Canada," March 12, 1973, National Correspondence 1972–1975, M7832, file 76, CYHA-GMA.

0  Quoted in Canadian Welfare Council, "Report on National Consultation on Transient Youth," May 2–4, 1970, 4, Circulars to Regions, M7832, file 113, CYHA-GMA.

1  Ibid., 3.

2  Ibid.

3  Memo from Dennis Lewis, Director, National Executive, Canadian Youth Hostels Association, to Lorne Hurst, Edmonton, and Don Campbell, Calgary, "Open Hostels

CYHA," November 30, 1971, 2, National Correspondence 1972–1975, M7832, file 76, CYHA-GMA.

164 Canadian Youth Hostels Association, "Task Force Visit, Vancouver," August 18, 1975, National Task Force 1974–1976, M7832, file 107, CYHA-GMA.

165 Letter from Ann McGougan, Executive Director, Association of British Columbia Hostels, to Ron Bradley, Hostel Association of South Western Ontario, August 8, 1974, National Task Force 1974–1976, M7832, file 107, CYHA-GMA.

166 Letter from Lianne Gusway to Dennis Lewis, June 25, 1974, Saskatchewan Regional Correspondence 1974–1977, M7832, file 190, CYHA-GMA.

167 Dennis Lewis, "Youth Hostelling's Bumpy Road," n.d., Youth Hostels, M7832, file 269, CYHA-GMA.

168 Canadian Youth Hostels Association, "President's Report, 1970–1971," Annual Reports 1965–1972, M7832, file 73, CYHA-GMA.

169 Memo from Peter Watts, President, Association of British Columbia Hostels, to David Simonsen, National President, Canadian Youth Hostels Association, "Re: First National Youth Conference on Travel and Exchange, Algonquin College, Ottawa, September 15, 1970," 2, National Task Force 1974–1976, M7832, file 107, CYHA-GMA.

170 David Simonsen, "President's Report," in Canadian Youth Hostels Association, *Annual Report 1970–71* (1971), 1, Annual Reports 1965–1972, M7832, file 73, CYHA-GMA.

171 In 1970 the types of Y's in Canada included the Young Men's Christian Association (YMCA), primarily for men, the family YMCA for people of all ages, the YWCA for women and girls, the amalgamated YM-YWCA, the Young Men's Hebrew Association, and the Young Women's Hebrew Association. Canada, Secretary of State, Committee on Youth, *It's Your Turn*, 81.

172 Andy Cohen and Opportunities for Youth were keen to work with the YMCA and YWCA because city-based "Y" programs could be easily "hooked into." Les Vipond, Ottawa Director, National YMCA, interview with Andy Cohen, August 6, 1971, in private possession of Byron Rogers. See also Canadian Welfare Council, *Transient Youth*, 20.

173 Les Vipond, Ottawa Director, National YMCA, interview with Andy Cohen, August 6, 1971, in private possession of Byron Rogers. See also Canadian Welfare Council, *Transient Youth*, 17; and "A Place for Young Transients," *Globe and Mail*, June 13, 1970.

174 The original statement of purpose said, "The YMCA is a worldwide fellowship united by a common loyalty to Jesus Christ for the purpose of building a Christian society." The revision read, "The Young Men's Christian Association is a worldwide fellowship dedicated to the growth of persons in spirit, mind and body, and in a sense of responsibility to each other and to the human community." The national president said, "We talk about involving youth but we never talk about changing youth." The motivation was for "a federal government committee to evolve a new policy on youth." "YMCA National Council Hears from Under 30s," *Regina Leader Post*, May 23, 1970.

175 The YMCA and YWCA did away with many forms of youth membership to become more involved with hostelling. "The Y – Get It On!" *Georgia Straight* (Vancouver), August 12, 1970.

176 Quoted in Canadian Welfare Council, "Report on National Consultation on Transient Youth," May 2–4, 1970, 3, Circulars to Regions, M7832, file 113, CYHA-GMA.

77  Dennis Lewis, "Executive Director's Report," in Canadian Youth Hostels Association, *Annual Report 1970–71* (1971), 4, Annual Reports 1965–1972, M7832, file 73, CYHA-GMA.

78  Ibid.

79  Letter from Dennis Lewis, Director, National Executive, Canadian Youth Hostels Association, to H. Schmidt, Minister of Culture, Youth and Recreation, March 24, 1972, 1–2, National Correspondence 1972–1975, M7832, file 76, CYHA-GMA.

80  Ibid.

81  Letter from National Executive, Canadian Youth Hostels Association, to Robert Stanfield, Leader of the Progressive Conservative Party, March 2, 1973, National Correspondence 1972–1975, M7832, file 76, CYHA-GMA.

82  Letter from Mrs. Grace Ivey, Canadian Youth Hostels Association, to Department of Health and Welfare and the Secretary of State, "Regarding a Permanent Youth Hostel in Thunder Bay," December 10, 1973, National Task Force 1974–1976, M7832, file 107, CYHA-GMA.

83  Canadian Youth Hostels Association, "Submission to Hugh Falker," July 1973, 6–7, National Task Force 1974–1976, M7832, file 107, CYHA-GMA.

84  "They are on shaky ground, particularly if the government changes hands in an election." Letter from Dennis Lewis, Director, National Executive, Canadian Youth Hostels Association, to John Parry, Canadian Youth Hostels Association, Great Lakes Region, London, Ontario, March 2, 1973, M7832, file 105, CYHA-GMA.

85  "Western Canadian Hostels Planning and Co-Coordinating Conference, Banff," May 24, 1973, Youth Hostels, M7832, file 76, CYHA-GMA.

86  Canadian Youth Hostels Association, "Task Force Visit, Vancouver," August 18, 1975, National Task Force 1974–1976, M7832, file 107, CYHA-GMA.

87  Grant application from Dennis Lewis, Director, National Executive, Canadian Youth Hostels Association, to Health and Welfare Canada, Fitness and Amateur Sports Branch, "National Inaugural Meeting and Conference, April 29–May 1, 1977," Health and Welfare, M7832, file 107, CYHA-GMA.

88  Ibid.

89  Richard James and John Roberts, "Hostelling in Canada," September 15, 1976, 8, National Task Force 1974–1976, drafts and proposals, M7832, file 108, CYHA-GMA.

90  Ibid., 4.

91  "We'll Make Hitchhiking a Sport and We'll Train Some Soldiers," *The Meliorist* (University of Lethbridge), March 26, 1971, 5.

92  "Threats Only Slightly Better than Bullets," *London Free Press*, July 2, 1971. See also "Drop-In Drop-Outs Doing Own Thing for Teens," *London Free Press*, July 26, 1970.

93  Canadian Youth Hostels Association, "Annual General Meeting," May 2, 1970, 1, 2, Executive Meeting Toronto, M7832, file 64, CYHA-GMA. See also Canadian Youth Hostels Association, "President's Report, 1968," Annual Reports 1965–1972, M7832, file 73, CYHA-GMA.

94  "Training Starts for Area Youth Centre Leaders," *London Free Press*, July 17, 1971.

95  Canadian Council on Social Development, *Transient Youth, 70–71*, 35.

96  Canadian Council on Social Development, *Youth '71*, 21–22.

97  Belford, "Summer Youth Hostel, London," 24.

198    Richard James and John Roberts said, "In 1970–71 ... one equated 'unstructured' with 'license,' 'irresponsibility,' and 'undesirability' and used the incorrect and unacceptable description of 'transient' to describe young travellers ... In 1972–74, the term 'unstructured' began to lose meaning. Persons concerned with operating hostels recognized that the learning experiences in them were real, but that opportunity for such experiences had necessarily to have some design ... The users of hostels changed from year to year, and by 1975, the hosteller had accepted planning and orderly use of hostels as a natural part of travel." Richard James and John Roberts, "Hostelling in Canada," September 15, 1976, 1–2, National Task Force 1974–1976, drafts and proposals, M7832, file 108, CYHA-GMA.

### Chapter 6: Head Out on the Highway

1    Martin Dorrell, "Winnipeg Walkaround," *Globe and Mail,* June 16, 1971.

2    "Youth in Canada: Drifting Around with the Government's Blessing," *New York Times,* April 22, 1973.

3    David Monaghan, *Canada's "New Main Street": The Trans-Canada Highway as Ideal and Reality, 1912–1956* (Ottawa: Canadian Science and Technology Museum, 2002).

4    "Newfoundland Wondering What Can Be Done: Quarters for Youth Hostels Hard to Find," *Globe and Mail,* May 31, 1971.

5    Canadian Council on Social Development, *Transient Youth, 70–71: Report of an Inquiry about Programs in 1970, and Plans for 1971* (Ottawa: Department of Health and Welfare, 1970), 5.

6    "Signs Point to Good Reception at Quebec Hostel for Canada's Wandering People," *Globe and Mail,* June 7, 1971. See also "Young Travellers Will Swarm Here This Summer," *Calgary Herald,* June 7, 1974, 69.

7    Canadian Welfare Council, *Transient Youth: Report of an Inquiry in the Summer of 1969* (Ottawa: Canadian Welfare Council, 1970), 27.

8    Martin Dorrell, "From North Bay to Sudbury: Two Rides and Peanut Butter," *Globe and Mail,* June 8, 1971.

9    The cheap day fare was $1.95. In Nanaimo the Salvation Army provided $1.50 meal vouchers. Martin Dorrell, "Vancouver Not the Mecca It Promised to Be," *Globe and Mail,* July 6, 1971. See also Canadian Welfare Council, *Transient Youth,* 27, 40.

10    Chaim Noy, "Performing Identity: Tourist Narratives of Self-Change," *Text and Performance Quarterly* 24, 2 (2004): 146.

11    Torun Elsrud writes, "Although risks in travelling are at times 'true,' mythology is vital to narrative survival ... Risk taking can be a device to construct a story." Torun Elsrud, "Risk Creation in Travelling: Backpacker Adventure Narration," *Annals of Tourism Research* 28, 3 (2001): 599–600.

12    Chandra Mukerji, "Bullshitting: Road Lore among Hitchhikers," *Social Problems* 25, 3 (1978): 250.

13    The federal government found that "groups feel capable of operating facilities themselves." Canada, Secretary of State, Committee on Youth, *It's Your Turn: A Report to the Secretary of State by the Committee on Youth* (Ottawa: Information Canada, 1971), 87.

14  "Lenient Attitude to Hitch-Hikers," *Regina Leader Post,* August 1, 1970.
15  Brian Gory, "Youthbeat," *Winnipeg Free Press,* May 5, 1971, 24.
16  "Young Travellers Will Swarm Here This Summer," *Calgary Herald,* June 7, 1974, 69.
17  "Lenient Attitude to Hitch-Hikers," *Regina Leader Post,* August 1, 1970.
18  Murray Milner Jr., *Freaks, Geeks and Cool Kids: American Teenagers, Schools, and the Culture of Consumption* (New York: Routledge, 2004).
19  Mike Featherstone, "Automobiles: An Introduction," *Theory, Culture and Society* 21, 4–5 (2004): 14.
20  Ibid. See also Mimi Sheller, "Automotive Emotions: Feeling the Car," *Theory, Culture and Society* 21, 4–5 (2004): 233; David Crouch and Luke Desforges, "The Sensuous in the Tourist Encounter," *Tourist Studies* 3, 1 (2003): 17; and Jay Vogt, "Wandering: Youth and Travel Behavior," *Annals of Tourism Research* 4, 1 (1976): 28.
21  Greg Ross and Hedley Swan, "Cross-Canada Jaunt," *The Fulcrum* (University of Ottawa), January 28, 1971.
22  Email correspondent 24, June 26, 2013.
23  Interviewee 99, Keith Perkins, Toronto, April 8, 2013.
24  Interviewee 85, Salt Spring Island, BC, June 29, 2011.
25  O'Regan adds that backpacking "is more than the mechanism through which mundane tasks are carried out and movement can itself become a performance through which we make statements about ourselves and acquire status." Michael O'Regan, "Backpacker Hostels: Place and Performance," in *Beyond Backpacker Tourism: Mobilities and Experiences,* ed. Kevin Hannam and Anya Diekmann (Bristol, UK: Channel View, 2010), 88.
26  Jo-Anne Hecht and David Martin, "Backpacking and Hostel-Picking: An Analysis from Canada," *International Journal of Contemporary Hospitality Management* 18, 1 (2006): 70–71; Marg Tiyce and Erica Wilson, "Wandering Australia: Independent Travellers and Slow Journeys through Time and Space," in *Slow Tourism: Experiences and Mobilities,* ed. Simone Fullagar, Kevin Markwell, and Erica Wilson (Bristol, UK: Channel View, 2012), 115, 117; Deborah Stevenson, Stephen Wearing, and Tamara Young, *Tourist Cultures: Identity, Place and the Traveller* (London: Sage, 2012), 47; Anders Sørensen, "Backpacker Ethnography," *Annals of Tourism Research* 30, 4 (2003): 852.
27  Richard Ivan Jobs, *Backpack Ambassadors: How Youth Travel Integrated Europe* (Chicago: University of Chicago Press, 2017), 152.
28  Bob Miller, "In Kanada by a Part-Time Transient," in student paper, Elmira District Secondary School, October 15, 1971, private collection of Robert Miller, Toronto, used with permission.
29  Ross and Swan, "Cross-Canada Jaunt," August 23, 1970, September 9, 1970, and January 28, 1971.
30  David Rideout and Ray Amiro, *Handbook Canada: A Traveller's Manual* (Toronto: Transglobular Functions, 1972), 1.
31  Paul DiMaggio, *The Hitchhiker's Field Manual* (London: Macmillan, 1973), 82.
32  Canada, Department of Health and Welfare, *On the Road: A Guide for Youth Travelling Canada* (Ottawa: Department of Health and Welfare, 1972), 2.

33  This phrase means, "to show off." Interviewee 91, Guelph, August 17, 2016.
34  Interviewee 99, Keith Perkins, Toronto, April 8, 2013.
35  Interviewee 93, Vancouver, June 22, 2011.
36  Interviewee 98, Duncan McMonagle, Winnipeg, August 24, 2012.
37  Simon Gibson, "Hitchhiking," *The Martlet* (University of Victoria), December 5, 1973, 12.
38  Interviewee 92, Vancouver, June 22, 2011.
39  Interviewee 98, Duncan McMonagle, Winnipeg, August 24, 2012.
40  DiMaggio, *Hitchhiker's Field Manual*, 10, 15.
41  Martin Dorrell, "Singin' the Espanola Blues," *Globe and Mail*, June 10, 1971.
42  Rideout and Amiro, *Handbook Canada*, 11.
43  "Error-Ridden 'Road' Booklet Still Valuable," *London Free Press*, July 22, 1972.
44  Canada, Department of Health and Welfare, *On the Road*, 11.
45  DiMaggio, *Hitchhiker's Field Manual*, 34–35.
46  Email correspondent 74, Rod Willmot, December 23, 2011.
47  Interviewee 86, Salt Spring Island, BC, February, 24, 2012.
48  Interviewee 94, Vancouver, June 22, 2011.
49  Douglas Williams, *Promised Lands: Growing Up Absurd in the 1950s and '60s* (Kingston, ON: Michael Grass House, 2012), 15.
50  Ross and Swan, "Cross-Canada Jaunt," January 28, 1971, 9.
51  Interviewee 26, Guelph, June 25, 2013.
52  Interviewees 81a and 81b, Vancouver, June 23, 2011.
53  Interviewees 32a and 32b, Gabriola Island, BC, February 22, 2012.
54  Email correspondent 74, Rod Willmot, December 23, 2011.
55  Interviewees 32a and 32b, Gabriola Island, BC, February 22, 2012.
56  Email correspondent 48, January 19, 2011.
57  Dorrell, "From North Bay to Sudbury."
58  Interviewee 34, Toronto, April 8, 2013.
59  Dorrell, "From North Bay to Sudbury."
60  Interviewee 63, Ladysmith, BC, February 17, 2012.
61  Dorrell, "From North Bay to Sudbury."
62  Email correspondent 48, January 19, 2011.
63  Email correspondent 24, January 19, 2011.
64  Interviewee 34, Toronto, April 8, 2013.
65  Interviewee 86, Salt Spring Island, BC, March 4, 2012.
66  Amie Matthews, "Young Backpackers and the Rite of Passage of Travel: Examining the Transformative Effects of Liminality," in *Travel and Transformation*, ed. Garth Lean, Russell Staiff, and Emma Waterton (Surrey, UK: Ashgate, 2014), 157.
67  H.J. Cody, "Foreword," in Canadian Youth Hostels Association, *Handbook* (1939–40), 3, Canadian Youth Hostels Association Handbook/Hostel Trails of Canada, 1939–1940, 1942, 1945–1946, M2169, file 11, Canadian Youth Hostels Association, Glenbow Museum Archives, Calgary (hereafter CYHA-GMA).
68  "What Is Hostelling?" Scrapbook 1959–1966, North West Region, Edmonton, M7832, file 296, CYHA-GMA.
69  Ron Verzuh, "Trip Tips," *The Peak* (Simon Fraser University), July 15, 1970, 3.

0 Myles Stasiuk, "Travelling and Living in Canada '73," *The Sheaf* (University of Saskatchewan), February 27, 1973, 4, 5.

1 Interviewees 32a and 32b, Gabriola Island, BC, February 22, 2012.

2 Interviewee 63, Ladysmith, BC, February 17, 2012.

3 Interviewee 94, Vancouver, June 22, 2011.

4 Dorrell "From North Bay to Sudbury."

5 "Unmarried Sex Ban Called Ludicrous by Disgruntled Travellers at Hostel," *Calgary Herald*, July 26, 1971.

6 "Cosy Snooze Out," *Montreal Star*, July 23, 1971, 44.

7 "Tom Terrifically Outraged at Transients and Ottawa," *Vancouver Province*, September 12, 1970.

8 "Persistent Bitching Starts Hostel Screw," *The Charlatan* (Carleton University), July 30, 1971, 1.

9 "Unmarried Sex Ban Called Ludicrous by Disgruntled Travellers at Hostel," *Calgary Herald*, July 26, 1971.

0 "Cosy Snooze Out," *Montreal Star*, July 23, 1971, 44.

1 "Hostel 'Cosy' Again," *Winnipeg Free Press*, July 31, 1971, 1–4.

2 Darya Maoz, "The Mutual Gaze," *Annals of Tourism Research* 33, 1 (2006): 235.

3 O'Regan, "Backpacker Hostels," 85.

4 George Orwell, *Down and Out in Paris and London* (London: Harcourt, 1933), 200–3.

5 "Traveling Youths Rely on Hostels," *Winnipeg Free Press*, August 9, 1971.

6 "Poll Changes Transient 'Pauper' Image," *Calgary Herald*, September 6, 1972.

7 Quoted in "50 Cents a Night Fee," *Brandon Sun*, July 18, 1974. See also Canadian Council on Social Development, *Transient Youth*, 70–71, 42.

8 "Canada's Youth Head for the Rockies," *Edmonton Journal*, July 30, 1971, 43. This article also reported, "The residents of Banff seem more than happy about the arrangement which grew out of public distaste for hordes of longhairs filling the town's streets and the freaks themselves are glad of the opportunity to handle their own affairs and enjoy themselves removed from the hassles of a 'straighter' society."

9 Patrick Esmonde-White, National Coordinator, National Youth Hostel Task Force, 1970, interview with author, December 5, 2012.

0 Marcel Martel, "'They Smell Bad, Have Diseases, and Are Lazy': RCMP Officers Reporting on Hippies in the Late Sixties," *Canadian Historical Review* 90, 2 (2009): 245. The lists of undesirables included leftists, homosexuals, trade union leaders, and members of the Black Power, Red Power, and Quebec separatist movements.

1 Doug Owram, *Born at the Right Time: A History of the Baby Boom Generation* (Toronto: University of Toronto Press, 1997), 195.

2 Canada, Department of Health and Welfare, *On the Road*, 8–9.

3 Vogt, "Wandering," 33.

4 Interviewee 34, Toronto, April 8, 2013.

5 Interviewee 96, Vancouver, June 23, 2011.

6 Interviewee 98, Duncan McMonagle, Winnipeg, August 24, 2012.

7 Interviewees 81a and 81b, Vancouver, June 23, 2011.

8 Duff Sigurdson, interview with author, Saskatoon, August 22, 2012.

9 Interviewee 26, Guelph, June 25, 2013.

100   Interviewee 11, Vancouver, June 22, 2011.
101   Interviewee 83, Saskatoon, March 8, 2012.
102   Ibid.
103   Interviewee 94, Vancouver, June 22, 2011.
104   Interviewee 83, Saskatoon, March 8, 2012.
105   Email correspondent 31, June 20, 2011.
106   Interviewee 99, Toronto, April 8, 2013.
107   Teddy Mahood, interview with author, Turtle Valley, BC, August 7, 2013.
108   Interviewee 63, Ladysmith, BC, February 17, 2012.
109   Interviewees 32a and 32b, Gabriola Island, BC, February 22, 2012.
110   Interviewees 84a and 84b, Toronto, April 8, 2013.
111   Interviewee 80, Salt Spring Island, BC, June 27, 2011.
112   Interviewee 99, Keith Perkins, Toronto, April 8, 2013; DiMaggio, *Hitchhiker's Field Manual*, 36.
113   "The Complete Youth Hosteller: Being Some Advice on Student Travel in Europe," *The Martlet* (University of Victoria), July 20, 1972, 4.
114   Greg Ross and Hedley Swan, "Exploring Western Canada – Part 3," *The Fulcrum* (University of Ottawa), February 8, 1971, 8. See also Greg Ross and Hedley Swan, "Across Canada by Thumb, Bus, etc. – Part 2," *The Fulcrum* (University of Ottawa), February 3, 1971, 10.
115   Interviewees 32a and 32b, Gabriola Island, BC, February 22, 2012.
116   Interviewee 92a, Vancouver, June 22, 2011.
117   Maoz, "Mutual Gaze," 221–39.
118   DiMaggio, *Hitchhiker's Field Manual*, 56.
119   Interviewee 99, Keith Perkins, Toronto, April 8, 2013.
120   Interviewee 85, Salt Spring Island, BC, June 29, 2011.
121   Interviewees 84a and 84b, Toronto, April 8, 2013.
122   Interviewees 32a and 32b, Gabriola Island, BC, February 22, 2012.
123   Email correspondent 74, Rod Willmot, December 23, 2011.
124   Ross and Swan, "Cross-Canada Jaunt," January 28, 1971.
125   Email correspondent 25, January 19, 2012.
126   Gibson, "Hitchhiking," 12.
127   Interviewee 85, Salt Spring Island, BC, June 29, 2012.
128   Email correspondent 19, December 21, 2011.
129   Interviewee 94, Vancouver, June 22, 2011.
130   Interviewee 83, Saskatoon, March 8, 2012.
131   Interviewee 96, Vancouver, June 22, 2011.
132   Interviewee 81b, Vancouver, June 23, 2011.
133   Sandra Lee Bartky, *Femininity and Domination: Studies in the Phenomenology of Oppression* (New York: Routledge, 1990), 72; Michel Foucault, quoted in Jennie Small, "The Emergence of the Body of Women and Girls," in *Tourism and Gender: Embodiment, Sensuality and Experience*, ed. Annette Pritchard, Nigel Morgan, Irena Ateljevic, and Candice Harris (Wallingford, UK: CABI, 2007), 84.
134   Interviewee 76b, Salt Spring Island, BC, June 29, 2011.
135   Interviewee 21, Toronto, April 16, 2013.

36  Kristine Alexander, "Agency and Emotion Work," *Jeunesse: Young People, Texts, Cultures* 7, 2 (2015): 124.

37  Peter Kelly, "The Entrepreneurial Self and 'Youth-at-Risk': Exploring the Horizons of Identity in the Twenty-First Century," *Journal of Youth Studies* 9, 1 (2006): 17.

38  Mukerji, "Bullshitting," 245.

39  "Got Them Old Half-Way between Carbonear and St. John's Blues Again," *The Muse* (Memorial University), June 9, 1972, 5.

40  Ibid.

41  Dorrell, "From North Bay to Sudbury."

42  Interviewees 34a and 34b, Toronto, April 8, 2013.

43  Ross and Swan, "Across Canada by Thumb." See also Ross and Swan, "Cross-Canada Jaunt," January 28, 1971, 9.

44  Interviewee 63, Ladysmith, BC, February 17, 2012.

45  "Wild Wacky BC, an Eastern View," *The Chevron* (University of Waterloo), August 17, 1972, 8.

46  Email correspondent 16, January 26, 2012.

47  Ross and Swan, "Cross-Canada Jaunt," January 28, 1971.

48  Chaim Noy, "Performing Identity: Touristic Narratives of Self-Change," *Text and Performance Quarterly* 24, 2 (2004): 146.

49  Email correspondent 18, December 21, 2011.

50  Interviewee 80, Salt Spring Island, BC, June 27, 2011. See also Annalee Grant, "History of the Point: The Jasper Internment Camp," *Jasper Fitzhugh*, February 3, 2011.

51  Interviewee 83, Saskatoon, March 8, 2012.

52  Crouch and Desforges, "Sensuous in the Tourist Encounter," 18.

53  Owram, *Born at the Right Time*, 170. See also "Canadians Seek to Spur National Consciousness," *New York Times*, May 11, 1975.

54  Interviewee 11, Vancouver, June 11, 2011.

55  Owram, *Born at the Right Time*, 170. See also "Canadians Seek to Spur National Consciousness," *New York Times*, May 11, 1975.

56  Interviewee 79, Salt Spring Island, BC, June 22, 2001.

57  Interviewee 11, Vancouver, June 11, 2011.

58  Interviewee 91, Vancouver, June 22, 2011.

59  Jobs, *Backpack Ambassadors*, 184.

60  Interviewee 23a, Erin, Ontario, March 7, 2013.

61  Interviewee 83, Saskatoon, March 8, 2012.

62  Interviewee 26, Guelph, June 25, 2013.

63  Interviewee 63, Ladysmith, BC, February 17, 2012.

64  Interviewee 11, Vancouver, June 11, 2011.

65  Johan Larson calls "dwelling in mobility" the psychological process that enables travellers to feel at home in environments that are transient, unfamiliar, and strange. Quoted in Crouch and Desforges, "Sensuous in the Tourist Encounter," 9.

66  Email correspondent 74, Rod Willmot, December 23, 2011.

67  Crowbar, "Tits Up on the Pavement," on the album *Larger Than Life* (Daffodil Records, 1972).

168 Wawa is often looked on as the watershed of cross-country travel and is notorious as the place to get marooned. "Army of Hitch-Hikers Already on the March," *Winnipeg Free Press,* June 22, 1972.
169 Interviewee 23b, Erin, Ontario, March 7, 2013.
170 Interviewees 34a and 34b, Toronto, April 8, 2013.
171 Crouch and Desforges, "Sensuous in the Tourist Encounter," 17; Vogt, "Wandering," 28.
172 Interviewees 32a and 32b, Gabriola Island, BC, February 21, 2012.
173 Interviewee 36, Toronto, June 23, 2011.
174 Interviewee 3, Edinburgh, Scotland, October 11, 2012.
175 Luke Desforges, "Travelling the World: Identity and Travel Biography," *Annals of Tourism Research* 27, 4 (2000): 938. See also Vogt, "Wandering," 39; and Erik Cohen, "Toward a Sociology of International Tourism," *Social Research* 39, 1 (1972): 176–77.
176 Interviewee 30, Tony Bonnici, Vancouver, March 1, 2012.

### Chapter 7: Car Sick

1 Michael Goss, *The Evidence for Phantom Hitch-Hikers* (1984; reprint, San Francisco, CA: Red Wheel/Weiser, 2015), 127. See also Alan Dundes, "Bloody Mary in the Mirror: A Ritual Reflection of Pre-Pubescent Anxiety," *Western Folklore* 57, 2–3 (1998): 130.
2 Dundes, "Bloody Mary in the Mirror," 122. See also Jan Harold Brunvand, *The Vanishing Hitchhiker: American Urban Legends and Their Meanings* (New York: Norton, 1981), 47.
3 Paul DiMaggio, *The Hitchhiker's Field Manual* (London: Macmillan, 1973), 14. See also "Travel into Danger on the Hitchhike Road," *Globe and Mail,* June 8, 1974, 6.
4 Richard Ivan Jobs, *Backpack Ambassadors: How Youth Travel Integrated Europe* (Chicago: University of Chicago Press, 2016), 198.
5 "Travel into Danger on the Hitchhike Road," *Globe and Mail,* June 8, 1974, 6.
6 Email correspondent 15, June 2, 2011.
7 "Travel into Danger on the Hitchhike Road," *Globe and Mail,* June 8, 1974, 6.
8 Interviewee 21, Toronto, April 16, 2013.
9 "Fifth Woman Found Slain Near Calgary," *Globe and Mail,* September 18, 1976, 16. This article reported that Melissa Rehorek was "found strangled and beaten near Cochrane near where at least one other woman has died violently or under mysterious circumstance since the start of this year." See also Vanessa Veselka, "Green Screen: The Lack of Female Road Narratives and Why It Matters," *American Reader* 4, 1 (2012): 4.
10 Interviewee 21, Toronto, April 16, 2013. See also Royal Canadian Mounted Police, "Melissa Ann Rehorek," in *Cold Case Files,* December 10, 2015, http://www.rcmp-grc. gc.ca/cc-afn/rehorek-melissa-eng.htm; and "Canada Highway Murders," in *Crimezzz: Serial Killer Crime Index,* n.d., http://www.crimezzz.net/serialkillers/C/CANADA_HIGHWAY_murders.php.
11 See Robert Hoshowsky, "Ingrid Bauer (1972)," in *Unsolved: True Canadian Cold Cases,* 57–63 (Toronto: Dundurn, 2010). Canada's highway murders involved 200 unsolved cases in western Canada between 1973 and 1981. The RCMP's ongoing investigation of highway murders has been superseded by the "Highway of Tears List," which refers to the route from Prince Rupert to Prince George, with some cases overlapping, including that of Melissa Rehorek. Royal Canadian Mounted Police, "Melissa Ann Rehorek."

12  "Travel into Danger on the Hitchhike Road," *Globe and Mail*, June 8, 1974, 6.

13  Veselka, "Green Screen," 4–6.

14  "Hitchhiking Perils Deter Youths," *Edmonton Journal*, July 17, 1974.

15  Canadian Welfare Council, *Transient Youth: Report of an Inquiry in the Summer of 1969* (Ottawa: Canadian Welfare Council, 1970), 9, 105.

16  "Travel into Danger on the Hitchhike Road," *Globe and Mail*, June 8, 1974, 6.

17  Don Wharton, "Thumbs Down on Hitchhikers! Too Many Rob and Kill," *Reader's Digest*, April 1950, 21–25.

18  Nathan Adams, "Hitchhiking – Too Often the Last Ride: Abduction, Rape, Murder – These Are the Chilling Hazards in Many Areas for Today's Young Thumbers," *Reader's Digest*, July 1973, 61.

19  Lester David, "Hitchhiking: The Deadly New Odds," *Good Housekeeping*, July 1973, 38–39.

20  Adams, "Hitchhiking – Too Often," 62–63.

21  Ibid., 63.

22  Dundes, "Bloody Mary in the Mirror," 130.

23  Jeremy Packer, *Mobility without Mayhem: Safety, Cars, and Citizenship* (Durham, NC: Duke University Press, 2008), 90.

24  Sanger's analysis of the role of cars in rape cases suggests that the law assumes that a woman who gets into a man's car or gives him a lift in hers also gives a proxy for consent to sex. Carol Sanger, "Girls and the Getaway: Cars, Culture, and the Predicament of Gendered Space," *University of Pennsylvania Law Review* 144, 2 (1995): 711, 715.

25  "But Where Is the Maple Leaf?" *Globe and Mail*, March 2, 1979.

26  Packer, *Mobility without Mayhem*, 101.

27  Anonymous [Beatrice Sparks], *Go Ask Alice* (1971; reprint, New York: Simon and Schuster, 2006), 87.

28  "Government Help Urged for Youth," *Edmonton Journal*, May 9, 1970.

29  Sanger, "Girls and the Getaway," 710, 715; Alexandra Ganser, "On the Asphalt Frontier: American Women's Road Narratives, Spatiality, and Transgression," *Journal of International Women's Studies* 7, 4 (2006): 160–61.

30  Anupriya Sethi, "Domestic Sex Trafficking of Aboriginal Girls in Canada," *First People Child and Family Review* 3, 3 (2007): 51–71.

31  James Greenley and David Rice, "Female Hitchhiking: Strain, Control, and Subcultural Approaches," *Sociological Focus* 7, 1 (1973–74): 87.

32  Ibid., 92.

33  Quoted in ibid., 93.

34  Ibid.

35  Abraham Miller, "On the Road: Hitchhiking on the Highway," *Society* 10, 5 (1973): 19.

36  Ibid., 21.

37  Ibid., 19.

38  Ibid., 18.

39  Ibid., 19.

40  Graeme Chesters and David Smith call Rinvolucri's attitude "dated and naïve" and at "times offensive." Graeme Chesters and David Smith, "The Neglected Art of Hitch-Hiking: Risk, Trust and Sustainability," *Sociological Research Online* 6, 3 (2001): sec. 2.3.

41  Mario Rinvolucri, "Wandering Hands," in *Hitch-Hiking*, ch. 7 (London: Mario Rinvolucri, 1974), https://prino.neocities.org/Mario%20Rinvolucri/chapter7.html. Rinvolucri adds, "The driver imagines *what he could do to a girl alone* and then goes on to imagine how she might expose him" (original emphasis).

42  Robert W. Johnson and James H. Johnson, "A Cross-Validation of the Sn Scale on the Psychological Screening Inventory with Female Hitchhikers," *Journal of Clinical Psychology* 34, 2 (1978): 366.

43  "Hitchhikers Are Flirting with Trouble ... Say Police," *Mississauga Times*, August 24, 1977. Helen Benedict identifies the factors that led the public and press to blame the victim for rape and to push her into the role of vamp. This occurred when the victim knew the assailant, when no weapon was used, and when she was the same age, race, social class, or nationality as the assailant. Helen Benedict, *Virgin or Vamp: How the Press Covers Sex Crimes* (New York: Oxford University Press, 1992), 19.

44  Elise Chenier, "The Criminal Sexual Psychopath in Canada: Sex, Psychiatry and the Law at Mid-Century," *Canadian Bulletin of Medical History* 20, 1 (2003): 75, 78.

45  Interviewee 89, Salt Spring Island, BC, June 21, 2011.

46  Interviewee 46, Vancouver, June 22, 2011.

47  Interviewee 82, Vancouver, March 1, 2012.

48  Karen Staller, "Constructing the Runaway Youth Problem: Boy Adventurers to Girl Prostitutes, 1960–1978," *Journal of Communication* 53, 2 (2003): 331, 337, 340–41.

49  Chenier, "Criminal Sexual Psychopath," 75, 78.

50  Canadian Welfare Council, *Transient Youth*, 31.

51  "But Where Is the Maple Leaf?" *Globe and Mail*, March 2, 1979.

52  Ibid.

53  DiMaggio, *Hitchhiker's Field Manual*, 58.

54  "Playing at the Eve Theatre in Winnipeg: Movie Poster Shows Two Scantily Dressed Young Women Hitchhiking," *Winnipeg Free Press*, June 8, 1974.

55  Canada, Department of Health and Welfare, *On the Road: A Guide for Youth Travelling Canada* (Ottawa: Department of Health and Welfare, 1972). See also the photos of the brochure on page 217.

56  Canada, Department of Health and Welfare, *On the Road*; Canadian Council on Social Development, *Transient Youth, 70–71: Report of an Inquiry about Programs in 1970, and Plans for 1971* (Ottawa: Department of Health and Welfare, 1970), 67.

57  DiMaggio said, "The phalluses in the heads of male drivers lead them to attempt in various ways to establish a sexual liaison with their quarry." DiMaggio, *Hitchhiker's Field Manual*, 58. See also Benedict, *Virgin or Vamp*, 16, 19.

58  "Offences on Hitch-Hikers during TTC Strike Studied: Women Who Are Sexually Assaulted Don't Provoke Attack, Toronto Psychologist Says," *Globe and Mail*, June 17, 1977, 15. See also Sheldon Geller, "The Sexually Assaulted Female: Innocent Victim or Temptress?" *Canadian Mental Health* 25, 1 (1977): 26–29.

59  Peter Stearns and Timothy Haggerty, "The Role of Fear: Transitions in American Emotional Standards for Children, 1850–1950," *American Historical Review* 96, 1 (1991): 83.

60  Tamara Myers, "Didactic Sudden Death: Children, Police, and Teaching Citizenship in the Age of Automobility," *Journal of the History of Childhood and Youth* 8, 3 (2015): 463.

51 Ibid., 465.

52 "Death Threat Makes Girls Leap from Car," *Hamilton Spectator,* November 28, 1974; "Guilty of Raping Hitchhiker," *Toronto Sun,* May 11, 1976; "Toronto Hitchhikers: 3 Raped at Knifepoint," *Toronto Sun,* September 4, 1977; "'Hand of Death' Signs Have Impact Designed to Make Hitchhikers Think," *Burlington Daily Times,* August 25, 1977, RG 23-32, file 12–15, Hitchhiking, 1978, Archives of Ontario.

53 "Hitchhike Victim Leaves Hospital," *Globe and Mail,* July 29, 1970; "Thousands on the Road This Summer," *Montreal Gazette,* August 25, 1970.

54 "RCMP Believe 18-Year-Old Montreal Girl Shot in BC," *Montreal Gazette,* August 13, 1970; "Girl Hitchhiker Killed," *Winnipeg Free Press,* August 11, 1970.

55 "Rape and Robbery: Hitchers Attract Crime," *Ottawa Citizen,* May 8, 1973, 5.

56 "Hitchhiking," *Edmonton Journal,* May 7, 1973. See also "14-Year-Old Girl Raped," *Edmonton Journal,* August 9, 1971; "Ride to Danger," *Edmonton Journal,* August 1, 1971; and "Hitchhiking Ban Urged on City Streets," *Edmonton Journal,* August 17, 1971. The RCMP discussed the deaths of at least six women found between September and June 1973: "The women were discovered nude and in a badly decomposed state. Three were last seen hitchhiking. Some were sexually assaulted." "Yellowhead Murders Topic of [RCMP] Conference," *Edmonton Journal,* July 10, 1974.

57 "Kamloops Girls Hitchhiked to Death," *Edmonton Journal,* July 2, 1974. See also "Slaying," *Edmonton Journal,* June 28, 1974; and "Similarities in Slaying Victims Puzzling Police," *Edmonton Journal,* June 28, 1974.

58 "Hitchhiking Ban Studies," *Winnipeg Free Press,* May 12, 1975.

59 "Hitchhiking in Saskatoon: The Reactionary – The Reaction," *The Sheaf* (University of Saskatchewan), March 21, 1972.

70 "Body in Swamp Inquest," *Ottawa Citizen,* November 20, 1972. See also "Jury Blames Teenager's Hitchhiking for Death," *Ottawa Citizen,* December 6, 1972.

71 The *Ottawa Citizen* reported that Tillack was "astonished when no branch of government or school board" came forward to finance the film. "Hitchhikers Run Risks of All Sorts on Roads," *Ottawa Citizen,* June 30, 1973.

72 Ontario Provincial Police, "BE AWARE ... ATTENTION!" RG 23-32, file 12–13, Published Bulletins, Posters, Pamphlets, 1978, Archives of Ontario.

73 "'Hand of Death' Signs Have Impact Designed to Make Hitchhikers Think," *Burlington Daily Times,* August 25, 1977, RG 23-32, file 12–15, Hitchhiking, 1978, Archives of Ontario.

74 "Hitchhikers Are Flirting with Trouble ... Say Police," *Mississauga Times,* August 24, 1977.

75 "For the Hitchhikers: Some Dos and Don'ts," *Edmonton Journal,* June 15, 1974.

76 "Toronto Hitchhikers: 3 Raped at Knifepoint," *Toronto Sun,* September 4, 1977.

77 "'Some of the Friendliest Faces Are Sex Maniacs': North York against Hitchhiking, Seeks Ban across Metro," *Globe and Mail,* June 11, 1974, 5.

78 Ibid.

79 Ann Landers, "She Agrees with Ann: Avoid Hitchhikers," *Montreal Gazette,* September 28, 1973; Abigail Van Buren, "Dear Abby: Hitchhiking Out for Girls, Boys," *Pittsburgh Press,* September 14, 1970; Ann Landers, "Dangers of Hitchhiking," *Edmonton Journal,* January 25, 1973.

80   Ann Landers, "Raped and Murdered," *Wainwright Star News*, May 13, 1974. See also Abigail Van Buren, "Dear Abby: Hitchhiking Out for Girls, Boys," *Pittsburgh Press*, September 14, 1970; and Ann Landers, "She Agrees with Ann: Avoid Hitchhikers," *Montreal Gazette*, September 28, 1973.

81   Abigail Van Buren, "World of Women," *Deseret News*, January 25, 1973.

82   "Hitchhiking Daughter Fighting Her Boredom, Elizabeth Thompson Advises," *Globe and Mail*, August 8, 1974, W7.

83   Benedict, *Virgin or Vamp*, 19, 162.

84   "Rape Charge Dismissed," *Edmonton Journal*, May 3, 1972. See also "Guilty of Raping Hitchhiker," *Toronto Sun*, May 11, 1976; and "Fifth Woman Found Slain near Calgary," *Globe and Mail*, September 18, 1976, 16.

85   "Guilty of Raping Hitchhiker," *Toronto Sun*, May 11, 1976.

86   *Hitch-Hiking*, film (Summerhill Productions, 1974); *Hitch-Hiking* movie poster, 1974, National Correspondence 1972–1975, M7832, file 76, Canadian Youth Hostels Association, Glenbow Museum Archives, Calgary.

87   "No Trace of Missing Girl during Search of Kleinburg Area," *Globe and Mail*, August 23, 1972. See also "Ingrid Bauer Reward Time Limit Extended," *Newmarket Era and Express*, April 4, 1973; Interviewee 62, Toronto, April 17, 2013; and Hoshowsky, "Ingrid Bauer (1972)," 60–63.

88   "No Trace of Missing Girl during Search of Kleinburg Area," *Globe and Mail*, August 23, 1972.

89   Cited in Linda Mahood, *Policing Gender, Class and Family: Britain, 1850–1940* (London: UCL Press, 1995), 3–5.

90   "'Hand of Death' Signs Have Impact Designed to Make Hitchhikers Think," *Burlington Daily Times*, August 25, 1977, RG 23–32, file 12–15, Hitchhiking, 1978, Archives of Ontario.

91   "Thunder Bay Boy Wins OPP Scholarship," *Kingsville Reporter*, February 11, 1976.

92   "'Hand of Death' Signs Have Impact Designed to Make Hitchhikers Think," *Burlington Daily Times*, August 25, 1977, RG 23–32, file 12–15, Hitchhiking, 1978, Archives of Ontario.

93   "Hitchhikers Are Flirting with Trouble ... Say Police," *Mississauga Times*, August 24, 1977.

94   The film came with a discussion guide that included questions for before and after a screening. "Discussion Guide – Rape: A Preventative Inquiry (1974)," 1. This guide said that the film's intended audience was high school juniors and seniors, college students, adults, and law enforcement. Ibid., 1.

95   *Rape: A Preventative Inquiry*, documentary (J. Gary Mitchell Film Company, Motorola Teleprograms, 1974).

96   "Indian Affairs Branch Said Blameless in Death," *Globe and Mail*, January 18, 1969, 49.

97   "Hitchhikers Are Flirting with Trouble ... Say Police," *Mississauga Times*, August 24, 1977.

98   Veselka, "Green Room," 10.

99   Greenley and Rice, "Female Hitchhiking," 91, 94.

100  Ibid., 99.

101  Ibid., 98.

02 On "historical biography," see Deborah Gorham, *Vera Brittain: A Feminist Life* (Oxford: Blackwell, 1996), 5–6.

03 Myrna Kostash, *Long Way from Home: The Story of the Sixties Generation in Canada* (Toronto: Lorimer, 1980), 170.

04 Interviewee 96, June 23, 2011.

05 "'Some of the Friendliest Faces Are Sex Maniacs': North York against Hitchhikers, Seeks Ban across Metro," *Globe and Mail*, June 11, 1974; Michael O'Regan, "Alternative Mobility Cultures and the Resurgence of Hitch-Hiking," in *Slow Tourism: Experiences and Mobilities*, ed. Simone Fullagar, Kevin Markwell, and Erica Wilson, 128–42 (Bristol, UK: Channel View, 2012).

06 In most women's narratives of the road, female protagonists realize that this is not a simple mission. Alexandra Ganser writes, "They find themselves 'prisoners of the white lines of the freeway,' as Joni Mitchell put it in her legendary road song 'Coyote' on her 1976 album *Hejira*." Ganser, "On the Asphalt Frontier," 160.

07 "Offences on Hitch-Hikers during TTC Strike Studied: Women Who Are Sexually Assaulted Don't Provoke Attack, Toronto Psychologist Says," *Globe and Mail*, June 17, 1977, 1.

08 Action Request from Commissioner of Ontario Provincial Police to Superintendent Jack Fullerton, November 10, 1978. This request stated, "Some films we are presently using are not recommended by this group."

09 "Travel into Danger on the Hitchhike Road," *Globe and Mail*, June 8, 1974, 6.

10 Interviewee 98, Duncan McMonagle, Winnipeg, August 24, 2012.

11 DiMaggio, *Hitchhiker's Field Manual*, 29–30.

12 Benedict, *Virgin or Vamp*, 16–17.

13 "Travel into Danger on the Hitchhike Road," *Globe and Mail*, June 8, 1974, 6.

14 "'Some of the Friendliest Faces Are Sex Maniacs': North York against Hitchhiking, Seeks Ban across Metro," *Globe and Mail*, June 11, 1974, 5.

15 Ibid.

16 "Travel into Danger on the Hitchhike Road," *Globe and Mail*, June 8, 1974, 6.

17 "Ban on Hitchhiking," *Globe and Mail*, June 1, 1974.

18 Marshall Franks, "Hikers Not Maniacs, Just People," *Globe and Mail*, September 23, 1977, 7. See also "Hitchhikers Are Flirting with Trouble ... Say Police," *Mississauga Times*, August 24, 1977; "A Hitch in OPP Campaign," *Charlottetown Guardian*, n.d., RG 23–32, file 12–15, Hitchhiking, 1978, Archives of Ontario; "'Hand of Death' Signs Have Impact Designed to Make Hitchhikers Think," *Burlington Daily Times*, August 25, 1977, RG 23–32, file 12–15, Hitchhiking, 1978, Archives of Ontario; Ontario Provincial Police, "Clippings," RG 23–32, file 12–5, Hitchhiking, 1978, Archives of Ontario.

19 Both quoted in Marshall Franks, "Hikers Not Maniacs, Just People," *Globe and Mail*, September 23, 1977, 7, original emphasis.

20 "A Hitch in OPP Campaign," *Charlottetown Guardian*, n.d., RG 23–32, file 12–15, Hitchhiking, 1978, Archives of Ontario.

21 "Hitchhikers," letter to the editor, *Globe and Mail*, September 21, 1977, 6.

22 "A Hitch in OPP Campaign," *Charlottetown Guardian*, n.d., RG 23–32, file 12–15, Hitchhiking, 1978, Archives of Ontario.

123 Paulo Jesus, Maria Formosinho, and Maria Helena Damião, "Risk-Taking in Youth Culture as a Ritual Process," *International Journal of Developmental and Educational Psychology* 5, 1 (2011): 457. Elaine Sharland, "Young People, Risk Taking and Risk Making: Some Thoughts for Social Work," *Forum: Qualitative Social Research* 7, 1 (2006): 16, http://www.qualitative-research.net/index.php/fqs/article/view/56/116. See also Jennie Small, "The Emergence of the Body in the Holiday Accounts of Women and Girls," in *Tourism and Gender: Embodiment, Sensuality and Experience*, ed. Annette Pritchard, Nigel Morgan, Irena Ateljevic, and Candice Harris, 73–91 (Wallingford, UK: CABI, 2007); and Paolo Mura, "'Scary but I Like It!' Young Tourists' Perceptions of Fear on Holiday," *Journal of Tourism and Cultural Change* 8, 1–2 (2010): 30–49.

124 Franca Iacovetta, "Gossip, Contest, and Power in the Making of Suburban Bad Girls: Toronto, 1945–60," *Canadian Historical Review* 80, 4 (1999): 595.

125 Packer, *Mobility without Mayhem*, 93.

126 Mary Louise Adams, *The Trouble with Normal* (Toronto: University of Toronto Press, 1997).

127 Quoted in Chenier, "Criminal Sexual Psychopath," 93.

128 Elise Chenier, "The Natural Order of Disorder: Pedophilia, Stranger Danger and the Normalising Family," *Sexuality and Culture* 16, 2 (2012): 174–75. See also Gayle Rubin, "Thinking Sex: Notes for a Radical Theory of the Politics of Sexuality," in *Pleasure and Danger: Exploring Female Sexuality*, ed. Carole S. Vance (Boston: Routledge and Kegan Paul, 1984), 281.

129 Chenier, "Natural Order of Disorder," 177.

130 Adams, *Trouble with Normal*, 129–35, 165; Chenier, "Natural Order of Disorder," 172.

131 Adams, *Trouble with Normal*, 129–30.

132 Packer, *Mobility without Mayhem*, 93.

133 Interviewee 99, Keith Perkins, Toronto, April 8, 2013.

134 Interviewee 93, Vancouver, June 22, 2011.

135 Interviewee 90, Vancouver, June 22, 2011.

136 Interviewees 32a and 32b, Gabriola Island, BC, February 22, 2012.

137 Interviewee 85, Salt Spring Island, BC, June 29, 2011.

138 Interviewee 99, Keith Perkins, Toronto, April 8, 2013.

139 Interviewee 89, Vancouver, June 22, 2011.

140 Interviewee 76a, Salt Spring Island, BC, June 21, 2011.

141 *Rape: A Preventative Inquiry*, documentary (J. Gary Mitchell Film Company, Motorola Teleprograms, 1974).

142 Kristine Alexander, "Agency and Emotion Work," *Jeunesse: Young People, Texts, Cultures* 7, 2 (2015): 120–28; Mona Gleason, "Avoiding the Agency Trap: Caveats for Historians of Children, Youth, and Education," *History of Education* 45, 4 (2016): 446–59; Mona Gleason, "'Knowing something I was not meant to know': Exploring Vulnerability, Sexuality, and Childhood," *Canadian Historical Review* 98, 1 (2017): 38; Linda Gordon, *Heroes of Their Own Lives: The Politics and History of Family Violence* (New York: Viking, 1988), 249.

143 Interviewee 5, Barrie, Ontario, May 29, 2016.

44 Florence Rush, *The Best Kept Secret: Sexual Abuse of Children* (New York: McGraw-Hill, 1980); Linda Gordon, *Heroes of Their Own Lives: The Politics and History of Family Violence, Boston 1880–1960* (London: Virago, 1988), 219.
45 Interviewees 81a and 81b, Vancouver, June 23, 2011.
46 Email correspondent 5, September 9, 2013.
47 Interviewee 78, Salt Spring Island, BC, June 27, 2011.
48 Interviewee 56, Vancouver, June 23, 2011.
49 Interviewee 84, Salt Spring Island, BC, February 16, 2012.
50 Interviewee 40, Saskatoon, July 4, 2013.
51 Veselka, "Green Screen," 8.
52 Ron Verzuh, "Trip Tips," *The Peak* (Simon Fraser University), June 10, 1970, 7.
53 "European Hitchhiker Finds It Possible to Live on $4 Daily," *Edmonton Journal*, August 13, 1971.
54 Martin Dorrell, "Singin' the Espanola Blues," *Globe and Mail*, June 10, 1971, 37.
55 Dane Archer and Lynn Erlich-Erfer, "Fear and Loading: Archival Traces of the Response to Extraordinary Violence," *Social Psychology Quarterly* 54, 4 (1991): 351.
56 Interviewee 21, Toronto, April 16, 2013.
57 Myers, "Didactic Sudden Death," 470.
58 "Angry and Repulsed," *The Chevron* (University of Waterloo), March 7, 1975.
59 "Free Announcement: 'Warning,'" *The Peak* (Simon Fraser University), August 4, 1971.
60 D. Chassels, "Mail," *The Peak* (Simon Fraser University), July 15, 1970.
61 Wanda Lust, "Drivers Bare Balls, Hearts to Hitchhiking Chick," *The Ubyssey* (University of British Columbia), October 7, 1969.
62 DiMaggio added, "Be civil and decent ... To know your country, you have to get to know your country's inhabitants." DiMaggio, *Hitchhiker's Field Manual*, 56.
63 Raymond Chouinard, interview with author, Vancouver, March 7, 2013.
64 David Rideout and Ray Amiro, *Handbook Canada: A Traveller's Manual* (Toronto: Transglobular Functions, 1972), 11.
65 "Hitchhiker Finds Friends," *Winnipeg Free Press*, August 21, 1971.
66 Interviewee 85, Salt Spring Island, BC, June 29, 2011.
67 Tamara Myers says that this approach is what public health nurses in the 1950s called "safety immunization," whereby adults used discipline to enforce safety regulations and taught children responsibility for their safety and that of others. Myers, "Didactic Sudden Death," 465.
68 The authors write, "The meaning produced through ritual always exists in problematic tension with the nonritual world." Adam Seligman, Robert Weller, Michael Puett, and Bennett Simon, *Ritual and Its Consequences: An Essay on the Limits of Sincerity* (New York: Oxford University Press, 2008), 26.
69 Packer, *Mobility without Mayhem*, 90.
70 Interviewee 99, Keith Perkins, Toronto, April 8, 2013.
71 Jesus, Formosinho, and Damião, "Risk-Taking in Youth Culture," 457.
72 "Hitchhikers Are Flirting with Trouble ... Say Police," *Mississauga Times*, August 24, 1977.
73 "'Hand of Death' Signs Have Impact Designed to Make Hitchhikers Think," *Burlington Daily Times*, August 25, 1977, RG 23–32, file 12–15, Hitchhiking, 1978, Archives of Ontario.

174  "Pretty Pair of Hitchhikers," *Winnipeg Free Press,* May 9, 1970. See also "Judie Crossing Canada," *Winnipeg Free Press,* May 9, 1970.
175  Paul Buhle, "No Laughing Matter: An Analysis of Sexual Humor," review, *Minnesota Review,* n.s., 25 (1985): 133–36.
176  Interviewees 81a, 81b, and 81c, Vancouver, June 23, 2011.
177  Folklorist Alan Dundes argues that the legend of the vanishing hitchhiker is a cautionary tale signifying that the hitchhiker who is raped will be ruined, punished, and doomed to spend eternity desperately unable to return to the safety of home and family. Dundes, "Bloody Mary in the Mirror," 130.

### Conclusion: The Vanishing Hitchhiker Eulogy

1  HitchBOT, "Travels in Canada," n.d., http://mir1.hitchbot.me/about/canada.
2  HitchBOT, "Travels in Germany," n.d., http://mir1.hitchbot.me/about/germany; HitchBOT, "Travels in the Netherlands," n.d., http://mir1.hitchbot.me/about/netherlands.
3  HitchBOT, "About HitchBOT," n.d., http://mir1.hitchbot.me/about; David Smith and Frauke Zeller, interviewed by Andrea Zeffiro, "Post-HitchBOT-ism," *Wi: Journal of Mobile Media* 10, 1 (2016): 4; Noreen Herzfeld, "Mourning HitchBOT," *Theology and Science* 13, 4 (2015): 377.
4  "HitchBOT the Hitchhiking Robot to Travel across Canada," *CBC News,* July 24, 2014, http://www.cbc.ca/news/canada/nova-scotia/hitchbot-the-hitchhiking-robot-to -travel-across-canada-1.2716476; Alexis Madrigal, "Meet the Cute, Wellies-Wearing, Wikipedia-Reading Robot That's Going to Hitchhike across Canada," *The Atlantic,* June 12, 2014.
5  HitchBOT, "Travels in the USA," n.d. http://mir1.hitchbot.me/about; Herzfeld, "Mourning HitchBOT," 377; Christopher Muther, "HitchBOT's Trip Comes to an End," *Boston Globe,* August 2, 2015.
6  Quoted in "HitchBOT the Hitchhiking Robot to Travel across Canada," *CBC News,* July 24, 2014, http://www.cbc.ca/news/canada/nova-scotia/hitchbot-the-hitchhiking -robot-to-travel-across-canada-1.2716476.
7  Smith and Zeller, interviewed by Zeffiro, "Post-HitchBOT-ism," 4.
8  Ibid., 6–7; HitchBOT, "About HitchBOT."
9  Albert Burneko, "HitchBOT Was a Literal Pile of Trash and Got What It Deserved," *The Concourse,* August 3, 2015; Smith and Zeller, interviewed by Zeffiro, "Post-HitchBOT-ism," 9–11; Herzfeld, "Mourning HitchBOT," 377–78; Muther, "HitchBOT's Trip"; Timothy Ignaffo and Christopher Dougherty, "HitchBOT's Last Lesson," *Full Stop: Reviews, Interviews, Marginalia,* August 5, 2015.
10  "HitchBOT, the Hitchhiking Robot, Gets Beheaded in Philadelphia," *CNN,* August 4, 2015, https://www.cnn.com/2015/08/03/us/hitchbot-robot-beheaded-philadelphia -feat/index.html.
11  Michael O'Regan, "Alternative Mobility Cultures and the Resurgence of Hitch-Hiking," in *Slow Tourism: Experiences and Mobilities,* ed. Simone Fullagar, Kevin Markwell, and Erica Wilson (Bristol, UK: Channel View, 2012), 136.
12  Torun Elsrud, "Risk Creation in Travelling: Backpacker Adventure Narration," *Annals of Tourism Research* 28, 3 (2001): 598.

13  Rory MacLean, *Magic Bus: On the Hippie Trail from Istanbul to India* (London: Penguin, 2007); Michael Hall, *Remembering the Hippie Trail: Travelling across Asia 1976–1978* (Newtownabbey, Northern Ireland: Island Publications, 2007).

14  "A Canadian's Journey: Hitch-Hiking Round the World," *The Scotsman* (Edinburgh), September 14, 1928.

15  Doug Owram, *Born at the Right Time: A History of the Baby Boom Generation* (Toronto: University of Toronto Press, 1997), 229; Mike Brake, *Comparative Youth Culture: The Sociology of Youth Cultures and Youth Subcultures in America, Britain, and Canada* (New York: Routledge, 1985), 156.

16  Interviewee 3, Edinburgh, Scotland, October 11, 2012.

17  "Army of Hitch-Hikers Already on the March," *Globe and Mail*, June 22, 1972. See also John Clarke, Stuart Hall, Tony Jefferson, and Brian Roberts, "Subcultures, Cultures and Class," in *Resistance through Rituals: Youth Subcultures in Post-War Britain*, ed. Stuart Hall and Tony Jefferson (London: Hutchinson, 1976), 9.

18  David Botterill, Shane Pointing, Charmaine Hayes-Jonkers, Alan Clough, Trevor Jones, and Cristina Rodriguez, "Violence, Backpackers, Security and Critical Realism," *Annals of Tourism Research* 42 (2013): 311–33; Erik Cohen, "Death of a Backpacker: Incidental but Not Random," *Journal of Tourism and Cultural Change* 6, 3 (2008): 209–26; Elsrud, "Risk Creation in Travelling."

19  Marg Tiyce and Erica Wilson, "Wandering Australia: Independent Travellers and Slow Journeys through Time and Space," in *Slow Tourism: Experiences and Mobilities*, ed. Simone Fullagar, Kevin Markwell, and Erica Wilson (Bristol, UK: Channel View, 2012), 115, 117; Deborah Stevenson, Stephen Wearing, and Tamara Young, *Tourist Cultures: Identity, Place and the Traveller* (London: Sage, 2012), 47; Anders Sørensen, "Backpacker Ethnography," *Annals of Tourism Research* 30, 4 (2003): 852. For the Canadian context, see Lawrence Aronsen, *City of Love and Revolution: Vancouver in the Sixties* (Vancouver: New Star Books, 2010), 18; Owram, *Born at the Right Time*, 206; and Jo-Anne Hecht and David Martin, "Backpacking and Hostel-Picking: An Analysis from Canada," *International Journal of Contemporary Hospitality Management* 18, 1 (2006): 70–71.

20  Lilly Fink Shapiro, "Pleasure and Danger on the Gringo Trail: An Ethnography of Bolivian Party Hostels" (Honor's thesis, Wesleyan University, 2009), http://wesscholar.wesleyan.edu/etd_hon_theses/375; Greg Richards and Julie Wilson, "Widening Perspectives in Backpacker Research," in *The Global Nomad: Backpacker Travel in Theory and Practice*, ed. Greg Richards and Julie Wilson (Clevedon, UK: Channel View, 2004), 265.

21  Amie Matthews, "Young Backpackers and the Rite of Passage of Travel: Examining the Transformative Effects of Liminality," in *Travel and Transformation*, ed. Garth Lean, Russell Staiff, and Emma Waterton (Surrey, UK: Ashgate, 2014), 157; Zygmunt Bauman, "From Pilgrim to Tourist – or a Short History of Identity," in *Questions of Cultural Identity*, ed. Stuart Hall and Paul du Gay, 18–36 (London: Sage, 1996); Elsrud, "Risk Creation"; Dean MacCannell, *The Tourist: A New Theory of the Leisure Class* (New York: Schocken Books, 1989).

22  Sørensen, "Backpacker Ethnography," 853, 852. See also Greg Richards and Julie Wilson, "Drifting towards the Global Nomad," in *The Global Nomad: Backpacker*

*Travel in Theory and Practice,* ed. Greg Richards and Julie Wilson (Clevedon, UK: Channel View, 2004), 6; and Kate Simpson, "Dropping Out or Signing Up? The Professionalization of Youth Travel," *Antipode* 37, 3 (2005): 448.

23 Cynthia Comacchio, *The Dominion of Youth: Adolescence and the Making of Modern Canada, 1920 to 1950* (Waterloo, ON: Wilfrid Laurier University Press, 2006), 17–18.

24 Quoting John Seeley, the director of California's Center for the Study of Democratic Institutions, Summer '71 member Rob Andras added that Opportunities for Youth represented a model of social services and the provision of meaningful employment for the "post-industrial society." Rob Andras and Cam Mackie, interview with Andy Cohen, June 3, 1970, Cabinet Documents, in private possession of Byron Rogers.

25 Lesley Andres and Johanna Wyn, *The Making of a Generation: The Children of the 1970s in Adulthood* (Toronto: University of Toronto Press, 2010), 30.

26 Draft memo from Cam Mackie to Secretary of State, January 28, 1970, Transient Youth Services Documents, in private possession of Byron Rogers.

27 Chandra Mukerji, "Bullshitting: Road Lore among Hitchhikers," *Social Problems* 25, 3 (1978): 246–47.

28 Mona Gleason, "Avoiding the Agency Trap: Caveats for Historians of Children, Youth and Education," *History of Education* 45, 4 (2016): 449, 450.

29 Brake, *Comparative Youth Culture,* 27.

30 Canadian Welfare Council, *Transient Youth: Report of an Inquiry in the Summer of 1969* (Ottawa: Canadian Welfare Council, 1970), 9, 105.

31 "Opportunities for Youth," *McGill Daily* (McGill University), September 20, 1971.

32 "From New Canada," *Arthur* (Trent University), February 19, 1970.

33 Canadian Council on Social Development, *Transient Youth, 70–71: Report of an Inquiry about Programs in 1970, and Plans for 1971* (Ottawa: Department of Health and Welfare, 1970), 21.

34 Carol Holden, "Transients," *Edmonton Journal,* August 9, 1971.

35 Darya Maoz, "The Mutual Gaze," *Annals of Tourism Research* 33, 1 (2006): 222, 225.

36 Barbara Jane Brickman, *New American Teenagers: The Lost Generation of Youth in American Film* (New York: Continuum, 2012), 4.

37 Ibid., 3; Elise Chenier, "The Natural Order of Disorder: Pedophilia, Stranger Danger and the Normalising Family," *Sexuality and Culture* 16, 2 (2012): 172–73, 180.

38 This image of the "new adolescent" was captured in American film by the androgynous actors Robby Benson and Jodie Foster. Brickman, *New American Teenagers,* 109–12.

39 Chenier, "Natural Order of Disorder," 172–73, 180.

40 Canada, Secretary of State, Committee on Youth, *It's Your Turn: A Report to the Secretary of State by the Committee on Youth* (Ottawa: Information Canada, 1971), 7. The Canadian Welfare Council's inquiry on transient youth described the youth in question as between thirteen and twenty-two years of age. Canadian Welfare Council, *Transient Youth,* 1.

41 Bernard Schissel, *Blaming Children: Youth Crime, Moral Panics and the Politics of Hate* (Halifax: Fernwood, 1997), 16.

42 Ibid., 31.

43  Peter Kelly, "The Entrepreneurial Self and 'Youth-at-Risk': Exploring the Horizons of Identity in the Twenty-First Century," *Journal of Youth Studies* 9, 1 (2006): 17.

44  Ibid. See also Johanna Wyn and Peter Dwyer, "New Directions in Research on Youth in Transition," *Journal of Youth Studies* 2, 1 (1999): 9, 16.

45  Gleason, "Avoiding the Agency Trap," 458.

46  Paulo Jesus, Maria Formosinho, Maria Helena Damião, "Risk-Taking in Youth Culture as a Ritual Process," *International Journal of Developmental and Educational Psychology* 5, 1 (2011): 457.

47  Ibid., 452; Susanne Schröter, "Rituals of Rebellion – Rebellion as Ritual: A Theory Reconsidered," in *The Dynamics of Changing Rituals: The Transformation of Religious Rituals within Their Social and Cultural Context*, ed. Jens Kreinath, Constance Hartung, and Annette Deschner (New York: Peter Lang, 2004), 44–47.

48  Jesus, Formosinho, and Damião, "Risk-Taking in Youth Culture," 452.

49  Jeremy Packer, *Mobility without Mayhem: Safety, Cars, and Citizenship* (Durham, NC: Duke University Press, 2008), 103.

50  Jonathan Swainger, "Teen Trouble and Community Identity in Post–Second World War Northern British Columbia," *Journal of Canadian Studies* 47, 2 (2013): 152. Youth studies pioneer John Springhall states, "There is a danger of minimizing the contemporary sense of worry and crisis ... by an account of its repetitious and historically relative character." Quoted in ibid.

51  Kristine Alexander, "Agency and Emotion Work," *Jeunesse: Young People, Texts, Cultures* 7, 2 (2015): 120–28; Gleason, "Avoiding the Agency Trap."

52  David F. Lancy, "Unmasking Children's Agency," *Sociology, Social Work and Anthropology Faculty Publications* (Utah State University), paper 277 (2012): 1, 11, http://digitalcommons.usu.edu/sswa_facpubs/277.

53  Ibid., 5. See also Schissel, *Blaming Children*, 105.

54  Alexander, "Agency and Emotion Work."

55  David Rideout and Ray Amiro, *Handbook Canada: A Traveller's Manual* (Toronto: Transglobular Functions, 1972), 4.

56  Gleason, "Avoiding the Agency Trap," 458.

57  Elaine Sharland, "Young People, Risk Taking and Risk Making: Some Thoughts for Social Work," *Forum: Qualitative Social Research* 7, 1 (2006), http://www.qualitative -research.net/index.php/fqs/article/view/56/116.

58  See "Thumbsploitation," *Popcorn & Sticky Floors*, May 14, 2008, http://spiltpopcorn. blogspot.ca/2008/05.

59  Richard K. Beardsley and Rosalie Hankey, "A History of the Vanishing Hitchhiker," *California Folklore Quarterly* 2, 1 (1943): 16; Ernest W. Baughman, "The Hitchhiking Ghost," *Hoosier Folklore* 6, 2 (1947): 77–78; Alan Dundes, "Bloody Mary in the Mirror: A Ritual Reflection of Pre-Pubescent Anxiety," *Western Folklore* 57, 2–3 (1998): 119–35.

60  Beardsley and Hankey, "History of the Vanishing Hitchhiker."

61  John T. Schlebecker, "An Informal History of Hitchhiking," *Historian* 20, 3 (1958): 316.

62  Packer, *Mobility without Mayhem*, 109, 101.

63  Beardsley and Hankey, "History of the Vanishing Hitchhiker," 22.

64  Dundes, "Bloody Mary in the Mirror," 130.
65  Vanessa Veselka, "Green Screen: The Lack of Female Road Narratives and Why It Matters," *American Reader* 4, 1 (2012): 6–8.
66  Federal Bureau of Investigation, "Highway Serial Killings: New Initiative on an Emerging Trend," April 6, 2009. https://archives.fbi.gov/archives/news/stories/2009/april/highwayserial_040609.
67  The RCMP's investigation of highway murders has been superseded by the "Highway of Tears List" for the route from Prince Rupert to Prince George, with some cases overlapping, including that of Melissa Rehorek. Royal Canadian Mounted Police, "Melissa Ann Rehorek," in *Cold Case Files*, December 10, 2015, http://www.rcmp-grc.gc.ca/cc-afn/rehorek-melissa-eng.htm. See also "Canada Highway Murders," in *Crimezzz: Serial Killer Crime Index*, n.d., http://www.crimezzz.net/serialkillers/C/CANADA_HIGHWAY_murders.php; and Robert Hoshowsky, *Unsolved: True Canadian Cold Cases* (Toronto: Dundurn, 2010).
68  Anupriya Sethi, "Domestic Sex Trafficking of Aboriginal Girls in Canada: Issues and Implications," *First Peoples Child and Family Review* 3, 3 (2007): 57–71; Highway of Tears, http://www.highwayoftears.ca.
69  Paolo Mura, "'Scary but I like it!' Young Tourists' Perceptions of Fear on Holiday," *Journal of Tourism and Cultural Change* 8, 1–2 (2010): 30–49; Jennie Small, "The Emergence of the Body in the Holiday Accounts of Women and Girls," in *Tourism and Gender: Embodiment, Sensuality and Experience*, ed. Annette Pritchard, Nigel Morgan, Irena Ateljevic, and Candice Harris, 73–91 (Wallingford, UK: CABI, 2007).
70  Michael W. Sherraden and Donald J. Eberly, "Reflections on Katimavik, an Innovative Canadian Youth Program," *Children and Youth Services Review* 8, 4 (1986): 283–303.

# Index

*Note:* "(i)" after a page number indicates an illustration. CWC stands for Canadian Welfare Council; CYHA stands for Canadian Youth Hostels Association; RCMP stands for Royal Canadian Mounted Police; UBC stands for University of British Columbia; VLF stands for Vancouver Liberation Front. Subentries for "Canadian Welfare Council (CWC)," "Canadian Youth Hostels Association (CYHA)," and "Jericho Beach hostel (Vancouver)" are arranged chronologically rather than alphabetically.

accidents, hitchhiking, 58–59, 158, 192, 193, 210
Adams, Mary Louise, 47, 264*n*110
Adams, Nathan, 208
Addy, Cenovia, 106, 114, 115
Adler, Judith, 36
adolescent wanderlust, 5, 6–10, 26–27, 87–88; and automobility, 4–5, 10–14, 69; in baby boom era, 4, 5, 11–12, 22, 64–99; and early travel/"tramping," 6–7, 43, 67, 82, 240; regulation/policing of, 9, 104, 222; and risk-taking, 9–10, 13–14, 17, 88; social work scrutiny of, 104–16; as stage of discovery/education, 137–38, 170; theories of, 8–10, 49, 87–88, 104
adventure hitchhiking/travel, 21–22, 26–61; and anti-hitchhiking campaigns, 57–60, 61; and automobility/road construction, 27–30, 48; dangers posed by, 56, 57–61; and delinquency/vagrancy, 47–51, 54–57; during Depression, 21, 26–27, 30–32, 36–37,

42, 49–51, 82, 240; as educational, 30, 34–35, 38–41, 42, 47, 60; and labour movement/activism, 36–38; in literature, 30, 60; by men/boys, 30–32, 42–44, 51–54; and "No Riders" rules, 57, 60–61; respectability of, 42–47, 85; by Scouts/soldiers, 42–43, 51–54; by women/girls, 32–35, 40–41, 44–47, 54–57, 59; by youth clubs/hostel associations, 35–41
advice, on hitchhiking, 92–97; in campus press, 14–15, 64, 94–96, 235; in guidebooks/manuals, 15, 64, 93–95, 177–81, 234–36; by newspaper advice columnists, 46–47, 55–56, 90, 219–20; for women, 85–86, 195–96, 234–36. *See also* guidebooks and manuals; Verzuh, Ron
Alexander, J.K., 141
Alexander, Kristine, 196, 246
Amaral, Everett, 56
Anderson, Judy, 141
Andras, Rob, 147, 314*n*24

Anka, Garry, 152
anti-hitchhiking campaigns: (1940s/
1950s), 57–60, 61; (1970s), 200, 216–
23, 227–28, 229
Armstrong, Jeannette: *Slash*, 78, 273*n*80
Aronsen, Lawrence, 131
automobility, 4–5, 10–14, 69; and anti-
car hitchhikers, 80–82; and car
culture, 11, 29–30, 66, 176–77; vs freedom, 18; and highway/road construction, 5, 11, 27–28, 48

baby boom era, hitchhiking in, 4, 5,
11–12, 22, 64–99; appeal of, 73–77;
background/context of, 64–69; and
car culture, 11, 66, 176–77; and environmentalism, 80–82; equipment
for, 92–93, 97–98; and generational
conflict, 86–92, 87(i), 98; guidebooks/
advice on, 92–97; and hippie subculture, 82–86; by Indigenous youth,
77–80; and music, 69–73, 80; Trudeau
as role model for, 97–98, 142, 239, 240
Bach, Richard: *Jonathan Livingston
Seagull*, 203
backpackers, 11, 13, 67; early adventure
travel by, 21, 27, 57; hippie image of,
64, 194, 241; and hostel movement,
137, 185–86; imagined travelscapes/
worlds of, 83–84; Israeli, 13, 19, 154,
243; Kerouac's "revolution" of, 92;
mobility subculture of, 19; negative
views of, 13, 93, 100, 132–33, 160, 165,
194, 243; rules/rituals specific to, 177;
women as, 19–20, 33, 40–41, 45–46,
85–86, 97–98, 141, 196, 221, 241
backpacks, 11, 64, 85–86, 92–93, 194,
197; advice on packing, 153; as androgynous, 85, 245; Canadian flags on,
201; contents of, 85, 93; "magic"/
transcendence of, 93, 194, 200; weight
of, 46, 86. *See also* haversacks;
rucksacks
Baez, Joan, 70; "The Hitchhikers' Song,"
71

Banff, 89, 116, 149, 169, 174; hitchhiking
to, 34, 35, 71
Banff National Park, 161, 182; CYHA
hostel in, 138; Echo Creek tent city in,
188, 301*n*88
Banks, Elizabeth: *The Autobiography of
a "Newspaper Girl,"* 7
bans on hitchhiking, proposed: in
Toronto, 219, 226, 227; in Vancouver,
4–5, 74
Barclay, Gary, 4, 5
Barclay, Mary and Catherine, 39, 137–
38, 165, 261*n*77
Barron, Sid: hitchhiker kiosk cartoon
by, 152, 152(i)
Bartky, Sandra Lee, 196
"Battle of Jericho." *See* Jericho Beach
hostel (Vancouver)
Bauer, Ingrid, 204, 205(i), 207, 221–22
The Beatles, 176; "The Long and
Winding Road," 70
Beatty Street drill hall (Vancouver),
118–21, 122, 123, 191
Beauvoir, Simone de: *The Second Sex*,
224
Belford, Joan, 159, 171
Bell, Gertrude, 33
Benedict, Helen, 220–21, 306*n*43
Bennett, R.B., 31, 37, 240
Berg, Dave: *Mad* magazine cartoon by, 4
Berger, Bennett, 83
Berger, Peter, 148
biopower (Foucault), 9, 104, 222
Birmingham, Lloyd, 36
Black, David, 134
Black Panthers, 81, 213
Blues Image: "Ride Captain Ride," 70
Bonnici, Tony, 203
*Born Innocent* (film), 209
boundaries: between drivers and pas-
sengers, 26; between locals and tour-
ists, 13–14, 93, 154, 243; for women/
girls, 207
Boy Scouts, 10, 39, 49, 83, 129, 137, 138–
39, 144, 166, 169; hitchhiking by, 52, 53

Bragg Creek, Alberta: CYHA hostel in, 43(i), 170
Brake, Mike, 2, 84, 262*n*90
Brand, Oscar: "Something to Sing About," 65
Braunstein, Peter, 113
Brickman, Barbara Jane, 244
Brookfield, Tarah, 65, 69
Burton, Helen "Lenny," 35, 46
buses, for hitchhikers (Summer '71 program), 149, 150–51, 153, 194, 208
Byles, John, 111

Cairenius, Mark, 228
Calgary, 39, 137, 138, 152, 192, 206–7; federal hostel space in, 116, 149, 186–87, 188; hitchhiking in, 96, 155, 161; hitchhiking to, 34, 174
Campbell, Alex, 156
Campbell, Lara, 30
Campbell, Tom: and federal hostel program (1970), 118–19, 121, 123, 124, 130, 157; on hippies, 129; hitchhiking ban proposed by, 4–5, 74; perceived bigotry of, 131–32, 156, 167
Canadian Council on Social Development (formerly CWC), 16, 105, 146. *See also* Canadian Welfare Council (CWC)
Canadian flag, 65, 121; as identifier, 201–2, 203, 248
Canadian Government Travel Bureau, 28
Canadian Hostel Association, 17, 23, 170
Canadian Union of Students, 74
Canadian University Press, 14–15, 75. *See also* newspapers, university
Canadian Welfare Council (CWC): and federal hostel program, 113–16, 119; and "hippie" organizations/youth workers, 108–16, 132, 136; history of, 105–6; National Youth Consultation hosted by, 22, 102, 114–16, 144, 242; problematic outlook/methods of, 106–13, 124, 132; as shut out of later

federal hostel program, 144–46; transient youth follow-up study (1970) by, 16, 132, 145–46, 242–43; transient youth inquiry (1969) by, 16, 17, 22, 78, 83, 88, 91–92, 100, 102, 106–13, 144, 148, 149, 207–8, 214
Canadian Youth Congress, 21, 35–36, 75
Canadian Youth Hostels Association (CYHA), 17, 21, 27, 35, 38–41, 47, 94, 96, 97–98, 108, 110, 111, 132, 136–71, 174, 185, 188, 191, 221; archival photographs of, 25(i), 38(i), 41(i), 43(i), 135(i), 139(i), 141, 164(i); vs federal hostel program, 22–23, 137, 144, 148–49, 153, 161, 163–71; fees of, 138, 163, 165, 168, 171; founding of, 39, 137–38; hostels/activities of, 136–44; houseparents/house rules of, 140, 144, 161, 164–65, 168–69, 171, 261*n*83; international affiliation of, 138, 140, 144, 168–69, 288*n*12; membership of, 138, 140, 144, 146; as merged with federal hostel associations, 17, 23, 169–70, 244; and transient youth movement, 142–44, 148; Trudeau's memo to, 98, 142, 143(i); values of, 137–38, 164–65, 170
Capra, Frank (dir.): *It Happened One Night*, 44
cars, 11, 29–30, 66, 176–77. *See also* automobility
Carter, Angela, 82–83
Catchpool, Jack, 39
Charlottetown, 72, 154, 156; federal hostel space in, 116, 117, 149, 155–56
Chenier, Elise, 214, 229, 244, 268*n*196
Chesters, Graeme, and David Smith, 19
Children's Aid Society, 78, 108, 109, 110, 111, 150, 162, 214
Citizenship, Department of, 116, 145, 147, 289*n*43
Cleaver, Eldridge, 81
clothing: as androgynous, 85, 196, 245; of baby boom era, 11, 83, 98, 129, 228, 237; as disguise, 7, 43, 49, 67, 82, 119,

197; as flashy/dangerous, 52–53; hippie, 64, 82–86, 113, 114, 117, 119, 157, 165, 166, 195–96; military/Scouting, 42–43, 51–54; as respectable, 42–43, 45–46, 51, 56, 85, 178; sexuality of, 195–96, 212–13, 215; of Trudeau, 97, 142; worn-out/ripped, 262n89, 274n105
Cochrane, Jacqueline "Johnny," 35, 46, 47
Cockburn, Bruce, 72
Cody, H.J., 40
Cohen, Andy, 115, 116, 147
Cohen, Erik, 67–68
Cohen, Leonard, 84
Cohen, Stanley, 10, 16, 105, 109, 131
Comacchio, Cynthia, 14, 49, 241, 261n78
Committee on Youth (Secretary of State), 115, 136, 144–45; *It's Your Turn*, 17, 71–72, 77–78, 98, 145, 148, 166
Committee Representing Youth Problems Today (CRYPT, Winnipeg), 109–10, 112, 132, 174
communitas, 12–13, 23, 175, 185, 198–200, 202, 203
Company of Young Canadians, 74, 78, 147
Cool-Aid (Moose Jaw hostel), 161
Cool Aid (Vancouver hostel network), 17, 109–10, 115, 119, 127, 132, 174, 191, 236
Cooper family, women of, as hitchhiking for work, 46
Co-operative Commonwealth Federation (CCF), 36
Corrigan, Dorothy, 156
Creedence Clearwater Revival: "Sweet Hitch-Hiker," 209
crimes: against hitchhikers, 58, 206–38, 244, 247–48; by hitchhikers, 27, 57–61, 208, 244, 267n184; as leading to anti-hitchhiking campaigns, 57–60, 61, 216–23, 227–28. *See also* female hitchhikers; rape/sexual assault; sexual predators
Criminal Code, 48, 56, 225–26, 229

criminalization of hitchhiking, 47–48, 95, 175–76, 218; in Ontario, 47–48, 51, 53, 54, 175; and proposed bans, 4–5, 74, 219, 226, 227; and vagrancy laws, 48, 56–57, 84, 112, 175
Cross, James, 133
Crowbar: "Tits Up on the Pavement," 202
Cull, Elizabeth, 226–27
Cyples, Ed, 52, 266n148

Dangelmajer, Charles, 31
Darlington, Pamela, 218
David, Lester, 208
*Dawn: Portrait of a Teenage Runaway* (film), 209
Dawson, Marilyn, 86
Dee, Sandra, 206
Dennison, Barbara, 54
Desmond, Jane, 12
*Diary of a Teenage Hitchhiker* (film), 209
Diefenbaker, John, 141–42
DiMaggio, Paul. See *The Hitchhiker's Field Manual* (DiMaggio)
dogs, hitchhiking with, 179, 211(i)
Dominion-Provincial Youth Training Programme, 50
Dorrell, Martin, 94, 96, 175, 182
Dowhan, Stanley, 160
Drader, Sam, 160
*Dragnet* (television series), 59
drifter: culture/persona of, 13, 35, 64, 67–68, 194, 203; negative image of, 53, 104, 118, 164, 165
drug dealers/pushers, 72, 112–13, 117, 158–59, 188, 189–90, 214
drug use: in baby boom era, 12, 20, 21, 82, 104, 107, 108, 147, 213, 237, 245, 246, 274n109; and bad trips, 117, 118, 190–91, 202; hippie subculture and, 117, 123–24, 129, 151, 188–92, 196, 209, 214; by hitchhikers, 93, 111–13, 158–59, 175, 188–92, 196, 202, 243; at hostels, 111–13, 123–24, 127, 129, 150, 157, 165, 186,

187, 188–92; parental/community concerns about, 90, 155, 158–59; prohibitions on, 123, 144, 248. *See also* hashish; LSD; marijuana

Dubree, L. Alfred, 180(i)

Dylan, Bob, 70

East Royalty, PEI: tent city in, 155–56

Edmonton, 31, 40, 41, 84, 177, 236; CYHA members/activities in, 25(i), 40, 138, 139(i), 140, 141–42; federal hostel space in, 116, 149, 161; and female hitchhikers, 218, 219, 234; hitchhiking in, 161, 192, 195; hitchhiking to, 25(i), 36, 141, 174

Elk, Flora Grace, 223

Elsrud, Torun, 20, 56, 255*n*89, 274*n*105

English, Jack, 97

"entrepreneurial self," 90, 119, 196–202, 245

environmentalism, 4, 71, 80–82, 119

Erasmus, Georges, 78

Erikson, Erik, 10, 88

Esmonde-White, Patrick, 17, 98, 116

Europe, hitchhiking in: in adventure era, 30–32, 34–35, 40–41, 45–47, 97, 137, 142; in baby boom era, 67, 75–76, 84, 93–94, 96, 107, 181, 189, 191, 202; and drug use, 189, 191; guidebooks on, 93–94

Expo 67 (Montreal), 65, 66, 138, 151, 157, 203

Farber, Jerry, 74

Federal Bureau of Investigation (FBI), 57, 119, 247

female hitchhikers, 23, 54–60, 206–38; as adventurers, 32–35, 40–41, 44–47, 54–57, 59; campaigns/publications aimed at, 216–23; clothes worn by, 45–46, 56, 85–86, 195–96; disappearances/murders of, 204, 205(i), 206–7, 208, 216, 218, 219, 220, 221–22, 247–48; feminists' support of, 224–28; as hippies, 85–86, 131, 181, 189, 195–96, 214–

15; as Indigenous, 209–10, 223, 248; and male gaze, 19–20, 55, 194–96, 207; in popular culture, 207–16; and resistance to predators, 228–36; risk-taking by, 207, 208, 210–11, 228, 235, 236–38, 245–48; and "secret lusts" of male drivers, 213–16, 219–20, 231–32; social theories of, 210–13; as vagrant/homeless, 56–57; as working or seeking work, 46–47. *See also* rape/sexual assault; sexual predators; vanishing hitchhiker

Fenyor, Mary, 107

films, 125, 184, 223; anti-hitchhiking, 221–22; hitchhikers in, 44, 59, 60–61, 206, 209, 268*n*199; soft porn, 215; "thumbsploitation," 59, 247. *See also* *specific films by title or director*

Fitzgerald, Frank, 47–48

Fodor's travel guides, 86, 94

"folk devils," hitchhikers as, 99, 137, 230, 287*n*7

Ford, Henry, 29, 30

Ford Motor Company, 32

Foucault, Michel, 196, 229; on biopower, 9, 104, 222

Fouquet, Monique, 225(i)

Francis, Edmund, 37

"Fred the Cook" (tent city organizer), 188

Fredericton, 149, 174

Friedan, Betty: *The Feminine Mystique*, 90, 224

Frommer, Arthur: *Europe on Five Dollars a Day*, 93

Front de Libération du Québec (FLQ), 133

Gardner, Penny, 97

Gaye, Marvin: "Hitch Hike," 206; "Mercy Mercy Me (The Ecology)," 80

gaze. *See* male gaze; mutual gaze; performance, of hitchhiking; tourist gaze

Geller, Sheldon, 216, 225–26

Gennep, Arnold van, 92

*Georgia Straight,* 4, 74, 100, 119, 125–26, 127, 167

Germany: and "The Happy Wanderer," 93, 277n167; hiking/camping clubs in, 38–39, 137; in Weimar era, 88; youth hostel movement in, 39, 165

Gibson, Simon, 178, 195

Gilbert, Lewis (dir.): *Loss of Innocence,* 125

Gilhuly, Brian, 147, 148, 153, 187, 188

Gimby, Bobby: "Ca-na-da," 65, 269n5

Ginsberg, Allen, 151; *Howl,* 75–76

Girl Guides, 10, 39, 83, 137, 138–39, 144, 166

Gleason, Mona, 242, 245, 246

Gooding, Stewart, 74

Goodman, Paul: *Growing Up Absurd,* 76–77

Grand Tour, of British/European nobility, 6, 42, 47, 67, 113, 153, 240

Grateful Dead, 151

Greater Vancouver Youth Communications Centre Society. *See* Cool Aid (Vancouver hostel network)

Greenley, James, and David Rice, 210–11, 224

guidebooks and manuals: and advice for women, 85–86, 195–96, 234–36; eating tips in, 179–81; mainstream, 86, 93–94; on performance of hitchhiking, 246–47; as written by hitchhikers/backpackers, 15, 64, 94–95, 177–78, 235–36. See also *Handbook Canada: A Traveller's Manual* (Rideout/Amiro); *The Hitchhiker's Field Manual* (DiMaggio); *On the Road: A Guide for Youth Travelling Canada* (Health and Welfare)

Gus (Jasper camp leader), 199

Gusway, Lianne, 165

Haddock, John, 117–18

Haggard, William, 58

Hall, G. Stanley, 8–9, 10, 49, 87–88, 104

Hamilton, Carmen, 122

*Handbook Canada: A Traveller's Manual* (Rideout/Amiro), 94–95, 178, 179, 236

"The Happy Wanderer," 93, 277n167; Trudeau as, 97–98

Harding, Jim, 74, 272n54

Harris, Nora, 34

Harry, Prince, 240

hashish, 127, 191, 200

haversacks, 67, 83, 92. *See also* backpacks; rucksacks

Hayes, Geoffrey, and Kirk Goodlet, 53

Health and Welfare, Department of, 16, 80, 108, 145, 147, 210; and National Youth Consultation, 102, 114–16; *On the Road* (brochure), 17, 94, 153, 178, 179–80, 189, 215, 217(i), 237

Hells Angels, 151

Henderson, Stuart, 20, 90, 113, 255n80

Heney, Denis, 141–42

Hennessy, Mickey, 158

Hepburn, Mitchell, 36

Herdman, Shirley, 40, 45

Herman, Kenneth, 222, 227–28

Higgins, Brian, 156

highway and road construction, 5, 11, 27–28, 48. *See also* Trans-Canada Highway

Highway Traffic Act (Ontario), 47–48, 51, 53, 54, 175

Hill, Joyce, 34, 47

Hill, William, 47–48

Hine, Thomas, 20

hippies, 4, 5, 20, 76, 97, 136, 199, 200–1, 240–41, 274n103; backpackers as, 64, 194, 241; culture/clothing and appearance of, 64, 82–86, 113, 114, 117, 119, 157, 165, 166, 195–96; as drug users, 117, 123–24, 129, 151, 188–92, 196, 209, 214; environmentalism of, 81; middle-class youth as, 111–12, 113, 209; opposition to, 72, 83, 88, 104, 117–19, 123–24, 129–32, 151, 154, 155–

61, 169, 194; parents of, 64, 88–92; poor personal hygiene of, 83, 84, 85, 131, 154, 159, 161, 184, 243; surveillance of, 119; and transient youth movement, 102–33; as unwanted tourists, 116–32, 153–64, 169; violence against, 122, 131, 158, 184; women/girls as, 85–86, 131, 181, 189, 195–96, 214–15; as youth workers/federal bureaucrats, 108–16, 132, 136–37, 147–48, 154, 171

HitchBOT (robot hitchhiker), 239–40

*The Hitchhiker's Field Manual* (DiMaggio), 4–5, 95, 158, 178–81, 191, 193, 215, 226, 235–36

hitchhiking, 4–23; and adolescent wanderlust, 5, 6–10, 26–27, 87–88; adventure, 21–22, 26–61; around the world, 30, 31–32, 43–44; and automobility, 4–5, 10–14, 18, 29–30; in baby boom era, 4, 5, 11–12, 22, 64–99; boundaries in, 13–14, 26, 93, 154, 207, 243; criminalization of, 47–48, 51, 53, 54, 95, 175–76, 218; and drug use, 93, 111–13, 158–59, 175, 188–92, 196, 202, 243; and "entrepreneurial self," 90, 119, 196–202, 245; in films, 44, 59, 60–61, 206, 209, 247, 268*n*199; in "gap year," 240, 241, 248; guidebooks/manuals on, 93–95, 177–81, 234–36; history/theories of, 4–13, 18–21; by homeless, 49–50, 56–57, 76, 78; and hostel movement, 22–23, 136–71; opposition to, 5, 47–54; as performance, 12, 19–20, 32–33, 34, 44, 55, 81, 95, 178–79, 194–97, 299*n*25; proposed bans on, 4–5, 74, 219, 226, 227; and risk-taking, 4, 9–10, 13–14, 17, 56–61; as rite of passage, 6, 11–14, 17, 23, 25–27, 92–93, 112, 175, 196, 240, 248; ritual(s) of, 5, 11, 18–19, 26, 175–82, 255*n*83; stories of, 14–18, 19, 23, 28, 30–35, 40–47, 174–203; and transient youth movement, 22, 102–33; as unwanted tourism, 13–14, 93, 102–3, 116–32, 153–64,

169, 243; by women and girls, 23, 32–35, 40–41, 44–47, 54–60, 195–96, 206–38. *See also specific topics and destinations*; vanishing hitchhiker

*Hitch-Hiking* (anti-hitchhiking film), 221–22

*Hitch-Hooker* (film), 215

Hitler, Adolf, 39, 74

Hoffman, Abbie, 119

homelessness, 49–50, 56–57, 76, 78; on the road, 155–57, 182–88

Hoogers, Evert, 130

Hoover, J. Edgar, 57

Hopper, Dennis (dir.): *Easy Rider*, 184

hostels, CYHA, 22–23, 136–71. *See also* Canadian Youth Hostels Association (CYHA)

hostels, federally-run (1970), 22, 102–33. *See also* Jericho Beach hostel (Vancouver); National Hostel Task Force (1970), *and entry following*

hostels, federally-run (1971–76), 22–23, 136–71. *See also* Independent Hostel Association; Summer '71 (federal program); Transient Youth Services, hostel program of (1971–76)

Houston, Susan, 6

Hughes, Roger, 218

Iacovetta, Franca, 105, 229

Independent Hostel Association, 22–23, 153, 165, 169–70, 242; and CYHA, 17, 23, 244

Indian Affairs and Northern Development, Department of, 78, 138, 210, 223

Indigenous peoples: women/girls, as hitchhikers, 209–10, 223, 248; youth, 8, 77–80, 273*n*80

Inner City Service Project (Vancouver), 109, 126, 127

International Youth Hostel Federation, 30, 39, 137; CYHA affiliation with, 138, 140, 144, 168–69, 288*n*12

Irving, Loraine, 41

*It's Your Turn* (Committee on Youth publication), 17, 71–72, 77–78, 98, 145, 148, 166
Ivey, Grace, 168–69

James, Richard, and John Roberts, 170, 298*n*198
Jasper, 35, 149, 174, 199
Jasper National Park, 161; CYHA hostel in, 97–98, 138, 142, 164(i); Morro Peak climbers in, 25(i), 141
Jeremiah, Clair, 165
Jericho Beach hostel (Vancouver), 122–33, 191, 232; aftermath/analysis of, 129–32, 133; as established on Canadian Forces property, 121, 123; labour support for, 123; opposition to, 121–23; Point Grey neighbourhood and, 121, 126; RCMP and, 102, 122, 123, 126, 127; residents' sit-in at, 17, 124(i), 124–26, 133, 147, 241, 242; UBC and, 126, 127, 128, 130–32, 242; violent police evictions at, 22, 101(i), 102, 126–29, 128(i); VLF and, 120(i), 123, 126, 127, 130, 133; YMCA's aid to refugees of, 132
Jewison, Norman, 42–43, 262*n*95
Jobs, Richard Ivan, 66, 201
Johns, Sammy: "Chevy Van," 209
Johnson, Robert, and James Johnson, 213
Joplin, Janis, 70; "Me and Bobby McGee," 71
Josephson, Eric, and Mary Josephson (eds.): *Man Alone: Alienation in Modern Society*, 76
Justice, Department of, 114
Juvenile Delinquents Act, 104

Katimavik, xi, 248
Keele, Paul, 93
Keller, Harry (dir.): *Tammy Tell Me True*, 206
Kelly, Peter, 245
Kelly, Vince, 115

Kennedy, Robert F., 67
Kent State University (Ohio), student killings at, 171
Kerouac, Jack: *Desolation Angels*, 76; *The Dharma Bums*, 92; *On the Road*, 11, 62
Kesey, Ken, and the Merry Pranksters, 151
Kettles, James G., 218
kiosks, for hitchhikers (Summer '71 program), 149, 150–52, 152(i), 153, 171, 241
Kitsilano (Vancouver), anti-hippie activism in, 117, 131
Kostash, Myrna, 224
Kubrick, Stanley (dir.): *2001: A Space Odyssey*, 189

Lake, Victor, 127
Lancy, David, 246, 270*n*11
Landers, Ann, 219–20
Lang, Otto, 146, 151
Lanyon, Richard I., 213
Laporte, Pierre, 133
Lastman, Mel, 219, 227
Laurence, Danielle, 70
Lebrec, Carole, 225(i)
Lennon, John, 84, 85
*Let's Go* travel guides, 94, 177
Levi, Charles, 15
Levine, Stanley, 31
Levitt, Cyril, 68, 74, 256*n*103
Lewis, David, 36
Lewis, Dennis, 167–68
Lexier, Roberta, 129
Lightfoot, Gordon, 70
liminality, 27, 32, 33, 42, 73, 187, 193, 194, 196; Turner on, 12–13, 92
*Little Ladies of the Night* (film), 209
London (Ontario), 52, 159, 171; federal hostel in, 116, 122, 154
Lothian, Jim, 141
LSD, 117, 151, 189, 190, 192, 213
Luckmann, Thomas, 148

Lupino, Ida (dir.): *The Hitch-Hiker,* 60–61
Luxton, Meg, 86–87

MacDonald, Heidi, 32
Mackie, Cam, 17, 147–48
*Mad* magazine: hitchhiking cartoon in, 4
Mahood, Teddy, 17, 121, 127–28
male gaze, 19–20, 55, 194–96, 207. *See also* mutual gaze; tourist gaze
The Mamas and the Papas: "California Dreamin," 70–71
Manpower and Immigration, Department of, 108, 114, 151, 290n55
Maoz, Darya, 13, 119, 154, 192, 243, 278n4, 285n146
Marchment, Diane, 40, 45
Marcino, Paul, 122
marijuana, 83, 93, 114, 117, 119, 127, 186, 189, 191–92, 193, 196
Martel, Marcel, 188
McGougan, Ann, 163, 169–70, 295n156
McMonagle, Duncan, 94, 178, 226
Meriguet, Henri, 58
Meyer, Herman, 219, 222
Middle East and Asia, hitchhiking in, 31, 32, 68, 97, 142
Miller, Abraham, 211–12
Miller, Bob, 178
Millett, Kate: *Sexual Politics,* 224
Milligan, Ian, 75
Minehan, Thomas: *Boy and Girl Tramps of America,* 49–50
Mitchell, Harriet, 40
Mitchell, Joni, 70; "Big Yellow Taxi," 80; "Carey," 71; "Coyote," 309n106; "Woodstock," 71–72
Mitton, Lloyd, 42
Möller, Friedrich-Wilhelm: "The Happy Wanderer," 93, 277n167
Montreal, 34, 43, 54, 67, 94, 138, 154, 159, 169, 202, 214–15; "bohemian" community in, 156–57; Expo 67 in, 65, 66, 138, 151, 157, 203; federal hostel space

in, 116, 149, 157–58; hitchhikers from, 70–71, 85, 93, 189, 191, 196; hitch-hiking in, 95, 107
Moorey, Darcy, and Iain Angus, 162–63
Morgan, David, 126
Morgan, James, 219
Morgan, Rik, 4, 5
Morrill, Don Sanami, 162
Mothers Against Drunk Driving (MADD), 193
motorcycle gangs, 122, 151, 158, 170–71
Mudle, William, 26
Mukerji, Chandra, 19, 175
music, 5, 69–73, 117, 151, 176, 200, 243; and drug use, 12, 72; and environmentalism, 71, 80; and rock festivals, 69(i), 72–73. *See also specific artists and songs*
mutual gaze: of drivers and hitchhikers, 192–96; of locals and travellers/tourists, 116–33, 196–97, 242, 285n146. *See also* male gaze; tourist gaze
Myers, Tamara, 11, 216, 234

Nalon, John, 31
National Advisory Council on Physical Fitness and Amateur Sport, 142
National Coalition of Provincial and Regional Hostelling Associations, 162, 169
National Council of Women, 40
National Defence, Department of, 116, 126–27
National Film Board, 28, 103, 105
National Hostel Task Force (1970), 12, 17, 144–45, 147; CWC and, 113–16, 119; CYHA and, 161, 169–70; formation of, 22, 102, 113–16; local opposition to, 116–19, 155, 157–58, 160; problems of, 122, 124, 132, 171, 242–43; RCMP and, 118–23, 126, 127; second iteration of, 169–70. *See also entry below*
National Hostel Task Force, hostels operated by, 116; Beatty Street

(Vancouver), 118–21, 122, 123, 191; Brighton Compound C (Charlotte-town), 116, 117, 155; London, 116, 122, 154; Thunder Bay, 116, 122. *See also* Jericho Beach hostel (Vancouver)

National Indian Brotherhood, 78

national parks, 28, 103; CYHA hostels in, 97–98, 138, 141, 142, 161, 164(i). *See also* Banff National Park; Jasper National Park

National Youth Conference on Travel and Exchange, 165

National Youth Consultation (CWC/Health and Welfare), 22, 102, 114–16, 144, 242

newspapers, university, 14–15, 75, 254*n*74; advice for hitchhikers in, 14–15, 64, 94–96, 235; *The Chevron*, 74–75, 96, 235; *The Fulcrum*, 177–78; *The Martlet*, 81, 96, 191, 195; *The Meliorist*, 70, 77, 81; *The Peak*, 70, 85–86, 95, 186, 234, 235; *The Sheaf*, 96–97, 186; *The Ubyssey*, 130, 235

Nicholas, Jane, 45, 263*n*99

*The Night Holds Terror* (film), 59

"No Riders" rules, 57, 60–61

Noxel, Jack, 26

Noy, Chaim, 19

Ocean: "Put Your Hand in the Hand," 72

October Crisis (1970), 133, 136, 145

Ogden, Sandi, 180(i)

*On the Road: A Guide for Youth Travelling Canada* (Health and Welfare), 17, 94, 153, 178, 179–80, 189, 215, 217(i), 237

On-to-Ottawa Trek, 37–38, 74

Ontario Provincial Police (OPP), 47–48; and anti-hitchhiking/rape prevention films, 221–22, 226; billboards of, 222, 227–28; brochures/pamphlets of, 94, 158, 218–19

Opportunities for Youth, 242, 296*n*172, 314*n*24; and Transient Youth Services,

12, 17, 137, 147, 153–54, 156. *See also* Transient Youth Services, hostel program of (1971–76)

O'Regan, Michael, 19, 177, 299*n*25

Orlowski, Paul, 179(i)

Orwell, George: *The Road to Wigan Pier*, 7

outdoor organizations, for youth, 137. *See also specific organizations*

Owram, Doug, 66, 189, 274*n*109

Packer, Jeremy, 19, 237, 247

Palmer, Bryan, 20, 79

Papas, Georgia, 41

Park, Robert E., 49

Parks, Emerson, 36

Parsons, Talcott, 110–11

*The Partridge Family* (television series), 209

*Pathfinder* (CYHA monthly), 97–98

Paush, Lydia, 40, 45

Pearson, Lester B., 146

Pelletier, Gérard, 116, 117, 121–22, 136, 145, 147, 154

Penkala, Joe, 218

performance, of hitchhiking, 95, 178–79, 194–97, 299*n*25; as anti-material-istic, 81; as "emotion work," 196, 246; as gendered, 19–20, 32–33, 34, 44, 55, 194–96; and tourist gaze, 12

Perkins, Keith, 177, 178, 191, 193, 230, 231

Pfeiffer, Daniel: "How the People Feel," 125–26

Phillips, Art, 117

Pitsula, James, 15, 70

Point Grey (Vancouver), 121, 126. *See also* Jericho Beach hostel (Vancouver)

Pon, Valeen, 41, 41(i), 45–46, 47

Post, Emily, 46–47, 55–56

Public Works, Department of, 151–52

Quebec, 72, 163; hitchhikers from, 58, 70–71, 96, 121, 192; hitchhiking in, 33, 34, 61, 89, 158, 189, 206; hostels in, 97, 139, 157–58; kiosks in, 150; October

Crisis in, 133, 136, 145; youth unemployment/unrest in, 146, 157 Quebec City, 116, 149, 174, 181, 190; female hitchhikers from, 218, 225(i)

Raadt, John van der, 161
*Rape: A Preventative Inquiry* (film), 222–23, 226, 231
rape/sexual assault, 58, 190, 206–38, 312*n*177; and anti-hitchhiking/educational campaigns, 216, 218–23, 226, 231; and disappearances/murders, 204, 205(i), 206–7, 208, 216, 218, 219, 220, 221–22, 247–48; and drivers as predators, 213–16, 219–20, 225–26, 228–36; and feminists' "right to hitchhike," 224–28; men/boys as targets of, 214, 223, 230–31, 237; reporting of, 208, 213, 216, 219, 220, 223, 231–33; and risks of hitchhiking, 207, 208, 210–11, 228, 235, 236–38, 245–48; stories of, 208, 216, 218, 219, 221–23, 230–36; and vanishing hitchhiker, 206–7, 210, 247–48. *See also* female hitchhikers; sexual predators; vanishing hitchhiker
Rasmussen, Lorna, 81
Reardon, Charles, 33
Red Cross, 10, 146
Red Power movement, 78, 79, 119, 273*n*80
Regina, 34, 149, 160; labour riot in, 37–38
Rehorek, Melissa, 206–7, 247–48
Rideout, David, and Ray Amiro: *Handbook Canada: A Traveller's Manual*, 94–95, 178, 179, 236
Rigby, Bella, 32–33, 44(i), 45, 55
Rinvolucri, Mario: *Hitch-Hiking*, 212–13
Rippon, C.L., 127
risk-taking: adolescent wanderlust/rebellion and, 9–10, 13–14, 17, 88, 222, 228, 236–37, 245–47; by both driver and passenger, 4, 18–19, 27, 56–61; hitchhiking stories of, 17, 19, 23, 28,

178, 255*n*89, 298*n*11; at hostels, 40; as inherent in hitchhiking, 240; by women/girls, 207, 208, 210–11, 228, 235, 236–38, 245–48
rite of passage, travel/hitchhiking as, 6, 11–14, 17, 25–27, 92–93, 240, 248; for boys vs girls, 112; communitas stage of, 12–13, 23, 175; liminality stage of, 12–13, 92, 196
ritual(s), of hitchhiking, 5, 11, 18–19, 26, 175–82, 255*n*83; advice on, 14–15, 64, 92–97, 177–81, 234–36; ambiguity/potential danger of, 23, 47–61, 206–38; as gendered, 192–96
Robidas, Marcel, 157
rock festivals, 69(i), 72–73
Rogers, Byron, 147, 148
Rome, Susan, 75, 89
Ross, Ellen, 10
Ross, Greg, and Hedley Swan: "Cross-Canada Jaunt," 176, 177–78, 181, 191–92, 194, 198, 199
Royal Canadian Mounted Police (RCMP), 15, 58, 89, 96, 108, 175–76, 185; and cases of murdered/missing hitchhikers, 206–7, 247–48, 304*n*11; and federal hostels, 102, 118–23, 126, 127, 156, 188–89; and On-to-Ottawa Trek, 37–38
Rubin, Jerry, 119
Rubin, Ken, 17, 107, 280*n*29
Rubin, Laurie, 110
rucksacks, 21, 27, 33, 46, 57, 67, 92. *See also* backpacks; haversacks
Russell, Connie, 227

Salvation Army, 35, 94, 103, 106, 108, 158, 159, 160, 214
Sangster, Joan, 56, 267*n*177
Saskatoon, 3(i), 67, 149, 160, 218
Schirrmann, Richard, 39
Schissel, Bernard, 244
Schlebecker, John T., 247
Schoedler, Lillian, 32
Scorsese, Martin (dir.): *Taxi Driver*, 209

Scotten, Anne, 226–27
Scull, Andrew, 59
Secretary of State, Department of. *See*
    Committee on Youth; National
    Hostel Task Force (1970), *and entry*
    *following*; Pelletier, Gérard; Transient
    Youth Services, hostel program of
    (1971–76)
Seligman, Adam, et al., 236
*Sex Brats* (film), 215
sexual predators, 213–16, 219–20, 225–
    26, 228–36; postwar anxieties about,
    229–30; reporting of, 219, 220, 223,
    231–32; stories of, 230–36; and van-
    ishing hitchhiker, 206–7, 209–10,
    247–48. *See also* female hitchhikers;
    rape/sexual assault
Sharland, Elaine, 247
Shebib, Donald (dir.): *Goin' Down the
    Road*, 72
Sheller, Mimi, 11, 80; and John Urry,
    54–55
Sigurdson, Duff, 188
Simon and Garfunkel: "Homeward
    Bound," 71
Simonsen, David, 144, 166
Skott-Myhre, Hans Arthur, 9, 251*n*29
Slipacoff, David, 147
"slumming," in Victorian/Edwardian
    eras, 7–8, 43, 67, 240, 250*n*17
Small, Jennie, 85, 263*n*103
Smallwood, Joseph (Joey), 174
Smith, Bob, 131–32
Smith, David (British social work
    professor), 19
Smith, David (Secretary of State Depart-
    ment), 169, 170, 239
Smith, David Harris (Canadian profes-
    sor), 240
Smith, Jack, 26
Smith, Margaret, 34, 47
social work profession, 104–6; and
    "hippie" organizations/youth workers,
    108–16, 132, 136–37; and transient
    youth movement/federal hostel

program, 106–16, 168–69. *See also*
    Canadian Welfare Council (CWC);
    National Hostel Task Force; transient
    youth movement
South and Central America, hitch-
    hiking in, 107, 189–90, 201
Sparks, Beatrice: *Go Ask Alice*, 209
Spearman, Marie, 54
Spock, Benjamin, 10, 65, 66, 82, 88,
    216
Spranger, Eduard, 9
Staller, Karen, 214
Stanfield, Robert, 168
Starnes, John, 119
Stasiuk, Myles, 96–97, 186
Steinbeck, John: *The Grapes of Wrath*,
    60
St. John's, 149, 156
Stollery, P.E., 30
stories of hitchhiking, 14–18, 19, 23,
    174–203, 255*n*89, 298*n*11; in adventure
    era, 28, 30–35, 40–47; as public talks,
    32, 43–44; and rape/sexual assault,
    208, 216, 218, 219, 221–23, 230–36; as
    urban legends/tall tales, 15, 24, 61,
    202–3, 206, 209–10, 247–48, 312*n*177.
    *See also* Trans-Canada Highway,
    stories of hitchhiking/hostelling on;
    vanishing hitchhiker
Strauss, William, and Neil Howe, 21
Student Summer Employment Program.
    *See* Summer '71 (federal program)
Students for a Democratic Society, 119,
    213
Summer '71 (federal program), 145, 147–
    52; "blue jean bureaucrats" in charge
    of, 147–48, 154; buses proposed by,
    149, 150–51, 153, 194, 208; hostel pro-
    gram of, 144–53; kiosk program of,
    149, 150–52, 152(i), 153, 171, 241;
    opposition to/problems of, 151–52,
    153–54, 171. *See also* Transient Youth
    Services, hostel program of (1971–76)
Sutherland, Betty, 226
Sutherland, Neil, 6

Swankey, Ben, 36
Sweezey, Alex, 227

Teale, Ernest, 58
tent cities: in Banff National Park, 188,
    301*n*88; in PEI, 155–56; as rejected in
    Toronto, 157
*The Texas Chain Saw Massacre* (film),
    247
Thompson, Elizabeth, 90–91, 220
Thomson, Lillian, 106, 110, 112, 113, 114–
    15, 132, 146, 242
The Three Stooges, 206
*Thumb Tripping* (film), 247
Thunder Bay, 154, 158, 222; federal
    hostel space in, 116, 122, 149, 186
Thunder Bay Travelling Youth Services
    Committee, 162
Tillack, Ralf, 218
Toll, Ellsworth and LeRoy, 31–32, 43–44
Toronto, 32, 36, 47, 52, 57, 76, 103, 104,
    107, 138, 157, 214–15, 218, 222, 228–29;
    federal hostel space in, 116, 149, 186;
    hitchhikers from, 63(i), 85, 89, 96,
    200, 219; hitchhiking in, 51, 95, 156,
    225(i); hitchhiking to, 173(i), 179(i);
    kiosk north of, 152; proposed hitch-
    hiking ban in, 219, 226, 227; transit
    strike in, 216, 225–26
tourism, 102–3; as unwanted, 13–14, 93,
    102–3, 116–32, 153–64, 169, 243; tran-
    scending "bubble" of, 13, 67–68, 93,
    175, 200–1
tourist gaze, 12, 203; vs local gaze, 116–
    33, 196, 242, 285*n*146. *See also* male
    gaze; mutual gaze
"tramping," in Victorian/Edwardian
    eras, 6–7, 43, 67, 82, 240
Trans-Canada Highway: creation/
    opening of, 5, 11, 28, 66; government
    information on, 94, 153; hitchhiking
    on, 12, 23, 83, 88, 96, 99, 100, 106, 107,
    113, 137, 206, 248; hostelling on, 139,
    149–51, 153–64; mile-zero marker of,
    199. *See also entry below*

Trans-Canada Highway, stories of
    hitchhiking/hostelling on, 94, 174–
    203; Canadian flag identifiers, 201–2;
    communitas, 198–200, 202; drug use,
    188–92; eating tips, 179–82; finding
    places to sleep, 182–88; rider-driver
    nexus, 192–98; road codes/etiquette,
    175–79; transcending "tourism bub-
    ble," 200–1
*Transient Youth: Report of an Inquiry in
    the Summer of 1969* (CWC), 16, 17, 22,
    78, 83, 88, 91–92, 100, 102, 106–13, 144,
    148, 149, 207–8, 214
*Transient Youth, 70–71: Report of an
    Inquiry about Programs in 1970, and
    Plans for 1971* (CWC), 16, 132, 145–46,
    242–43
transient youth movement, 22, 102–33;
    and federal hostel programs, 113–24,
    136–71; and "hippie" youth workers/
    "blue jean bureaucrats," 108–16, 132,
    136–37, 147–48, 154, 171; and Jericho
    Beach hostel standoff, 124–33; as "new
    style of vagrancy," 102–4, 279*n*8; and
    social work profession, 104–16; as
    term, 106; types of travellers identi-
    fied in, 111–12; as unwanted tourism,
    13–14, 116–32. *See also entries above
    and entry below; Canadian Welfare
    Council (CWC); Canadian Youth
    Hostels Association (CYHA); Jericho
    Beach hostel (Vancouver); National
    Hostel Task Force, and entry
    following*
Transient Youth Services, hostel pro-
    gram of (1971–76), 15, 144–53, 157,
    174, 208; "blue jean bureaucrats" in
    charge of, 147–48, 154; and bus/kiosk
    programs, 149, 150–52, 152(i), 153;
    CYHA vs, 22–23, 137, 144, 148–49, 153,
    161, 163–71; and drug use, 150, 157,
    165, 186, 187, 188–92; opposition to/
    problems of, 153–61, 186–88, 242–44;
    RCMP surveillance of, 188–89; as run
    with Opportunities for Youth, 12, 17,

137, 147, 153–54, 156; sex segregation at, 132, 150, 157, 186–87. *See also* Summer' 71 (federal program)
*Travellers' Cheques* (NFB tourism film), 103
Trevelyan, Sir Charles Philips, 33
Trevelyan, Katharine, 33–34, 45
Trudeau, Pierre Elliott, 2, 126, 130, 146; encouragement of travel by, 98, 118, 148, 174; memo to CYHA from, 98, 142, 143(i); and October Crisis, 133, 136, 145; as veteran hitchhiker/ hosteller, 97–98, 142, 239, 240; and youth issues, 136, 144–45
Truth, Sojourner: "Ain't I a Woman," 224
Turner, Victor, 12–13, 92
Tyson, Ian, 70

Ulmer, Edgar (dir.): *Detour*, 59, 268*n*199
unemployment: in baby boom era, 21, 73, 75, 78, 116, 129–31, 168, 175, 195, 225(i), 241–42, 290*n*52; during Depression, 5, 12, 27, 32, 37–38, 49, 51–52, 74; of early women hitchhikers, 56–57; and federal hostel program (1971), 144–53, 157, 163
United States, hitchhiking in: in adventure era, 26, 30, 31, 32–34, 42–45; in baby boom era, 70–71, 84, 89, 107, 189, 199–202; with Canadian flag identifier, 201–2; and lure of California, 32–33, 44(i), 44–45, 54, 70–71, 189, 200–1; by servicemen/women, 42–43, 54
universities: Alberta, 40, 140, 161; British Columbia, 82, 126, 127, 128, 130–32, 242; Carleton, 116, 187; Dalhousie, 186; Guelph, 176; Kent State, 171; Lakehead, 162; Lethbridge, 70, 77, 81, 154, 171; McGill, 242; McMaster, 240; Memorial, 96, 156; New Brunswick, 36; Ottawa, 154, 176, 177; Oxford, 36; Regina, 70; Saskatchewan, 96–97, 186; Simon Fraser, 69,

70, 81, 85–86, 95, 119, 130, 186, 225, 234, 235; Toronto, 31–32, 40, 111, 224, 227; Trent, 242; Victoria, 81, 96, 97, 178, 191, 195; Waterloo, 74–75, 96, 130, 235; Western Ontario, 36; Wisconsin, 210–11; York, 226–27
university presses, Canadian, 14–15, 75. *See also* newspapers, university
Urry, John, 12; Mimi Sheller and, 54–55

vagrancy, 48, 56–57, 84, 112, 175; "new style" of, 102–4, 279*n*8
Van Buren, Abigail, 219–20
Vancouver, 30, 31, 32–33, 34, 35, 58, 214–15; anti-hippie activism in, 117, 118–19, 121–24, 131; federal hostels in, 118–21, 122, 123, 124–32, 191, 232; as popular postwar destination, 64, 76, 89, 90, 118, 174–75, 191, 197(i), 199; proposed hitchhiking ban in, 4–5, 74. *See also* Jericho Beach hostel (Vancouver)
Vancouver Liberation Front (VLF), 119–21, 120(i), 123, 126, 127, 130, 133, 167
vanishing hitchhiker: legend of, vi, 61, 206, 210, 240, 247, 312*n*177; in popular culture, 207–16, 247; and real-life disappearances/murders, 206–7, 210, 247–48; robot as, 239–40; sexual predators and, 209–10, 247–48; social theories of, 210–13; as "unadjusted girl," 54–60
Vanity Fare: "Hitchin' a Ride," 70
Vansickle, Alexander, 58
Verry, H.L., 30–31
Verzuh, Ron: "Trip Tips" column by, 70, 85–86, 95, 186, 234
Veselka, Vanessa, 20, 55, 234, 247
Victoria, 31, 34, 75, 81, 89, 110, 199, 203, 239; federal hostel space in, 116, 117–18
Vietnam War, 201–2; protests against, 83, 171
*The Violent Years* (film), 59
Vipond, Les, 166
Vogt, Jay, 68, 189

Wadleigh, Michael (dir.): *Woodstock*, 71
Waisberg, Harry, 221
Walker, Imogene, 40, 45
Walkowiak, Christine, 218
Walsh, Mary, 57
Wandervogel (German hiking/camping club), 38–39, 137
Warden, Randy, 223
Watson, John B., 9, 40, 65, 216
Watson, Rheta, 32–33, 44(i), 45, 55
Watt, Brian, 188
Watts, Peter, 165
Wawa, Ontario, 84, 174, 203, 237, 304*n*168; stories/urban legends of, 15, 172, 202–3
Weather Underground, 213
Weaver, Sharon, 80
*Welcome, Neighbour* (NFB tourism film), 103
Westhues, Kenneth, 68
Weys, Gale, 218
Wharton, Don, 58, 208
Wheeler, Bernelda, 79–80
Wheeler, Michael, 106, 112–13
White Paper on Indian policy (1969), 78
Whitehorn, Katharine, 73, 74
Whitton, Charlotte, 105
Whyte, William H.: *The Organization Man*, 76–77
William, Prince, 240
Williams, Douglas: *Promised Lands*, 75–76, 84, 93, 181
Willmot, Rod, 67, 91, 181, 194, 202
Willows, Richard, 160

Winnipeg, 34, 36, 37, 91, 109, 168; hitchhiking in/near, 63(i), 89, 96, 154–55, 160, 173(i), 174, 198, 211(i); youth hostel in, 107, 116, 149, 154, 159–60, 180(i), 183(i), 184(i)
Wolf, Naomi, 90, 276*n*153
Wolfe, Tom: *The Electric Kool-Aid Acid Test*, 151
women and girls, hitchhiking by. *See* female hitchhikers
Woodsworth, Ken, 42

Yellowhead Highway, 113, 174
YMCA/YWCA, 10, 21, 27, 209, 296*n*171; conservative/structured approach of, 35–36, 39, 50, 108–9, 110, 111, 132, 138, 166; and facilities for transient youth, 94, 108–9, 110, 111, 132, 146, 153, 154, 160, 161, 162, 174, 282*n*92; modernization of, 166–67, 296*nn* 174–175; and rescue of Jericho Beach refugees, 132
Young, Neil, 70
Young Communist League, 21, 35, 36, 75
Youth International Party (Yippies), 119, 127
youth mobility, 6–10; and automobility, 4–5, 10–14; as problematic, 11–12, 102–4, 279*n*8; and women's "right to hitchhike," 224–28. *See also* adolescent wanderlust; transient youth movement

Zeidman, Samuel, 43
Ziolkoski, Kel, 197(i)
zoot suits, 52–53